DEVILS AND ANGELS

Youth Justice is a key area of the criminal justice policy in England and Wales and has been the subject of an inordinate amount of recent legislation seeking to enhance the criminal courts' powers to punish and prevent offending and re-offending by young people. This legislation uses criminal justice measures to prevent offending, but there has been little attempt to use non-criminal or civil law procedures to achieve the same result. This book challenges this approach and questions why delinquency in young people has been so firmly criminalised in this jurisdiction. At an individual level criminalisation has a critical impact on our attitudes towards the young, and the criminalisation of young people's behaviour results in them being labelled as criminal, and often leads to the loss of 'childhood'. In policy terms children become merely part of a crime problem rather than the product of failing social policies in employment, education and youth culture. For society at large the identification of young people with criminal activity and the negative public image that results creates a culture of fear and distrust which may in turn create further possibilities for criminalisation of their behaviour. A comparative perspective in this work examines responses to youth crime in other jurisdictions and questions whether the criminal justice process is an appropriate context in which to deal with young people's problematic behaviour.

Devils and Angels:
Youth Policy and Crime

JULIA FIONDA

Law School
Southampton University

·H A R T·
PUBLISHING

OXFORD AND PORTLAND, OREGON
2005

Published in North America (US and Canada) by
Hart Publishing
c/o International Specialized Book Services
920 NE 58th Avenue, Suite 300
Portland, OR 97213-3786
USA

Tel: +1 503 287 3093 or toll-free: (1) 800 944 6190
Fax: +1 503 280 8832
E-mail: orders@isbs.com
Web Site: www.isbs.com

Hart Publishing, Salters Boatyard, Folly Bridge,
Abingdon Rd, Oxford, OX1 4LB
Telephone: +44 (0)1865 245533 Fax: +44 (0) 1865 794882
email: mail@hartpub.co.uk
WEBSITE: http//:www.hartpub.co.uk

British Library Cataloguing in Publication Data
Data Available

ISBN-13: 978–1-84113–374–4 (paperback)
ISBN-10: 1–84113–374–4 (paperback)

Typeset by Hope Services, Abingdon Ltd., in Minion 10/12 pt
Printed and bound in Great Britain by
Biddles Ltd, UK Ltd

In fond memory of Allan Levy QC
1942–2004

CONTENTS

Acknowledgements   xi

Part I – Devils and Angels   1

1 Introduction   3

2 Youth   8

Incapable of Evil?   8
  Minimum Ages   9
  Presumptions of *Doli Incapax*   12
    Legal View   15
    Policy View   17
Childhood   20
  Constructions of Childhood   20
  Perceptions of Childhood   26

3 Policy   33

Models of Youth Justice   34
  The Punishment Model   34
  The Welfare Model   35
  The Treatment Model   37
The 1980s – A 'Velvet Revolution'   38
Policy Conflicts   40
Who Makes Youth Justice Policy?   44
  'Minimal Intervention' in Discretion in the 1980s   44
  Called to Account in 2004   46
New Labour and the Policy Making Process   49
  Influences   49
  Consultation   54
  Using Youth Justice Models   55

4 Crime   59

Measuring Youth Crime   59
The Extent of Youth Crime   63
  Young People and Crime (1995)   63

Youth Lifestyles Survey (1998/99)   65
Crime and Justice Survey (2003)   65
Official Statistics   66
Crime Trends   67
Desistance and Growing Out of Crime   68
Explanations   69
The Research   69
Family Life   70
Education   71
Other Lifestyle Factors   72
Theoretical Explanations   74
Anomie and Strain   74
Conflict and Subcultures   76
Labelling, Outsiders and Deviance Amplification   79
Control Theories   81
Perceptions of Youth Crime   82

Part II – Youth Justice Policy and Practice   85

5 Diversion   87

Diversion in Policy   88
Diversion in Practice   95
Cautioning   96
Reprimands and Warnings   98
Crown Prosecution Service   101
Discussion   105
Due Process and Crime Control   106
Formality and Informality   108
Net-widening   109
The Politics of Diversion   113

6 Tribunals   115

The Youth Court   116
The Development of a Jurisdiction   116
The youth court in action   120
Reforming the youth court: issues and development   123
Philosophical Issues   123
Participation   125
Openness and Shaming   126
The Referral Order and Youth Offender Panels   128
The Crown Court   132

7 **Sentencing** 140

Guiding Sentencers 140
The Statutory Framework 145
A Principal Principle? 148
Punishment in the Community? 151
   The Community Orders 155
   Welfare Agencies and the Implementation of Community
      Punishment 157
   Social Control 161
Custody 164
   Custodial Orders 168
   Critique 169
Sentencing Policy 172

8 **Restorative Justice** 174

Restorative Justice in Theory 174
Restorative Justice in Practice 181
   The Referral Order 184
   The Reparation Order 186
   Reprimands and Warnings 188
Comparative Perspectives 189
   Family Group Conferencing in New Zealand 190
   The Youth Diversion Project in the Republic of Ireland 193
Discussion 195
   Conflicting Principles 196
   Ethnocentricity 197
   Social Exclusion 198
   The Role of the State 201

9 **Parents, Schools and Youth Crime** 204

Introduction 204
Parental Responsibility 206
   The 'Scientific' Rhetoric 206
   The Political Rhetoric 211
   The Reality 214
Schools and Youth Crime 219
   Introduction 219
   The Rhetoric 220
   The Reality 223
Conclusion: 'Holding On'? 228

Part III – Alternatives   231

10 Alternatives   233

England and Wales   234
  Crime, Disorder and Zero Tolerance   234
  Controlling Children under 10   237
    Curfews   237
    Child Safety Orders   238
  The AntiSocial Behaviour Order   239
  Discussion   242
Scotland   245
  Children's Hearings in Context   245
  The Provisions   247
  Discussion   250
The Children Act 1989: A Way Forward?   252
  The 1989 Act in Context   253
  Themes   255
  Provisions   257
  Potential   259

11 Conclusion   262

Bibliography   271
Index   287

ACKNOWLEDGEMENTS

The research for this book began in October 1988, as I sat in an undergraduate Juvenile Justice class in the Law Faculty of Southampton University and furiously took notes as Andrew Rutherford beguiled us all with his erudite and often sardonic observations on criminal policy-making. It was an exciting time in policy terms, and Andrew's significant influence on that exciting and productive era, inspired a captivation and enthusiasm for this subject that I have never lost. This was my first introduction to the field of youth justice and to Rutherford's classic text *Growing Out of Crime*, which remains the most inspirational book on youth justice that I have ever read. Much has happened since that time, both in personal and policy terms, and it is now I that stand before students of Youth Justice at Southampton, at 9 am on a Tuesday morning, imparting a rather more gloomy message about the efficacy of the government's attempts to deal with youth crime. Andrew not only taught me a great deal substantively and ideologically, but also schooled me in scholarly endeavour and the ways of academic life. I owe such an enormous debt of gratitude to Andrew as my tutor, my mentor, a colleague and a friend. His contribution to making me what I have become cannot be over estimated. I shall always aspire to his talent for policy analysis and his inimitable academic flair.

This book is dedicated to Allan Levy, in appreciation for his inspiration as a friend and a colleague. His tireless and life-long campaign for the protection of children in the legal system will ensure that we will all remember him as we discuss the issues addressed in this book and he has left a profound legacy in developing a child-centred focus to the law in this field. On a personal level he gave generously of his time, took a great interest in the development of this book and became my sage as well as a good friend. He will be sorely missed for his generous friendship, entertaining and lively company and his intellectual influence and I am only sorry that I did not work hard enough to ensure that he saw the final product.

I would like to thank Rob Jago for his constant support and companionship over many years. As a friend you have never ceased to give without expectation, to provide constant support and warm-hearted companionship and to offer fun, laughter and good times. As the Jean Paul Sartre to my Simone de Beauvoir, you shared with me your wisdom, insight and humour as we sampled the culture and bars of London, New York and Paris. You taught me what friendship really means and I value the changes that you have inspired in my life. My family have continued to provide unconditional and unstinting love, putting up with my bad moods when I wasn't able to write and tolerating my aloofness when I was. Thanks, mum, for keeping my life, soul and house together and thanks Jacqueline, my treasured big sister, for friendship, fun and frolics. Roobarb, Custard and Ollie helped with the typing—four paws are undoubtedly faster than two fingers and sometimes make more sense. Thanks to all my friends who kept me in their thoughts, even when they did not see me for months at a time because I was so busy. You have given me the space to write this book, and I appreciate that more than you could know.

I am, as always, proud and honoured to work at Southampton University and I am grateful to that institution for their support in providing funding for my research and leave, so that I had time out to read, think and write. In the Law School I have enjoyed the support of colleagues and a scholarly and friendly environment in which to work. I am also grateful to the many students I have taught over the years, from whom, probably unbeknown to them, I learnt so much in our many discussions of the issues in this book. The academic world has introduced me to many friends in this field, books that I have read and enjoyed, and countless scholars who have informed, persuaded and challenged me in my views. They appear at the end of the book and are far too numerous to mention individually here. I am ever grateful to Richard Hart and the editorial team at Hart Publishing for their patience in waiting for the manuscript, and for all the hard work in taking a stream of consciousness and turning it into a book.

Finally thanks to Ernest Gallo, Mr Kipling and Philip Morris, my best friends.

Julia Fionda
Dorset, May 2005

Part I
Devils and Angels

1

Introduction

The photograph on the front cover of this book shows two people sitting on what we suppose is a wall. What do we know about these people? Nothing. We cannot even see their faces. What do we assume about them? That they are young? That they are offenders? We may reasonably assume this because we know that this book is about young offenders, and they appear on the cover. Once we have made this assumption we may look further at the image and find evidence to corroborate our initial assumption. We look at their dress (the jeans, the hat, the hooded sweatshirt). One of them is holding a skateboard. There is graffiti on the wall. They are not doing anything, they are 'hanging about'. The reality is that we know very little about them. Their back is turned to us so we cannot see their faces. We do not know their names or their age and we do not know anything of their history or background. However, such is the power of the image, that we instantly make associations and assumptions about them. Within seconds we may have created a mental image of these two people as part of a deviant group or 'devils'. We may have decided that we do not like them, that we may be afraid of them, that we may blame them for many things (possibly including the graffiti on the wall). They are guilty by association. We categorise them in a social group and they take on the characteristics we have assigned to that social group. There were many pictures to choose from for the front cover, and an alternative choice may have produced very different assumptions. What, for example, might we have assumed if I had chosen a picture of James Bulger for the cover? Or a picture of younger children, with more 'baby-like' faces, playing games, dressing up or going to school? We may then have placed those children in the box labelled 'angels' and assumed those children to be innocent by association.

The problem addressed in this book goes beyond mere labelling; we are all labelled in one way or another and assigned to social groupings with whom we are presumed, rightly or wrongly, to share characteristics. The problem with the labelling of young people is that, in an adult-centric society, it tends to be carried out judgmentally, through fear of the young, and the label assigned to the majority of them is inherently negative. What does it mean to be a devil or an angel in contemporary society? The distinctions between the two groups are dichotomous and over-simplistic, as stereotypical labels often are. To be an angel means to be acceptable to adult society and to embrace the characteristics that adults value, regardless of what is 'normal', acceptable or valued among young people themselves. This means being innocent (morally and legally), vulnerable, quiet, competent, healthy, dependent and independent of adults in appropriate contexts, and intellectually able (in terms of what is culturally valued as intellectual in adult society). Devils are determined by their failure to live up to these characteristics—they are noisy and boisterous, unruly, lacking in original innocence, 'knowing' in an adult sense, under-achievers educationally and socially, anti-social and problematic. Of course, the dichotomy breaks down, as the angels are sometimes devilish (all children are naughty sometimes) and the devils are sometimes acknowledged to be a product of our social and moral neglect. The murder of James Bulger in 1992 demonstrated how this throws the adult world into confusion and crisis. James Bulger, depicted as the innocent, 'angelic' victim, was being naughty on the day of his murder, proving difficult for his mother to control and facilitating his own abduction. Venables and Thompson were vilified as the 'devils', but not universally; as discussion of the case progressed, more details of their background emerged that led us to question our own social responsibility for the apparent breakdown of moral order among our children and young people. The problem lies in the fact that the falsely dichotomous labels are defined from an adult perspective and framed upon a false memory of our own childhood and unrealistic expectations of what young people can be or indeed, are, in their own social world.

As young people inevitably fail to live up to these impossible expectations, our adult perceptions of them are inherently negative and young people are viewed as problematic, rather than celebrated as a group with cultural value. Both youth social policy and youth justice policy perpetuate the labels of 'devils' and 'angels'. For example, cultural policy directed towards young people in England and Wales, tends largely to address their 'failings' rather than promote youth culture as a fundamental part of our national heritage. The Department of Culture, Media and Sport, and its associated Ministry for Young People, is currently promoting increased investment in sports and 'healthy living' centres for young people, but as part of the government's wider strategy to tackle obesity, crime and educational problems among young people. Announcing an Activity Co-ordination Team as a government initiative to encourage children to play more sport, Tessa Jowell, Secretary of State for Culture Media and Sport stated:

> Tackling the 'couch potato' culture amongst children and young people is a priority for us. We know that physical activity can be an important way of getting young people more engaged. We know that it can help achieve this Government's objectives in health, education and law and order.[1]

---

[1] Department of Culture, Media and Sport, *Speech by Tessa Jowell, Secretary of State for Culture, Media & Sport to the Tackling Obesity in Young People Conference* Press Release (25 February 2004).

Similarly, cultural activities for young people are being promoted as a means of cutting youth crime, as the success of the government's Splash Extra Scheme boasted that:

> Organised sports and cultural activities for young people in some of the country's most deprived areas last summer helped to reduce street crime and robbery, new figures show.[2]

The promotion of state-funded sporting and recreation facilities for those young people who lack the resources to otherwise participate in them is a welcome development, but as these examples show, the promotion of such schemes seems to have to be justified in relation to encouraging devils to alter their behaviour and engage in what adults perceive to be worthy and appropriate leisure activities.[3] In contrast, what some view as the 'art form' of graffiti, the leisure activities of 'hanging out' in public, skateboarding, listening to loud music and other teenage preferences have been declared 'anti-social', even criminal, as they are considered to be annoying or threatening.[4]

Elsewhere in Europe a more positive perception of youth has been recognised. In the Netherlands for example it is acknowledged that young people are failing to engage in politics, demonstrating growing dissatisfaction with their social situation and developing 'symptoms of psychological instability and abnormal behaviour':

> There are two ways out of this problematic situation. One of them is to intensify control over young people by using repressive measures against abnormality in young people and to reinforce ideology in order to strengthen internal norms. The basic underlying approach is a negative or problem-oriented understanding of young people as a risk group. The alternative is the opposite, namely to rely on young people's creative potential, the capacity for self-confidence of young people, of youth involvement. This approach can be called positive.[5]

Examples of such a 'positive' approach can be found in jurisdictions in Europe where youth policy has been the subject of more proactive and focused government initiatives and legislation. For example, in Sweden, legislation passed in 1999 enacted a wide-ranging set of policies directed at young people, formulated in a white paper entitled *On Their Terms*. The paper sets out the following three underlying objectives of the policy:

---

[2] Department of Culture, Media and Sport, *Culture Can Cut Crime Says Tessa Jowell* Press Release (13 January 2002).

[3] For example in April 2004 the government announced the investment of £7 million in museums and galleries to 'create opportunities to enrich the learning of school-age children and young people across the country . . . and provide value added learning experiences—through the use of cultural resources—in a classroom, museum or other setting.' Department of Culture, Media and Sport, *Boost for Children and Young People's Learning as Government Announces £7 million for Museums and Galleries Education* Press Release (22 April 2004).

[4] See further Ch 10.

[5] Council of Europe, *Youth Policy in the Netherlands* (Strasbourg, Council of Europe, 2000) p 15.

Objective 1: young people should be given good opportunities for living independent lives;
Objective 2: young people should be given genuine opportunities for participation
and influence;
Objective 3: young people's capacity for commitment, creativity and critical thinking is a resource for society and should be made good use of.[6]

The contrasting negative public image of young people in England and Wales may
not only be unfair but also damaging, especially in the field of youth justice.

Youth justice has been the subject of intense political interest for many decades,
but never more so than in England and Wales since 1997. It has been the focus of
inordinate amounts of legislation, seeking to enhance the criminal courts' powers
to punish and prevent offending and re-offending by young people. However, the
legislation assumes as a given that the predominant means of preventing crime
must be the use of criminal measures and that presupposes the definition of
troublesome behaviour in young people as 'crime'. Policy makers have become
blinded by the label of crime and keep their eyes tight shut in the face of different
ways of defining and perceiving it. The criminalisation of young people's behaviour results in them being labelled as 'devils', losing their identity as individuals,
much as the two people on the front cover have lost their individuality and are
assumed to be members of a distinct social group, sharing common characteristics
with all young people who behave, dress and appear in that way. They are
commodities to be processed, feeding the criminal justice machinery with its raw
material. The youth justice process increasingly denies young offenders their
childhood, since as devils, they are assigned adult-like attributes of evil and the
competence of free will. Much of the criminal justice process focuses on encouraging them to be accountable for their rational choice of lifestyle and behaviour. If
the devilish nature of offending young people can be banished—by coercion if
necessary—then the assumption is that they can reclaim their 'childhood' and
rejoin the 'angels'. However, the chapters of this book will demonstrate how that
process is flawed.

Part I examines how the labels of devils and angels have been developed and
applied to young people, through a discussion the development of youth justice
policy over the last century, and of social constructions of childhood and their
influence over youth justice procedures, particularly the minimum age of criminal
responsibility. Part I also examines the nature and extent of youth crime, according to statistical and research evidence and assesses the extent to which the label of
devil is appropriate given the aetiology and nature of the youth crime problem.
What emerges from Part I is a sense of perceptions about young people and their
criminal behaviour which may be more responsible for the application of the label

---

[6] Faktablad Ministry of Culture, *On Their Terms* (Stockholm, Ministry of Culture, 1999).

of 'devils' than the 'reality' of youth crime. Part II then examines the youth justice process, stage by stage, to assess the impact of the labelling process on reforms to youth justice procedures and their practical application. Finally, in Part III, the possibility of undermining the labels of devils and angels, by re-focusing our response to young people's behaviour is considered, through the assessment of comparative approaches and other civil law approaches in England and Wales.

Overall, this book seeks to examine how the labels of devils and angels, and youth justice policy based on the politics of fear has resulted in increasing attempts to control, regulate and intervene in the lives of young people. The late twentieth and early twenty-first centuries have witnessed an unprecedented expansion in the scope and extent of youth justice measures, notwithstanding relatively modest changes in the levels of quantified youth crime.[7] It is argued that as youth justice policy is increasingly influenced by public fear, public opinion and media hysteria, and less and less on ideology and criminological discourse, that policy becomes more focused on socially excluding deviant young people identified as 'devils'. Intervention methods, which exacerbate their exclusion from conventional society, prompt further suspicion and fear, further expansion of the youth justice process and a vicious cycle ensues. Caught in the whirl of this vicious cycle, governments remain committed to the use of criminal measures as a means of protecting the public from the threat of youth.

At the same time, our social construction of childhood and youth reveals a confused and ambiguous approach to understanding the behaviour of this group, which informs an ambivalent approach to youth justice: in addition to its punitive, actuarial approach, youth justice seeks to reform and remould young people into an adult perception of the acceptable citizen, or 'angel'. We, therefore, see policy in this area meandering between two familiar models of welfare and punishment, and sometimes a bifurcated attempt to implement both at the same time, but have only rarely witnessed a radically different approach. The concluding chapter considers whether, if we look behind the labels of 'devils' and 'angels', and abandon stereotypical and irrational perceptions of young people, we may be able, firstly, to be more tolerant of behaviour, much of which is different to how we as adults would behave, but not necessarily threatening or dangerous, and, secondly, to deal with the more serious behaviour in a more constructive, nurturing way.

---

[7] See further Ch 4.

2

Youth

Incapable of Evil?

Since 'youth' is the subject of this book, we need to understand what we mean by this term. This prompts a discussion of when 'youth' begins and ends, at least for legal purposes. Further, since this book focuses principally on youth justice policy, the age at which we attribute criminal responsibility for children's actions is as good as any other notional starting point for this discussion. The age of criminal responsibility and the ages at which children appear in the criminal just-ice system reflect social and legal constructions of childhood and tell us much about what we may expect of children at various ages. This symbolic 'age' may be based on capacity for criminal behaviour (the legal view) or on the extent to which we choose to protect children from the responsibilities which arise from attaining a legal identity (the policy view). Since our construction of childhood is fluid over time and between contexts, so too may the age of criminal responsibility be sub-ject to change to reflect such constructions. This chapter begins with an analysis of what we mean by the age of criminal responsibility and the recent debate over whether the age ranges currently applicable in the English youth justice system are appropriate. In order to inform this debate, it is then necessary to discuss the var-ious historical, social and legal constructions of childhood. Haines and Drakeford begin their book with the bold but significant statement that: 'Our society does not like young people. In comparison with our continental partners Britain shows little of the warmth and tolerance which extends to young people in public places or on communal occasions.'[1] Why is this? And what implications does this have for youth justice policy? An examination of popular or media perceptions of child-hood are discussed at the end of this chapter in order to assess to what extent these 'perceptions' both derive from the constructions of childhood and contribute to the resulting ages at which we require children to take responsibility for their actions.

---

[1] K Haines and M Drakeford, *Young People and Youth Justice* (Basingstoke, Macmillan, 1998) p 1.

Minimum Ages

The minimum age of criminal responsibility denotes the age at which any criminal justice system permits itself to bring criminal proceedings against a child who commits a crime. Children below that minimum age are universally deemed to be *doli incapax* or 'incapable of evil'. The minimum age is a complete bar to prosecution, regardless of any behaviour committed by the child, even where such behaviour would be an offence if committed by someone who exceeds that minimum age. Children below the minimum age are not held legally responsible for such 'criminal' behaviour or, where necessary, civil proceedings may be invoked to protect the child's welfare or to protect society from that child.[2] The minimum age does not suggest any physical incapacity to commit offences (indeed very young children may be capable of extreme levels of violent or unsociable behaviour) but rather an incapacity to be held responsible or accountable for such behaviour.

The minimum age of criminal responsibility in England and Wales is currently 10. Until 1933 the minimum age had been 7 but section 50 of the Children and Young Persons Act 1933 raised it to 8. The Criminal Justice Act 1963 then raised it to 10[3]. Historically then, the trend has been to raise this age. Indeed section 4 of the Children and Young Persons Act 1969 would have raised it further to 14 as part of the de-criminalisation agenda of that legislation,[4] but this part of the Act was never implemented.[5] If it had been, one wonders whether the recent debate on *doli incapax* would ever have taken place. Successive governments have reviewed the current position but all have resolved to maintain the status quo. For example, in 1990 a government white paper on criminal justice considered both the minimum age of criminal responsibility as well as the presumption of *doli incapax* between the ages of 10 and 14 and concluded:

> The government does not intend to change these arrangements which make proper allowance for the fact that children's understanding, knowledge and ability to reason are still developing.[6]

---

[2] Eg, s 31 Children Act 1989 enables a child of any age under 16 to be placed in the care of a local authority where the relevant criteria are met, and such criteria include where the child is suffering or likely to suffer harm due to them receiving insufficient parental care or being beyond the control of their parents.

[3] Section 16.

[4] See further Ch 3.

[5] See further A Rutherford, 'A Statute Backfires: The Escalation of Youth Incarceration in England during the 1970s' in J Doig (ed) *Criminal Corrections: Ideals and Realities* (New York, Lexington, 1983). Section 4 was finally repealed in the Criminal Justice Act 1991, s 72, having lain dormant on the statute books for over 20 years.

[6] Home Office, *Crime Justice and Protecting the Public* Cm 965 (London, HMSO, 1990) para 8.3.

More recently, concern was expressed as to whether this age was appropriate in the light of the murder of James Bulger by two 10-year-olds in 1993. For example, an article in *The Times* reporting the judgment of the Queen's Bench Division in *C v DPP*[7] appeared alongside a (largely irrelevant) picture of James Bulger and stated: 'The rule was highlighted in the James Bulger murder trial in which two boys were convicted of murdering the two-year-old. They were both aged 10 at the time.'[8] The implicit suggestion there was that, had the defendants in that case, Venables and Thompson, been a few months younger, English law would have prevented criminal proceedings being brought against them (though there would have been no bar on civil care proceedings if that was deemed necessary). The outcry during their subsequent prosecution and trial was vehement enough; it would have been even more hysterical had no prosecution been brought.

Much has been made of the comparative view of this minimum age. It is clear from a perusal of minimum ages of criminal responsibility across Europe that the current position in England and Wales is rather out of line. Not only do most countries have a higher minimum age, but the general European trend is to raise that age rather than reduce it. In Ireland, for example, the minimum age was raised from 7 to 12 in 2001.[9] Elsewhere minimum ages in the early to mid teens are the norm as Table 2.1 demonstrates.

Exceptionally Belgium and Luxembourg do not prosecute young people under the age of 18 at all.[10] On a more global scale, Table 2.1 enables a comparative view of where the policy in England and Wales stands on the world stage; notably lower in this 'league table' than most of Europe, the United States and many other jurisdictions.

A simple comparison of minimum ages, however, gives us only a partial view of the way that young offenders are treated elsewhere. In addition to the minimum age, many countries, in practice, do not prosecute young people immediately after attaining this age, but operate a *presumption* against *doli incapax* which presumes that children will not be subject to prosecution proceedings unless that presumption can be rebutted. For example, on raising the minimum age to 12, the Irish Parliament established such a presumption for children aged over 12 but under 14.[11] The Scottish Law Commission similarly proposed a presumption against the prosecution of children aged under 16 in their discussion of the age of criminal

---

[7] [1994] 3 All ER 190. This decision is discussed further below.

[8] F Gibb, 'High Court Throws Out "Age Rule" Escape for Child Criminals' *The Times* (30 April 1994).

[9] Children Act 2001 s 52(1).

[10] The figure of 18, as the minimum age for Belgium, is rather misleading. Children below this age may be prosecuted, but are automatically found not guilty in order to prompt a diversion of the child to a welfare agency, which is able to tackle 'dangers' in the child's environment—see further J Christiaens, 'A History of Belgium's Child Protection Act of 1912: The Redefinition of the Juvenile Offender and His Punishment' (1999) 7 *European Journal of Crime, Criminal Law and Criminal Justice* 5.

[11] Children Act 2001 s 52(2).

TABLE 2.1 *Minimum ages of criminal responsibility*

Europe		Worldwide	
Cyprus	7	India	7
Liechtenstein	7	Nigeria	7
Switzerland	7	Singapore	7
		South Africa	7
Northern Ireland	8	Gibraltar	8
Scotland	8	Kenya	8
		Sri Lanka	8
		Malta	9
England/Wales	10	Australia	10
		Fiji	10
		Malaysia	10
		New Zealand	10
Greece	12	Canada	12
Ireland	12	Jamaica	12
Netherlands	12	Morocco	12
Turkey	12		
France	13		
Austria	14	China	14
Bulgaria	14	Mauritius	14
Germany	14	Taiwan	14
Italy	14	Vietnam	14
Latvia	14		
Lithuania	14		
Romania	14		
Slovenia	14		
Czech Republic	15	Egypt	15
Denmark	15	USA (Connecticut)	15
Estonia	15	USA (New York)	15
Finland	15	USA (S Carolina)	15
Iceland	15		
Norway	15		
Slovakia	15		
Sweden	15		
Andorra	16	Argentina	16
Poland	16	Japan	16
Portugal	16	Macau	16
Spain	16	USA (Illinois)	16
		USA (Louisiana)	16
		USA (Georgia)	16
		USA (Texas))	16
		USA (Massachusetts	16
Belgium	18	Brazil	18
Luxembourg	18	Colombia	18
		Congo	18
		Peru	18

Source: http://www.unicef.org

responsibility.[12] Until 1998 such a presumption acted as a proviso to the English minimum age in relation to children aged under 14. The discussion of, and ultimate abolition of, this presumption added to the general debate on the age of criminal responsibility in England and Wales.

Presumption of *Doli Incapax*

Under common law, a presumption operated in England and Wales to prevent children under 14 being prosecuted for any crime unless it could be established that they knew that their actions were 'seriously wrong'. This presumption against prosecution operated for this age range regardless of the minimum age of criminal responsibility and effectively created a discretionary age range in which it was possible, but not the norm, to prosecute children between whatever the minimum age was at the time and the age of 14. The presumption had existed for many centuries and was referred to in the first edition of *Blackstone's Commentaries on the Laws of England*[13], which cited a heritage for the presumption dating back to the time of Edward III.

The presumption suggests that a 'normal' child under 14 will not appreciate that their actions, whilst amounting to a criminal offence, were seriously wrong as opposed to merely naughty or mischievous. The burden lay with the prosecution to adduce evidence that the child possessed the requisite understanding and knowledge to realise that their actions were seriously wrong: 'gravely wrong, seriously wrong, evil or morally wrong.'[14] Such evidence, therefore, must seek to demonstrate a moral awareness in the child, advanced for the norm for their age, rather than any legal knowledge of the criminal nature of their actions. The doctrine was described in *Blackstone's Commentaries* thus: 'the capacity of doing ill, or contracting guilt, is not so much measured by years and days, as by the strength of the delinquent's understanding and judgement'.[15] This led to a wealth of case law, cited extensively in *C v DPP*,[16] in which the appropriate strength and nature of required evidence was discussed. In summary, such evidence must be adduced from the child's general moral awareness and capacity to understand the consequences of their actions, rather than from the seriousness of the criminal behaviour itself (although, circumstantial evidence surrounding the criminal act, such as running away from the scene of the crime, may suggest such awareness of the wrongfulness of the behaviour). In practice, however, in later years, the

---

[12] Scottish Law Commission, *Discussion Paper on Age of Criminal Responsibility* Discussion Paper no 115 (Edinburgh, TSO, 2001).

[13] *Blackstone's Commentaries on the Laws of England* 1st edn (1769) Bk IV, p 23.

[14] *Archbold, Criminal Pleading Evidence and Practice* (1993) vol 1, p 52.

[15] *Blackstone's Commentaries* above n 13 at Bk IV, p 24.

[16] [1994] 3 All ER 190.

presumption posed less and less of a bar to prosecution especially since a large majority of children appearing in the youth courts plead guilty. The case law suggests that, where guilt was contested, minimal evidence of a child's moral understanding of their actions sufficed to allow the trial to continue.[17]

Notwithstanding the weakening of the presumption in recent years, its application and conceptual obscurity exercised Laws J to such an extent in *C v DPP* in 1994 that he felt compelled to abolish it. As the presumption existed in common law, this radical step was, in the view of Laws J, within his remit since 'The common law is not a system of rigid rules, but of principles whose application may alter over time, and which themselves may be modified.'[18] He cited a number of vehement criticisms of the doctrine to justify this decision. His arguments will be analysed in more depth below, but in summary six arguments may be elicited from his judgment. First, the rule assumes as a position of normality that a child under 14 will not know the moral 'obliquity' of his actions. Such a position in modern times is 'unreal and contrary to common sense'.[19] The second, more practical, concern was that evidence of an assumed abnormal level of understanding may be difficult to ascertain, particularly if the child exercises his right to silence during the investigation and trial. Third, the requirement that the prosecution not just prove all elements of the offence against the child, but also an extra mental element of moral awareness is 'conceptually obscure' since this is never required in the case of an adult facing criminal charges.[20] Further, Laws J was concerned at the risk of injustice perpetrated by the doctrine on two grounds: that children brought up in 'good homes' to know the difference between right and wrong were more likely to be subject to prosecution than those not taught such rudiments by their parents; and that to fail to hold a child to account for their criminal actions simply because they are 'morally irresponsible' is 'perverse'.[21] Finally, he believed that the rule was outdated, since it originated at a time when children, in common with adults, may have been subject to more barbaric and often violent punishments for even minor crimes. Children in the late twentieth century, he argued, require no such protection from a comparatively benign criminal justice system.

The defendant in *C v DPP* appealed to the House of Lords where the presumption was reinstated.[22] This decision, however, should not be confused with a statement of sympathy for the *doli incapax* presumption, since the House of Lords based their decision almost entirely on constitutional grounds concerning the rightful authority of the Divisional Court to abolish such a long-standing common

---

[17] *B v R* (1958) 44 Cr App R 1. Note that in the trial of Venables and Thompson, for the murder of James Bulger in 1993, the seriousness of their conduct rendered the question of their moral understanding virtually academic.

[18] [1994] 3 All ER 190, 199.

[19] *Ibid* 196.

[20] *Ibid* 197.

[21] *Ibid* 198.

[22] [1995] 2 WLR 383.

law doctrine. Indeed, Lord Lowry expressed some agreement with the logic of Laws J's arguments regarding the presumption but the House unanimously concurred that:

> The distinction between the treatment and the punishment of child 'offenders' has popular and political overtones, a fact which shows that we have been discussing not so much a legal as a social problem, with a dash of politics thrown in, and emphasises that it should be within the exclusive remit of Parliament.[23]

Hence the presumption was briefly resurrected for reasons of legal propriety but Parliament was urged to review the doctrine as a matter of urgency. Shortly after the general election in 1997, New Labour responded to this call. In their first consultation paper on youth justice, *Tackling Youth Crime*,[24] the *doli incapax* presumption was considered under the general theme of 'taking responsibility' for youth crime, the suggestion being that the presumption against prosecution prevented young people being held accountable for their actions. At this stage, views were invited as to whether the presumption should be abolished, retained or reversed, so that it could, in effect, operate as a defence to some children who claimed to lack moral responsibility. However, the government's white paper, published shortly afterwards, announced a decision to abolish the presumption in order to 'remove the practical difficulties prosecutors and courts face under the current law and which they would continue to face if the presumption were reversed rather than abolished.'[25] The presumption was finally abolished in section 34 of the Crime and Disorder Act 1998.

The debate over the existence of this presumption, which in reality rarely posed such practical difficulties for prosecutors and the courts, was rather more symbolic than substantive and Lord Lowry's assertion that it had political overtones was appropriate. Academics, politicians as well as members of the senior judiciary contributed to a wide-ranging discussion of the treatment of young children in the criminal justice system in the late twentieth century and a number of views emerge as to the extent to which punishment for criminal behaviour, in whatever guise, is appropriate at this age, as well as underlying assumptions about what the minimum age of criminal responsibility should be. Elsewhere these arguments have been analysed in terms of two broad views of the minimum age: a legal view and a policy view.[26]

---

[23] *Ibid* 403 (Lord Lowry).

[24] Home Office, *Tackling Youth Crime: A Consultation Paper* (London, Home Office, 1997)

[25] Home Office, *No More Excuses: A New Approach to Tackling Youth Crime in England and Wales* Cm 3809 (London, TSO, 1997) p 12.

[26] J Fionda, 'Youth and Justice' in J Fionda (ed) *Legal Concepts of Childhood* (Oxford, Hart Publishing, 2001) pp 85–88.

Legal View

The legal view of *doli incapax* takes a literal translation of the Latin phrase (incapable of evil) and suggests that the non-prosecution of children under a certain age derives from their lack of capacity to form criminal intent or to understand the moral implications of their actions. Debate over the minimum age and the existence of a presumption of *doli incapax* therefore involves an assessment of the mental capacities of children of different ages and, in particular a more general assessment of the growing-up process to ascertain at what age we might consider greater mental capacity the norm. The choice of a minimum age of criminal responsibility must reflect a consensus on the social construction of childhood and any perception that children are maturing any earlier or later than in previous times. Laws J summed up this view in *C v DPP*:

> Whatever may have been the position in an earlier age, when there was no system of universal compulsory education and when, perhaps, children did not grow up as quickly as they do nowadays, this presumption at the present time is a serious disservice to our law ... the effect of the presumption is then that a defendant under 14 is assumed to possess a *sub*normal mental capacity, and for that reason to be doli incapax. There can be no justification for such a bizarre state of affairs.[27]

Thus, without empirical evidence or further sociological analysis, Laws J based a large part of his judgment on the sense that children in the late twentieth century grow up more quickly than they did earlier in the century. As they grow up the assumption is that they develop a greater moral awareness and a greater capacity to understand the implications of their behaviour. The presumption of *doli incapax* certainly operated in practice on this view, the case law demonstrating the difficulties in recent years of adducing evidence (often without psychological or psychiatric reports) on a child's capacity to understand their actions. This is, no doubt, the view that prompted Professor Andrew Ashworth to comment that the abolition of the presumption in the Divisional Court was a result of the operation of the rule which 'had become "a bit silly" in practice, with little difference between cases either side of the line.'[28]

Adducing evidence in individual cases, to indicate an abnormal mental capacity in young children, may indeed have been a difficult task for lawyers, resulting in a minute analysis of a child's words and behaviour to elicit signs of such mental capacity. Laws J was offended, in particular, by the illogicality of setting a minimum age of criminal responsibility at 10, but then assuming all others (bar the few exceptions) also shared the incapacity of the under-10s and could not, in practice, be prosecuted. Indeed, the simpler position, in the legal view, would be to set a minimum age of criminal responsibility at an appropriate age for the social era and

---

[27] [1994] 3 All ER 190, 196–97.
[28] Quoted in C Dyer, 'Judges Close Child Crime Loophole' *Guardian* (30 April 1994).

operate a complete bar to prosecution below that age. This seemed to be Laws J's preferred option, but his preference for the minimum age was 10. A similar method, but with different results, was used by the government in the late 1960s. Following the white paper *The Child, The Family and the Young Offender*, the Children and Young Persons Act 1969 proposed to abolish the presumption against prosecution for the under-14s by raising the minimum age to 14. This view was supported by Paul Cavadino in his critique of the decision in *C v DPP* where he stated that:

> [F]ar from being an outmoded survival from an earlier era, the doli incapax rule is fully consistent with our increasing knowledge of child development and learning which tells us that children mature and learn over differing time spans. A presumption of this kind acknowledges that there are variations in the speed of the maturation process.[29]

Even Lord Lowry queried Laws J's assumption that universal compulsory education necessarily suggested that children 'will more readily distinguish right from wrong'.[30]

Adherence to the legal view of *doli incapax* will inevitably produce such contrary views on the rightful limits of moral responsibility of children. This perhaps explains why a number of governments have reviewed the rule and its consequent presumption from time to time but taken different views on whether it should be amended or not, in line with the contemporary social perception of childhood and children's capacities. Shortly before Laws J took his extreme view, the government had considered the issue in their white paper in 1990[31] but concluded that the age limits in operation were satisfactory. New Labour, in 1997, also took a legal view of the *doli incapax* issue, concluding that the presumption of incapacity for the under-14s was 'contrary to common sense'.[32] They not only abolished the presumption but created the child safety order for children under 10 who committed, inter alia, acts which could amount to a criminal offence in older perpetrators, as a means of circumventing the minimum age of criminal responsibility and to 'nip crime in the bud' where children's behaviour became a concern at this very early age.[33]

Since the abolition of the presumption in 1998, the issue of children's mental capacity to commit criminal offences has resurfaced in relation to proof of *mens rea* in criminal trials. It is one thing to remove the bar to prosecution of very young children, but it remains the burden of the prosecution to prove that the child was

[29] P Cavadino, 'Goodbye, *doli*, Must We Leave You?' (1997) 9 *Child and Family Law Quarterly* 165 at 168.
[30] *C v DPP* [1995] 2 WLR 383, 396.
[31] See above, n 6.
[32] *No More Excuses* above n 25 at p 12.
[33] Crime and Disorder Act 1998 s 11. See further Ch 10, and J Fionda, 'New Labour, Old Hat: Youth Justice and the Crime and Disorder Act' [1999] Crim LR 36 at 45.

capable of forming *mens rea*. In *R v G*[34] the House of Lords were asked to consider whether two boys, aged 11 and 12, could be convicted under the Criminal Damage Act 1971 on the basis that they were reckless as to whether property was damaged or destroyed by the fire that they had started. At their trial, applying the current test of recklessness set out in *R v Caldwell*,[35] the trial judge had reluctantly convicted them since, regardless of their age or mental incapacity, they gave no thought to the risk of damage that would have been obvious to the ordinary reasonable (adult) person. In overturning the decision in *Caldwell* the House of Lords expressed concern at the injustice that the *dicta* in *Caldwell* was apt to produce: 'It is neither moral nor just to convict a defendant (least of all a child) on the strength of what someone else would have apprehended if the defendant himself had no such apprehension.'[36] Lord Steyn went further and, citing the UN Convention on the Rights of the Child, argued that the criminal law was obliged to consider the mental incapacity of children in assessing their responsibility for criminal acts: 'Ignoring the special position of children in the criminal justice system is not acceptable in a modern civil society.'[37] These statements of policy are all the more ironic given that just 10 years previously the defendants in *R v G* might not have been prosecuted by virtue of the presumption of *doli incapax*, criticised by the courts for exactly the sentiments expressed here by the House of Lords.

Policy View

The policy view of *doli incapax* largely ignores issues regarding children's mental capacity but rather takes a more protective view of the age at which a society chooses to subject young children to its criminal justice procedures and punishments. Glanville Williams suggested in 1954 that arguments reflecting the legal view were often confused with 'the theory of moral responsibility, and the right to inflict retributive punishment . . . No one whose opinion is worth considering now believes that a child who does wrong ought as a matter of moral necessity to expiate his wrong by suffering'.[38] Therefore the minimum age reflects a capacity to accept punishment for wrongdoing, rather than a capacity to understand the moral implications of that wrongdoing. This view can be most clearly seen in the European and other jurisdictions where the minimum age of criminal responsibility is much higher than that operating in England and Wales. Are we to believe, as proponents of the legal view would have it, that children under 18 in Belgium or under 16 in Spain, are incapable of understanding that their actions are seriously wrong? The only sensible way of understanding these higher minimum

---

[34] [2001] 1 AC 1034.
[35] [1982] AC 341.
[36] [2001] 1 AC 1034, 1055 (Lord Bingham).
[37] *Ibid* 1061.
[38] G Williams, 'The Criminal Responsibility of Children' [1954] Crim LR 493 at 495–96.

ages is in relation to the policy view that has been taken in such jurisdictions, that it is wrong, as a matter of policy, to subject young people under that age to the rigours of the criminal justice process.

In England and Wales the policy view has been used to support the abolition of the presumption of *doli incapax* and possibly a reduction in the minimum age. Glanville Williams saw merit in subjecting young children to the punishments afforded by the criminal justice system in order to give them access to welfare opportunities to tackle their offending behaviour: 'Thus *at the present day* the 'knowledge of wrong' test stands in the way not of punishment, but of educational treatment.'[39] Emphasis is added to the words 'at the present day' since Williams was writing in 1954, about a youth justice system steeped in the welfare tradition. It may indeed have been true to say at that time that '[*doli incapax*] saves the child not from prison, transportation, or the gallows, but from the probation officer, the foster-parent or the approved school'.[40] Changes to the tenor of youth justice policy in recent years suggest that prison is not such an unlikely destination after trial, and changes to the role and working ideology of the probation service (and latterly Youth Offending Teams[41]) mean that saving a child from these organisations may be seen as all the more necessary. At the very least this argument against the presumption can only be justified where there is sufficient confidence that youth justice punishments are remedial rather than retributive.[42]

Laws J expressed such confidence in 1994 in *C v DPP* in arguing that 'the philosophy of criminal punishment has, very obviously, changed out of all recognition' since the inception of the presumption many centuries ago and that therefore 'This presumption has no utility whatever in the present era.'[43] However, Mr Justice Laws was in a position to know better; since 1991 criminal punishment has been based on desert and principles of proportionality which, strictly speaking, prevents the more utilitarian use of punishment to provide access to welfare agencies. Indeed, whilst based on the most benevolent of intentions, the use of prosecutions of children to draw them to the attention of welfare agencies such as social services and probation was criticised by many long before Laws J made this

---

[39] G Williams, 'The Criminal Responsibility of Children' [1954] Crim LR 493 at 496.

[40] *Ibid* at 496.

[41] See eg W McWilliams, 'Probation, Pragmatism and Policy' (1987) 26 *Howard Journal* 97; M Nellis, 'Probation Values for the 1990s' (1995) 34 *Howard Journal* 19.

[42] A view which is doubted by Sue Bandalli, amongst others: 'Abolition of the Presumption of *doli incapax* and the Criminalisation of Children' (1998) 37 *Howard Journal* 114 at 119. Indeed, the abolition in *C v DPP* was presented at a time when the government were already restricting the use of cautions (Home Office Circular 18/1994), introducing the use of custodial penalties for 12–15-year-olds (Criminal Justice and Public Order Act 1994 ss 1–15) and when the CPS amended their Code of Practice by deleting the paragraph suggesting that prosecution of young children should always be a last resort (see A Ashworth and J Fionda, 'Prosecution, Accountability and the Public Interest: The New CPS Code' [1994] Crim LR 894; see further Chs 5 and 7).

[43] [1994] 3 All ER 190, 198.

rather old-fashioned statement.[44] It is perfectly possible for welfare intervention to be prompted without the assistance of a criminal prosecution and, since 1989, social services have a more proactive statutory duty to investigate children deemed to be 'in need' under the Children Act and intervene where necessary (but as minimally as possible) to alleviate that need.[45] This is the approach taken in jurisdictions where the minimum age is higher. Evidence of 'criminal' behaviour by young people under the minimum age is not ignored, but is perceived by policy makers as evidence of a welfare need. Civil procedures may be invoked to deal with that need, without any requirement that the criminal courts alert them to the problem. This more tolerant perception of 'criminal behaviour' enables the policy view of *doli incapax* to dominate and facilitates a higher minimum age of criminal responsibility.

The abolition of the presumption of *doli incapax* in the Crime and Disorder Act 1998 is indicative of a contrary view. The presumption acted as a bar to punishment for offending behaviour which meant that not only could young offenders not 'take responsibility' for their actions but that they could not subject themselves to action on the part of criminal justice agencies to get 'tough on the causes of crime.'[46] Developments in the Republic of Ireland have taken a different turn, where the minimum age of criminal responsibility has been raised from 8 to 12. This amendment was justified by the Irish Minister of Justice, Mr O'Donoghue, in presenting the Children Bill to the Díal Éireann in March 2000, on grounds of principle and pragmatism. On a point of principle, the Irish government believed 'that as a society we should not criminalise children under 12 years of age' and that it is wrong that children 'may have been criminalised for the wrong reason, however well meant. There may be a temptation to bring charges for sole purpose of ensuring the child received care and protection in an institutional setting. That cannot happen under this Bill.'[47] The pragmatic reasons for raising the minimum age of criminal responsibility reflected quantitative evidence on youth crime indicating that the average age of onset of offending for young males in Ireland was 13 and that therefore the youth crime 'problem' for children under the age of 12 did not merit the resources of the criminal justice process. Since Graham and Bowling's research tells us that the average age of onset of offending for young males in England and Wales is 13.5,[48] we can assume that the concern to facilitate the prosecution of children from the age of 10 was somewhat misplaced.

---

[44] See eg A Rutherford, *Growing Out of Crime* (Harmondsworth, Penguin, 1986) ch 2.
[45] See further Ch 10.
[46] Home Office, *Tackling Youth Crime* above n 24.
[47] Díal Éireann Debates vol 517 col 35 (29 March 2000).
[48] J Graham and B Bowling, *Young People and Crime* HORS 145 (London, HMSO, 1995) p 23.

Childhood

The discussion over *doli incapax* mirrors debates over the nature and extent of childhood. Mr Justice Laws, in *C v DPP* instinctively felt childhood has been short-ened in recent years since children are growing up more quickly in contemporary society than in previous eras.[49] He justified the abolition of the presumption of *doli incapax* on that view. Others[50] argued he had misconceived the nature of childhood and took the view that the immaturity of youth persists beyond the minimum age of criminal responsibility. Disparate as these views are, they share a sense that childhood is a construction, not a biological given. Such constructions of childhood will differ amongst those of different political, social and age groups in any society and the controversial debate over *doli incapax* may have symbolised a social disagreement over whether our perception of childhood has fundamen-tally changed in recent years. Discussion over the Bulger case represented a pinna-cle in this disagreement and caused many to question whether this case signalled a death knell in the innocence and purity commonly associated with childhood. Goldson argues it prompted (or possibly exacerbated) a growing adult anxiety about the 'demonization' of children and the increased fear of their capacity for evil.[51] There is certainly an erosion of childhood in youth justice policy[52] but is this reflective of wider sociological perceptions of what it means to be a child in con-temporary society and whether young people mature any more quickly today than in the past? Or is youth justice policy founded on a manufactured perception of fear of children which justifies politically authoritarian responses to youth crime?

Constructions of Childhood

A number of academic disciplines in which the study of childhood is of key inter-est provide less instinctive and rather more 'scientific' insights into how childhood has been and is currently constructed. Historian Philippe Ariés prompted this academic interest in his seminal study of childhood through the centuries, in which he not only asserted that childhood was a social and cultural construction, but was also a relatively modern concept in historical terms which emerged amongst the upper classes in late medieval times.[53] Since then a social history of

---

[49] [1994] 3 All ER 190, 196.

[50] Eg, Paul Cavadino above n 29.

[51] B Goldson, 'The Demonization of Children: From the Symbolic to the Institutional' in P Foley *et al* (eds) *Children in Society: Contemporary Theory, Policy and Practice* (Basingstoke, Palgrave, 2001).

[52] Fionda described this theme in youth justice policy in the 1990s as 'a lack of emphasis on "youth" and the greater emphasis on "justice"' in 'The Age of Innocence?: The Concept of Childhood in the Punishment of Young Offenders' (1998) 10 *Child and Family Law Quarterly* 77 at 77.

[53] P Ariés, *Centuries of Childhood* (London, Cape, 1973).

childhood has been well documented and discussed.[54] Hendrick has traced a number of models of childhood through recent historical perspectives.[55] These are important models as we can learn much from historical accounts of perceptions of childhood in terms of how they influence government policy on both welfare and crime, as well as the extent to which society frames its construction of childhood in any particular time or social circumstances. Beginning in the late eighteenth century, childhood was viewed as a manifestation of original innocence and growing up was associated with loss of innocence and the acquisition of adult capacities for evil (Hendrick's 'Romantic Child'[56]). A less clear perception of childhood emerges in the nineteenth century. Hendrick notes a resurgence, chiefly amongst the Evangelical movement, of the belief in the depraved and savage nature of children and their innate immorality.[57] However, this was also a period during which the Factory Acts and the emerging welfare approach to youth justice and child welfare reform indicated a lamenting at the loss of original innocence amongst children and a perceived need to protect children from the horrors of the adult world with which they were becoming acquainted at too early an age. The first Factory Act in 1833 therefore protected children under the age of 9 from the brutal conditions of the workplace. Similarly Mary Carpenter sought to provide education and care to young people whose delinquent behaviour was a symptom of a premature adoption of adults' values and behaviour: 'children's delinquency was to be dealt with in such a way that the child may be "turned again into a child" '.[58] Indeed Sheila Brown notes that: 'with a schizophrenic dualism so redolent of the Victorians, childhood was at the same time idealized, worshipped and protected, feared, regulated and punished, and debased, exploited and appropriated'.[59]

During the late nineteenth and twentieth centuries, childhood was constructed through the need, not only to protect the child's innocence from adult contagion, but also to provide them with the necessary tools to grow into more civilised and competent adults (hence Hendrick's 'Schooled Child', 'Child of the Nation' and 'Child of the Welfare State'[60]). This involved, over time, providing them with free education, access, in their own right, to the welfare state and even, later in the twentieth century, with rights. This perception recognises a certain lack of capacity in the child and a need for both adult family members and the state to take

---

[54] See eg, H Cunningham, *Children and Childhood in Western Society since 1500* (London, Longman, 1995); C Heywood, *A History of Childhood* (Cambridge, Polity Press, 2001).

[55] H Hendrick, 'Constructions and Reconstructions of British Childhood: An Interpretative Survey, 1800 to Present' in J Muncie *et al* (eds) *Youth Justice: Critical Readings* (London, Sage, 2002).

[56] *Ibid* pp 24–25.

[57] *Ibid* pp 25–26.

[58] M Carpenter, *Juvenile Delinquents: Their Condition and Treatment* (London, Cash, 1853) quoted in H Hendrick above n 55 at p 29.

[59] S Brown, *Understanding Youth and Crime* (Milton Keynes, Open University Press, 1998).

[60] Hendrick, above n 55 at pp 30–38.

responsibility for their developing needs. On the other hand a greater sense of their competence to possess rights[61] and in youth justice terms, a greater sense of their own responsibility as citizens of society to be accountable for their behaviour suggest a less protective and more independent perception. However, Davin remains convinced that dependence was the key feature that distinguished childhood from adulthood in the nineteenth century, even where children were expected to work from an early age, look after younger siblings and, in the case of young girls, become housekeepers for the better off. Whilst this may appear to suggest that children gained social, emotional and financial independence, Davin argues that this in fact merely reinforced the power relationship between adults and children which kept children in a subordinate role:

> Early engagement with work does not necessarily mean children 'grow up' faster . . . Where young people's labour was part of a shared domestic economy to which they were bound by loyalty, duty or perhaps a stake in the future, they might be stuck for years in the contributory and subordinate position of a child though physically and subjectively adult.[62]

Later in the twentieth century, as the middle-class indulgence in a 'natural' childhood began to be extended to working-class children through the development of welfare legislation and children's rights, dependency on adults was further reinforced.

Such a multiplicity of constructions of childhood may reflect the complexities of the society in which those children lived and the varying hopes, expectations and responsibilities of children at different times. Moreover, Brown suggests that historical constructions of childhood may have been symbolic of a wider sense of social order and stability (or lack of it), which may explain the contradictory nature of such constructions:

> The construction of the child as a particular kind of social category in Victorian society . . . culminated in a series of linked, if often confused and contradictory, conceptions of childhood identity. These focused on the potential and hope represented by childhood to restore a sense of lost order, innocence and simplicity; and the potential threat represented by childhood to undermine ideals, moral health and social order.[63]

In adult perceptions, therefore, children as unfinished and developing beings may have represented both anxiety and optimism in a rapidly changing social world. Given this symbolic perception of childhood, it is little wonder that sociologists have recently taken a greater interest in children as a social group.

---

[61] Though Onora O'Neill is doubtful of this competence—see 'Children's Rights and Children's Lives' (1988) 98 *Ethics* 445.

[62] A Davin, 'What is a Child?' in A Fletcher and S Hussey (eds) *Childhood in Question: Children, Parents and the State* (Manchester, Manchester University Press, 1999) p 25.

[63] S Brown above n 59 at p 11.

The last two decades have witnessed a new interest in childhood amongst sociologists, although two broad schools of thought have emerged. The first, more 'naturalistic' view, derives from the historical perspectives discussed above as well as from developmental psychology.[64] This school is described by Jenks as the 'pre-sociological' view.[65] Children under this model are seen as undeveloped or unfinished human beings, or 'human becomings'.[66] They are effectively on a journey, the destination being complete and fully developed adulthood. In this sense, this model reflects both the biological and psychological view of childhood in which children are yet to be physically fully grown and are psychologically in the process of developing personality and identity. As children are in an unfinished state, this perception of childhood requires that children will always be viewed by reference to adults; childhood exists only as far as can be measured in relation to adulthood as the standard norm:

> As long as adulthood could be treated as a fixed point that everybody understood, children could be defined in relation to this certainty. Thus, children were often defined as whatever adults were *not*.[67]

Childhood is therefore defined as the opposite of adulthood and childhood ends when children metamorphose into adults. This, in turn, creates an adult-centric society in which children must be managed by adults and moulded into their own form. Children are not only dependent on adults, but, as Davin argues, are subordinate to them.[68]

The style in which children are managed by adult society may vary according to 'natural' moral position assigned to childhood. Where children are perceived to be innately innocent the process of growing up involves a gradual loss of their original innocence and an adoption of adult capacity for immorality or evil. Since children are corrupted by the evil of the adult world, management of the angelic child will therefore aim to preserve that innocence for as long as possible and the management style will be protective. Conversely, where children are perceived to be innately evil and savage, the growing up process becomes akin to the 'taming' of the savage and the style of adult management of the demonic child is controlling and authoritarian. Within the 'pre-sociological' view Jenks finds both moral perspectives. A prevailing belief in the inherent innocence of childhood, stemming from Rousseau's belief that 'God makes all things good; man meddles with them and they become evil', is still, in Jenks' view, the dominant moral position in

---

[64] In particular the work of Jean Piaget; see *The Psychology of the Child* (London, Routledge, 1973).

[65] C Jenks, 'Sociological Perspectives and Media Representations of Childhood' in J Fionda (ed) *Legal Concepts of Childhood* above n 26 at pp 23–33.

[66] N Lee, *Childhood and Society: Growing Up in an Age of Uncertainty* (Milton Keynes, Open University Press, 2001) p 7.

[67] *Ibid* p 8.

[68] See above n 65.

contemporary society, despite being rather 'anachronistic'.[69] Nevertheless, a 'Dionysian'[70] childhood, in which children are wilful, unruly and inherently sinful is also evident in contemporary views, and enjoyed(?) a resurgence in the early 1990s after the murder of James Bulger by Venables and Thompson, who were decried in the press as 'the spawn of Satan'[71] and 'little devils'[72].

The second sociological view derives from the seminal work of Jenks[73], Stainton Rodgers *et al*[74] and James and Prout.[75] Their 'new sociology of childhood'[76] takes a more anthropological approach and assesses children as a discrete, though marginalised, group of social actors, and childhood as an infinitely variable social construction. As such, it is claimed that childhood does not exist as a universal truth, but rather as a state of being that derives meaning from a child's interaction and relationships with others. As those interactions and relationships change, either over time or within the discourse of societies and cultures, so too will the construction of childhood. In this sense, the 'new' sociological view departs radically from any notion of a 'natural' childhood. Neither do these sociologists agree that childhood can be properly understood only in relation to an adult-centric world. The anthropological approach precludes such a view, and prefers that children are understood in relation to their own world and based on their role as 'active and interactive practitioners of social life'.[77]

James and Prout assert that not only is childhood a social construction, but children exist in their own social world:

> The children's world is . . . not unaffected by, but nevertheless artfully insulated from the world of adults; it is to be understood as an independent place with its own folklore, rituals, rules and normative constraints.[78]

Jenks views this as the 'Tribal Child', and in the anthropological tradition, whilst adults may have a limited understanding of the child's social world, Jenks warns against ethnocentrism in the study of childhood. Rather, as with other tribes, children should be studied ethnographically in order to inform policy from a more child-centred position: 'There will be homologies, but the purpose of such a model

---

[69] C Jenks, *Childhood* (London, Routledge, 1996) p 124.

[70] *Ibid* p 126.

[71] *Guardian* (27 November 1993).

[72] *Sunday Times* (28 November 1993).

[73] C Jenks (ed) *The Sociology of Childhood: Essential Readings* (London, Batsford, 1982).

[74] W Stainton Rogers, D Harvey and E Ash (eds) *Child Abuse and Neglect* (Milton Keynes, Open University Press, 1989).

[75] A James and A Prout, *Constructing and Reconstructing Childhood* (London, Falmer Press, 1990).

[76] So named by M Lavalette and S Cunningham, 'The Sociology of Childhood' in B Goldson *et al* (eds) *Children, Welfare and the State* (London, Sage, 2002).

[77] C Smart *et al*, *The Changing Experience of Childhood: Families and Divorce* (Cambridge, Polity Press, 2001) p 12.

[78] James and Prout, above n 75 at p 29.

as this is to ensure that the homologies do not legislate or stand in a dictatorial relationship to the child's world.'[79]

Further, this 'tribal child' exists in a social group which is marginalised, and oppressed in an adult-centric world. This is a characteristic which, firstly, suggests that whilst childhood itself is not a universal construction, children as a social group do have a universal set of needs and interests. Secondly, it is a characteristic that children share with other minority groups[80] in a social structure which is inherently discriminatory. In this sense the child may be seen to belong to a sub-culture whose norms and values conflict with the dominant adult culture.[81] The child's dependence and relative powerlessness, according to this view, derive from their minority status and their political oppression. This new sociological view is therefore claimed to be a 'sociology for children rather than of children'.[82] Research under this model would involve a more active participation for children, in which they are given a voice rather than being mere 'subjects' of observation and comment, although Jenks acknowledges that 'Methodology . . . is a constant problem.'[83]

Conceptually, therefore, the two sociological schools of thought are diametrically opposed in terms of their perspective; one adult-centric, the other child-centric. This juxtaposition of perspectives is symbolised in the final scene of Golding's *Lord of the Flies:*

> A naval officer stood on the sand, looking down at Ralph in wary astonishment. On the beach behind him was a cutter, her bows hauled up and held by two ratings. In the stern-sheets another rating held a sub-machine gun.
>
> The ululation faltered and died away.
>
> The officer looked at Ralph doubtfully for a moment, then took his hand away from the butt of the revolver.
>
> "Hello."
>
> The officer nodded, as if a question had been answered.
>
> "Are there any adults—any grown-ups with you?"
>
> Dumbly Ralph shook his head. He turned a half-pace on the sand. A semicircle of little boys, their bodies streaked with coloured clay, sharp sticks in their hands, were standing on the beach making no noise at all.
>
> "Fun and games," said the officer.
>
> The fire reached the coco-nut palms by the beach and swallowed them noisily. A flame, seemingly detached, swung like an acrobat and licked up the palm heads on the platform. The sky was black.

---

[79] Jenks, 'Sociological Perspectives' above n 55 at p 39.

[80] Oakley, eg, suggests this may explain why women and children are so often discussed concurrently in academic discourse—'Women and Children First and Last: Parallels and Differences between Women's and Children's Studies' in B Mayall (ed) *Children's Childhood* (London, Falmer Press, 1994).

[81] The criminological implications of this are discussed in Ch 4.

[82] James and Prout, above n 75 at p 31.

[83] Jenks, 'Sociological Perspectives' above n 55 at p 39.

The officer grinned cheerfully at Ralph.

"We saw your smoke. What have you been doing? Having a war or something?"

Ralph nodded.

The officer inspected the little scarecrow in front of him. The kid needed a bath, a hair-cut, a nose-wipe and a good deal of ointment.[84]

Whilst Ralph and the boys depicted in the novel represent the tribal child (both in terms of appearing savage, but also in terms of regulating and creating a social structure in their own world on the island) the officer brings to the island the adult-centric, paternalistic view of them as playful, harmless and in need of care. Once on the island the officer takes control and manages the 'rescue' of the boys.

Perceptions of Childhood

This scene also demonstrates what we may learn from the sociological perspectives in terms of formulating youth justice policy. At first the officer is wary of the boys and even arms himself and his colleagues against a discovered 'tribe' on the island, which through lack of understanding and recognition, he inherently fears and does not trust. Once he recognises that 'tribe' as children, he perceives their innate innocence and disarms himself. It was clear from the first part of this chapter that contemporary perceptions of childhood, and particularly the end of childhood, and our perception of children as 'grown up' may impact on our perception of young offenders and their capacity to take responsibility for their actions. How we view young offenders is inextricably tied to our collective view of childhood, on the one hand, but results in some collective confusion and anxiety on the other when children's criminal behaviour reflects what we perceive as adult-like behaviour. Goldson describes this confusion as:

> [A] curious ambivalence [that] underpins adult conceptualizations of children and childhood. Sentimentality and anxiety are polarized. Constructions of innocence and vulnerability necessitating protection contrast sharply with conceptualizations of a threatening and dangerous childhood demanding correction.[85]

This confusion is evident in youth justice policy as successive governments struggle to decide whether to protect or punish children who offend.[86] However, as will be seen in chapter 3, youth justice policy in the late twentieth century has become more authoritarian and repressive, and sociological and historical constructions of childhood may help us to understand why that is so.

The pre-sociological construction of childhood, being inherently adult-centric in its perspective, takes adulthood as a normative standard and perceives children

---

[84] W Golding, *Lord of the Flies* (London, Faber, 1954) p 221.

[85] Goldson, 'The Demonization of Children' above n 51 at pp 40–41.

[86] See further Ch 3.

against that norm. Therefore children, who do not reflect that norm, are viewed as inferior, marginal, 'no-things.'[87] This is an inevitably negative perspective. Indeed, Smart *et al* remind us that 'to call someone 'childish' is not a neutral or descriptive observation: it is almost a term of abuse.'[88] Children, according to this construction, are therefore inevitably deviant, a subordinate and lesser social group. Whether they are assigned moral purity or feral savagery, as 'little angels' or 'little devils', they remain secondary beings. This can be contrasted with the new sociological position that children are 'people' in their own right and who are more positively viewed as members of a distinct social group, which may be different to adults, but not necessarily inferior.

The pre-sociological view thus creates in children a social group which adult society perceives as 'the other'. A sense of social identity for any social group necessitates, according to Abrams and Hogg[89], fear and mistrust of 'out groups'. A lack of understanding of the tribal child, as well as a sense of danger posed by the difference of the child, may prompt the anxiety and fear of children that appears to be prevalent in contemporary media and popular opinion:

> Childhood, placed at a tangent to adulthood, perceived as special and magical, precious and dangerous at once, has turned into some volatile stuff—hydrogen, or mercury, which has to be contained.[90]

Children who misbehave are therefore demonised and feared for their capacity to challenge both adult social identity and a stable social order. This may in turn necessitate social exclusion and oppression of delinquent youth or children as a social minority. Since we have already seen that adults, as a result of their superior social position, wield significant power over more vulnerable, dependent and marginalised children, for youth justice policy the volatility of the dangerousness of children is all the more potent when combined with the power of adults to contain that danger. Lee suggests that the pre-sociological construction of childhood, and its concomitant adult-centric construction of social power results in the following process: 'The more one is in a position to make decisions for children, to speak on their behalf, the more one is able to silence their voices. Abusive, cruel or unfair treatment of children can hide behind this wall of silence.'[91] Cultural conflict between the two social groups may result, not only in the definition of child-like behaviour as deviant, but also autocratic and controlling mechanisms to ensure that children retain their subordinate and innately 'innocent' social position. As Brown has suggested, children

[87] Fionda (ed) *Legal Concepts of Childhood* above n 26 at p 12.

[88] Smart *et al* above n 77 at p 8.

[89] D Abrams and M Hogg (eds) *Social Identity Theory: Constructive and Critical Advances* (London, Harvester Wheatsheaf, 1990) ch 1.

[90] M Warner, *Managing Monsters: Six Myths of Our Time* The Reith Lectures 1994 (London, Vintage, 1994) p 35.

[91] Lee, above n 66 at p 10.

have been constructed through policy not as citizens, but as objects of increasingly repressive modes of governance. As adult anxiety and punitive desire escalate, the (metaphorical) body of the delinquent is carved up to serve popular appetites, and effectiveness and rationality are increasingly subsumed under ideological imperative.[92]

Pearson's historical review of media perceptions of young people suggests that it was ever thus. The 'hooligan', he argues, is not a modern phenomenon and the 'respectable' fears of adult society have a long-standing heritage rendering the sense of youthful misbehaviour as a worsening problem something of an urban myth:

> The grumbling of older generations against the folly of youth—in which the rising generation is accused of breaking with the 'timeless' traditions of the past—has all the appearance of being a 'timeless' phenomenon itself.[93]

However, a historical review of youth justice policy reveals a less timeless obsession with the social control of young people. Whilst youth justice policy has always had to respond to the 'hooligan' there is a sense that such policy was becoming more authoritarian and less benevolent in the early twentieth century. Lee attempts to explain this phenomenon through an analysis of the state of adulthood in late modernity. He claims that we have witnessed a weakening of adult authority over children as socio-economic and cultural change have de-stabilised adulthood:

> [I]t is clear that stable, complete, standard adulthood can no longer be presumed to exist. It can no longer be relied upon to form the basis of our understanding of childhood and . . . it can no longer form the basis of adult authority over children.[94]

Adults have become even more confused regarding their role in relation to children, and in particular how to treat them, in modern society. Citing Dencik, he suggests that their 'uncertainty is chronic'.[95] Such uncertainty may exacerbate their fears of losing control, order and identity as a group which in turn results in the need to re-assert authority and power. Garland noted that, on a more global scale, governments rendered weak by the 'criminology of everyday life' resorted to a more 'volatile' and authoritarian criminal justice policy.[96] This political 'chest-beating' seeks to mask and deny the weakness of governments to win the war against crime and reinforces a sense that the 'sovereign state' is not so limited. In this context we have witnessed, according to Lee, a similar sense of inadequacy and weakness in adulthood which may have produced a similarly obdurate response.

---

[92] S Brown above n 59 at p 116.

[93] G Pearson, *Hooligan: A History of Respectable Fears* (Basingstoke, Macmillan, 1983) pp 219–20.

[94] Lee above n 66 at p 19.

[95] L Dencik, 'Growing Up in the Postmodern Age' (1989) 32 *Acta Sociologica* 155 at 174, cited in Lee, above n 66 at p 20.

[96] D Garland, 'The Limits of the Sovereign State: Strategies of Crime Control in Contemporary Society' (1996) 36 *British Journal of Criminology* 445–71.

Children, as passive, submissive (and non-enfranchised) subjects have little choice but to remain the silent recipients of such a response.

The politics of fear, justifying the assertion of power over children, was used to the full in the societal response to the murder of James Bulger by two 10-year-old boys in 1993. This crime was hysterically over-reported and analysed in the British press at the time and analysis of these reports,[97]and their influence on subsequent youth justice policy, demonstrates the full impact of the pre-sociological view of childhood on constructions of children as a deviant group. Media reporting of this case served not only to provide an outlet for the collective anxiety of adults in contemporary society (albeit irrationally[98]), but also an opportunity for politicians to step in and utilise those fears to justify a youth justice policy which sought to protect society from the 'monsters' it had created. On the one hand Venables and Thompson were vilified as 'freaks' and anomalous to perceptions of normal childhood, since their capacity for violence and evil transcended childlike behaviour and thrust them into the realm of corrupted adulthood (note that they were tried as adults in the Crown Court). Such a view is reconcilable to pre-sociological constructions of childhood and the dominant idea that it is normally characterised by 'original innocence'. The hysteria of the time may be accounted for by this shocking sense of the extraordinary and the consequent 'conceptual eviction'[99] of the two murderers from the category of children.

However, on the other hand, subsequent academic analysis demonstrates that in many ways the perception of the Bulger case generated such hysterical fear because is was symbolic of the norm in pre-sociological constructions. That Venables and Thompson were the rule and not the exception was what gave rise to the level of horror expressed in popular discourse at the time. Their capacity for evil represented the puritanical assumption that all children were possessed by such sinful urges and powers to destruct, evident to witnesses of children's behaviour in everyday life:

> The theory that children need to compensate for their own hapless dependence by imagining themselves huge and powerful and cruel has also normalised all manner of frightening playacting, equating children with monsters, childhood with a savage state . . . Lots of toys appeal to the idea of children's savagery: from huge furry, clawed slippers for tiny tots to wear to bed to warn off any other beasts in the night, to dinosaur lunchboxes.[100]

---

[97] See eg B Franklin and J Petley 'Killing the Age of Innocence: Newspaper Reporting of the Death of James Bulger' in J Pilcher and S Wagg (eds) *Thatcher's Children: Politics, Childhood and Society in the 1980s and 1990s* (London, Falmer Press, 1996). Also M Freeman 'The James Bulger Tragedy: Childish Innocence and the Construction of Guilt' in A McGillivray (ed) *Governing Childhood* (Aldershot, Dartmouth, 1997).

[98] As suggested by Michael King in *A Better World for Children: Explanations in Morality and Authority* (London, Routledge, 1997) ch 5.

[99] Jenks, *Childhood* above n 69 at p 128.

[100] Warner above n 90 at p 40.

The Bulger case merely served to demonstrate that children were as much a danger to each other as to adult society and James Bulger himself became the epitome of the fragile, vulnerable, injured child victim.[101] Jenks concludes that 'It was not just two children who were on trial for the murder of a third but childhood itself.'[102]

The consequences of this interpretation of the tragic events in 1993 were manifold. Firstly, the murder became at once both ordinary and extraordinary. For Jenks this was evident in the CCTV footage of James Bulger being led away from his mother by Venables and Thompson in the shopping centre, representing '[t]he transgressive juxtaposition of mundanity and magnitude'.[103] If we suspend our hindsight of what took place after the abduction, the CCTV image reveals the most ordinary of situations. A child is being led away, holding hands with two older children. This is an image that is not just ordinary, but which, in other circumstances, may represent the security of the child. The fact that this took place outside a Mothercare store is both a painful irony and a reminder of the image's mundanity. For Young the CCTV image symbolised the 'trauma of the visible'. The offence was unusually highly visible to the public; from the initial abduction caught on film in the shopping centre, through the long walk around the city centre that they subjected James Bulger to and which was witnessed by at least 38 eye-witnesses that gave evidence at the trial, through to the television and news images of the screened off body lying beside the railway tracks after the murder had taken place. 'The killing of James Bulger took place beside a railway track, in the dark, seen only by Venables and Thompson. Everything else, before and after, is re-presented.'[104] The visibility of this crime is traumatic in the sense that it reveals the powerlessness and failure of adults to control and prevent the violent behaviour of young people:

> Simply seeing an image does not lead to action. The sight of violence cannot determine any intervention against violence. The replaying of the image promises the possibility of intervention; trauma is experienced due to the gap between the image's promise and the substance of its referment.[105]

So this event was traumatic for adults because it reminded them of the everyday savagery of children, their powerlessness to control it and the destruction in social order when their vigilance fails and their backs are turned. The consequence of this has been to restore the vigilance of adult society; they must *watch* children with ever more care and assert their authority even more powerfully. It is ironic that Young notes how the trauma of the visible has resulted in adults 'imagining crime' in the deviant groups around them:

---

[101] Alison Young discusses this dichotomous view of children in *Imagining Crime* (London, Sage, 1996) ch 5.

[102] Jenks, *Childhood* above n 69 at p 127.

[103] *Ibid* p 125.

[104] Young, *Imagining Crime* above n 101 at p 137.

[105] *Ibid* p 132.

The only way we can watch out for ourselves is by being on the look-out for the criminal. The citizen must be alert at all times. Being alert involves keeping eyes open for risk, for danger, for crime.[106]

Imagining crime amongst children serves to increase adult fears and distrust of this social group, since all children represent the potential deviant, the potential criminal or the potential monster.

Secondly, the murder enabled politicians to capitalise on the fears and anxiety of adult society in justifying a youth justice policy that had political as well as (apparently) criminological capital. In 1992, John Major as Prime Minister had launched the Back to Basics political campaign to raise the popularity of his Conservative government. Back to Basics involved returning to a government policy founded on the traditional or 'basic' right-wing values of the moral majority, such as the centrality of the nuclear family, the enforcement of law and order, and the pursuance of a free market economy. Michael Howard, MP, a known proponent of far right politics, was appointed Home Secretary to ensure that the Back to Basics message featured as much in criminal justice policy as elsewhere. He embarked on implementing this brief in the Conservative Party Annual Conference in October 1993 when he famously introduced his speech with the line 'Crime is caused by criminals'. In some ways a meaningless soundbite, this can be read alternatively as a more significant statement of the retreat from any sense of welfare or leniency in the government's approach to young offenders, justified by a view that youth crime could be explained simply through their free will and the innate sinfulness of children. The subsequent murder of James Bulger could have provided no finer example of this. What followed will be discussed in more detail in Chapter 3, but the tone of official discourse on the 'problem' of youth crime became more risk oriented and protective of public safety in order to address the fear and anxiety exacerbated by the case which epitomised the potential threat posed by misbehaving youth.

This event, coupled with a sense of the dismemberment of the nuclear family in postmodern society, prompted some to go further and argue that childhood had disappeared. Postman propounded this thesis as a precursor to his later work, which sought to demonstrate that in the postmodern *Technopoly*[107] citizens (and children in particular), are *Amusing themselves to Death*.[108] The escalation of violent and sexual (or 'adult') material broadcast through the electronic media, is he claims, corrupting children to the extent that they are losing their childhood altogether:

> As for childhood, I believe it must, in the long run, be a victim of what is happening. Electricity makes nonsense of the kind of information environment that gives rise to and nurtures childhood.[109]

[106] *Ibid* p 209.
[107] N Postman, *Technopoly* (London, Vintage, 1993).
[108] N Postman, *Amusing Ourselves to Death* (London, Methuen, 1987).
[109] N Postman, *The Disappearance of Childhood* (London, Vintage, 1982).

Of course, what Postman is suggesting has disappeared is pre-sociological child-hood. His thesis echoes the view of Mr Justice Laws in *C v DPP* outlined above, that children are growing up more quickly. That is, the gap between adulthood and childhood is allegedly narrowing and children are being corrupted by the adult world at an earlier age. Whilst Postman's views are disputed by some,[110] his views were redolent not only in Laws J's landmark decision, but more widely in youth justice policy after the early 1990s in which Fionda discerns a distinct 'adul-teration'[111] and the tendency to eradicate child-specific procedures for dealing with youth crime which were the original hallmark of the youth justice system.

It has therefore been demonstrated that any contemporary construction of childhood has a significant impact on the treatment of young offenders and the formulation of youth justice policy. A consequence of the pre-sociological, adult-centred construction is that children are debased and rendered inferior and attributed with expectations of innocence and childishness which may or may not be realistic. When their behaviour is defined as criminal they face legal sanctions which reflect their moral culpability as well as the disappointments they engender in adult society in failing in those expectations. Furthermore, the pre-sociological construction of childhood, with its subordinate view of children, tends to prompt a youth justice policy which is marked by its authoritarian nature and tendency for social control of children. The 'new sociological' view, however, provides a con-trasting construction in which children are understood in relation to their own social world and therefore assigns children a more primary position and active role. It also does not presuppose any adult-centred moral awareness in the child, but assesses their behaviour in the child's own terms. A youth justice policy which embraced this construction of childhood would be significantly different. The tribal child, understood by reference to child-like norms, would prompt a more tolerant and child-centred policy. As Jenks concludes:

> One way of discovering why children commit acts of violence, what motivates them or what stays their hands, would be to know more from children themselves about crime and violence . . . the adult world finds itself in a state of ignorance about what ordinary children do ordinarily to one another . . . children are rarely seen as advocates of their own experiences. Children as social actors may gradually become visible and acceptable within sociology but in the public world children themselves may still have little oppor-tunity to have their voices listened to.[112]

A youth justice policy founded on this new sociological view may enable the adult community to understand more and condemn less.

---

[110] See eg, D Buckingham, 'Television and the Definition of Childhood' in B Mayall (ed) above n 80.
[111] J Fionda, 'The Age of Innocence?' above n 52 at p 84.
[112] Jenks, *Childhood* above n 69 at p 135.

3

Policy

The 1908 Children Act marked the 'birth' of a formal youth justice system in England and Wales, as it established the first Juvenile Court on a nationwide basis to deal with young offenders separately, both in terms of the trial forum and in terms of a more benevolent approach to that extended to adults. However, youth justice policy began to emerge some 50 years earlier than that, as penal reformers began to push for a more enlightened and individualistic approach to young offenders and greater appreciation of the special care and sensitivity required in dealing with a crime problem which stemmed from the particular difficulties faced by young people in their formative years. We can therefore trace over 150 years of 'slings and arrows' in youth justice policy, culminating in the radical overhaul that the system has received under New Labour. It is not proposed here to review that entire history, which has been so exhaustively researched and analysed in the growing number of texts on this subject.[1] This chapter aims to provide more of a thematic overview of this history and further details of it can be found *en clair* throughout this book in the discussion of the development of policy in relation to particular issues and areas of youth justice.

Here the focus is on the key questions of who makes youth justice policy, what influences it and how it is made. This will involve focusing on certain eras in history and taking a closer examination of these questions. First, the chapter takes an overall look at general approaches and over-arching models of youth justice and how these have been utilised at various times. Then it looks at the emergence of a new approach in 1980s which, given its practitioner focus, prompts the question 'who makes youth justice policy?' The focus on New Labour examines what has influenced their thinking on youth justice issues and how their landmark changes to youth justice have come about.

---

[1] For particularly good discussions of the history of youth justice see A Rutherford, *Growing Out of Crime: The New Era* (Winchester, Waterside Press, 2002) ch 3; A Morris and H Giller, *Understanding Juvenile Justice* (London, Croom Helm, 1987) chs 1, 3 and 4; and L Radzinowicz and R Hood, *The Emergence of Penal Policy* (Oxford, Oxford University Press, 1990) chs 6 and 7.

Models of Youth Justice

The Punishment Model

In the first part of the nineteenth century, the philosophy underlying the response to youth crime was 'punishment'. Children at this time, particularly those of the working class, who were more readily identified as offenders, were largely treated no differently from adults in society[2] and this model of youth justice reflected that social attitude. Not only were children expected to work at an early age and bear many of the other responsibilities of an adult, they were treated similarly to adults in terms of responding to their offending behaviour. They would be tried and sentenced in the adult courts (there being no alternative at that time) and would be eligible for all the adult penalties, including imprisonment, the death penalty, whipping, transportation and fines.

Under this model it is felt that to be lenient on children simply because they are young would be inconsistent with the criminological idea that crime is a product of free will. This idea was very much the product of classical criminology which was in vogue in the eighteenth century, having been developed by the likes of Beccaria[3] and Jeremy Bentham[4]. Classical criminology is based on notions of free will, rational choice and the social contract ideal. These theorists had argued that crime was the result of a rational choice on the part of the offender who had weighed up the benefits or otherwise of both crime and obedience to the law and had concluded that crime was more advantageous. The punishment inflicted under this theory seeks to condemn the infringement of the rights of others and reinforce the social contract to deter the individual and others from making a similar choice on subsequent occasions.

In the nineteenth century such a model had obvious appeal. Criminology had not advanced much beyond classicism at this time and alternative approaches were therefore not immediately apparent. Crime was also felt to be synonymous with sin and the punishment for youth crime was partly based on religious ideas. Sin required a response of retribution, and punishment was meted out according to the gravity of the sin. Further, developments in the criminal justice process at the time lent themselves to a punishment and retribution (as opposed to rehabilitative) approach. The punishment of children in the middle of the nineteenth century coincided with a general expansion of the prison system alongside the

---

[2] See further Ch 2.

[3] C Beccaria, *On Crimes and Punishments* (1764; reprinted Cambridge, Cambridge University Press, 1995).

[4] J Bentham, *An Introduction to the Principles of Morals and Legislation* reprinted (London, Athlone Press, 1970).

continued use of corporal, financial and banishment forms of punishment. In more recent times we have witnessed occasional returns to the nineteenth century punishment approach, when penalties involving the loss of liberty become a more prominent response to youth crime, along with denials that the only relevant aetiological factor in youth crime is free choice. In the mid-1990s both the Prime Minister, John Major, and his Home Secretary, Michael Howard, offered soundbites to the media indicating their preference for the punishment approach when they said respectively: 'We should understand less and condemn more' and 'Crime is caused by criminals'.

Therefore the key features of this model are that crime is viewed as an object of the free will of the offender, who makes a rational choice between the benefits of committing the crime and the resultant punishment. Regardless of the age of the offender, they are responsible for that rational choice and must be held accountable for it. Punishment therefore relates to the offence rather than the offender, the latter being largely irrelevant to the choice of punishment given, and any punishment should reflect society's disapproval and will be based on retribution and deterrence.

The Welfare Model

During the latter part of the nineteenth century a new model began to emerge alongside the punishment model; the welfare model. The emergence of this model was part of the individualisation of justice generally; that is, a movement away from emphasis on punishing the offence and towards dealing with the offenders themselves. It coincided with the development of the new positivist school of criminology. Positivism sees human behaviour as being largely determined by forces in the social world. For positivists, the government of society becomes akin to a technical enterprise, while for classicists it is a moral-political activity. Whereas the classicist saw breaches of the criminal law largely as offences against the social contract and the rights of other members of the pact, the positivist saw offending as a symptom of social pathology, a departure from the norm which could be responded to as a valuable symptom of pathology either in the individual or in the social process. This was particularly so with youth crime which, it was recognised, may not be a matter of rational choice. Rather, it was acknowledged that young people may commit crimes as a result of bad parenting, a lack of education, unemployment and poor living conditions.

The movement towards individualisation also reflected the changing social view of children at the end of the nineteenth century. Children were beginning to be seen as an object of concern with special needs,[5] including in the criminal justice

---

[5] See further Ch 2.

system. The opening of Parkhurst prison, specially reserved for young offenders, was indicative of this. It was seen that children may become tainted by adults in prison and the need to segregate children for proper deterrence was clearly recognised. In this way, the welfare approach first emerged alongside the punishment model, not as a distinct approach replacing the latter. Mary Carpenter[6] is often associated with the development of the welfare model. She expressed some disillusionment with the capacity of imprisonment to deter and reform young offenders. Instead, she argued:

> Proper training can counteract the imposition of poor family life, a corrupt environment and poverty, while at the same time toughening and preparing delinquents for the struggle ahead.[7]

Such 'proper training' was to be offered in a number of Reformatories which she established between 1850 and 1870. These were residential schools providing education and skills training, at first to young offenders after their prison sentence had been served, and later to young people who were considered to be at risk of offending, but who had not yet done so. In this way the welfare model emerged at first in the form of an after-care institution, not as a replacement for imprisonment. Also the Reformatories were a form of institutionalisation: welfare at this early stage did not involve non-custodial alternatives. The process of individualisation under the welfare approach came to a climax in 1908 with the Children Act (known as the children's charter), which created the Juvenile Court, the first court to deal specifically and only with children, and the 1907 Probation of Offenders Act, which provided the court with their first non-custodial alternative under which young offenders could be supervised in the community.

Therefore the key features of the welfare model are that crime is viewed as a product of the offender's environment and the offender is seen as neglected, poor or deprived, rather than depraved. The criminal justice system therefore seeks to help young people by identifying their welfare needs and the response to their crime is based on prevention by the alleviation of the offender's disadvantages. This response is offender-based rather than offence-based. Common features of a modern welfare-oriented youth justice system include a focus on community or non-custodial penalties which are designed to facilitate intervention by welfare agencies such as social services or the probation service (now the youth offending team (YOT) in England and Wales), which aims to combat 'risk' factors associated with re-offending. Welfare approaches may, indeed, by-pass the criminal justice process altogether, since notions of blame, criminal liability and punishment may

---

[6] Mary Carpenter (1807–77) was the daughter of a Unitarian Minister who devoted much of her life to pioneering free schools for children from deprived families. See further Rutherford, *Growing Out of Crime* (2002) above n 1 at pp 40–42.

[7] Mary Carpenter, *Reformatory Schools, for the Children of the Perishing and Dangerous Classes and for Juvenile Offenders* (London, Gilpin, 1851).

be seen as irrelevant in the task of preventing further offending. The development of the Children's Hearing System in Scotland in the late 1960s aimed to achieve just that.

The Treatment Model

Towards the end of the nineteenth century the treatment approach also emerged alongside the welfare model. This model emerged coincidentally with the development of both the profession of psychiatry and the development of a branch of positivist criminology called biological determinism. This type of positivism, pioneered by the likes of Lombroso[8], viewed offenders as biologically determined to commit crimes as a result of physiological defects or psychological maladjustments. Young people suffering from such disorders therefore did not rationally choose to commit crime but suffered an illness which needed to be cured. There was less focus on class and environmental conditions, but it was similar to the welfare model in that it did not replace punishment at first. Rather, psychiatric treatment was to be provided inside institutions such as the prison or the asylum.

As the twentieth century progressed, the history of youth justice policy began to reflect a debate over welfare and punishment, as successive governments changed their approach and adopted either a liberal, welfare/treatment model seeking to prevent youth crime through constructive intervention, or to punish it with a more hard-line, deterrent approach. To some extent this followed the pattern of political events as the welfare/treatment model is generally associated with the left of the political spectrum and tended to make an appearance as a Labour government was elected, while the punishment approach, with its belief in retribution and deterrence, tends to be a feature of the right and can be associated at various times with the election of a Conservative government. This does not always follow; the Labour government elected after the Second World War, for example, while pursuing a liberal social policy that created the welfare state, were not so liberal in relation to youth crime and invented the 'short sharp shock' and the detention centre. In the late 1980s and early 1990s we also witnessed a Conservative government who appeared to be dedicated to the reduction on the use of custodial penalties and pursued what was regarded as a surprisingly liberal approach to youth justice. However, broadly the trend has been that the models have been utilised and discarded over time, rather like a pendulum swing[9] between welfare and punishment. Liberal-minded policy makers pursue a non-custodial, rehabilitative

---

[8] Cesare Lombroso (1835–1909) was a psychiatrist and professor of legal medicine at the University of Turin. His key work on crime causation was published in numerous editions of his book *L'uomo delinquente* [*The Criminal Man*].

[9] This analogy was previously used in J Fionda, 'Youth and Justice' in J Fionda (ed) *Legal Concepts of Childhood* (Oxford, Hart Publishing, 2001) p 80.

agenda, swinging the pendulum to the left, followed shortly after by a sharp return to a law and order approach, swinging the pendulum to the right. The welfare ideal, criticised for its leniency and net-widening effect, is rejected and we see custodial penalties of different types being developed as the pendulum swings to the right. At certain times, however, governments have attempted to pursue a mixture of both ideologies and the pendulum swing became more complex. New Labour, in the late 1990s, pledged to bring the pendulum swing to a stop, promising us a third way, though it was not initially clear what that actually consisted of. Both of these phenomena are discussed below. There has been only one period in this history when the pendulum swing appeared to be abandoned and a new approach was applied briefly in the 1980s.

The 1980s—A 'Velvet Revolution'

After the initial enthusiasm for 'short, sharp, shock' during the 1970s,[10] reaffirmed by William Whitelaw in 1980,[11] we see that, towards the middle of the 1980s, an unprecedented decarceration occurred in youth justice. The proportion of young offenders sent to custody decreased dramatically as the proportion of young offenders cautioned almost doubled. All this happened without an increase in the extent of youth crime; indeed the number of known offenders (those either convicted or cautioned) dropped slightly towards the end of the decade.[12] How and why did this downward trend occur after the escalation of custodial sentences in the 1970s? Four main elements contributed towards this phenomenon: demographic changes, legislative changes, changes in the working philosophy of practitioners working with young offenders and the emergence of a new model of juvenile justice, the developmental model.

One reason for the fall in the use of custody during the mid-1980s was demographic change. There was an 18 per cent drop in the population of 14- to 16-year-old males. It has been suggested this 'clearly' had an impact on the overall numbers sentenced, and yet, this cannot be the only reason because, as Newburn points out, the figures do not explain the fall in the number of 14- to 16-year-old males sentenced to custody, from 12 per cent in 1985 to 7 per cent in 1990.[13] Legislative changes may have contributed to the lower use of custody and the higher use of cautioning in the 1980s. In 1980 the Home Office white paper,

---

[10] See further N Tutt, 'A Decade of Policy' (1981) 21 *British Journal of Criminology* 246.

[11] See Home Office, *Young Offenders* Cmnd 8045 (London, HMSO, 1980) para 46.

[12] For a fuller analysis of the figures see Rutherford, *Growing Out of Crime* (2002) above n 1 at ch 1.

[13] T Newburn, 'Young People, Crime and Youth Justice' in M Maguire, R Morgan and R Reiner, *The Oxford Handbook of Criminology* 3rd edn (Oxford, Oxford University Press, 2002).

Young Offenders, described the paradox that had arisen at the end of the 1970s: namely, that non-custodial alternatives needed to be developed because the prison-building programme (and resources allocated to youth custody), were unable to keep up with the extent to which custody was being ordered. Hence, although supporting the short sharp shock form of detention for some young offenders, the white paper also advocated the end of the use of remand custody for 14-year-olds and argued that restrictions should be imposed on magistrates in the use of custody for those over 15 years old. The result was the Criminal Justice Act 1982, section 1(4) of which imposed criteria which had to be satisfied before a custodial order could be made for a young offender.[14] Partly as a result of these criteria, magistrates were prevented from using custody to the same extent as they had in the previous decade.

However, Rutherford argues that there was also a 'sea-change' in the attitude of magistrates which made them reluctant to use custody, notwithstanding the restrictive criteria. Rutherford argues that, as a body, magistrates across the country became disillusioned with custody as a means of reforming young offenders.[15] Perhaps what also prompted such a 'sea-change' was another official initiative which increased the non-custodial alternatives available. In 1982, the Department of Health and Social Security made available £15 million to local authorities, to fund intermediate treatment (IT) projects.[16] Over 100 IT projects were set up in 62 local authority areas in England and Wales, providing magistrates with credible, rehabilitative, non-custodial alternatives. In 1985, the Home Office also gave official backing to (and guidance on), the practice of cautioning by the police, which played its part in greatly increasing the use made of this option, for non-serious offences, thereby reducing the number of offenders appearing before the magistrates in the juvenile court.[17]

The 'sea change' in the attitude of sentencing magistrates, shared by the staff of the welfare agencies at the time, demonstrated how a new model of youth justice had emerged, the developmental model. The key features of this model are that crime is viewed as part of the adolescent or traumatic 'storm and stress' phase in a teenager's life. Therefore, most (though not all) young offenders are likely, in normal circumstances, to grow out of their offending behaviour as they grow out of their adolescent years. The response to youth crime therefore needs to be as non-stigmatising and informal as possible in order to assist in the maturing process, and not to hinder the child's growth. Where official intervention is necessary, it should be as minimal as possible and should not involve separation from the family environment. Where official intervention is not necessary, informal

---

[14] See further Ch 7.
[15] See *Growing out of Crime* (2002) above n 1 at ch 1.
[16] For a description of such a project see Rutherford, *Growing Out of Crime* (2002) above n 1 at pp 112–20.
[17] See further Ch 5.

mechanisms (such as the family and the school) should be the preferred method of dealing with youth crime. As custody stunts a child's emotional growth and the development of a child into a mature adult, it should therefore be abolished for all but the most dangerous and serious offenders. The key to this approach is that, if all young offenders are presumed to grow out of crime, then the more problematic youngsters who require a more interventionist approach will be identified, without hindering the growth of the majority. Through their commitment to this model, practitioners worked hard to keep young offenders out of the juvenile court and wherever possible out of custody.[18] The important thing to remember about this approach, as its greatest supporter reflected in 2002, is that:

> The developmental approach was never a recipe for radical non-intervention but should instead be seen as a plea for understanding the full consequences of intervening in the lives of young people.[19]

Policy Conflicts

As stated above, at certain times during the last century, the pendulum swing between justice and welfare has become more complex as governments have tried to combine the two in a bifurcated policy approach. At these times the pendulum may be said to spiral. Youth justice policy witnessed significant growths in custodial sentencing and the social control of young people immediately after both the 1969 Children and Young Persons Act and the 1991 Criminal Justice Act, both of which had liberal foundations. The historical and political processes which took a proclaimed commitment to welfare and yet produced unprecedented practice of the justice approach were similar in both decades, and are founded in the drafting of ambiguous legislation, based on an inability to choose one approach over the other.

During both eras, the government spent several years designing a proactive new framework for youth justice policy and in both cases an overriding theme was decarceration and greater focus on non-custodial alternatives. The two governments had different reasons for rejecting custody as a viable and effective response to youth crime: in 1969 the government were proposing a more general treatment-based youth justice system, which would entail a minimal use of criminal procedures and, thereafter a focus on providing the courts with treatment options aimed at addressing the family and educational problems associated with youth crime.[20]

---

[18] Some of their personal experiences of this time are described in *Growing Out of Crime* (2002) above n 1.

[19] Rutherford, *Growing Out of Crime* (2002) above n 1 at p vii.

[20] See Home Office, *The Child, the Family and the Young Offender* Cmnd 2742 (London, HMSO, 1965) and *Children in Trouble* Cmnd 3601 (London, HMSO, 1968).

While the courts were to have some powers to issue short custodial sentences to older offenders, the use of custody did not fit neatly within the treatment approach. In 1991, the government was principally concerned about resources and the expense of custodial penalties, especially given their ineffectiveness in addressing the welfare needs of the offender. They famously concluded that prison is 'an expensive way of making bad people worse.'[21] So both governments set about designing a youth justice system in which less emphasis was placed on custodial measures (and in 1969, this also involved a gradual phasing out of criminal proceedings for many of the younger age range of offenders).

Both governments took their time in formulating proposals and the reforms were re-drafted in a series of discussion papers. However, by the time the final white papers had been published, the tone of the policies and their liberal, even abolitionist, stance had already been weakened and the language of those white papers began to take on a more punitive tone. In the 1960s there is a distinct change in tone between the title of the two white papers, moving from *The Child, the Family and the Young Offender* in 1965 to *Children in Trouble* in 1968. The former paper, as the title suggests placed a great deal of emphasis on the family as the appropriate forum for addressing the offending behaviour of young people and proposed to replace criminal proceedings for children under 16 (to be the new minimum age of criminal responsibility) with local family councils, which would adopt a non-criminal, non-adversarial, non-judgmental and constructive approach.[22] By 1968, however, the reference to the family had disappeared from the title of the later white paper, as indeed had reference to it in its proposals. By then the Home Office had, in response to a hostile response from the Magistrates' Association, proposed to retain the juvenile court for the over-14s (a slightly lowered new minimum age of criminal responsibility), albeit preferably using their civil powers in relation to care proceedings rather than their criminal powers. Detention centres and borstals, as penal institutions, would be *gradually* phased out as Intermediate Treatment was more fully developed as a community alternative but:

[T]he 1969 Act and the discussions and debates that preceded it did not directly address the issue of incarceration. Indeed, the issue as such did not exist. Certainly the term incarceration was not used, and there was a general blurring of issues around custody.[23]

In 1990 the government published a white paper, whose title was *Crime, Justice and Protecting the Public*, rather different from the preceding green paper entitled *Punishment, Custody and the Community*.[24] Whilst the green paper had emphasised

---

[21] Home Office, *Crime, Justice and Protecting the Public* Cm 965 (London, HMSO, 1990) para 2.7.
[22] *The Child, the Family and the Young Offender* above n 20 at pp 5–9.
[23] A Rutherford, 'A Statute Backfires: The Escalation of Youth Incarceration in England during the 1970s' in J Doig (ed) *Criminal Corrections: Ideals and Realities* (Massachusetts, Lexington, 1983) p 75.
[24] Home Office, *Punishment, Custody and the Community* Cm 424 (London, HMSO, 1988).

the greater use of a strengthened set of community sentences in order to avoid detaining young people in custodial institutions, the white paper, as the title suggests, placed some emphasis on the merit of custody as a means of protecting the public through incapacitation. The juggling of sentencing options at this time was discussed firmly within the criminal justice context and was to be managed through a new sentencing framework which would impose tight restrictions on the use of both.

The result in both eras was legislation which was forced into a compromise by political expediency both before and during the legislative process. The Magistrates' Association during both decades, fearing for the loss of their powers to use custody where they felt it was appropriate and necessary, voiced opposition to the liberal tone of the reforms. In the 1960s the Conservative Party in opposition to the government also found the reform measures to be anathema to their traditional law and order approach. What emerged from the Parliamentary process was legislation which had a principal focus on non-custodial responses, for both welfare and managerial purposes, but with some emphasis on giving magistrates the opportunity to use custody in what were thought to be the rare cases where serious young offenders needed to be incapacitated. Neither piece of legislation was ultimately committed enough to a decarcerative policy to remove entirely the custodial powers of the magistrates, nor to close penal institutions.[25] Both the 1969 Children and Young Persons Act and the 1991 Criminal Justice Act had left the mechanisms and apparatus for custodial sentencing intact.

Between enactment and implementation of these Acts there occurred similar changes in the political climate. In 1970 a general election replaced the Labour authors of the 1969 Act with a new Conservative government which had made manifesto promises to implement a tougher law and order policy. The implementation of the liberal-oriented legislation of 1969 therefore became the task of a different government to that which had enacted it. Their priorities were different and they were in a position to manipulate the implementation to ensure that the justice elements legitimised greater custodial sentencing while the liberal elements remained on the statute books to gather dust until 1991 when they were finally repealed.[26]

In 1992, John Major, who had previously replaced Margaret Thatcher upon her resignation in 1990, had just won his first election as Prime Minister in his own right, and had thereby been given the mandate of the people to place his own stamp on youth justice policy. His narrow election victory, and a series of by-elections soon after, revealed his political weakness and a country which felt it had been governed for too long by the Conservatives was beginning to lose its faith in the government. This, together with later media panics over youth crime,

---

[25] On the 1969 legislation see further Rutherford, *Growing Out of Crime* (2002) above n 1 at p 59.
[26] See further Rutherford 'A Statute Backfires' above n 23.

including after the murder of James Bulger in 1993, prompted John Major to announce a political initiative called Back to Basics, in which he promised to return his policies to the more traditional right-wing values of his party, which included a hard-line approach to crack down on youth offending.[27] The new Home Secretary appointed to implement this ideology, Michael Howard, also had a different priority to the previous administration which had drafted the 1991 Act, and the liberal intentions of that legislation threatened to be politically embarrassing. The government therefore sought to distance themselves from it by, first, repealing the most restrictive elements of the just deserts approach in the Criminal Justice Act 1993[28] and then, by enacting the Criminal Justice and Public Order Act 1994 which gave magistrates heightened powers to use custodial sentences for young people, including a new power to imprison the under-15s in Secure Training Units.[29]

Further, the behaviour of the judiciary in both eras was significant and the extent to which juvenile or youth court magistrates continued, despite more liberal policy rhetoric, to flex their custodial muscles was influential in the implementation of the legislation. In both the early 1970s and mid-1990s they felt inclined to do so, whether through an ideological commitment to prison as an effective option, or through their own reaction to the political scare-mongering over the threat of increasing youth crime at those times. We can therefore trace an escalation in the use of imprisonment and rising youth prison populations almost immediately after these apparently decarcerative Acts had been implemented. In the 1970s magistrates still had detention centres in place and made full use of them. After 1992 sentencing guidance from the Court of Appeal[30] lowered rather than raised the thresholds which were supposed to minimise the use of custody, not least through resurrecting deterrence as a sentencing principle despite the government's rejection of it in 1991.

The experience in these two eras shows us two things: internal conflicts within policy can badly misfire as ambiguous legislation is subject to changes in political whim. Unless a clear focus is adopted and other approaches rejected, the way remains clear for future administrations to prioritise different parts of the legislative provisions. Further the legislation is open to interpretation by the judiciary and other practitioners, whose task it is to turn the written word on the statute books into a reality. At that level, other ideologies and priorities may intervene to circumvent the government's intentions. This shows that a great deal of power to

---

[27] The tendency of politically weak governments to turn to 'strong' law and order policies is discussed by David Garland, 'The Limits of the Sovereign State: Strategies of Crime Control in Contemporary Society' (1996) 36 *British Journal of Criminology* 445.

[28] Which repealed the unit fine system and the requirement for magistrates to ignore previous convictions when sentencing.

[29] See further Ch 7.

[30] See further Ch 7.

determine policy lies with the practitioner in the youth justice system. They may
then apply their own ideology in interpreting and applying the statutory agenda,
prompting the question, who really makes youth justice policy?

Who Makes Youth Justice Policy?

There are two ways of viewing youth justice policy; agendas from the top, in the
form of white papers, legislation and government guidance, and agendas from the
ground level, in the form of practice initiatives, discretion in dealing with individual offenders and the application of working ideologies that pervade amongst the
practitioner agencies. Policy from the top, according to David Downes,

> is only one variable among others in governing what actually happens. Policy may be
> influential only to a degree or not at all. It may be clear or fudged. It may work success-
> fully at some stages of the criminal justice process and misfire badly at others.[31]

As scholars of youth justice, it is tempting to focus merely on this 'policy' view and
ignore the 'practice' view. The policy view is easier to determine, taking the form
of public documents and statements, and carries a certain weight, as it is officially
sanctioned. However, this policy may be remote and misleading as to what
actually takes place in the youth justice system, in much the same way that a
King's-and-Queen's approach to history provides a narrow and deceptive view
which obfuscates the real impact of events on a nation. There have been periods in
the history of youth justice when the divergence between policy and practice has
widened and when the real picture emerges from the 'coal face'.[32]

'Minimal Intervention' in Discretion in the 1980s

During the 1980s, the policy approach described above did not appear to be
entirely (if at all) responsible for the extraordinary decarceration of young offenders in that decade, not least because of its ambiguous approach to custodial
sentencing. The other official initiatives, the funding of Intermediate Treatment
and the sanctioning of cautions, still relied on impetus from the ground to take
effect. Many commentators on this period agree that what most contributed to the
decarcerative trend, was the commitment of ground-level probation officers
and social workers to reduce (or even eradicate) the use of custody. A marked feature of this period was the unison of practitioners across agencies in a working

---

[31] D Downes, *Contrasts in Tolerance* (Oxford, Clarendon Press, 1988) p 190.
[32] As Rutherford describes the ground level view—see *Growing Out of Crime* (2002) above n 1 at p 20.

ideology, based on the developmental ideal, which embraced a firm anti-custody ethos. A focal point for this ideology was the formation of the Association for Juvenile Justice, established in 1983 with an initial membership of 500, drawn mainly from basic-grade social workers, probation officers and members of voluntary organisations such as NACRO (National Association for the Care and Rehabilitation of Offenders) and the Children's Legal Centre. Through the publication of their journal *AJJUST*, the message that custodial sentences for young people were not only ineffective but also highly damaging to the developmental process, was disseminated among practitioners, in what could be described as the nearest equivalent to the Utrecht School in the Netherlands.[33] As a result Rob Allen describes how:

> The success of the . . . effective reduction of custody for juveniles in many parts of the country has been due in no small part to the energy, enthusiasm and the commitment of practitioners and managers 'on the ground'—the 'alternatives to custody' movement has developed an almost crusading zeal.[34]

Moreover, as the decade progressed this view was shared by magistrates in many localities. The Magistrates' Association was broadly supportive of the new ideology, not least because the welfare agencies had provided them with credible alternatives to custody. Rutherford describes how youth justice practitioners constructed viable community packages which kept young people out of prison.[35] McLaughlin and Muncie argue that one of the reasons for presenting more viable community packages was that, just as the powers of magistrates were more readily scrutinised during this period, so was the discretion of social workers.[36] The criticisms of the welfare approach had been noted, and a growing ethos of 'alternatives to custody' was being employed, this time through minimum intervention and maximum diversion either to the developmental institutions of the family and the school, or to Intermediate Treatment which made rigorous attempts to address the behaviour of even the most serious of young offenders. These latter alternatives, developed with the funding from the DHSS Initiative, focused on those at most risk of custody and provided constructive intervention at the 'deep end' of youth crime, where diversion from court may have been inappropriate. As Rutherford pointed out: 'Intermediate Treatment had come a long way from being associated in the minds of magistrates with "treats" such as rural outings in a mini-bus.'[37]

---

[33] See further W de Haan, *The Politics of Redress* (London, Unwin Hyman, 1990).

[34] R Allen, 'Out of Jail: The Reduction in the Use of Penal Custody for Male Juveniles 1981–88' (1991) 30 *Howard Journal* 30 at 49.

[35] *Ibid* pp 109–20.

[36] E McLaughlin and J Muncie, 'Juvenile Delinquency' in R Dallos and E McLaughlin (eds) *Social Problems and the Family* (London, Sage, 1993) p 178.

[37] A Rutherford, 'The Mood and Temper of Penal Policy' (1989) 27 *Youth and Policy* 27 at 30.

The reforms at this time therefore took the form of localised agendas to persuade magistrates to avoid custody and use the alternatives, even where custody may have been justified under the national criteria, producing 'custody-free zones' in some areas such as Hampshire, and contributing to the nationwide decarceration. This was an agenda that on a national scale would have been more difficult to achieve, but locally succeeded as informal relationships between the local courts and welfare agencies blossomed. Further, the practice of diversion from court was enhanced as relationships between the welfare agencies and the police were cemented by the local formation of multi-agency teams, Juvenile Liaison Bureaux,[38] in which the decision to caution could be discussed and arrived at through the pooling of expertise. These were less formal than the current youth offending teams, but did pave the way for what is often termed 'joined up' thinking and planning. Probation, social services, police, education, local authorities and voluntary sector organisations worked together to assist the young person. This was a real move away from the conflicts between those agencies that had been present during the 1970's and early 1980's.

Called to Account in 2004

The 1980s experience demonstrated that whilst national, official policy could be ambiguous or 'fudged', agendas on the ground, although less explicit, may be more directed and uniform and therefore make a greater impact on the way in which young offenders are actually dealt with. There has recently been some evidence that the anti-custody ethos is still alive and kicking at the ground level, despite New Labour's commitment to punishing offenders in the name of the classicist agenda of 'taking responsibility' and accepting 'no more excuses'. New Labour's approach has been to provide a clear and coherent framework for youth justice policy, in creating youth offending teams to implement their punishment ideology, and a Youth Justice Board, whose function it is to oversee the implementation on behalf of the Home Office, and to ensure that the ideology is appropriately ensconced in practice at the ground level. When the National Audit Office (NAO) reviewed the implementation of the newly designed community and custodial penalties since 1998,[39] representatives of both the Youth Justice Board and the welfare agencies were called to account by the House of Commons Public Accounts Committee, to justify some of the less positive conclusions that had been reached. On 2 February 2004, Mark Perfect, the Chief Executive of the Youth Justice Board (YJB) and Martin Narey, Chief Executive of the new joint probation and prison service, the National Offenders Management Service

---

[38] See further R Smith, *Youth Justice: Ideas, Policy, Practice* (Cullompton, Willan, 2003) pp 11–14.

[39] See National Audit Office, *Youth Offending: The Delivery of Community and Custodial Sentences* HC 190 (London, TSO, 2004).

(NOMS), were summoned to appear before the Committee and subjected to some rigorous questioning on the effectiveness and costs of delivering youth justice penalties.

The minutes of the meeting reveal an interesting tension for Perfect and Narey, between their loyalty to good practice and their perception as practitioners of what works, and their loyalty to the government to whom their respective institutions are accountable. The discussions therefore reveal a commitment that:

> I do not think that custody can make an impact in a very short space of time, in some circumstances I believe a short custodial sentence can be more damaging and community penalties are always likely to be more effective.[40]

However, moments later, Narey reveals a belief that rehabilitative intervention in the prison setting is more effective than it was before, making custodial sentences a more attractive option:

> [Y]oung people are leaving prison much better equipped to avoid re-offending, many more with educational qualifications than was the case a few years ago . . . I think there are things being done in custody now which were not happening a few years ago and that has been as a result of these reforms and the investment we have had from the YJB.[41]

This ambivalence made both Narey and Perfect ill-prepared to respond to later questions posed by the Committee regarding the results of the National Audit Office survey of YOT managers, in which 48 out of 146 managers revealed that they operated a policy at their local level of *never* recommending custodial sentences in pre-sentence reports presented to the youth court. This survey data came as a shock to both Mark Perfect (who evidently had not read this part of the NAO's report[42]) and to the MPs who were questioning him, who stated that 'That is outrageous!'[43] However, Perfect did acknowledge that this practice, which was ongoing in 2003, was a throw-back to the anti-custody ethos practised by the same ground-level workers in the 1980s. This had happened, despite efforts by both the YJB and the government to restrict the discretion of the practitioner and to offer a more directed statutory framework within which they practiced. Indeed, Mark Perfect's view of the practice was that it was a cultural 'problem':

> The culture that we had in the Seventies and Eighties was to divert young people away from the courts to not very much, and from custody to not very much, and that is what we are busy trying to change . . . The Youth Justice Board was established to change and challenge this culture.[44]

---

[40] Narey in response to Qu 2 from the Committee—Public Accounts Committee, *Youth Offending: The Delivery of Community and Custodial Sentences* 40th Report of Session 2003–04 HC 307 (London, TSO, 2004) Evidence p 1.

[41] *Ibid* Evidence p 1.

[42] See *Ibid* Evidence p 16, question 145.

[43] *Ibid* Evidence p 7.

[44] *Ibid* Evidence p 7. Martin Narey also described the practice as 'very worrying', p 17.

The discussion at this point revealed that whilst practitioners in many areas[45] had clearly not changed their practices since the 1980s, despite the more stormy political climate erupting above their heads, the senior management responsible for their practice adopted an Orwellian stance in re-writing this period of history, distancing themselves from it and describing it in a more critical tone.

This episode informs us that practitioners can still find opportunities to practice their working ideology 'beneath the radar', which may, in their quiet, subtle yet determined way, circumvent policy directives from above. The government's emphasis on controlling the discretion of these unruly social workers was manifest in the following exchange of views in the Committee hearing:

> **Mr Ian Davidson:** Who decides this policy as to whether or not custody ever works? A group of these teams take the view that custody never works, so who decides that? Are they left to decide that themselves or do they take their line from you?
>
> **Mr Mark Perfect:** The Youth Justice Board identifies what is good practice and if any YOT failed to engage with that then I will engage with the chief executives [of the local authority] and they have always been responsive.
>
> **Mr Ian Davidson:** . . . if they [YOTs] are under the direction of the appropriate chief executive of a local authority, there is no difficulty about instructions being given, so that actually will no longer prevail. These are employees, are they not? It is not as if you have to persuade them what has to be done. They can be instructed.[46]

For the respondents this was a question of 'managing' (or controlling) the teams more effectively. Martin Narey suggested that 'funding can be withdrawn if performance deteriorates' among these rogue YOTS,[47] while Mark Perfect lost no time, the following day, in writing to all YOT managers across the country, instructing them to behave themselves:

> The National Audit Office reported that 48 out of 146 Youth Offending Teams responding to their survey have a policy of not recommending custody in any circumstances. The MPs were shocked. Some young people do need to be held in secure facilities for the safety of themselves and/or the public. We have reached the point now where it is not acceptable to make no recommendation when a custodial sentence is appropriate . . . failure to do so undermines confidence in pre-sentence reports . . . The Board expects youth offending services to deliver a service based on assessment and reasonable recommendations to courts. Public confidence in our approach will be damaged if services are seen to adopt positions based not on the facts of the individual case but on a previously determined opinion.[48]

---

[45] 48 YOT managers had been extraordinarily honest in revealing this practice in a survey submitted to the NAO. It is possible that others were aware of the practice but had less courage to admit to it.

[46] Public Accounts Committee above n 40 Oral Evidence p 16.

[47] *Ibid* Evidence p 8

[48] *Ibid* Evidence p 23.

YOT managers have already demonstrated that the authority of the government can be undermined. The expression of dictatorial chastisement in this letter may similarly be ignored, especially where recent legislation has provided an increasing menu of alternative community arrangements such as the Intensive Supervision and Surveillance Programme which can be recommended to the courts in place of custody, in much the same way that IT was used in the 1980s. However, unlike during the 1980s, the Magistrates' Association no longer appears to be working with YOTs in their diversionary attempts; custodial sentences have increased during this period suggesting that the pleas in the pre-sentence reports are going unheard. However, this experience does demonstrate that opportunities do still exist to present a credible alternative rhetoric and practice to that prescribed from the top down. The government ministers and senior management may well believe that it is only they who have a legitimate policy-making role, but the practitioners have proved otherwise.

New Labour and the Policy-Making Process

The following discussion of New Labour's contribution to the history of youth justice seeks to demonstrate how contemporary youth justice policy, which is discussed further throughout this book, has been made. Detailed analysis of the provisions of legislation enacted and other policy initiatives can be found in later chapters. Here, the purpose is to discuss the policy-making method that is associated with the current government, the influences that they have drawn from in designing their approach to tackling youth crime and the thematic approach they have taken. Having pledged to 'end the confusion over welfare and punishment at local and national levels'[49] whilst in opposition prior to 1997, New Labour appeared to be pledging to end the pendulum swing that has been such a feature of youth justice history. What follows is an account of how their views were formulated in opposition, translated into policy proposals and then enacted in legislative form.

Influences

New Labour had been thinking a great deal about youth justice issues and what works in this field for many years before they won the 1997 election. During this time they had the opportunity of learning from the mistakes they perceived the previous administration were making, to make their critical views known in a

---

[49] Labour Party, *Tackling Youth Crime, Reforming Youth Justice* (London, Labour Party, 1996).

series of informal policy papers and to read the growing body of research and enquiry that was emerging during the 1990s on effective youth justice practice. When in government, a number of these influences were explicitly cited and quoted in their discussion papers, other influences were not made public but were clearly evident in the changes they proposed.

Throughout the long period in opposition, New Labour published a large number of discussion papers starting in 1988[50] and culminating in a pre-election manifesto in 1996.[51] These papers developed the sound-bite that Tony Blair had offered the media as Shadow Home Secretary in 1993: 'we must be tough on crime, tough on the causes of crime', into a more reasoned set of proposals. On the one hand there is a clear pledge to be tough, in a punishment style, on youth offending. A paper produced for the 1995 Party Conference declared: 'We are now the party of law and order' and proceeded to set out 'proposals for measures for tough action against crime in England Wales'.[52] The message in this and other papers was that we could expect 'firm action'[53] involving 'getting a grip on youth crime'[54] to restore confidence in the youth justice system and a reduction in the economic and other costs that crime incurred. This involved a 'fair deal for victims'[55] and a commitment to secure facilities for young people whose offending was serious or persistent, though local authority secure accommodation was preferred to secure training centres, to which they had publicly objected.[56] At the same time, other papers promised a programme of social and criminal policy aimed at alleviating causes of crime since the punishment approach of the Conservative government was seen as ineffective:

> [L]ong term, sustained reductions in crime may not be forthcoming unless much more attention is paid to the link between crime on the one hand and social conditions and restricted opportunities on the other.[57]

These papers promised a crime prevention package which would involve strengthening schools, supporting parents, combating drug and alcohol abuse, creating employment opportunities for young people leaving school, the provision of

---

[50] Labour Party, *Protecting Our People* (London, Labour Party, 1988).

[51] Labour Party, The Road to Manifesto Press Release (20 May 1996). The election manifesto proper was published in the form of a credit-card-sized slip of paper bereft of detail, but pledging merely to tackle youth crime and reform youth justice.

[52] Labour Party, *Safer Communities, Safer Britain: Labour's Proposals for Tough Action on Crime* (London, Labour Party, 1995) p 1.

[53] *Ibid* p 6.

[54] A Michael, *Getting a Grip on Youth Crime* (London, Labour Party, 1993).

[55] *Safer Communities, Safer Britain* above n 52 at p 4.

[56] *Ibid* p 7. Interestingly, Labour MPs sitting on the Public Accounts Committee debate discussed above criticised local authority secure accommodation for being too expensive and questioned the witnesses on why more use was not being made of YOIs which were cheaper—see report Evidence p 2.

[57] Labour Party, *Tackling the Causes of Crime: Labour's Crime Prevention Policy for the 1990s* (London, Labour Party, 1991).

leisure activities for teenagers and a pledge to restore state benefits to 16- and 17-year-olds.[58] They also promised a more efficient, cost-effective youth justice system that would deliver both welfare and justice speedily, especially necessary since they refused to believe Home Office statistics which were already showing a downturn in youth crime.[59]

Once in power, the government appointed a Youth Justice Task Force on 17 June 1997 to advise the Home Secretary on the development of their youth justice proposals. Membership of the Task Force included senior representatives of the relevant welfare and education agencies involved with young people, as well as civil servants from a variety of government departments and others from the judiciary and voluntary agencies. They published a number of reports between August and October 1997, too late to inform the drafting of the first round of consultation papers, but their final report states that they did influence the white paper, the drafting of the Crime and Disorder Bill, as well as implementation issues.[60] Their recommendations were almost identical to the policy proposals that had already been drafted into the consultation paper, which was not surprising given that the Chair of the Task Force was Norman Warner who had previously advised Jack Straw on criminal policy, and who, no doubt, was influential in the drafting of some of the previous papers discussed above.

The consultation papers and white paper drew explicit attention to sources of critique of the youth justice system in its current form and to sources of information on youth crime in order to inform policy and the problems which needed addressing. These included Graham and Bowling's study of youth crime[61] and the Audit Commission's 1996 report *Misspent Youth*.[62] The former had suggested that significant factors causing youth crime were associated with parenting behaviour and education experience[63] and had calculated the ages at which young people begin and end their offending career as well as the types and extent of their crimes. The consultation paper *Tackling Youth Crime* selectively cites parts of this research, particularly data which suggested that a small minority of young people begin offending early and evolve into serious and persistent offenders.[64] The Audit Commission had reviewed the extent to which the youth justice system was providing a value-for-money service in preventing and dealing with youth crime. Their criticisms that the system was disorganised, inefficient and expensive were

---

[58] See *Ibid.* These pledges are repeated in papers such as *Tackling the Causes of Crime: Labour's Proposals to Prevent Crime and Criminality* (1996); *Partners against Crime: Labour's New Approach to Tackling Crime and Creating Safer Communities* (1994) and *Parenting: A Discussion Paper* (1996).

[59] *Partners against Crime*, previous n at p 9.

[60] Home Office, *Final Report of the Youth Justice Task Force* (London, Home Office, 1998) para 4.

[61] J Graham and B Bowling, *Young People and Crime* HORS 145 (London, HMSO, 1995).

[62] Audit Commission, *Misspent Youth . . . Young People and Crime* (London, Audit Commission, 1996).

[63] See further Ch 4.

[64] Home Office, *Tackling Youth Crime* (London, Home Office, 1997) para 47.

also taken on board in that consultation paper,[65] particularly its recommendation that greater use be made of less expensive community penalties, that practitioners pool their resources and expertise and that delay and waste should be reduced.

Other influences are not explicitly acknowledged, but ideas in the government's proposals appear to have been 'borrowed' from other sources. The previous Conservative Home Secretary, Michael Howard, had published a consultation paper just a few months before the 1997 election setting out further reforms to the youth justice system.[66] As these proposals had no hope of resulting in legislation, unless his party won the forthcoming election in May, these proposals can only be read as an early form of manifesto. Howard's paper (which also cited Graham and Bowling's research) proposed a new framework for preventing offending to include multi-agency child crime teams[67] as well as a new parental control order.[68] At one time, the sharing of policy ideas between political parties at either end of the political spectrum may have been extraordinary. However, New Labour had already announced themselves as the 'new' law and order party (as discussed above) and had quoted the views on youth justice of prominent Tory Ministers, with approval, in their earlier discussion papers.[69] Further more, the only criminological theory that appears to have influenced New Labour's ideology on crime was that of the American right realists James Q Wilson and George Kelling. Resonance of their 'broken windows' theory[70], and the zero-tolerance approach to neighbourhood disorder that it advocates, can be found in the Labour paper *A Quiet Life* and in the consultation paper *Community Safety Order*[71] which ultimately produced the anti-social behaviour order.[72]

A further influence over policy, for a government to whom 'spin' and public image is so important,[73] was public opinion. Throughout the discussions of their proposals for a new youth justice system, was an underlying theme that the system must instil the confidence of the public and allay their fears of crime. The consultation paper *Tackling Youth Crime* was concerned at the lack of 'public credibility' in the system and its inability to prevent, deter and punish the victimisation of that public.[74] The protection of the public has become a strong theme in youth justice

---

[65] Home Office, *Tackling Youth Crime* (London, Home Office, 1997) p 1.

[66] Home Office, *Preventing Children Offending* (London, TSO, 1997).

[67] *Ibid* ch 3

[68] *Ibid* ch 5.

[69] In *Tackling the Causes of Crime* above n 57 for example, Michael Howard, Lord Tebbit and Kenneth Clarke are all quoted discussing the need to address the social causes of youth crime—see p 7.

[70] JQ Wilson and G Kelling 'Broken Windows: The Police and Neighbourhood Safety' (1982) 249 *The Atlantic Monthly* 29.

[71] Home Office, *Community Safety Order* (London, Home Office, 1997).

[72] See further A Rutherford, 'An Elephant on the Doorstep: Criminal Policy without Crime in New Labour's Britain' in P Green and A Rutherford *Criminal Policy in Transition* (Oxford, Hart Publishing, 2000).

[73] See A Rawnsley, *Servants of the People: The Inside Story of New Labour* (London, Penguin, 2001).

[74] Home Office, *Tackling Youth Crime* above n 64 p 2.

policy, which increasingly focuses on the persistent and 'dangerous' or serious young offender. The white paper had proposed not only greater focus on the members of the public who had been victims of crime and the community harmed by offending, giving the youth justice system more of a restorative tone, but had also suggested that the system, especially the youth court, needed to be more open so that the public would have greater faith in it:

> There must be more openness in youth court proceedings . . . present practice places too much emphasis on protecting the identity of young offenders at the expense of the interests of the victim and the community. Justice is best served in an open court where the criminal process can be scrutinised and the offender cannot hide behind a cloak of anonymity.[75]

By 2000 this concern had gone beyond the respective interests of the offender and victim, and the government were keen to address problems highlighted by the British Crime Survey's results on the attitudes of the general public towards the system. In this survey, the public had expressed their most critical views in respect of the youth justice system, but had also revealed that this was the part of the criminal process that they knew least about.[76] The government put two and two together and repeated their calls for the youth court to admit the public to hearings.[77] More recently, the government have been keen to involve the public generally in the policy-making process, by directly asking their views on what needs further reform. In a brief survey of just six questions, the public, and young people especially, were asked to give their views on how various hypothetical offenders in particular scenarios should be dealt with by the system.[78] The survey asked about issues such as how to 'punish young people involved in crime'[79], whether money for training youth court magistrates 'would be better spent elsewhere'[80], and whether it was 'a good idea to punish some violent young people without sending them to prison'[81]. Respondents had to tick an appropriate answer to these and other, sometimes leading, questions. The government received 8000 replies, and set out their responses to this in the form of a series of action points, directly adopting the suggestions made by the public.[82]

---

[75] Home Office, *No More Excuses* Cm 3809 (London, TSO, 1997) para 9.7.

[76] J Mattinson and C Mirless-Black, *Attitudes to Crime and Criminal Justice: Findings from the 1998 British Crime Survey* HORS 200 (London, TSO, 2000).

[77] Home Office, *The Youth Court 2001: The Changing Culture of the Youth Court—Good Practice Guide* (London, Home Office, 2001).

[78] Home Office, *Got Something to Say about Youth Crime?—So SayIt* (London, Home Office, 2003).

[79] The answers stated: in a way that prevents future offending.

[80] The overwhelming answer was 'no'.

[81] The majority answer was 'yes', with appropriate supervision, although when asked if this was fair to victims, a majority agreed that it was not.

[82] Home Office, *Stopping Youth Crime—Tell Us What You Think: Summary of Responses from Children and Young People and the Government Response* (London, Home Office, 2004).

Consultation

After their election in May 1997, the government spent a busy summer drafting four consultation papers on youth crime and another on anti-social behaviour orders, all drawing on the influences set out above. *Tackling Youth Crime*[83] set out wide-ranging changes proposed to the youth justice system, drawing together previous pledges they had made to address the causes of youth crime as well as achieving appropriate standards of punishment. *Getting to Grips with Crime*[84] responded to the Morgan Report[85] which had acknowledged that the community as a whole needed to join forces with the police and criminal justice agencies to fight crime and this consultation paper proposed a framework for local consultation between the public and local authorities in statutory crime-fighting partnerships. *New National and Local Focus on Youth Crime*[86] proposed the new management structure of the youth justice system, the creation of a Youth Justice Board and the move towards statutory multi-agency working through youth offending teams. *Tackling Delays in the Youth Justice System*[87] responded to the Narey Report[88] and proposed 'fast-track' youth justice which would be more efficient and in which young offenders would more speedily progress from arrest to conviction and sentencing. Finally, *Community Safety Order*[89] built on the concern previously voiced in the Labour Party's 1995 paper, *A Quiet Life*, and sought to tackle disorder, nuisance neighbours and anti-social behaviour through what was then termed a community safety order, but later became the anti-social behaviour order.

Those interested to do so were invited to respond to the policy ideas set out in the papers, as has always been the case where government publish early policy ideas in green papers, as they were formerly known, and wish to consult with experts and the public before they draft firmer legislative proposals. However, a significant feature of New Labour's method of legislating is a considered disregard for the views of those who responded. Each consultation paper gave details of where responses were to be directed and by when. The deadline for such responses to these papers were all between 31 November 1997[90] and 10 November 1997.[91] However, the white paper *No More Excuses*, which set out more detail on the

---

[83] Published in September 1997.
[84] Published in September 1997.
[85] Home Office, *Safer Communities: The Local Delivery of Crime Prevention through the Partnership Approach* (London, Home Office, 1991).
[86] Published in October 1997.
[87] Published in September 1997.
[88] Home Office, *Review of Delay in the Criminal Justice System: A Report* (London, Home Office, 1997).
[89] Published in September 1997.
[90] The deadline for responses to *Getting to Grips with Crime*.
[91] The deadline for *New National and Local Focus on Youth Crime*.

proposed legislation, drawing from all the consultation papers, was published in November 1997. This paper must have been drafted, re-drafted, discussed within the Home Office and printed, long before the deadlines for responses to the consultation papers, leaving little or no time for the responses to inform the second round of proposals. The white paper also offered the opportunity to respond to the government, this time by a deadline of 31 March 1998. By this time, however, the Crime and Disorder Bill was already progressing through the Parliamentary process, having been introduced in the House of Lords by Lord Williams on 2 December 1997.[92] Whilst paying lip-service to the democratic process of consultation, therefore, the government evidently either did not anticipate adverse comment on its policy agenda, or was not prepared to listen to the same. The last time that a government published discussion papers on reforms that ultimately became legislation was in the early 1990s, when the 1988 green paper allowed six months for responses to return and then a further year before the white paper proposals were published.

Using Youth Justice Models

As discussed above, the overall purpose behind all of the policy proposals set out in the papers and the Bill, was to end the confusion over welfare and punishment and to bring the pendulum swing to a stop. It was not clear at first whether it was the government's intention to choose one or other of the models, or to offer a third alternative. This became no clearer as the proposals emerged and the Bill was drafted. The plethora of consultation papers addressed a variety of issues from different policy perspectives and the Bill covered a multitude of youth justice, criminal law and other criminal justice issues. From this profusion of reforms and their multiplicitous origins, it is perhaps not surprising that no clear ideology is discernible and that the overall approach in the Crime and Disorder Act 1998 was described as 'a melting pot of principles and ideologies'.[93] The themes of *Tackling Youth Crime* included taking responsibility, being tough on crime and its causes and preventing youth crime, which applied both welfare and justice principles. On the one hand the Home Office stated that 'Punishment is important as a means of expressing society's condemnation of unlawful behaviour and as a deterrent'[94] and the theme of 'taking responsibility' reflects classicist thinking in holding young people accountable for their decision to commit an offence. On the other hand we are told that:

---

[92] HL Debates vol 583 col 1245 (1997/98).
[93] J Fionda, 'New Labour, Old Hat' [1999] Crim LR 36 at 46.
[94] Home Office, *Tackling Youth Crime* above n 64 at p 3.

[T]he strongest influences on starting to offend are low parental supervision, persistent truancy and associating with offenders. Effective intervention to prevent children and young people turning to crime and, if they do, to prevent re-offending, needs to address the causes of offending as well as punishing the offender.[95]

Thus the Home Office acknowledges that welfare has an equally important part to play in its legislative scheme, so that amendments to arrangements for custodial sentences for young offenders, sit alongside a greater variety of community sentences with greater or lesser focus on alleviating the underlying causes of crime. The white paper continues the bifurcated approach, although the language has become more dogmatic and the title of the paper, *No More Excuses,* indicates a shift towards justice, as the welfare approach smacks of leniency and justification for criminal conduct:

An excuse culture has developed within the youth justice system. It excuses itself for its inefficiency, and too often excuses the young offenders before it, implying that they cannot help their behaviour because of their social circumstances. Rarely are they confronted with their behaviour and helped to take more responsibility for their actions . . . The White Paper seeks to draw a line under the past and sets out a new approach to tackling youth crime.[96]

Not only did many commentators argue that his was not new at all[97] but that it emphasised punishment and denied any value in the welfare approach.

Hence the pendulum continued to swing after 1998, but it became a three-dimensional swing, or spiral, as further principles and objectives were added to the welfare/justice debate. Managerialism takes a clear priority in these reforms, since speed and efficiency are continually cited as essential policy objectives. We were promised not just effective and tough action on both crime and the causes of crime but also a fast-track and less expensive means of achieving those aims:

Delays will be cut by introducing **streamlined procedures** and **better case management** and by setting **mandatory time limits** for all criminal proceedings involving young people. Strict time limits for persistent young offenders backed by performance targets, will ensure fast-track justice and a speedy response to the offending of those from whom the public most needs protection.[98]

The swift administration of justice takes pole position in the list of objectives to be pursued in achieving the principal aim of the youth justice system[99] and the referral order, introduced in the Youth Justice and Criminal Evidence Act 1999

---

[95] Home Office, *Tackling Youth Crime* above n 64 at p 3.

[96] Home Office, *No More Excuses* above n 75, see 'Preface'.

[97] See J Fionda, 'New Labour, Old Hat' above n 93; A Morris and L Gelsthorpe, 'Something Old, Something Borrowed, Something Blue, but Something New? A Comment on the Prospects for Restorative Justice under the Crime and Disorder Act 1998' [2000] Crim LR 18.

[98] Home Office, *No More Excuses* above n 75 at p 2.

[99] See further Ch 7.

ensured that the more timely processes of rehabilitation and reparation would not burden the youth court, but would be diverted to an alternative youth offender panel.

Reparation and the principle of restorative justice were also key concerns of the government, who argued that the public not only required protection from offenders but were owed something back, either in their position as victims of crime or as members of a wronged community. Restorative justice received scant attention in the discussion papers in 1997, but was evident in the subsequent legislation in the form of referral orders, reparation orders and reparation requirements to be annexed to community sentences and warnings.[100] Protection of the public has become a greater focus, particularly since 2000, as new sentencing legislation, the Criminal Justice Act 2003, embraces the European trend towards actuarial justice.[101] That Act provides for longer prison sentences, indeterminate detention and intensive supervision in the community with electronic monitoring in an attempt to manage the risk posed by young offenders perceived to be dangerous.

New Labour have therefore provided a youth justice system in which the welfare/justice debate continues to rage. Whilst their reform process has been more considered than the 'scattergun'[102] approach of the previous Conservative administration, in that it is proactive and forward thinking, rather than reactive to media hysteria, their policy lacks clear ideology and a decisive stand on what they believe is the most appropriate means of dealing with youth crime. The government pointed out in the white paper in 1997 that the two models of welfare and justice were not incompatible:

> The Government does not accept that there is any conflict between protecting the welfare of a young offender and preventing that individual from offending again. Preventing offending promotes the welfare of the individual young offender and protects the public.[103]

This is not what they had said in 1996. However, they are not alone in arguing that a broad-brush approach can be more useful in this field. The government of the Republic of Ireland, in designing a similarly newly structured youth justice system suggested that:

> Opinion swings full circle when the harsh measures are not seen to work and a more liberal approach is then followed. When this does not work there is a return to the harsher measures and a cycle of juvenile justice oscillation between the two traditional

---

[100] See further Ch 8.

[101] See further R van Swaaningen, 'Back to the "Iron Cage": The Example of the Dutch Probation Service' in P Green and A Rutherford (eds) *Criminal Policy in Transition* (Oxford, Hart Publishing, 2000).

[102] Rutherford, *Growing Out of Crime* (2002) above n 1 at p vi.

[103] Home Office, *No More Excuses* above n 75 at para 2.2.

approaches, the juvenile justice delinquency model and the welfare model. It is accepted that this country and this Bill [The Children Bill 1999] embraces that the most appropriate system for this country is a modified form of a justice model which incorporates suitable elements of the welfare model. This is the best way to break out of the cycle earlier described.[104]

No doubt, to policy makers there are benefits to each model which make it difficult to abandon either in preference for the other. However, historical precedent demonstrates that there are problems with the failure to adopt a clear focus in youth justice policy. Bifurcated approaches in the past, such as in 1969 and in 1991, suffered for a lack of *equal* focus on the two models, and a tendency to give one greater priority. As the political climate changed in both 1970 and 1993, the anxieties of governments in relation to political power, and the public in relation to the perceived threat of crime, dictated that the punitive aspects of the bifurcated policies should take precedence and the socio-liberal aspects were sidelined. In recent years, anxiety over youth crime has not diminished, and is exacerbated by a more vague, global threat of criminal action. Further, the influence of public opinion and media comment over youth justice policy, previously the realm of officialdom and government ministers, has led to justice or punishment being the favoured priority for both resources and political energies. The justice model has also invaded the territory of welfare, tainting rehabilitative agendas with tough action to restrict liberty and incapacitate young offenders. Policy on youth justice has therefore begun to express a political form of double-speak in which punitivism and correctionalism are combined (together with restoration, managerialism and a lot more besides) in an effort to be kind to be cruel. Welfare may be used as the sweetener for punishment, to please all sides of the political spectrum.

The expression of mixed messages in youth justice policy also tends to result in increased intervention and expansion of the system. The historical pendulum swing emerged as governments tried one approach, found it unpalatable, and then tried another. Contemporary policy attempts to try all approaches at the same time, offering a greater variety of intervention methods for different types of offenders in the hope that within that melting pot we will discover that 'something works'. Not only does this deter the search for alternatives to criminal justice approaches, since the belief prevails that we have everything covered, but it ensures that more 'devils' are drawn into a wider net with a thinner mesh[105] and the distinction between 'devils' and 'angels' becomes greater.

---

[104] Dáil Éireann Debates vol 517 cols 700–1 (5 April 2000).
[105] See S Cohen, *Visions of Social Control* (Cambridge, Polity Press, 1987).

4

Crime

Young people are undoubtedly a criminogenic group. Statistically they commit a large proportion of all known crimes, and as a society we are now accustomed to a perception of young people as dangerous and unruly; James Dean's 'rebel without a cause' had a profound impact in our recognition of youth as a threatening social group. Research, both empirical and theoretical, would also suggest that young people are more prone to deviance, either because, from a positivist perspective, their environment and transition into adulthood propels them into it, or, from a radical perspective, because the perceptions and structures of society identify them as a deviant social group. This may, to some extent, justify the fact that youth justice policy is so unremittingly politically dynamic and young people the focus of so much control and intervention. The difficulty with this justification is that the evidence is somewhat questionable. We are well aware that statistics are subject to manipulation and even (or especially) official statistics cannot be fully trusted to be truthful. More than this, however, they are inextricably intertwined with our perceptions of the criminality of youth and a chicken and egg situation arises: do our perceptions emerge from the statistical information that we are presented with, or do the statistics reflect perceptions already formed, particularly with the growing emphasis on self- or victim- report studies? The discussion of the extent of youth crime must be mindful, therefore, of how youth crime is measured and presented for public consumption. This is especially so if the youth justice policy discussed in the rest of this book is, in any way, informed by the extent and nature of the 'crime problem' it is seeking to address. In this chapter, we can explore whether it is the statistical data or public (and media) perception of youth crime which informs policy. This is an important issue, since, as will be demonstrated, the two present very different criminological scenarios and will therefore pre-empt policies of contrasting emphasis on control and exclusion.

Measuring Youth Crime

Measuring youth crime has become something of a growth industry in recent years. As youth justice policy and law has expanded, the need to know more about how much crime young people commit, and why, has similarly grown. The Home Office now commit enormous levels of resources into gathering crime statistics as well as a multitude of crime surveys. Official statistics have, since the late nineteenth century, collected data on crimes reported to and recorded by the police, as well as data on whether and how the courts have dealt with those incidents. This statistical data is published bi-annually by the Home Office in increasing numbers of volumes of tables of figures, charts and graphs. Notwithstanding the wealth of information in those volumes, they continue to be criticised for the incomplete picture of crime that they present. In particular, the 'dark figure of crime', the notion of unreported and unrecorded crime omitted from the statistics, is thought to lurk dangerously beneath the official figures, rendering them inaccurate and unsafe as a basis for policy decisions.[1] This 'dark' figure comprises the crimes that victims do not report to the police, for a variety of reasons, and further offences that the police, in their discretion, do not record for statistical purposes or fail to recognise as crime for the purposes of proceeding with an investigation and prosecution.[2] Furthermore, as criminal policy changes, we can expect crime rates to change as the courts are encouraged to deal with greater or lesser volumes of young offenders, in the name of welfare or justice.[3]

Estimates of the volume of the 'dark figure' vary widely, but there is some consensus among commentators that it is large.[4] The Home Office themselves are concerned about this 'dark figure' and have taken steps to find more accurate ways of ascertaining a more precise picture of the crime problem. Surveys of both young people themselves and the general public, often funded by the Home Office, seek to do just that. Self-report surveys, such as Graham and Bowling's study[5] and the Youth Lifestyles Survey (YLS) ask young people about their involvement in crime. As an anonymous survey, it is hoped that crimes which remained undetected by the police and unreported by victims (or victimless) can be counted to present a fuller picture, as well as ascertaining more qualitative data than the official statistics can supply, on aetiological factors affecting the onset of offending and desistance. While methodological issues inevitably arise in such surveys,[6] if carried out with a reasonably representative sample and according to sophisticated research designs, these surveys present a great deal of more 'accurate' and valuable

---

[1] See further J Muncie, 'The Construction and Deconstruction of Crime' in J Muncie and E McLaughlin (eds) *The Problem of Crime* 2nd edn (London, Sage, 2001).

[2] See further C Coleman and J Moynihan, *Understanding Crime Data* (Milton Keynes, Open University Press, 1996).

[3] J Muncie, *Youth and Crime* 2nd edn (London, Sage, 2004) pp 17–19.

[4] For example, the British Crime Survey has estimated that a majority of crime reported to the police is never recorded, and that this proportion is increasing—to 70% in 2002/3: J Simmons and T Dodd, *Crime in England and Wales 2002/2003* (London, Home Office, 2003).

[5] J Graham and B Bowling, *Young People and Crime* HORS 145 (London, HMSO, 1995).

[6] For example, it is impossible to corroborate information presented to the researchers and there may be good reasons why young people over- or under-exaggerate their involvement in crime. See Graham and Bowling, above n 5, pp 8–9.

data on youth offending patterns. Similarly victim surveys, such as the annual British Crime Survey (BCS), interview members of the general public about their experiences as victims of crime. Again, subject to methodological issues, these surveys can reveal incidences of crime that went unreported to the police or that were not recorded by them, as well as further qualitative data on attitudes to crime and the criminal justice process as victims perceive it or have witnessed it. The BCS may not, however, uncover the true extent of victimless crimes, nor does it investigate child victimisation.[7] This has been researched to a limited extent by privately funded studies, although interviewing young children on such sensitive, and often technical subjects, can be difficult.[8]

The BCS has overtaken the Home Office criminal statistics in presenting the 'official' picture of crime, now being cited by Home Secretaries as evidence for the need for further policy action, and the results being more widely discussed in the media upon publication than those of the criminal statistics. This reflects a general sense among Home Secretaries, beginning with Jack Straw, that the public need to be aware of a fuller, more 'honest', picture of the youth crime problem. Straw announced changes to the 'counting rules' in 1998, prompting police officers to submit fuller records of the number of crimes reported to them to the government's statistical office.[9] This was followed by a wider review of criminal statistics commissioned by the Home Office in 2000.[10] This review suggested that there should be an overarching purpose to the gathering of crime statistics, namely 'to make governments accountable and to reduce the impact of crime on society'.[11] This, it is claimed, is best achieved by changing the definition of 'crimes' to be reported and to move towards 'problem oriented statistics'. The review therefore recommended that police should record or 'count' incidents reported or 'calls for service' rather than identified crimes:

> Incidents or 'calls for service' should be understood to include both crimes and non-crimes, and in particular should consider the capture of non-crime events brought to the attention of the police.[12]

This essentially moves the counting process back to the point at which a victim or a witness makes contact with the police and removes filtering discretion of the police not to count incidents that they have not interpreted as crime. This is a shift,

---

[7] Although the 1992 BCS did pursue a mini-survey of young people aged 12 to 15—see N Aye Maung, *Young People, Victimisation and the Police* HORS 140 (London, HMSO, 1995).

[8] J Hartless *et al*, 'More Sinned Against than Sinning: A Study of Young Teenagers' Experience of Crime' (1995) 35 *British Journal of Criminology* 114.

[9] Previously allowed to count only one offence, where an individual perpetrator had committed a series of offences, and to ignore many minor offences, in 2002 they were instructed to 'count' each offence reported, including the minor ones.

[10] J Simmons, *Review of Crime Statistics: A Discussion Document* (London, Home Office, 2000).

[11] *Ibid* recommendation 1.

[12] *Ibid* recommendation 4.

described in the review, from the 'evidential' approach to the 'prima facie' approach.[13] The review appropriately points out that the counting rules, applied inconsistently by different police force areas, render it impossible to state with certainty what definitions of crime are being counted around the country. However, the answer, in their view, lies in recording everything just in case, including suspicious or anti-social behaviour and demands for police assistance. Whilst, on the one hand, this may reveal operational needs for the police, to include this information in the *crime* statistics will inevitably ensure that 'crime' figures rise, particularly in relation to young people, whose behaviour, given public perceptions of young people, may be subject to more suspicion than that of other groups.

Why would a Home Office, committed to reducing youth crime and 'preventing offending by children and young persons'[14] wish to radically change the collection of criminal statistics to reveal a larger volume of crime. The review speaks of honesty and nationwide consistency in criminal statistics and responds to criticism that existing statistics make 'what is measurable important, not what is important measurable'.[15] We may, indeed, discover not only the true extent of the 'dark figure' of crime but much more besides. This may include the extent to which the public are not prepared to tolerate the behaviour of young people, criminal or otherwise, which may, in turn, inform youth justice policy. The distinction between crime and non-crime has less significance in the proposed collection of statistics, although Nils Christie asserted over 20 years ago that the distinction was rather haphazard in any event:

> Crime is not a "thing". Crime is a concept applicable in certain situations where it is possible and in the interests of one or several parties to apply it. We can create crime by creating systems that ask for the word. We can extinguish crime by creating the opposite types of systems.[16]

This illustrates the policy conflict here. A Home Office wishing to pursue a politically useful, expanding youth justice policy, needs some raw material. As crime rates for young people appear to fall, they can create a system of counting which turns that trend around. Added to this, the government has created a whole new set of deviant incidents, in the form of anti-social behaviour, which is so loosely defined it can neither be properly measured nor reach any optimum level.[17] In this way, Christie's later work suggests that governments can find a 'suitable amount of crime' from an 'unlimited natural resource'. Christie, in common with

---

[13] J Simmons, *Review of Crime Statistics: A Discussion Document* (London, Home Office, 2000) para 24.

[14] The principal aim of the youth justice system, Crime and Disorder Act 1998, s 37.

[15] S Jenkins, 'Criminal Conspiracies' *The Times* (1 December 1999).

[16] N Christie, *Limits to Pain* (Oxford, Martin Robertson, 1982) p 74.

[17] See further Ch 10.

Garland,[18] attribute the need to find this raw material as a feature of modern weak governments:

> Today, in the suitably weakened state, it is a dream of most politicians to be involved with law, particularly penal law . . . There are so few other arenas left, arenas for the national exposure of the politicians as political figures, and for the party line. Where the dominant goal of life is money and the dominating idea is that an unregulated market economy is the road to this goal, in such a system crime becomes the major arena for what remains of politics. Here it is possible to present oneself as a person deserving votes, with values common to a population of affluent consumers.[19]

So while the government will inevitably wish to demonstrate that their youth crime prevention policies are effective, a rising youth crime problem can inform an expanding youth justice policy and further social control and exclusion of young people as a social group.

The Extent of Youth Crime

In this section the currently held research and statistical data on the extent of youth crime will be examined. This tells us what is known about the age at which young people begin offending, the types of crime they commit and the extent to which crime trends in this area are changing. This data can be found in the self-report and victim surveys discussed above, as well as from official statistics. While there may be differences in the extent to which these sources evaluate the true number of crimes committed by young people, upward and downward trends in youth crime are broadly similar across each source.[20]

Young People and Crime (1995)

The study by Graham and Bowling[21] reveals that there is a pattern of trivial but prevalent offending amongst young people. They interviewed a sample of 1721 young people aged between 14 and 25 in 1992 about their background, their family life, school, their lifestyle, any offending behaviour and whether they were using controlled drugs of any sort. As well as finding evidence of the risk factors which cause young people to offend, this study is one of few which have asked detailed

---

[18] D Garland, 'The Limits of the Sovereign State: Strategies for Crime Control in Contemporary Society' (1996) 36 *British Journal of Criminology* 445.

[19] N Christie, *A Suitable Amount of Crime* (London, Routledge, 2004) p 37.

[20] Simmons, *Review of Crime Statistics* above n 10 at Fig 1, p 10.

[21] *Young People and Crime* above n 5.

questions to non-offenders about their behaviour. Thus their conclusions include interesting and important information about why some young people *do not* offend. A large proportion of the young people questioned in the study had offended at some time, indicating that offending behaviour amongst young people is widespread. 55 per cent of the males and 31 per cent of the females surveyed admitted to having committed an offence at some time in their lives, although the figures were 28 per cent and 12 per cent respectively when confined to the year during which the study took place.[22] As expected, female offending rates were lower, with young women committing roughly half as many offences as young men.[23] The majority of young people surveyed (56 per cent of males and 57 per cent of females), however, had only committed one or two offences during that year, while much smaller proportions (26 per cent of males and 9 per cent of females) admitted to committing more than 5 offences.[24] This may suggest that offending behaviour amongst young people is largely not as persistent as policy makers often claim.[25] Property offending was much more common than violence (males were twice as likely to commit property offences as violence, and females were three times more likely to commit property offences).[26] Where young people did admit to violent offences, most admitted to only one or two offences of this type.[27] Half of the males and one third of the females also admitted to drug use although few used drugs regularly and most of this drug use was confined to the consumption of cannabis. The authors of this study asked about drug use simply as an indicator of young people's lifestyle—they did not attempt to link drug use and crime in any way. Asians had the lowest rates of both offending and drug use, which confirms previous research findings,[28] but interestingly, and contrary to some previous findings, Afro-Caribbeans and white young people had roughly similar rates of offending and drug use.[29] In terms of the age at which offending occurs, the average age of onset, according to this study was 15 for both males and females, which is a year later than the onset of truancy and alcohol consumption and a year earlier than the onset of drug-taking.[30] Males reached a peak level of offending at 14 for property offences, 16 for violent offending, and 17 for serious offending while females peaked at 15 for both property and serious offending, 16 for violent offences and 17 for drug use.

---

[22] *Young People and Crime* above p 11.

[23] *Ibid* p 20.

[24] *Ibid* p 18.

[25] See also Hagell and Newburn who reach the same conclusion in their research study—A Hagell and T Newburn, *Persistent Young Offenders* (London, Policy Studies Institute, 1994).

[26] *Young People and Crime* above n 5 at p 12.

[27] *Ibid* p 18.

[28] M Fitzgerald, *Ethnic Minorities in the Criminal Justice System* Royal Commission on Criminal Justice Research Paper no 20 (London, HMSO, 1992).

[29] *Young People and Crime* above n 5 at pp 20–21.

[30] *Ibid* p 29.

Youth Lifestyles Survey (1998/99)

In 1998–99 the Home office funded a further, similar self-report study, the second Youth Lifestyles Survey.[31] In this study a wider sample of 4848 young people aged between 12 and 30 were interviewed about their offending behaviour, background and lifestyle. This study revealed similar patterns to Graham and Bowling's earlier study, with some significant variations. Among this sample 57 per cent of young men and 37 per cent of young women admitted to offending at some point, representing similar levels to Graham and Bowling's study, and the offending rates in the year preceding the study were also similar (26 per cent of males and 11 per cent of females.)[32] The average age of onset of offending revealed here was slightly lower, however, at 13½ for males and 14 for girls.[33] Offending was more prevalent in older members of the sample and those aged 14 to 21 also revealed that males offended at around three times the rate of females. Peak ages for offending were 18 for males and 14 for females.[34] Again, most of the offending amongst young people under 18 involved property offences, including shoplifting, criminal damage and buying stolen goods. Violent offences increased in males over the age of 16, and for both sexes the rate of fraudulent offending increased as offenders reached their 20s as other types of offences decreased, although for young women over 21 any type of offending was very low.[35] This survey did reveal that a large part of the youth crime problem is committed by a very small number of persistent offenders. Half of all the known youth crime reported was committed by approximately 10 per cent of those admitting offences, representing a mere 2 per cent of all males and less than 1 per cent of all females in the overall sample.

Crime and Justice Survey (2003)

A much larger-scale self-report study was initiated by the Home Office in 2003. The Crime and Justice Survey questioned 12,000 people of all ages (between 10 and 65) about their offending behaviour. About 4500 of these were young people under 25, who, though a disproportionate sample in relation to the general population,[36] were a booster sample who could provide data on youth crime which was of specific interest to the researchers. The results are still being collated, but to

---

[31] C Flood-Page, S Campbell, V Harrington and J Miller, *Youth Crime: Findings from the 1998/99 Youth Lifestyles Survey* HORS 209 (London, TSO, 2000). A previous Youth Lifestyles Survey had been conducted in 1992/93.

[32] *Ibid* p 10.

[33] *Ibid* p 10.

[34] *Ibid* p 10.

[35] *Ibid* p 10.

[36] Young people aged between 10 and 17 inclusive account for about 10% of the general population of England and Wales—see Office for National Statistics, *Census 2001: National Report for England and Wales* (London, TSO, 2003).

date, some figures on crime and anti-social behaviour by young people have been released. Rates of commission of anti-social behaviour[37] are similar to crime rates found in the above studies (29 per cent overall admitted to this type of behaviour within the previous year; a third of the male sample and a fifth of the female sample).[38] Anti-social behaviour appears to reach a peak at the 14- to 19-year-old age range (within which, on average, 38 per cent admitted to incidents).[39] The majority of young people behaving anti-socially only did so once (68 per cent) with only 9 per cent admitting to two or more and only 3 per cent admitting to five or more incidents.[40] There was little evidence to corroborate the claim that anti-social behaviour was a precursor to later criminal offending, with only 12 per cent of those committing anti-social behaviour also admitting to criminal offences. The most common forms of anti-social behaviour asked about were causing a public disturbance, accounting for 15 per cent of incidents, followed by causing neighbours to complain (13 per cent).[41] More serious forms such as joyriding and carrying a weapon were far more rare, although racial harassment was most likely to be committed on more than one occasion.[42]

Official statistics

Home Office statistics from the police and the courts, present a similar overall pattern, in that most youth offending is property based; theft and handling stolen goods, burglary, criminal damage and fraud collectively accounted for 43 per cent of all known youth crime amongst males aged 10 to 17 in 1999, 58 per cent amongst females. The remainder was a combination of a small number of violent and sexual offences (11 per cent for males, 9 per cent for females), drugs and motoring offences. Other summary offences (which would include public order offences) accounted for the largest proportion of youth crime for both sexes; 35 per cent for males and 28 per cent for females.[43] Overall, in 1999 the official statistics recorded 145,700 known male offenders under 18 and 35,900 female offenders of the same age. The peak age for offending was 18 for males and 15 for females, both sexes showing a sharp decline in offending after those ages.[44]

---

[37] Defined for the purposes of this survey as noisy or rude behaviour in public, joyriding, behaviour resulting in complaints by neighbours, graffiti and racial harassment. Of course, anti-social behaviour may take an indefinite number of forms since the definition of it is victim led and depends upon the tolerance or otherwise of witnesses to the behaviour.

[38] R Hayward and C Sharp, *Young People, Crime and Antisocial Behaviour: Findings from the 2003 Crime and Justice Survey* Home Office Findings no 245 (London, Home Office, 2005) p 2.

[39] *Ibid* p 2.

[40] *Ibid* p 3.

[41] *Ibid* p 1.

[42] *Ibid* p 2.

[43] Home Office, *Criminal Statistics for England and Wales 2000*, Annex B, Table 1.

[44] *Ibid* Annex B, Table 2.

Crime trends

Self-report surveys that are not replicated on a regular basis cannot reveal a great deal about whether youth crime is increasing or decreasing. As the Youth Lifestyles Survey has been repeated twice, the second survey was able to assess a change over a six-year period. Official criminal statistics, whilst inaccurate as to the full extent of youth crime, can, providing they are consistently inaccurate, tell us about levels of youth crime over longer periods. A Home Office study of official statistics between 1981 and 1999[45] shows a decrease in the number of known young offenders aged between 10 and 17 inclusive, a fall of 37 per cent for males and 15 per cent for females.[46] Taking into account demographic factors (such as the fall in numbers of young people in this age range in the general population) that study found a decrease of 23 per cent in the number of known male offenders but an increase of 8 per cent of female offenders.[47] The extent of the crime committed by these offenders remained relatively steady over the period 1981 to 1999 but decreased particularly between 1998 and 1999 (a 2 per cent decrease in male crime and a 7 per cent decrease in female crime).[48]

The Youth Lifestyles Survey compared the rates of crime reported to them in 1992/93 with those in 1998/99. This presents a rather different picture. One reason for this is that, as a self-report study, it can collate data about crime rates whether or not the offenders were proceeded against, whereas the Home Office statistics will not include offenders against whom no further action was taken or who were given informal cautions (those formally cautioned are included in the official figures). The YLS, like the Home Office, found that overall crime rates had not changed significantly over the period in question. However, when their results were broken down into more specific age ranges, they found that male offenders aged 14 to 17 reported 14 per cent more crime in 1998/99 than in 1992/93. Offending rates for males aged 18 to 25, however, fell by 6 per cent. Figures for female offenders rose by 4 per cent in the 14 to 17 group, but fell by 4 per cent in the older age group.

These studies do reveal a general picture of youth crime, albeit with minor variations. Young people are a highly criminogenic group; although not the most criminogenic group, since adults commit 75 per cent of all known crime.[49] It is a

---

[45] K East and S Campbell, *Aspects of Crime: Young Offenders 1999* (London, Home Office, 1999).

[46] *Ibid* para 3.1.3

[47] *Ibid* para 3.1.3. A problem with these types of statistics in relation to female offending is that they can produce rather startling percentages where the actual numbers remain very small. The 8% increase here is accounted for by an increase from 1300 to 1400 female offenders per 100,000 of the population.

[48] *Ibid* para 3.1.3.

[49] Admittedly a large proportion of this is committed by 'young adults' aged between 18 and 21, who are represented in the self-report surveys, although not in the official statistics and the youth justice system.

predominantly male problem (although young females are committing more offences now than before). The problem consists predominantly of young men aged over 14 who commit property offences, occasionally persistently, and rarely commit violent or sexual offences. Overall youth crime has not significantly increased in the last two decades, some figures even suggest it has fallen.

Desistance and Growing Out of Crime

Early self-report studies did not examine the extent to which and reasons why many young people do not offend. Further, of course, official Home Office statistics would not reveal data on this since they are inevitably only concerned with young people who do offend. However, in the study of youth crime, desistance may be of great importance, not only in assessing how young people can be encouraged to cease offending, but also in relation to the developmental ideal, to test whether youth crime is indeed a temporary, adolescent phase which declines as a young person makes the transition from childhood to adulthood. Graham and Bowling's study reversed the trend and uncovered data on both issues.

In that study, those who were least likely to offend in the first place, were those who revealed fewer of the 'risk' factors identified, involving mainly problems in the home and at school. These are discussed below. However, the age at which offending for each sex reaches a peak denotes the point at which desistance begins to occur, and this is usually associated with the growing-up process. Young women most commonly stopped offending after their mid-teens and by the time they reached their early 20s, their offending rate was five times lower than for females in the 14 to 17 age group.[50] For males, offending reached a peak later, at the age of 18, and remained high into their mid-20s. Only after this age did serious offending begin to fall. Property offending decreased in quantity in older males but tended to change in character, from acquisitive crime such as theft and handling stolen goods, to fraud and workplace theft, leaving Graham and Bowling to hypothesise that 'some males may switch from relatively risky property offences such as shoplifting and burglary, to less visible and thus less detectable forms of property crime . . .'[51] The Youth Lifestyles Survey also examined whether there was evidence that crime decreased with age, and found that overall there was a decline in offending for both sexes after the age of 21. They concurred with Graham and Bowling in finding that men persisted in property offending until the age of 25, but after that a decrease was found to take place, and by then the property offences had become more fraudulent or involved more hidden theft from the workplace.

[50] *Young People and Crime* above n 5 at p xi.
[51] *Ibid* p xi.

These findings suggest that young females do appear to grow out of crime as they leave their adolescence. However, for young men, the growing-up process appears to commence later, after the age of 25.

Qualitatively, Graham and Bowling examined why young people stopped offending. First, of those who had admitted offending at least once in the previous year, young people were asked whether they would be likely to offend again. Two-thirds answered in the negative, most claiming that offending behaviour was 'childish', they were frightened of being caught, they acknowledged it was wrong or felt that their 'life had changed'.[52] In relation to those who reported that they had already stopped offending as they grew older, the reasons for desistance were consistent with making a successful transition into adulthood and greater maturity. For females, key desistance factors were leaving education and finding stable employment, leaving home, forming stable relationships (lasting more than a year) and having children. Other, slightly less influential, desistance factors included finding a sense of direction and meaning in life, realising the consequences of their actions and learning that crime doesn't pay. For males, however, these desistance factors were less associated with a decline in offending, although there was some evidence that those who remained living with their parents or who had married or were living with a long-term partner were more likely to stop offending.[53] Since there was evidence that a degree of desistance did occur in older males (albeit later than for females) this could only be explained by the increased absence or avoidance of onset factors as they grew older. For example, those older males who drank heavily or used controlled drugs, had partners or peers in trouble with the police or had been themselves a heavy offender or a victim of violent crime, increased their offending behaviour at this age. So those young men who were successfully able, in their mid- to late-20s, to avoid these onset factors were more likely to begin the desistance process.[54]

Explanations

The Research

The study by Graham and Bowling and the Youth Lifestyles Survey, through which young people were interviewed to ascertain their involvement in criminal behaviour, have been able to elicit qualitative data on the reasons why young people offend. Asked about aspects of their home life, education and social life, the

---

[52] *Ibid* p 51.
[53] *Ibid* p 59.
[54] *Ibid* p 63.

researchers were able to test whether there were statistical correlations between certain background or lifestyle factors and offending behaviour. The results of the two studies reveal common aetiological correlations. Information so far released from the 2003 Crime and Justice Survey has also revealed aetiological or 'risk' factors associated with anti-social behaviour in young people, which again broadly reflect those revealed by the previous two studies. These commonly identified factors which correlate strongly with offending behaviour relate to parental and other family relationships, attendance and achievement at school and other lifestyle factors such as alcohol and drug use, the behaviour of friends and socio-economic status.

Family Life

Graham and Bowling found a strong correlation between a young person's relationship with their parents and siblings and the onset of offending behaviour. Family structure also had some influence. Young people who lived with both natural parents were the least likely to start offending, (these accounted for 42 per cent of male offenders and 17 per cent of female offenders). Those living with a one natural parent and one step-parent were the most likely to offend (57 per cent of male offenders and 36 per cent of female offenders), while those living with a single parent fell in between (49 per cent male and 23 per cent female, respectively).[55] Family size, and the number of siblings that the young person lived with did not significantly affect offending behaviour, except that there was some evidence that the larger the family, the greater the risk of offending. However, these figures are more revealing in the light of correlations between parental attachment and supervision. Both male and female young offenders who did not get on well with either parent were approximately twice as likely to offend as those who had good relationships with them. Those who were strongly attached to their parents produced an offending rate of only 42 per cent whereas the offending rate for those less attached was 70 per cent overall.[56] The pattern is similar in relation to parental supervision, where those who experienced low levels of supervision were almost twice as likely to offend.[57] Young females in the sample were more likely to be closely supervised than males, and this helps to explain their relatively low offending rates overall. Where either a parent or a sibling were in trouble with the police, young people were much more likely to offend themselves. This was particularly so for young females, who were almost five times more likely to offend where they knew someone who was in trouble with the police. Young males were approximately twice as likely to offend in this situation.

---

[55] *Young People and Crime* above n 5 at p 36.
[56] *Ibid* p 37.
[57] *Ibid* p 38.

The Youth Lifestyles Survey only tested aetiological factors in relation to persist-ent or serious offenders (those who had offended three times or more) but their results confirm Graham and Bowling's findings. There were strong correlations between young people offending and living with one step- and one natural parent (and to a lesser extent those living with single parents), lack of parental supervision and weak attachments. Indeed, the researchers concluded that a key determining factor in the onset of offending was the relationship between the young person and their parents since this may also affect the level of supervision they receive:

> The degree to which teenagers are supervised by their parents is directly related to the number of evenings that they go out: generally young teens who went out several evenings during the week or who went to pubs, night-clubs or parties, were more likely to be offenders. On the other hand, those young people who spent most of their leisure time in the home, for example, reading or watching TV, were less likely to be offenders. Thus, this analysis points towards a close link between poor family relationships and a higher risk of offending.[58]

The suggestion here is that those who got on well with their parents were more likely to spend more time in their company and therefore their parents knew where they were and what they were doing. Those with poor relationships were more likely to wish to leave the home environment and seek activities in environ-ments where they are not only unsupervised but where opportunities for offend-ing are greater.

The Crime and Justice Survey 2003 has examined 'risk factors' prompting the onset of both crime and anti-social behaviour. Not only did a negative parental relationship represent a 'high risk factor' in relation to anti-social behaviour but parents with a relaxed attitude towards certain inappropriate behaviours (such as starting a fight, using graffiti, skipping school or smoking cannabis) were also more likely to have offending children. The researchers in this study, however, have questioned whether the poor relationship with a parent prompts offending behaviour or results from it.[59] Whilst offending and poor relationships correlate in these studies, given the greater responsibilities being placed on parents by the courts to take responsibility for their children's misbehaviour, the offending may cause, or contribute to, a poor relationship.

Education

Both the Graham and Bowling study and the YLS examined the extent to which experiences in school may trigger the onset of offending behaviour. In this area attendance and attachment were significant indicators of a young person's likelihood of offending, suggesting that in common with parental influences,

[58] C Flood-Page *et al* above n 31 at p 33–34.
[59] Hayward and Sharp above n 38 at p 4.

attachment and good relations are crucial, as is supervision and some element of social control over young people. The YLS confirmed the results of Graham and Bowling's study in relation to attachment to school, finding that males disaffected from their educational experience were twice as likely to offend, females three times as likely.[60] The 2003 Crime and Justice Survey also found that 'poor school environment' presented as a high risk factor in anti-social behaviour.[61] Poor school environment included factors such as a lack of clear rules, poor teachers who do not praise good work and a school regime which made it easy to truant. Attendance at school was also found to have a strong correlation with offending behaviour in all three studies, where regular truancy and exclusion from school rendered young people much more likely to offend. Graham and Bowling and the YLS researchers, however, have indicated that further research needs to be done to ascertain whether truancy and school exclusion are *causal* factors in offending or *coincidental* factors, tending to occur at the same time in a young person's life as the onset of offending.[62] Linked to both attachment and attendance was the issue of achievement. The YLS found significant differences in offending behaviour between those who performed at an above average level at school (of whom 6 per cent of males and 4 per cent of females offended) and those whose performance was below average (18 per cent of males offended, 9 per cent of females).[63] Similarly in the older range of respondents, those who left school with some qualifications were half as likely to offend as those who left with none.[64] Those who do not attend school and who do not enjoy their experience of school are likely to suffer academically and together these factors render the school environment an important determinant in whether a young person offends or not.

Other Lifestyle Factors

Each study has examined a variety of other factors connected with a young person's lifestyle and their relationships with their offending behaviour. Graham and Bowling examined the impact of the socio-economic status, and poverty in particular, on youth crime, but found little significant difference in offending rates between young people (males in particular) from higher or lower socio-economic groups. For females, offending was more common amongst those from lower socio-economic groups, but when examined in conjunction with other family factors such as supervision and attachment, these class differences became less significant.[65] Some forms of anti-social behaviour were found to be associated

---

[60] C Flood-Page *et al* above n 31 at p 36.
[61] Hayward and Sharp above n 38 at p 4.
[62] For example see Flood-Page *et al* above n 31 at pp 37–38.
[63] *Ibid* p 36.
[64] *Ibid* p 36.
[65] *Young People and Crime* above n 5 at p 33–34.

more often with young people facing financial difficulties, in the 2003 Crime and Justice Survey. Those living on 'council estates' and in low-income areas were more likely to cause neighbour complaints, racial harassment and to carry weapons.[66] However, overall the prevalence of anti-social behaviour was no higher in low-income and urban areas than it was in higher-income and rural areas. Council estates were reported to produce only slightly higher levels of anti-social behaviour than non-council areas.[67]

Although Graham and Bowling studied drug use amongst young people, and found levels of use similar to offending rates, no link between the two was made, and we cannot assume that those who used drugs were the same young people who reported offending behaviour. The YLS and the Crime and Justice Survey, however, have examined whether there is a link between the consumption of controlled drugs and alcohol and crime. The YLS found a high correlation between drug use and serious or persistent offenders, especially amongst those aged 12 to 17, in which age group drug users were five times more likely to offend than non-drug users.[68] Alcohol use in this same age group correlated with higher offending rates, especially with violent behaviour and the more regular their reported drinking, the more likely they were to be involved in acts of violence. This correlation was lower in the 22 to 30 age group. Social activities such as playing darts, pool and snooker were also associated amongst the under-18s with higher levels of offending, although this may be attributed to the fact that these activities often take place in drinking environments such as pubs and are therefore linked with alcohol consumption. Gambling, in the form of betting or playing the National Lottery, also produced higher offending rates.

In relation to anti-social behaviour, drug use was identified as the highest risk factor amongst all age groups, although it was more of a factor in the 17 to 25 age group.[69] For younger people, alcohol use was also a very high risk factor. It was unclear from these results, however, whether the consumption of drugs or alcohol *caused* the anti-social behaviour, or actually *was* the anti-social behaviour. Young people seen drinking in public maybe reported as acting anti-socially, whether or not the alcohol affects their behaviour. Associating with delinquent peer groups was identified in all three studies as having some influence (but not as significant as other factors) on offending behaviour and anti-social behaviour, although, again, it is difficult to ascertain a cause and effect relationship with this factor. Whether young people associating with delinquents *become* delinquent

---

[66] Hayward and Sharp above n 38 at p 5. However, since anti-social behaviour is very much determined by victim perception, this may tell us more about victims living in these areas than the young people themselves.

[67] *Ibid* p 5.

[68] C Flood-Page *et al* above n 31 at p 40.

[69] Hayward and Sharp above n 38 at p 4.

themselves, or whether delinquent youths seek to associate with other like-minded groups, is unclear.

Theoretical Explanations

Since this is not intended to be a textbook on criminology, it is not proposed here to review the entire literature on criminological theory. This has been done comprehensively elsewhere in relation to youth crime.[70] Rather those criminological theories have been selected which most closely corroborate and provide further explanations of the picture of youth crime depicted in the statistical data set out above. The theories chosen fit with the results of research set out above and also demonstrate the relationship between criminological theory and the thematic analysis of policy throughout this book. Perceptions of young people as 'devils' or 'angels' and the resulting labelling, exclusion, condemnation and state control of the 'devils' has done little in the last few decades to reduce levels of youth crime. Crime for this group remains a relatively static phenomenon. The theories set out below provide analytical tools with which to explore the failure of much of the youth justice policy to date and the extent to which criminal policy may in fact manufacture or pre-empt as much crime as it seeks to reduce. They may also, together with the statistical explanations above, suggest viable ways forward for a more credible and effective approach to the troublesome behaviour of young people.

Anomie and Strain

Emile Durkheim (1858–1917), the French sociologist, moved criminological thinking, at the end of the nineteenth century, from focus on the individual to an examination of social structures and their impact on deviant behaviour. His theory of anomie was developed through two key works *The Division of Labour in Society* (1893) and *Suicide* (1897). Through these works, Durkheim argued that western societies were in a state of transition between their early 'mechanical' form and towards a post-industrial 'organic' form. A mechanical society is one that features a series of small communities, socially bonded through common customs and traditions. While there is some division of labour integral to these communities, there is little division of labour between them. These communities are self-sufficient and founded on cohesive belief systems and a common sense of morality. Deviance, in such a society, is a healthy phenomenon, which contributes to the social solidarity of the group through the expression of collective sentiments of condemnation, and reinforces collective norms through repression of deviance.

---

[70] See further Muncie, *Youth and Crime* above n 3 at chs 3 and 4; S Brown, *Understanding Youth and Crime: Listening to Youth?* (Milton Keynes, Open University Press, 1998) ch 2.

Mechanical societies feature a large, but constant, set of criminal sanctions aimed at maintaining a moral and social order. Further, deviance allows, over time, the progression of norms and social change as opposition to diversity gradually gives way to acceptance and the reinvention of those norms:

> There is no occasion for self-congratulation when the crime rate drops noticeably below the average level, for we may be certain that this apparent progress is associated with some social disorder.[71]

In organic societies, as industrialisation transforms systems of labour, these small communities give way to increased division of labour in the society as a whole. Attachment to social solidarity and collective belief systems is weakened and society becomes more centrally regulated. As industrialisation transforms society and the economic prospects of those living in it, regulation of transactions and relations between individuals may fall behind the progress of social change, creating a sense of 'lawlessness' or 'normlessness' which Durkheim called anomie (from the Greek *anomos* meaning 'lawless'). Observing that rates of suicide in France increased during times of both economic prosperity and economic decline, Durkheim concluded that deviance might result from a lack of social regulation. In a state of economic crisis (either through over- or under-production), the individual is unable to achieve equilibrium between his needs and his means and the state lacks the capacity to regulate either. The individual, forced to adjust his aspirations according to his means, suffers pain and misery, and social maladies, such as suicide, result.

In the 1930s Robert Merton developed the concept of anomie in his criminological work on strain. He argued that an individual's means are not determined by social structures and economic forces, as Durkheim had done, but rather they were a product of cultural aspirations or socially defined goals. Society determines goals according to what is culturally valued and specifies institutional, or accepted, means of attaining those goals. For Merton in the America of the 1930s, the cultural goal was the accumulation of wealth, through the institutional means of education, the gaining of employment, careful husbandry and honest diligence.[72] Crime can be understood in relation to the *strain* that occurs when an individual in that society aspires to the cultural goal, pursues the institutionalised means, but where social structures limit the opportunity for that individual to achieve it.[73] Merton suggested that individuals subject to that strain may react in a number of ways, some of which would result in delinquent or criminal behaviour.

---

[71] E Durkheim, *The Division of Labour in Society* (1893; reprinted New York, Macmillan, 1933) p 156.

[72] At that time, the cultural goal of America was idealised in the American Dream, in which people believed that any American citizen could make something of their lives, despite any disadvantage, and ultimately become President.

[73] R Merton, 'Social Structure and Anomie' (1938) 3 *American Sociological Review* 672.

'Innovation', whereby the individual finds new and innovative means to acquire wealth, may result in workplace theft, fraud and tax evasion. However, 'rebellion' results in that individual rejecting the cultural goal and replacing it with their own, alternative, goal. Their behaviour in pursuing their own goal may, therefore, fall outside the norm for that society and be viewed as 'alternative' or, more importantly, may fall outside the bounds of legitimacy and be viewed as 'deviance'.

It is this sub-cultural aspect to Merton's work that may have most significance in relation to youth crime. Young people, particularly those most disaffected from the education system and the labour market, may find themselves living in a social structure which conspires to deny them the opportunity to join the prosperous classes. Facing this inevitable truth, young people collect into sub-cultural groups in which they can pursue their own cultural goals and norms, although this may be viewed as deviant by the rest of society. Albert Cohen, in developing Merton's theory further, attributed this analysis to the cultural goal of youth gangs in America in the 1950s. Far from seeking wealth or material success, the cultural goal within these sub-cultures was status. Unable to attain status vicariously through that of a middle-class family, low-status youths pursued this goal through other, deviant means.[74] In the US, this sub-cultural analysis of deviance in young people can also be seen in the work of Cloward and Ohlin in the 1960s in which they suggest that a lack of opportunity for youth sub-cultures to attain status through aspiring to middle-class, conventional and legitimate means, either pursue status through joining the adult criminal underworld, or if that too is impossible, by acquiring status by coercion.[75] Muncie assesses the degree to which this sub-cultural analysis can explain the formation of youth gangs in Britain in the late twentieth century in the form of Teddy Boys, Mods and Rockers, Punks, Skinheads and Rastafarians.[76]

Conflict and Sub-Cultures

Criminological theorists in the 1960s and 1970s developed a new radical explanation for crime, which centred on the structure of power and the inequalities it produces in society, and moved away from explanations based on the pathologies of individuals. Collectively these theories, some based on the work of Karl Marx, argued society's norms are not only established by the powerful groups in that society, but are also enforced by the powerful ruling groups in a way that maintains their power and represses challenges to it. The enforcement of a dominant culture in society creates conflict between that culture and other, less powerful sub-cultural groups, who are marginalised and socially excluded from mainstream society in the name of repressing their alternative culture and their perceived

---

[74] A Cohen, *Delinquent Boys: The Culture of the Gang* (Chicago, Chicago University Press, 1955).

[75] R Cloward and L Ohlin, *Delinquency and Opportunity: A Theory of Delinquent Gangs* (London, Routledge, 1961).

[76] Muncie, *Youth and Crime* above n 3 at pp 166–73.

threat to the dominant group. These interactionist theories are, therefore, based on class structure and the use of power to control minority groups through the application of notions of deviance.

Thorsten Sellin's 1938 work, *Culture Conflict and Crime*, argued that as each society or culture established its own norms, rules of behaviour were enacted in criminal laws, defined according to the moral code of those norms. Individuals within that culture are socialised to uphold and abide by those laws, which represent a social consensus. Where this consensus is truly present in any society, crime rates will be low. However, more realistically, where that consensus is not shared by all, a conflict arises between two groups holding different cultural values and acting according to a different set of norms. Inter-cultural conflicts are the 'primary' conflicts identified by Sellin, where in neighbouring societies conflict arises, as a dominant society invades the territory of another and attempts to impose its cultural norms. We witness many such primary conflicts on a global scale. However, secondary conflicts are intra-cultural and arise between a dominant culture and sub-cultures within a particular society. Through a similar process, the dominant culture 'invades' and attempts to impose its norms, through the criminal law and deviant labels, on the accepted behaviour of sub-cultural groups. Youth may be one of a number of such sub-cultures within a society and this theory reflects the 'new sociology' of childhood discussed in Chapter 2. Indeed, Vold argued that social identity determines that human beings will inevitably congregate in like-minded groups, even if only transiently and for a specific purpose, to respond to crisis or challenge (such as a Trade Union or political pressure group). Therefore while youth may be a transient state, young people may share cultural norms, which differ from those of the adult world. Where the balance of power between different cultural groups is relatively equal, Vold[77] argues they may resolve their conflict through compromise and discussion. However, where the power imbalance is great, as between youth and adults in an adult-centric society, revolution occurs in which the more powerful group use the criminal law to suppress the interests of the less powerful culture.

The methods used for the suppression of weak sub-cultural groups, have been further developed by Quinney and Steven Box. Quinney's 'social reality' of crime asserts that the criminalisation of cultural groups is part of the political process. The powerful culture in a society not only has the means to define what is criminal and attach deviant labels but also has control over the criminal process and can use it to reinforce its position and weaken that of opposing groups:

> Crime is a definition of human conduct created by authorised agents in a politically organised society . . . Criminal definitions describe behaviour which conflicts with the interests of segments of society which have power to shape public policy.[78]

---

[77] G Vold, *Theoretical Criminology* (New York, Oxford University Press, 1958).
[78] R Quinney, *The Social Reality of Crime* (Boston, Little Brown, 1970) pp 15–23.

> Criminal definitions are applied by the segments of society that have the power to shape the enforcement and administration of criminal law.[79]

Similarly Steven Box similarly argues that the criminal statistics and criminal justice policy focus, inappropriately, on the activities of certain sub-cultural groups, at the expense of revealing and tackling more serious crime problems that are less visible, such as white collar crime. His critique of criminal policy, from the liberal 'scientism' perspective, suggests that the criminal statistics reveal no more than a policy on the part of powerful groups in society to perpetuate the image of deviance among less powerful groups through only counting incidences of deviance committed by the latter, and through representing the activities of the police and the courts which are mainly concerned with the deviance of the powerless:

> The process of law enforcement, in its broadest possible interpretation, operates in such a way as to *conceal* crimes of the powerful against the powerless, but to *reveal* and *exaggerate* crimes of the powerless against 'everyone'.[80]

The radical 'reflexiveness' perspective, however, delves further into the misrepresentation of 'the crime problem' as a problem of deviance among subcultures, and suggests that 'artful criminal definitions' are employed so that the criminal law is designed to criminalise the behaviour of those sub-cultures and leave de-criminalised the deviant behaviour of more powerful groups:

> Rather than being a fair reflection of those behaviours objectively causing us collectively the most avoidable suffering, criminal law categories are artful, creative constructs designed to criminalize only some victimizing behaviours, usually those more frequently committed by the relatively powerless, and to exclude others, usually those committed by the powerful against subordinates.[81]

In this way, definitions of criminal offences are not a scientific given, but a product of perception and the use of the power of the legislators to marginalise subcultural groups by defining their cultural norms as criminal. The Criminal Justice and Public Order Act (CJPOA) 1994 provided a stark example of this process, when the lifestyles of some cultural groups were manifestly criminalised; the gathering of young people in public places to listen to a particular type of music, for example, were categorised in that Act as 'raves' and were criminalised.[82] The gathering of 100 or more persons to listen to amplified music in open, public places, whether or not trespassing, could equally have been applied to open air orchestral concerts attended over the summer months by a more middle-class audience, but the use of the descriptor 'rave' precluded application of the criminal label to such concerts. As a consequence, the 'crime problem' is perceived as

---

[79] R Quinney, *The Social Reality of Crime* (Boston, Little Brown, 1970) pp 15–23.
[80] S Box, *Power, Crime, and Mystification* (London, Routledge, 1983) p 5.
[81] *Ibid* p 7.
[82] CJPOA 1994 ss 63–66.

manifesting from the behaviour of certain social groups. The more generic notion of harm being caused to members of a community, which may, in Box's view, result extensively from the behaviour of powerful groups, is absent from criminal definitions which have a political purpose.

Labelling, Outsiders and Deviance Amplification

In a similar vein, Howard Becker, Edwin Lemert and Stanley Cohen have developed theories of crime which emphasise the role of society's response to deviance, rather than role of the individual's psychology, physiology or reaction to their social circumstances. These are more individual-focused labelling theories, which suggest that penal responses to crime can exacerbate criminal behaviour through their stigmatising effect or through a process of social exclusion of deviant groups to the margins of society, which prompts a vicious circle in which their behaviour, thus marginalized is regarded with greater suspicion and the law is more heavily enforced against them.

For Edwin Lemert the labelling process was related to the psyche of the individual and their self-concept. If minor, primary acts of deviance are ignored by others in authority, an individual who is not assigned a deviant label does not change their self-concept or their set of ideas and attitudes about who they are. However, where those acts of deviance attract a label, such as 'criminal', 'truant' or 'troublemaker', the individual's self-concept alters to accommodate this label. This in turn may affect their behaviour, their self-concept influencing repetition of the deviant act. Through this process of labelling in relation to criminal deviance, authorities' condemnation and attempts to control criminal acts, causes what Lemert referred to as secondary deviance, repeated deviant behaviour prompted by the deviant label and the 'self-fulfilling' prophecy that it produces.[83] In this way, a heavy-handed response to early delinquency can actually exacerbate criminal behaviour and it is the control of crime that may be said to have caused further delinquency. Proponents of the developmental approach to youth justice argue that the stigma of the rituals of the criminal justice system and its labels in the form of criminal convictions can alter self-concept to a degree which inhibits the developmental process of growing up, and causes criminal behaviour to become a less transient and entrenched form of behaviour.

For Howard Becker and Stanley Cohen, the process of 'manufacturing crime' occurs at an institutional level. In a similar vein to Quinney's conflict theory above, it is the labelling by society of certain acts or groups as deviant, that creates a crime problem. Since no act is intrinsically criminal, its deviant status rests on society's perception of either an act or those committing it as deviant. Put simply, the law enforcement apparatus creates crime by labelling it at such. Howard

---

[83] E Lemert, *Human Deviance, Social Problems and Social Control* (Englewood Cliffs, NJ, Prentice-Hall, 1967).

Becker, a sociologist from the Chicago School in the 1960s, studied both dance music and the use of marijuana as examples of activities which foster cultural identities, complete with behavioural codes, belief systems and moral values. Their values and norms differ from those of mainstream society, who cast them in the role of deviants or 'outsiders':

> Deviance . . . is created by society. I do not mean this in the way that it is ordinarily understood, in which the causes of deviance are located in the social situation of the deviant or in 'social factors' which prompt his action. I mean, rather, that *social groups create deviance by making the rules whose infraction constitutes deviance*, and by applying those rules to particular people and labelling them as outsiders. From this point of view, deviance is *not* a quality of the act the person commits, but rather a consequence of that application by others of rules and sanctions to an 'offender'. The deviant is one to whom that label has successfully been applied; deviant behavior is behavior that people so label.[84]

Whether an act is deviant, is therefore, dependent on how other people perceive it, and whether an individual is a deviant depends on how others react to their behaviour. Perceptions of young people and crime will be discussed below, but it is significant that the legislation on anti-social behaviour takes Becker's view to its logical extreme in creating a form of deviance out of any behaviour perceived as such, whether or not it infringes any code of norms or causes any greater harm than annoyance or hatred. It is, in a very true sense, a result crime.

Cohen studied this labelling theory in relation to public perceptions of youth sub-culture in Britain in the 1960s, and in particular the impact that the media have on the labelling process. His work, *Folk Devils and Moral Panics*,[85] related the moral panic that ensued in response to the behaviour of groups of Mods and Rockers, who had descended upon Clacton for a Bank Holiday weekend in 1964. Inclement weather restricted the activities of these youths and, as they became bored, they committed minor acts of vandalism and became involved in minor skirmishes between rival groups. As the media reported this behaviour as threatening and out of control, so the police responded with a more authoritarian and controlling approach. As they arrested further young people behaving suspiciously, the media's fears were confirmed, a moral panic ensued and the vicious circle of more authoritarian policing continued. In this way, the groups of youths had been demonised as 'folk devils' who threatened social order, and social anxiety increased through the intensified response of the police and the hysterical reaction of the media. Here again, the response of institutions to deviant behaviour can manufacture or 'amplify'[86] deviance rather than reduce it.

---

[84] H Becker, *Outsiders: Studies in the Sociology of Deviance* (New York, Free Press, 1963) p 9.

[85] S Cohen, *Folk Devils and Moral Panics: The Creation of the Mods and Rockers* (London, MacGibbon and Kee, 1972).

[86] See further L Wilkins, *Social Policy, Action and Research: Studies in Social Deviance* (London, Tavistock, 1964).

Control Theories

Whereas the other theories discussed above emphasise 'otherness', or deviants as different, social control theories begin from an alternative perspective, that criminal behaviour represents normality. The assumption inherent in these theories is that we would all commit crime as a natural human impulse, but the important question to ask is not why that is so, but why so many of us resist that impulse. These theorists are, therefore, more concerned with the issue of desistance from crime. Desistance implies some form of control over human behaviour and the lack of such controls may explain why some individuals do not successfully desist from crime. Theorists in this branch of criminology have identified both internal and wider, external social controls both of which known offenders may lack.

David Matza argued that the approach of traditional criminological theories which emphasise the difference of individuals who commit acts of delinquency tends to over-diagnose crime and explain too much delinquency. They also ignore the tendency in youth, borne out by evidence set out above, to begin offending at a particular stage in life, but to desist later as they move into a different life stage and he sought to ask why young people grow out of crime. Matza's alternative theory, therefore, was that young people 'drift' into criminality when their internal moral control is weakened through 'neutralisation'.[87] Neutralisation inhibits the young person's 'moral bind to law', prevents them from perceiving their actions as immoral or harmful and prompts them to deny personal responsibility for their actions. They become 'irresponsible' in the true meaning of that word. This can, in Matza's view, be exacerbated by an institutional response which does not seek to restore their internal conscience and sense of responsibility. The maturation process tends to reverse neutralisation in most young people, as Graham and Bowling's identified desistance factors would confirm.

Travis Hirschi's later work on control theory focused on the absence of social controls over young people's behaviour.[88] Where individuals are closely bonded to their social group and identify with that group's norms, they are more likely to conform and therefore resist delinquent behaviour. Where those social bonds are weakened, social institutions such as the family, peers or the school are less able to control their behaviour and ensure conformity, and criminal behaviour results. Strong social bonds rely on four essential elements: attachment to others; commitment to the conventional society and a reluctance to risk deviant behaviour; involvement in conventional activities; and a belief in the values and moral rules of that conventional society. Detachment from social groups that a young person most closely identifies with and disaffection from conventional society render a young person more likely to offend. Hirschi's research on young people in Calfornia revealed similar results to the recent British research outlined above,

[87] D Matza, *Delinquency and Drift* (New York, John Wiley & Sons, 1964).
[88] T Hirschi, *Causes of Delinquency* (Berkeley, University of California Press, 1969).

namely that weak attachments to parents, disaffection from school and attachment to delinquent peers (a non-conventional society) produced higher offending rates. Strengthening the bonds with developmental institutions may therefore be a key crime reduction strategy.

Perceptions of Youth Crime

From the above discussions we can conclude that, from a positivist perspective, the youth crime problem principally stems from problems at home and a lack of attachment and positive relationships between parents and their children as well as disaffection from school; lack of educational achievement there resulting in truancy and exclusion. Both factors compromise the extent to which young people can be nurtured, supervised or, in the most benevolent sense, socially controlled. The statistical evidence portrays a problem which is low key in terms of the seriousness of the offending behaviour, largely a transient problem as desistance sets in upon maturity (even though this may be much later than previously thought) and overall the level of crime is gently falling. The theoretical evidence points to youth crime emanating from the behaviour of a sub-culture which is neither valued nor tolerated and is perceived as threatening. The problem may be further escalated by policy makers and authorities through the labelling process, and the inability of the developmental institutions to 'hold on' and nurture young people through the growing-up process.

Despite this 'reality' of youth crime, the perception of youth crime as dangerous, violent and increasing persists both in policy circles and popular discourse (including the media). The Home Affairs Committee received a great deal of evidence from policy makers and practitioner representatives which smacked of a disbelief that the problem of youth crime could possibly be understated. Despite evidence to the contrary from pressure groups and organisations representing the welfare agencies, the Committee were told by representatives of the judiciary and the police that the problem was escalating and needed urgent control:

> [T]here is plenty of evidence that the number of offences committed by juveniles is going up substantially and . . . it is nonsense to say that the picture is media created.[89]

Tony Blair, then Shadow Home Secretary, was also sceptical of the statistical evidence and found it 'difficult to believe Home Office claims that offending by young people has actually gone down across the country'.[90] Indeed, the Association of Chief Police Officers attempted a more scientific approach to refuting the statistical evidence, claiming that given the decline in the number of young people in the population, the general increase in crime overall and the reduction

---

[89] Evidence of a circuit judge to the Committee—Home Affairs Committee, *Juvenile Offenders* Sixth Report HAC 221–I (London, HMSO, 1993) p viii.
[90] *Ibid* p ix.

in detection rates 'the true rate of offending has probably increased by 54 per cent in the 10 years from 1980 to 1990.'[91] This was an ingenious manipulation of statistical data, in which they appeared to be not only counting crimes committed by juveniles that had never been born, but also counting crimes that may or may not have taken place, but, by their own admission, the police had failed to discover. The 'statistic' that they put forward therefore was no more than an estimate and was ignorant of the fact that the Home Office trends had been calculated in terms of crimes committed per 100,000 of the juvenile population, thereby building in a comparable set of figures notwithstanding the decline in the population generally. What this reveals is a perception of youth crime among politicians, the police and the judiciary, all of whom have some interest in maintaining the view that youth crime persists as a problem and requires their intervention to tackle it. Michael Cavadino, commenting on the Committee's report, argued that 'knee-jerk' reactions to that perception were inevitable,

> when media and politicians alike insist that the country is threatened by a tidal wave of young offenders and that this menace requires drastic governmental and legislative action to remedy it.[92]

This period reflected the process that had been predicted by many who wrote of the explosive combination of self-interest of the police, political expediency and media hype in creating moral panics.[93]

The 'rhetoric' of youth crime therefore appears at odds with the 'reality'. Muncie reviews media reporting of youth crime, which reveals a rather different picture.[94] Indeed, we are all too familiar with headlines which portray young offenders as threatening, violent and persistent and which suggests that the youth crime problem is serious and increasing, a view diametrically opposed to the reality. This is not surprising given that Steve Chibnall has identified that the selection of crime news tends to reflect the commercial concerns of newspaper editors rather than a concern to 'inform' readers of the true nature of youth crime.[95] However, the perceptions of the public who consume media reports demonstrate that they often believe the essence of the headlines that confront them. Hough and Roberts conducted a survey of 1800 people aged over 16 about their views on the nature of the youth crime problem, the nature of young offenders, and trends in and the efficacy of the youth justice system. The survey revealed a sense that youth crime was increasing (75 per cent of respondents reported this[96]) and that young

---

[91] *Ibid* p ix.
[92] M Cavadino, 'Persistent Young Offenders' (1994) 6 *Journal of Child Law* 2 at 2.
[93] See eg, S Cohen, *Folk Devils and Moral Panics* above n 85; T Mathiesen, 'Contemporary Penal Policy: A Study in Moral Panics' Lecture at the Annual Meeting of the Howard League (25 November 1992).
[94] Muncie, *Youth and Crime* above n 3 at pp 39–41.
[95] S Chibnall, *Law and Order News* (London, Tavistock, 1977).
[96] M Hough and J Roberts, *Youth Crime and Youth Justice: Public Opinion in England and Wales* (Bristol, Policy Press, 2004) p 9.

people were responsible for a disproportionate amount of recorded crime (74 per cent believed that young offenders committed more than 30 per cent of known crime, when the true figure is around 12 per cent[97]). Also there were (false) perceptions that drug crime among young people was increasing faster than other types of offence, and that over 40 per cent of youth crime involves violence.[98] Despite that, youth crime was only identified as the most important crime problem facing the government by 15 per cent of the respondents, others believing that drug crime, sex crime and terrorism were more urgent concerns.[99] Research by Cromer suggests that not only does the moral panic regarding youth crime present a fear of an escalating problem that is out of control, but that it is more widespread in terms of class and is no longer confined to the unruly children of the underclass.[100]

There are, therefore, clearly diverging views of the problem that the youth justice system is tasked to deal with. The important question is, which view informs policy, the rhetoric or the reality? This is important, because a policy that seeks to provide a solution to a problem which is misconceived sets itself up for failure, and, more significantly, could cause damage to the young people who find themselves subject to misguided intervention. Not only is there theoretical evidence that such interventions may exacerbate general crime levels and an individual's propensity to offend, but at societal level, these interventions can generate hostility towards youth as a social group, excessive social control of their behaviour and social exclusion which pushes them further towards the margins of citizenship from where their proven social disadvantages and lack of opportunities are compounded. Notwithstanding references to some criminological data on youth crime, recent government policy discussions tend to assume the rhetorical perception as the foundation for their proposals for change. In the mid-1990s a series of 'knee jerk' enactments followed the discussion of the Home Affairs Committee, which evidently followed the advice of the likes of the Association of Chief Police Officers (ACPO) and the judiciary and ignored the pleas of the welfare agencies for a more considered and restrained approach. In 1997, Jack Straw, in the preface to the white paper *No More Excuses*, also denied clear evidence that young people grow out of crime:

> For too long we have assumed that young offenders will grow out of their offending if left to themselves. The research evidence shows this does not happen.[101]

The result has been a number of enactments which lack a clear ideology and a clear, honest, perception of the problem they claim to be 'tackling'.

---

[97] *Ibid* p 12.

[98] *Ibid* p 13.

[99] *Ibid* p 7.

[100] G Cromer, ' "Children from Good Homes": Moral Panics about Middle-Class Delinquency' (2004) 44 *British Journal of Criminology* 391.

[101] Home Office, *No More Excuses: A New Approach to Tackling Youth Crime in England and Wales* Cm 3809 (London, TSO, 1997).

Part II
Youth Justice Policy and Practice

5

Diversion

At the pre-trial stage of the youth justice system, practitioners wield a powerful discretion to divert offenders out of that system. The agencies empowered with such discretion may vary between jurisdictions, but most systems will operate some form of diversion at this stage and the policy has historically been an important temperance measure in the punishment of youth crime. The minimum age of criminal responsibility, discussed in Chapter 2, may be seen as a primary diversionary tactic in the sense that young people falling below that minimum age are dealt with (if at all) without resort to criminal justice measures. The higher the minimum age, the more likely that the jurisdiction take a *policy* view of criminalisation[1] which involves keeping young people out of the criminal justice system in order to avoid inappropriate outcomes of punishment on the more vulnerable, or to facilitate a more constructive response to behaviour offered by civil law measures. In these cases young people simply may not be charged at all with criminal offences and the procedures of the youth justice system are never invoked. In Belgium, for example, the apparent minimum age of criminal responsibility of 18 is in fact a mechanism through which young people may be charged with an offence but are immediately, and virtually automatically, diverted out of the criminal process.[2]

Diversion may alternatively take place after a charge has been levied but serves to prevent the young person being processed beyond the pre-trial stage. The police or the public prosecutor thus act as 'gatekeepers', using their discretion at the front door of the system to control input into it. Diversion is therefore more commonly discussed as diversion from court, often, though not always, on to a non-criminal alternative agency or procedure. In policy terms the importance of this practice lies principally in its capacity to limit the negative impact of the youth justice system on an offender and ensures that constructive action can be taken to prevent re-offending without the effects of stigma or labelling. In the 1980s in England and Wales the practice of cautioning was consequently key in ensuring that the youth

---

[1] The policy view was discussed in Ch 2. This view regards the minimum age as a tool for protecting young people from the rigours of the criminal justice process, rather than assessing the age at which children become competent to commit criminal offences.

[2] See further Ch 2.

justice system provided minimal intervention in implementing the developmental approach. For policy makers, however, the managerial benefits of diversion cannot be ignored; restrictions on the flow of cases to the youth courts, and the extensive use of a less costly alternative to prosecution, can provide a pressure valve in easing delay in the court process. It is not surprising that the Home Office have been highly supportive of the diversion process, recognising both types of benefit for the system and for the offender.

Notwithstanding such advantages, diversion has been recognised as problematic in other respects. The extensive use of policies of expediency that offer a less formal and therefore less stigmatic response to minor offending may give rise to allegations of net-widening and expansion in the remit of social control of the youth justice system. Whilst the intervention offered under diversionary schemes may be benevolently constructed, their implementation at the early, hidden stages of the criminal process provides potential for expansion in the level and extent of intervention, a criticism often levelled at welfare-oriented alternatives to justice. The informality of diversionary procedures becomes problematic in terms of the legal principle of due process and has produced allegations that relatively unaccountable practitioners may exercise their discretion in a discriminatory and inconsistent way. The recent retraction from high levels of diversion in England and Wales has been justified by further challenges to its effectiveness as a crime prevention measure and to its apparent inconsistency with a youth justice policy based on classical punitive notions of taking responsibility.

Diversion in Policy

In the latter half of the twentieth century diversion played a central role in youth justice policy and practice. As the century progressed, not only did the Home Office give greater recognition and support for the practice, but it also developed greater regulation of it and the trend has been towards formalising a previously highly informal process. In the early history of the youth justice system, however, diversion was not initially encouraged. As the juvenile court was established on welfare principles, there was a perception that young offenders did not need to be diverted from a court process that was inherently benevolent and concerned with addressing the welfare needs of the child. Consequently in 1927, the Malony Committee were strongly disparaging of a practice which they identified as a cause for concern:

> A conference is held in the Chief Constable's room at which the child and his parents, the police officer concerned in the inquiry and sometimes the probation officer or other social worker are directed to appear. This practice seems to us objectionable, as

usurping the functions of a tribunal, and we think it is outside the proper duties of the police . . . when it is realised that these courts are specially equipped to help rather than punish the young offender, we hope that the reluctance to bring such children before them will disappear.[3]

In an era when youth justice policy was so firmly welfare oriented and there were genuine attempts to implement that ideal through the courts, this intolerance of any informal and hidden procedure which seeks to undermine the work of the juvenile court was understandable. However, some 40 years later this perception had radically changed as the powers and practice of the juvenile court had been injected with a more punitive ethos and the need to avoid that arena was more keenly felt.

By the mid-1960s the Home Office began to acknowledge that cautioning could play a central role in the broadly abolitionist policy that was being developed in this field. As the juvenile court was to be increasingly sidelined as a forum for dealing with youth crime, and eventually to be replaced by care proceedings for young offenders, cautioning took on a more significant role not only as a more routine official response to offending behaviour but also as a mechanism for diverting offenders to informal networks, such as the family, where the real preventive and rehabilitative work was to be done. The 1965 white paper *The Child, the Family and the Young Offender* emphasised a family approach to crime prevention:

> We . . . propose to remove young people so far as possible from the jurisdiction of the court, and to empower each local authority, through its children's committee, to appoint local family councils to deal with each case as far as possible in consultation and agreement with the parents.[4]

It was to be the cautioning procedure which would perform that 'removal' for those young offenders not already barred from the court by a raising of the minimum age of criminal responsibility. By 1968, when the Home Office were developing more concrete plans for legislation, the abolitionist stance had weakened somewhat[5] but the support for diversion from court was still as powerful. The white paper *Children in Trouble* envisaged a cautious approach to the prosecution of young offenders above the new minimum age of criminal responsibility, with restrictive statutory criteria for prosecution to be satisfied before the offender could appear in the juvenile court, and even then court proceedings were to be focused on care and protection rather than punishment based on criminal

---

[3] Malony Committee, *Report of the Departmental Committee on the Treatment of Young Offenders* Cmnd 2831 (London, Home Office, 1927) pp 22–23.

[4] Home Office, *The Child, the Family and the Young Offender* Cmnd 2742 (London, HMSO, 1965) para 11.

[5] The 1968 white paper *Children in Trouble* proposed raising the minimum age of criminal responsibility to 14 rather than 16 and abandoned the idea of family councils as an alternative to the juvenile court.

responsibility.[6] Subsequently the 1969 Children and Young Persons Act gave statutory recognition for the first time to cautioning (although it did not exactly provide a statutory schema in the way that more recent legislation has). Section 5 of the 1969 Act imposed restrictions on prosecution of young offenders and provided for a presumption in favour of cautioning in appropriate cases:

> 5(2) A qualified informant shall not lay an information in respect of an offence if the alleged offender is a young person unless the informant is of the opinion that . . . it would not be adequate for the case to be dealt with by a parent, teacher or other person or by means of a caution from a constable . . .

The letter of section 5, along with many other parts of the 1969 Act, was never implemented,[7] but it may be said that its spirit was. The rate of young people cautioned rose sharply through the 1970s, although, as Table 5.1 illustrates, so too did the number of young people found guilty in the juvenile courts.

TABLE 5.1 *Young persons cautioned and found guilty 1964–74*

Year	Cautioned (1000s)	Found Guilty (1000s)	Cautioned (%)
1964	15	67	18.2
1969	20	65	23.5
1974	47	84	36.1

Source: Home Office, *Criminal Statistics, England and Wales 1964–74*

This would suggest that the 1970s was an era of general expansion in the application of youth justice procedures, and the escalation of cautioning rates may have been as much a product of net-widening, or diversion *to* cautioning, as of diversion *from* the court. In Rutherford's view, far from keeping young offenders away from the punitive measures available to the courts, the Act rather enabled police officers to tinker with cautioning at the 'shallow end of the juvenile justice process' while magistrates exercised their custodial powers to the full at the deeper end.[8] The fusion of the dual care and punishment roles of the juvenile court, with an emphasis on the former whilst phasing out the latter, as envisaged by the Labour reformers of the 1960s, did not materialise.

---

[6] Home Office, *Children in Trouble* Cmnd 3601 (London, HMSO, 1968) paras 12 and 17.

[7] A change of government in 1970 and the election of the Conservatives, with a hard-line law and order agenda, saw to it that the liberal ethos of the legislation never saw the light of day.

[8] A Rutherford, 'A Statute Backfires: The Escalation of Youth Incarceration in England during the 1970s' in J Doig (ed) *Criminal Corrections: Ideals and Realities* (New York, Lexington, 1983) p 75.

Nevertheless, despite continued Home Office commitment to the expansion of incarceration through the 1970s and 1980s (after the election of Margaret Thatcher as Prime Minister in 1979) developments in the use of cautioning at 'the coal face'[9] took a surprisingly escalatory turn. As practitioners adopted a developmental approach to dealing with youth crime cautioning again took on a central role as the epitome of minimal formal intervention and as a mechanism by which offenders could be diverted to the developmental institutions of the family and the school where offending behaviour could be addressed in a more nurturing way. Practitioners at this time, committed to a clear and forceful working ideology, surreptitiously achieved the implementation of diversionary aims of the 1969 Act, 'beneath the radar' and without the use of legislative measures.[10] Policy makers, until this time, had had neither the political courage nor the ideological inclination to do so. Not only did cautioning rates rise to unprecedented levels, but many regions of England and Wales became 'custody-free zones' as the practitioners tackled even the deep-end of youth offending using this diversionary strategy. Juvenile Liaison Bureaux (JLB) enabled agencies to collaborate in implementing this strategy according to coherently agreed principles.[11] Further, the development of Intermediate Treatment programmes[12] for those 'at risk' of custody gave diversion sufficient gravity and credibility for even the more persistent and serious offenders. Repeat cautions were utilised in some cases[13] in order to persist in attempts to prevent re-offending while avoiding the more punitive alternatives used by the juvenile court which, it was acknowledged, did little to enable young people to 'grow out of crime'.

The statistical evidence in Table 5.2 is testimony to the commitment of practitioners to this diversionary strategy. Perhaps even more extraordinary was that by 1985 the Home Office demonstrated a keen support for the policy by issuing a Circular to Chief Constables promoting the practice.[14] The Home Secretary at the time

> commends to chief officers the policy that prosecution of a juvenile is not to be taken without the fullest consideration of whether the public interest and the interests of the juvenile concerned may be better served by a course of action which falls short of prosecution Thus chief officers will wish to ensure that their arrangements for dealing with juveniles are such that *prosecution does not occur unless it is absolutely necessary*.[15] (emphasis added)

---

[9] A Rutherford, *Growing Out of Crime: The New Era* (Winchester, Waterside Press, 2002) p 20.

[10] This extraordinary period in the history of the youth justice system is discussed in more depth in Ch 3.

[11] See further R Smith, *Youth Justice: Ideas, Policy, Practice* (Cullompton, Willan, 2003) pp 11–17.

[12] These were more intensive rehabilitative programmes which burgeoned around the country after the DHSS made funds of £15 million available, with which local authorities could develop initiatives.

[13] Though perhaps not to the extent that scare-mongering reports later claimed—see R Evans, 'Cautioning: Counting the Cost of Retrenchment' [1994] Crim LR 566.

[14] Home Office, 'The Cautioning of Offenders' Circular 14/1985 (London, Home Office, 1985).

[15] *Ibid* para 1.

TABLE 5.2 *Persons cautioned 1980–90 as a proportion of known offenders aged 10–17*

Year	Male offenders (%)	Female offenders (%)
1980	44	69
1981	46	71
1982	49	75
1983	51	77
1984	54	83
1985	59	84
1986	61	85
1987	66	86
1988	69	84
1989	71	86
1990	75	89

Source: Home Office, *Criminal Statistics, England and Wales, 1980–1990*

However, this support came with provisos and there was concern in the Home Office that the expansion of the cautioning practice was accompanied by the extension of inconsistent decision making around the country as well as the potential for net-widening and discrimination against minority groups of offenders. The Circular therefore set out a series of guidelines for police officers which took the form of suggested criteria for making the decision to caution. Hence cautioning was not just officially recognised but, for the first time, had a quasi-legislative format. These were not legal criteria and the Circular had no force in law[16], but this began a gradual process of formalising the procedure, culminating in the statutory scheme set out in the Crime and Disorder Act 1998. Initially the criteria suggested that there should be sufficient evidence that an offence has been committed, that the young person should admit the offence, that neither the offence nor the offender's record should be serious and that the parents of a young person should consent to the caution being given. It was hoped that by applying a uniform set of criteria, cautioning practice would become more consistent nationwide and that police officers would avoid the temptation to abuse their discretion. Evans and Wilkinson point out, however, that this did not happen, not least because the guidelines lacked force and could be adopted fully, partially or not at all according to the operational preferences of any Chief Constable. Police forces already

[16] Although Hilson suggests that later forms of the criteria were attributed with a quasi-legal status in that some offenders were able to appeal against the decision not to caution them—see further C Hilson, 'Discretion to Prosecute and Judicial Review' [1993] Crim LR 739.

operating varying forms of the practice, adopted the guidelines to different extents and the result was further inconsistency and 'justice by geography'.[17]

The Home Office attempted again to reign in unacceptable variations in practice by issuing a further Circular in 1990.[18] This time the Home Office were more prescriptive in tightening the guidance and issuing National Standards for the practice. Whilst remaining broadly supportive of diversion, NACRO noted at the time that:

> It appears from the Circular that the underlying principle in support of cautioning is not based solely on the notion that young people will, in most cases, grow out of crime and that entry into the formal system of criminal justice may be counter-productive. It also rests on the view that cautioning is an efficient, effective and economic response to offending behaviour which is relatively minor, opportunistic and transient.[19]

As the 1980s drew to a close, there were already signs that support for the developmental approach was weakening but also that diversion had other, more managerial, benefits that justified some continued support. So much so that in 1993 both the Home Affairs Committee (HAC) and the Royal Commission on Criminal Justice (RCCJ) recommended that the process be fully recognised in law and placed on a statutory footing. The former were impressed by the strength of the commitment to the practice from practitioners and pressure groups who gave evidence to them, as well as by the estimated re-offending rates of 20–30 per cent, which suggested that cautions were effective in preventive terms.[20] Their preference, however, was for formal rather than informal cautioning, and, in order to avoid the problems of net-widening, inconsistency and abuse of discretion already identified by the Home Office, they recommended a set of statutory regulations for the practice.[21] The RCCJ had been charged with investigating problems in the pre-trial stages of the criminal justice process that had given rise to prominent miscarriages of justice in the 1970s (prompted by the recent quashing of the convictions of the Guildford Four and the Birmingham Six). Their inquiry, however, went beyond the protection of due process rights for defendants at this stage and became a wider consideration of the crime control and managerial benefits of diversionary justice administered at these stages.[22] Their support for cautioning[23]

---

[17] R Evans and C Wilkinson, 'Variations in Police Cautioning Policy in England and Wales' (1990) 29 *Howard Journal* 155.

[18] Home Office Circular 59/1990.

[19] NACRO, *The Home Office Circular on the Cautioning of Offenders: Implications for Juvenile Justice* Briefing Paper (London, NACRO, 1990) p 2.

[20] Home Affairs Committee, *Juvenile Offenders* Sixth Report HAC 441–I (London, HMSO, 1993) para 63.

[21] *Ibid* para 76.

[22] See further J Fionda, *Public Prosecutors and Discretion: A Comparative Study* (Oxford, Oxford University Press, 1995) p 62; S Field and P Thomas, *Justice and Efficiency? The Royal Commission on Criminal Justice* (Oxford, Blackwell, 1994).

[23] They recommended a statutory footing for cautioning under which guidelines could be drawn up by the CPS and the police to promote nationwide consistency—RCCJ, *Report* Cm 2263 (London, HMSO, 1993) ch 5, para 57.

was therefore also driven by economy rather than a commitment to the developmental ideal.

Even those managerial concerns took secondary priority over politics a few years later when the incumbent Home Secretary, Michael Howard, began a campaign to toughen up youth justice policy as part of the 'Back to Basics' political campaign of John Major's government. The relatively lenient and informal practice of cautioning had no place in such a policy and a further Circular in 1994 had a distinctly more discouraging flavour:

> People who commit crime should expect to be punished. If they are cautioned once they should regard it as a chance to get back on the straight and narrow. But they should also know that it could be their last chance . . . I share the widespread public concern about the inappropriate use of cautions.[24]

Home Office Circular 18/1994 provided a radically restrictive set of guidelines, essentially discouraging the use of repeat cautions, which 'send completely the wrong signal to offenders';[25] cautioning for so-called serious offences which 'bring the cautioning system into disrepute'; and caution plus[26]: 'Under no circumstances should police officers become involved in negotiating [with the victim] or awarding reparation or compensation'.[27] The National Standards and criteria were left relatively unchanged but the tone of the Circular left no doubt that the new Home Secretary was not in favour of widespread use of the practice. Research conducted by Roger Evans demonstrated that police forces had taken heed of these harsh words and cautioning did begin to decrease, especially where offenders had already received a caution.[28]

By the late 1990s, New Labour were keen to pick up on these issues and to give cautioning an appropriate place in their plans for a newly designed youth justice system. Their consultation paper was supportive of cautioning as an early form of intervention to 'prevent young offenders from graduating into adult criminals'.[29] However, they concurred with the view of formal cautions formed by the Audit Commission that repeat cautioning was likely to be ineffective and plagiarised this statement from *Misspent Youth*:

> While cautioning works well with most first time offenders (about 80% of whom do not reoffend within two years), it becomes progressively less effective once a pattern of offending sets in.[30]

---

[24] Michael Howard MP, quoted in a Home Office press release announcing proposed changes to the cautioning guidance (29 October 1993).

[25] *Ibid*

[26] 'Caution plus' constitutes a caution 'plus' an additional penalty offered as a condition of non-prosecution. See further below p 00.

[27] Home Office Circular 18/1994, note 4C.

[28] Evans 'Cautioning' above n 13.

[29] Home Office, *Tackling Youth Crime* (London, Home Office, 1997) p 3.

[30] *Ibid* p 3, but also see Audit Commission, *Misspent Youth . . . Young People and Crime* (London, Audit Commission, 1996) p 22.

Plans for the future development of the diversion process were discussed in the consultation paper under the theme of 'Taking responsibility' alongside the abolition of the *doli incapax* presumption and the action plan order, indicating that the new form of cautioning was to be a part of a graduated *punishment* process aimed at forcing a young offender to confront the consequences of their offending behaviour, beginning with an attempt at diversion but clearly intended to culminate more quickly with an appearance in court and expanded powers for the court to ensure that young people do not 'offend with impunity'.[31] Chapter 5 of the subsequent white paper expanded on their plans to abolish the cautioning procedure and replace it with a 'Final Warning' scheme, making it clear that they were adopting the same approach as Michael Howard in 1994 in ensuring that a first chance to escape prosecution was clearly a last chance: 'if a first offence results in a Final Warning, any further offence would automatically lead to criminal charges.'[32] Whilst the statutory scheme actually implemented a 'two strikes and you're out' approach, rather than a single strike, the effect of it has been as restrictive of diversion as the previous administration had been in 1994.[33]

Diversion in Practice

In England and Wales it is the police that are referred to as the 'gatekeepers' of the criminal justice system because it is they (rather than the public prosecutor) who exercise the important discretionary power to admit young offenders into it or divert them out of it. They effectively hold the key to the front door of the criminal process. The decisions involved in exercising that discretion include deciding whom to arrest, which cases to investigate, how to investigate offences, whom to interview and whom to charge with which offence. Once they have decided to charge a young person with an offence, they have three options in the disposal of the case. First, they may take no further action at all; this will be their decision if they do not have enough evidence to make a conviction more likely than an acquittal at court or if, where there is enough evidence, it is not in the public interest to prosecute. This latter decision involves the consideration of non-legal criteria, for example, is the offence too trivial to justify the expense of prosecution, is the offender mentally or physically ill, or has the offender volunteered to make reparation? Second, if there is sufficient evidence to prosecute, the police may decide to issue a reprimand or a warning to a young offender under the new statutory procedure for diversion by the police in the Crime and Disorder Act

---

[31] *Ibid* p 3.
[32] Home Office, *No More Excuses: A New Approach to Tackling Youth Crime in England and Wales* Cm 3809 (London, TSO, 1997) p 17.
[33] See further R Evans and K Puech, 'Reprimands and Warnings: Populist Punitiveness or Restorative Justice?' [2001] Crim LR 794.

1998. Finally, where a reprimand or warning is inappropriate the police may decide to prosecute the young offender and will pass the file to the Crown Prosecution Service (CPS).

Cautioning

Prior to the 1998 enactment of the statutory system of reprimands and warnings, police cautioning operated without formal legal authority and on a highly discretionary basis. An official acknowledgement of the central role of cautioning in a strongly abolitionist statutory schema, enacted in the 1969 Children and Young Persons Act, was never implemented. Rather the procedure emerged from the development of police discretion in relation to non-prosecution, over a period of time dating back at least as far as 1833.[34] Whilst it is possible to describe general principles in the operation of the system, local practices may have differed widely since, prior to the early 1980s, there was little official guidance on the practice nor, it appears, any formal limit on its operation.

The old non-statutory system enabled a police officer to issue a caution. This was essentially a verbal warning given to a young offender by a senior officer. Cautions may have taken one of a number of forms, varying in formality and legal consequences. The practice originated with the use of informal cautions in very trivial cases of law-breaking. There were no criteria for their use, no requirement to assess the evidence against the offender, no requirement to charge the offender and no admission of guilt was formally required. Indeed, these were warnings which, in the case of a young offender, may have even been given at the scene of a crime and took the form of a brief 'telling off' for a suspected offender in the hope that such action would deter them from re-offending. Since they were rarely recorded in any way we have no indication of the precise extent to which they were used or which types of offenders received them. That said, the Audit Commission conducted a survey of police force areas and in their 1996 report *Misspent Youth* they noted that 11 out of 43 police force areas were still making use of informal warnings.[35] As the practice of cautioning increased, it gained an element of formality. By the 1980s the Home Office began issuing the guidelines discussed above and criteria were suggested to render their use more consistent between police force areas. By this time formal cautions were also recorded, albeit locally, and were citable in court as previous cautions (though not as previous convictions, which should have been regarded as more serious evidence of persistence by

---

[34] Home Office Evidence submitted to the Royal Commission on Criminal Procedure cites an instruction issued by the Metropolitan Police Commissioner in 1833, condemning the practice. See Royal Commission on Criminal Procedure, *Police Cautioning* Memorandum no VI, Evidence no 240, Evidence from the Home Office (London, HMSO, 1979) p 34.

[35] Audit Commission, *Misspent Youth* above n 29 at p 20.

magistrates). Formal cautions were delivered by a senior police officer, in uniform, in the police station and therefore were used only after a suspect had been arrested and had been charged with an offence to which they admitted their guilt. Since these formal cautions were recognised by the Home Office as an official (though still not legally sanctioned) disposal and were recorded, official statistics contain data indicating the extent of their use.

Once the caution acquired a formal identity, some police force areas developed the procedure further to maximise its rehabilitative effect. In Northamptonshire, for example, in 1984, the police joined forces with a number of other agencies in an early example of multi-agency co-operation in determining which offenders should be cautioned. The JLB established there became a nationwide model for collaboration between welfare agencies in implementing the minimal intervention ideal of the time. The decision to caution in many cases was deferred while the JLB undertook a wider examination of the offender's background and behavioural history and assessed what informal networks, if any, the offender should be diverted to.[36] Since the working ideology of the JLB was minimalist and no intervention was preferred, where appropriate, even to non-criminal intervention, decisions were being made by these teams as to not only what the offender should be diverted *to* but also what they should be diverted *from*, including advocating the use of informal, in preference to formal, cautions in suitable cases. Even a formal caution therefore was viewed as a form of intervention away from which offenders could be diverted.

A third form of caution was developed in some areas and was called 'caution plus' where additional penalties could be offered, effectively as a condition of non-prosecution. These additional penalties may have included making reparation to the victim, participation in mediation proceedings with the victim or the payment of compensation. The practice developed as part of the evolution of police discretion, most notably in the Thames Valley police force area, but was considered in policy circles in 1990 when the HAC considered a Home Office proposal to implement the scheme nationally.[37] The Committee were in favour of such an extension to the cautioning power, especially where a formal caution without additional requirements had been offered previously but the offender continued to offend, although they acknowledged that not only might the scheme produce an unduly heavy and disproportionate response to the offending behaviour but might also provide too heavy an inducement on the young offender to plead guilty to an offence.[38]

---

[36] See further A Bell *et al*, 'Diverting Children and Young People from Crime and the Criminal Justice System' in B Goldson (ed) *Youth Justice: Contemporary Policy and Practice* (Aldershot, Ashgate, 1999).

[37] Home Affairs Committee, *Juvenile Offenders* above n 20.

[38] *Ibid* paras 74 and 75.

Reprimands and Warnings

The system of police diversion has undergone major revision in the Crime and Disorder Act 1998. The new Labour government have responded to calls[39] to place the system on a statutory footing so that there is now legal authority for the police to divert offenders instead of prosecuting them. The 1998 Act introduces a two-tier system of reprimands and warnings set out in sections 65 and 66. The old and new systems are not greatly different and the reprimand essentially replaces the formal caution while the warning introduces the 'caution plus' on a national basis (both for those aged 17 and under only).

The reprimand is broadly similar to the old formal caution. It is less serious and less onerous than the warning and will be given where the offender has committed his/her first offence. It will be given only where the offence is not serious enough to warrant a warning (a warning can also be given for a first offence where that offence is serious). The reprimand will usually be given in the police station[40] by a uniformed police officer of the rank of Inspector or above and, where the offender is aged under 17. An appropriate adult must be present (usually a parent, guardian, social worker or other responsible adult). The police officer must explain to the offender 'in ordinary language' that the reprimand is citable in court upon subsequent conviction. No further action is taken after a reprimand has been given (unlike the warning—see below). The white paper in which the Home Office first mooted the new system[41] stated very clearly that no offender would be eligible for two reprimands. After receiving a reprimand, any subsequent offence, if not prosecuted, would merit a warning. Both the provision in section 65(2) and the Home Secretary's rhetoric has stressed that reprimands should be one-off penalties.

A warning is available for more serious first offences or for second offences where a reprimand was previously given. In the white paper, this disposal was called the 'final' warning. In the 1998 Crime and Disorder Act the word 'final' has been dropped but section 65(3) states that a second warning will not be given unless the previous offence was committed over two years before and the current offence is not so serious as to merit a prosecution. The first part of the warning is the same as a reprimand—that is, it is a warning given to the offender, like the old

[39] Eg from the Home Affairs Committee, *ibid* para 76.

[40] Section 56 Criminal Justice and Court Services Act 2000 amends this requirement and allows for the reprimand to be given in some place other than in the police station, eg, in the young person's school or youth club. The Home Secretary's guidance on this suggests that the venue should be carefully chosen as a place which bears some meaning for the offender (e.g. the venue where the offence took place) but a reprimand or warning should never be given in the street or in the offender's home. The venue should also be an appropriate place for the victim to attend, where relevant, and should not be seen as threatening or traumatic for the victim—Home Office, *Final Warning Scheme: Further Guidance for the Police and Youth Offending Teams* (London, Home Office, 2001) paras 5–9.

[41] Home Office, *No More Excuses* Cm 3809 (London, Home Office, 1997).

formal caution, and given in the same circumstances as the reprimand. However, there is a second element to a warning set out in section 66. All offenders given a warning are referred to the Youth Offending Team (a local multi-agency team with responsibility for the rehabilitation of the offender) for assessment for participation in a local rehabilitation programme. In this respect the warning is similar to the old 'caution plus' system where in some police force areas an offender could be required to undertake further rehabilitation or make some reparation as well as receiving a caution. There is one important difference between the warning and the old caution plus. Having been given a warning, the offender, on any subsequent prosecution within two years, will not be eligible for the sentence of conditional discharge (section 66(4)). This may seem a trivial, technical provision but in fact it has very important consequences. First, it inherently suggests that a warning and a conditional discharge are similar penalties (otherwise there would be no objection to the offender receiving both). As the warning is given where there is no conviction in a court of law this suggestion is clearly wrong. The warning is deliberately designed to be a less formal penalty than the conditional discharge. Many young offenders on their first appearance in court were given conditional discharges (in 1997 32.5 per cent of young offenders sentenced were given the order).[42] It was seen as a useful penalty for a first, non-serious offence, essentially involving no penalty but with conditions attached to prevent the young offender from getting into further trouble. This provision will therefore affect a high proportion of young offenders who re-offend after being given a warning. There then remains the question of how the youth court sentences these offenders if they cannot use a conditional discharge. They will have two choices: to use an absolute discharge (previously extremely rarely used) or they will have to give a fine or even a community penalty. This means that the court will have to either up-tariff or down-tariff the offence and it remains to be seen which option the courts will take.

The criteria for both reprimands and warnings are set out in section 65(1) of the Crime and Disorder Act 1998. Most importantly, the police must have enough evidence to be able to prosecute the young person (that is, evidence that there is a 'realistic prospect of conviction'). This must be the first and paramount criterion in order to prevent net-widening.[43] As the reprimand or warning is recorded and citable in court, this is a fundamental protection of the offender's civil liberties. Equally importantly, the offender must admit the offence. This is a necessary criterion in order to justify giving a penalty without a formal adjudication of guilt. It effectively makes the reprimand or warning voluntary and prevents the police making unjustified presumptions of guilt. Note that the Act requires the police

---

[42] Home Office, *Criminal Statistics* (London, Home Office, 1997).

[43] Net-widening is the process by which offenders who previously would have received no further action because there is not evidence against them to be able to prosecute, are now proceeded against using some less formal measure—this is discussed further below.

officer to explain to the young offender the consequences of the reprimand or warning but not until he/she is in the process of giving the reprimand or warning. It used to be a requirement that this advice was given prior to the admission of guilt, which was particularly important since most young offenders do not receive legal advice in the police station. The offender must not previously have been convicted of an offence and the police officer must be satisfied that it is not in the public interest to prosecute (the public interest is undefined but police officers will probably consider similar factors to those considered by public prosecutors.)[44]

It is noticeable that these statutory criteria fall short of those set out in the Home Office Circular 18/1994 in some very important respects. First, the offender's record was not to be serious and the Home Office, in Circular 18/1994, stated that offenders should only ever receive one caution unless the second or subsequent offence took place a long time after the first offence or was very different in nature.[45] Despite the criticism that this provision attracted, the Act has gone further and prohibited the offender from having any official record at all. Second, the interests and views of the victim had to be taken into account (although they were not paramount) and the caution had to be explained to the victim under the 1994 guidelines. Despite New Labour's apparent commitment to the principles of restorative justice, there is no mention of the victim in the statutory criteria. Third, the offender's family and background circumstances were taken into account in deciding whether a caution was appropriate. Although application of this criterion had the potential to exacerbate stereotypical and possibly discriminatory decision making if abused,[46] it was nevertheless aimed at encouraging decisions informed by the circumstances of the offender in order to assess the extent to which informal networks (such as the family or the school) may be the most appropriate forum for preventive intervention. The new formal guidelines do not specifically refer to the background of the offender and have produced a rather more rigid set of gatekeeping criteria. Finally, there is no longer any requirement that the parent or guardian of the young offender give their consent to the reprimand or warning. This was considered important under the old guidelines given that the consent of a person aged under 16 is largely invalid in many other fields (such as medicine).

It remains to be seen whether the police will continue to use their discretion to offer non-statutory informal warnings alongside the new system. There is nothing specifically in law which prevents a police officer from using their discretion to issue an informal warning, but, given the new statutory procedures, a police officer may prefer to avoid a legal challenge and opt for a more formal response. No further action may be preferred where a reprimand is considered too 'heavy handed' or disproportionately severe as a response to very trivial first time

---

[44] See *Code for Crown Prosecutors* (London, CPS, 2004).

[45] See further Evans, 'Cautioning' above n 13.

[46] See further T Bennett, 'The Social Distribution of Criminal Labels' (1979) 19 *British Journal of Criminology* 134.

offences. The practice of informal warnings, if it does continue, will be entirely unofficial and the 1998 Act does not sanction their use. As they are unrecorded it will be impossible to know whether they are still being used or not.

Crown Prosecution Service

Rather unusually by European standards diversionary discretion invested in the public prosecutor in England and Wales is very limited. Whereas in many other jurisdictions it is the public prosecutor who is invested with a wider variety of diversionary options,[47] in England and Wales the key gatekeeping responsibility rests with the police. For historical and cultural reasons, the Crown Prosecution Service (CPS) never adopted this role when it was established in 1985 and the police retained their autonomy and independence in relation to decision making at the very early stages of the youth justice process.[48] Prior to the Prosecution of Offences Act 1985, the police used to carry out both the investigation and prosecution function on behalf of the Crown in the absence of any other suitable agency for the task. The Philips Commission had recommended the establishment of an independent prosecution agency in England and Wales in their 1981 report,[49] largely as a result of their critique of that dual function of the police, which, they claimed, resulted in a lack of objectivity in decision making at this early stage, inadequate independent review of police investigations and consequent miscarriages of justice. The CPS was therefore established as a second, independent filter in the pre-trial stage. Their statutory independence was designed to prevent an unhealthy collaboration between agencies and to facilitate the objective review of evidence before cases proceeded to court, but also resulted in the CPS being wholly removed from the investigation process and they notably have no control or supervisory capacity over police activity in cases before the submission to them for review.

The CPS therefore is unlikely to review any of the cases which the police initially consider appropriate for a reprimand or warning (or indeed no further action). It is only where the police decide to prosecute that the CPS receives the file for a second, apparently independent review of it merits for diversion. Even after receipt of the file the CPS have few opportunities to divert a young offender away from court. Their decisions are limited to taking no further action and dropping the case or continuing with the prosecution process and preparing for a court hearing. In this regard the CPS apply two key criteria: the evidential sufficiency test and the public interest test. The *Code for Crown Prosecutors* offers published guidance on

---

[47] See Fionda, *Public Prosecutors and Discretion* above n 22.
[48] *Ibid* ch 2.
[49] Royal Commission on Criminal Procedure, *Report* Cmnd 8092 (London, HMSO, 1981).

the requirements of each test.[50] First, and most importantly for due process reasons, the CPS must assess whether there is sufficient evidence to prosecute. After various re-draftings since 1986[51] the test now involves considering objectively whether there is a realistic prospect of conviction given the weight of the evidence, its reliability and admissibility and the likelihood of further evidence coming to light, bearing in mind the early stage at which this review takes place.[52] Where there is insufficient evidence to proceed the CPS should drop the case against the accused at this point to protect the young offender from an unnecessary appearance in court which results in a directed acquittal.

Where there is sufficient evidence to proceed the CPS must then consider whether it is in the public interest to do so. This involves considering a number of non-legal criteria to assess whether an expedient approach to the case should result in its termination at this point. The *Code for Crown Prosecutors* sets out the public interest factors as lists of considerations weighing in favour of and against prosecution.[53] The original draft of the *Code* in 1986 presented a clear presumption against prosecution,[54] quoting Lord Shawcross's famous statement that 'It has never been the rule in this country—I hope it never is—that suspected criminal offences must automatically be the subject of prosecution . . . public interest is the dominant consideration.'[55] The quote remains in the *Code* and, indeed, prosecution is not automatic since Crown Prosecutors are charged with the task of carefully weighing up factors for and against prosecution. However, since the 1994 draft of the *Code* there has been a more explicit statement that there is a presumption in favour of prosecution unless there are serious public interest reasons for not proceeding. Paragraph 5.7 of the current edition of the *Code* states this clearly:

> The public interest must be considered in each case where there is enough evidence to provide a realistic prospect of conviction. Although there may be public interest factors against prosecution in a particular case, often the prosecution should go ahead and those factors should be put to the court for consideration when sentence is being passed. *A*

---

[50] The current edition of the *Code* was published in 2004. The *Code* is produced for public consumption, although the CPS themselves use more detailed guidance in their own policy manuals which, for policy reasons, are not published. See further A Ashworth and J Fionda, 'Prosecution, Accountability and the Public Interest' [1994] Crim LR 894.

[51] The *Code* was re-drafted in 1990, 1994, 2000 and 2004. See Ashworth and Fionda previous n.

[52] The early review of evidence by the CPS was criticised since they might not have been in a position to consider possible defences open to the defendant or, in the case of young offenders before 1998, evidence of *doli incapax*. This has been addressed in the new edition of the *Code* which instructs prosecutors to consider changes to the weight of the evidence in the light of future developments in the case—see A Ashworth and M Redmayne, *The Criminal Process* 3rd edn (Oxford, Oxford University Press, 2005) pp 182–83.

[53] *Code for Crown Prosecutors* (London, CPS, 2004) paras 5.9 and 5.10.

[54] Crown Prosecutors in this edition of the *Code* were cautioned not to prosecute unless the public interest 'requires' them to do so—*Code for Crown Prosecutors* (London, CPS, 1986) para 8. See further A Ashworth, 'The "Public Interest" Element in Prosecutions' [1987] Crim LR 595.

[55] HC Debates vol 483, col 681(1951); G Mansfield and J Peay, *The Director of Public Prosecutions: Principles and Practices for the Crown Prosecutor* (London, Tavistock, 1987).

prosecution will usually take place unless there are public interest factors tending against prosecution which clearly outweigh those tending in favour, or it appears more appropriate in all circumstances of the case to divert the person from prosecution.[56] (emphasis added)

The tone of this guidance is discouraging to prosecutors in exercising their already limited diversion discretion, the preference being that mitigating factors that might previously have kept young offenders out of the youth courts should now be considered at the sentencing stage. Indeed, some have argued that a momentum for prosecution is inherent in the pre-trial review process, since the CPS become involved only after the police have already decided to prosecute and may feel deterred from reversing that momentum.[57] Research by Gelsthorpe and Giller revealed that the content of police files were likely to add to that momentum: 'The Crown Prosecution Service remains dependent upon the police for information. Since the raison d'être of the police is to detect and prevent crime we might reasonably expect a presumption in favour of prosecution with respect to those cases they refer to the Crown Prosecution Service.'[58]

In relation to young offenders, the reluctance to divert has been more clearly stated in recent editions of the *Code*. Prior to the establishment of the CPS there had been a long-standing reluctance to prosecute young offenders, the stigma of a court appearance and the long-term negative effects of a criminal conviction rendered the practice unfair and inappropriate, and by the mid-1980s when the CPS was established, youth justice policy was, in practice at least, firmly rooted in the developmental ideal to which prosecution was antithetical. Indeed, in the House of Lords debates on the Prosecution of Offences Bill in 1985, Baroness Lucy Faithfull moved an amendment requiring specially trained prosecutors to use prosecution in juvenile cases as a last resort, with a heavy presumption in favour of cautioning in suitable cases, thereby carrying the ethos of police practice into the policy of the new prosecution service.[59] Lord Elton[60] responded with a promise that that 'ethos' would be clearly reflected in the *Code for Crown Prosecutors*, as it duly was. The youth of the offender was a public interest criterion weighing strongly against prosecution:

---

[56] The last part of this paragraph refers to the new statutory cautioning system for adults, introduced in the Criminal Justice Act 2003, and not to the reprimand and warning system for young offenders. Para 8.9 of the *Code*, discussed below, sets out the policy on diversion for young offenders.

[57] See further Fionda, *Public Prosecutors and Discretion* above n 22; M McConville, A Sanders and R Leng, *The Case for the Prosecution: Police Suspects and the Construction of Criminality* (London, Routledge, 1991).

[58] L Gelsthorpe and H Giller, 'More Justice for Juveniles: Does More Mean Better?' [1990] Crim LR 153.

[59] HL Debates vol 458 col 1112 (1985).

[60] HL Debates vol 458 col 1114 (1985).

[T]here may be positive advantages for the individual and society in using prosecution as a last resort and that in general there is in the cases of juvenile offenders a much stronger presumption in favour of methods of disposal which fall short of prosecution unless the seriousness of the offence or other exceptional circumstances dictate otherwise. The objective should be to divert juveniles from court wherever possible. Prosecution should always be regarded as a severe step.[61]

By 1994, however, youth was removed from the list of factors weighing against a prosecution, and was replaced by a short paragraph elsewhere in the *Code* which stated that the youth of the offender needed to be weighed carefully against the seriousness of their offending behaviour or their propensity to re-offend.[62] It was notable that this amendment to the *Code* was published within days of the Home Secretary's circular on cautioning[63] which was similarly discouraging of extensive diversion of young offenders, although the CPS have vehemently denied any deliberate collusion in policy making with the Home Office.[64]

In between the two extremes of prosecution and non-prosecution, the CPS were, prior to the 1998 legislation, able to refer a case back to the police and request that they reconsider a caution. This provided them with their only diversionary possibility where a prosecution was felt to be inappropriate or too heavy-handed, but where non-prosecution may fail to address the offending behaviour in any way. Since the statutory reprimand and warning scheme has been introduced, the prosecutor will rarely be able to exercise this discretion. The statutory scheme explicitly and strictly prohibits repeat reprimands or warnings except in the most exceptional of cases. Indeed the current *Code* has been revised to take into account the new scheme and provides updated guidance on the limits to diversionary possibilities thus:

Case involving youths are usually referred only to the Crown Prosecution Service for prosecution if the youth has already received a reprimand and final warning, unless the offence is so serious that neither of these were appropriate or the youth does not admit committing the offence. Reprimands and final warnings are intended to prevent re-offending and the fact that a further offence has occurred indicates that attempts to divert the youth from the court system have not been effective. So the public interest will usually require a prosecution in such cases, unless there are clear public interest factors against prosecution.[65]

Where the 'two-strikes' of this procedure have been wielded previously, and young offenders consequently finds themselves subject to prosecution, the CPS clearly

---

[61] *Code for Crown Prosecutors* (London, CPS, 1986) para 16.
[62] *Code for Crown Prosecutors* (London, CPS, 1994) para 6.8.
[63] Home Office Circular 18/1994—discussed above.
[64] See Roger Daw's spirited response to Ashworth and Fionda's comments in this regard—[1994] Crim LR 904.
[65] *Code for Crown Prosecutors* (London, CPS, 2004) para 8.9.

consider themselves powerless to request any further diversion and are left with the choice between not proceeding at all or playing the trump card of prosecution.

It therefore seems that a consequence of the legislative formula for police diversion has had a further limiting effect on the potential for the CPS to avoid prosecution. They will no doubt be relieved, since their reluctance to involve themselves in the diversion of young offenders has been clearly voiced in the past. During the early 1990s, when the practice of cautioning had escalated to unprecedented levels, questions arose as to whether the police were the appropriate agency to administer diversionary decisions, given their lack of accountability and possibly objectivity. Suggestions were therefore made that, as in other European jurisdictions, perhaps the CPS were better placed to adopt the role. The Royal Commission on Criminal Justice (RCCJ) discussed this possibility in 1993. In two very brief paragraphs[66], the Commission discussed the system of prosecutor fines in other jurisdictions such as Scotland and concluded that the CPS should be empowered to caution an offender with view to offering a discretionary fine as a penalty.[67] At that time the CPS suggested in their evidence to the Royal Commission that unless and until cautioning was placed on a statutory basis they were reluctant to develop their own diversionary role within that context.[68] Now that the statutory scheme excludes them from any active diversionary role, the possibility of these developments being resurrected in policy circles is remote.

Discussion

The history of diversion in England and Wales, both in policy terms and in the development of it in practice, reveals some inherent tensions and conflicts which may explain why youth justice policy has persisted in pursuing a diversionary strategy but with widely varying enthusiasm at different times. Support for such a strategy has never, for example, been so committed that prosecution of young offenders has truly been an exception to the rule. Rather, diversion has been perceived as a temporary concession to leniency, a privilege of welfare which may be withdrawn at any time. Conversely, other jurisdictions neighbouring England and Wales, such as the Republic of Ireland and Scotland, have demonstrated a firmer commitment to diversion such that criminal proceedings have become a rarity in youth justice practice and the failure of diversion to prevent further offending is perceived as a failure to address welfare needs rather than a failure on the part of

---

[66] The Commission were clearly not guided by the caution in 'transplanting' procedures from comparative jurisdictions advised by academics in the field of comparative research—see eg L Zedner 'Comparative Research in Criminal Justice' in L Noaks, M Levi and M Maguire (eds) *Contemporary Issues in Criminology* (Cardiff, University of Wales Press, 1995).

[67] RCCJ, *Report* above n 23 at ch 5, para 63.

[68] Crown Prosecution Service, *Evidence to Royal Commission* (London, CPS, 1991) p 98.

the individual offender to take advantage of the privilege they have been offered. This may be because diversion is regarded by both practitioners and policy makers in England and Wales as a double-edged sword, rendering their faith in it somewhat half-hearted. Further discussion of those tensions may explain the concomitant enthusiasm and anxiety for the practice.

Due Process and Crime Control

Herbert Packer first used these terms to describe two competing value choices facing criminal justice policy makers.[69] Packer developed these two models or value systems as a convenient means of representing the conflicting nature of those choices and the competing considerations that underlie decision making in criminal law. The due process model perceives the criminal justice system as an 'obstacle course' through which any case must overcome a series of impediments designed to protect the defendant's rights and liberties before a conviction can be satisfactorily obtained and before any punishment can be wholly justified. The possibilities of false accusations or a miscarriage of justice are of paramount importance in a system where cases should be heard by an objective court before which the defendant is given a full opportunity to defend himself and dispute the charges against him. A system based on this model is designed to err on the side of caution and allow all criminal prosecutions to run their full course before the state is satisfied that an adjudication of guilt is just. In contrast, the crime control model focuses on repressing crime and on the swift, administrative punishment of it. For the purposes of speed and effective management of a crime problem a justice system based on this model will seek to process suspects and punish them at the earliest possible stage of the criminal justice process, avoiding wherever possible the opportunity for dispute, contention or appeal. To this end Packer suggests:

> It follows that extra-judicial processes should be preferred to judicial processes, informal operations to formal ones. But informality is not enough; there must also be uniformity. Routine, stereotyped procedures are essential if large numbers are to be handled.[70]

These models were never described as realities, rather as artificial theoretical extremes to demonstrate tensions in making policy choices in this area. Furthermore, Packer's models have been subject to more recent criticism for their inherent contradictions,[71] their undue simplicity, and their failure to appreciate

---

[69] The models are explained and discussed in his seminal work *The Limits of the Criminal Sanction* (Stanford, Stanford University Press, 1969).

[70] *Ibid* p 159.

[71] Packers models have been subject to rigorous scrutiny and critique by Stuart MacDonald in his, as yet unpublished, PhD thesis *Analysing Criminal Justice Policy: The Anti-Social Behaviour Order and the Pervasive Effect of Packer's Two Models of the Criminal Justice Process* (University of Southampton, 2004).

wider considerations (such as victim-centred restoration or managerialism) facing policy makers in a more contemporary world.[72]

Despite their over-simplicity, the models are illustrative of the existence of the conflict inherent in choices to be made in the youth justice system regarding diversion. When you add into this conflict the further choices and concerns that Packer did not address, the conflict is heightened. The practice of diversion appears to accord most closely with Packer's crime control model in the sense that firstly, in the true sense of crime control, many believe that the preventive merits of diversion for young offenders lie in opportunities it affords to take constructive, though informal action to address offending behaviour without the stigma of a court appearance or the threat of carrying it out under court order. Secondly, the informal and extra-judicial adjudication of guilt and issue of penalties at the early stages of the youth justice process, for the purposes of achieving a finite and speedy conclusion to a case, epitomise Packer's description of this model. The closer the policy accords with the crime control model, the greater the anxiety felt by policy makers and practitioners that they may be retreating from the due process model.[73] In short, the greater the enthusiasm for the welfare, crime control and managerial benefits of diversion, the greater the anxiety in a post Human Rights Act world over the dangers and demerits of the practice.

An analysis of the varied history of diversion in policy demonstrates that while policy makers and governments have lent support to the practice, research on the process has provided stark warnings on its due process dangers. During the 1980s, for example, while cautioning expanded as an officially sanctioned tool of the developmental approach, a number of research projects examining the use of police discretion in this area revealed practice that was discriminatory, unaccountable and persistently inconsistent despite burgeoning Home Office guidance. Racial discrimination was found to be rife in the exercise of this discretion in London,[74] wide-scale class discrimination has been discovered,[75] and unjustifiable net-widening and inconsistency in decision making has led to suggestions that the police may abuse their unfettered powers in this context.[76]

The ruminations of the Royal Commission on Criminal Justice in 1993 provides explicit evidence of the tensions in this area. On the one hand, their brief

---

[72] See eg Ashworth and Redmayne, *The Criminal Process* above n 51 at pp 38–40.

[73] Although Packer was never clear about the relationship between his models or the extent to which adoption of one necessarily meant retrenchment from the other.

[74] See F Landau, and G Nathan, 'Selecting Delinquents for Cautioning in the London Metropolis Area' (1983) 23 *British Journal of Criminology*128.

[75] See Bennett, 'The Social Distribution of Criminal Labels' above n 45.

[76] See J Mott, 'Police Decisions for Dealing with Juvenile Offenders' (1983) 23 *British Journal of Criminology* 249; Evans and Wilkinson, 'Variations in Police Cautioning Policy' above n 17; C Fisher and R Mawby, 'Juvenile Delinquency and Police Discretion in an Inner-City Area' (1982) 22 *British Journal of Criminology* 63; A Sanders, 'The Limits to Diversion from Prosecution' (1988) 28 *British Journal of Criminology* 513.

to investigate means of preventing miscarriages of justice at the pre-trial stages of the criminal justice process rendered their support for cautioning somewhat guarded. On the other hand their zeal in utilising these early stages in designing efficient crime control methods meant that the value of cautioning could not be ignored and neither could the practice be denounced. This resulted in a recommendation to support the practice, but only provided it was given legal regulation and placed as far as possible in the hands of a fully accountable agency. When the new Labour government addressed the issue four years later the thought process was similar. Unable to deny the benefits of a diversion process, but mindful of the fact that, according to their own legislative agenda elsewhere, the Crime and Disorder Act 1998 had to be compatible with the Human Rights Act 1998, the result was to support a diversionary strategy, but only with full legal regulation. Consequently the drive to expand and fully utilise a policy of diversion is inevitably tempered by a need to formalise the process in order to minimise breaches of due process rights. The development of formal regulation of the process, however, tends to have the effect of controlling, restricting and reigning in the practice of diversion.

Formality and Informality

In addition to fears over the due process rights of the offender, official support for the diversion process has been restrained by anxiety over the uncontrolled use of discretion. Early disapproval of those police force areas that developed the practice in the late nineteenth and early twentieth century was partly a disapproval of the police adopting a judicial and social work, rather than law enforcement, role. The Malony Commission's objection to the practice, quoted above, suggested it was 'outside the proper duties of the police.'[77] By the 1950s, when the police were using cautioning as a tool of the welfare approach, even social workers shared this mistrust of police discretion:

> The police are in this way taking the place of the professional experts who assess the child's needs before the Order is made and of the trained social case workers who help him afterwards. They are not trained to recognise or to deal with cases where deep emotional disturbance is present, and as police the only tool they have is the threat of a court charge.[78]

Indeed, Covington and Giller's study of cautioning in Hampshire noted that police decisions on cautioning were often influenced by gut reaction or instinct.[79]

---

[77] See above n 3.
[78] W Cavenagh, *The Child and the Court* (London, Gollancz, 1959) p 203.
[79] C Covington and H Giller, *Hampshire Constabulary Youth Help Scheme: Report of Research Findings* (Winchester, Hampshire County Council, 1985).

Later critique of the use of discretion in this area spread to the inconsistency which emerged from practice in different police force areas. Home Office statistics in 1985 revealed diverse practice around the country, some police forces clearly adopting a more diversionary strategy than others. In that year, the average cautioning rate was 66.04 per cent of all known young offenders being diverted. However, the rates ranged from 40.75 per cent in Dorset or 57.06 per cent in South Wales to 76.71 per cent in Thames Valley and 75.52 per cent in Warwickshire. Inconsistency was regarded as unprofessional, but more worrying was the lack of equity in the application of justice in different areas where offences of similar types may or may not be prosecuted depending on where they were committed.

It is therefore no surprise that during the 1990s, when policy makers considered their dilemma over whether to encourage or discourage diversion, their guarded support hinged on some form of legal regulation of it. The call for statutory authority came from a string of government or Parliamentary reports including the Royal Commission on Criminal Justice, Home Affairs Committee, the Audit Commission and New Labour themselves. Bureaucratically legitimated procedures provided the comfort blanket of law, under which the use of the procedure could be carefully controlled to ensure it was appropriately applied, but which could also ensure that the extent of its application could be regulated according to the political barometer. Rutherford, however, sounded an early warning that formalisation would result in further net-widening[80] and according to Evans and Wilkinson, the regulatory guidance distributed in 1985 actually provoked more inconsistency in practice.[81] As early forms of formalisation appeared to do nothing to ease policy makers' feelings of insecurity regarding diversion, the pressure to increase control has been great and the formalities have increased.

Net-widening

The benefits of diversion have been acknowledged and tested since the practice first emerged, and help to explain the early development of it in the face of much official opprobrium.[82] The drive to expand the practice on the part of practitioners has been attributed to its two key advantages over formal processing in the courts, namely the avoidance of labelling and stigma. The labelling theory, developed by sociologists, suggests that identifying a person as 'deviant' can set in motion a process of alienation. The offender finds himself cut off from the normative values of society, and forms a social identity or a sub-cultural 'outgroup' of offenders. This group develops their own values which conflict with

---

[80] A Rutherford, *Growing Out of Crime: The New Era* (Winchester, Waterside Press, 2002) p 108.
[81] Evans and Wilkinson, above n 17.
[82] See Malony Committee above n 3.

those of the rest of society.[83] This results in an 'amplification of deviance' whereby the deviant group's norms become intolerant to the rest of society, law enforcement is increased to express that intolerance, and hostility of the deviant group towards law enforcers results in further deviant behaviour.[84] The theory was tested in a study conducted by David Farrington in 1977, based on the self-reported delinquency of 400 working-class youths in London.[85] The delinquency scores were significantly higher for those youths who had been publicly labelled, after which they were more willing to admit to further delinquent acts. There was also evidence that the effects of labelling at an earlier age last longer than those publicly labelled later. The study, though, further revealed that public labelling through official cautions, as opposed to labelling by court procedures and a criminal conviction, did not result in deviance amplification.

The results of this study gave credence to official statements supporting cautioning for its anti-labelling merit. The Black Committee, for example, proposing legislation on youth justice in Northern Ireland in 1979, warned of the spiralling effects of the delinquent label:

> Once labelled a delinquent, a child is more likely to see himself as such, to associate with kindred spirits, to be a focus of attention for the police, to become stereotyped. It is now widely accepted that convictions can have the effect of increasing rather than diminishing juvenile criminality.[86]

A year later, in England and Wales, the Home Office also acknowledged that cautioning was likely to have a positive, preventive advantage over prosecution:

> Juvenile Offenders who can be diverted from the criminal justice system at an early stage in their offending are less likely to re-offend than those who become involved in judicial proceedings.[87]

Public labelling, however, is not the only damaging effect of those judicial proceedings. The adversarial nature of the court process has long been felt to be inappropriate and increases the feeling of isolation and rejection of the young person. The domination of lawyers and officials in the proceedings leave the young person feeling confused and insignificant. As McCabe and Treitel observed in their study:

> The children sit at the centre of this bustle, unoccupied and unnoticed. There is evidence of carelessness, high-handedness on the part of those who serve the court, only the dedication of each one to the particular job he has to do. Parents and children have no job to do—no part to play.[88]

---

[83] H Becker, *Outsiders: Studies in the Sociology of Deviance* (New York, Free Press, 1966)

[84] L Wilkins, *Social Policy, Action and Research: Studies in Deviance* (London, Tavistock, 1964)

[85] D Farrington, 'The Effects of Public Labelling' (1977) 17 *British Journal of Criminology* 112.

[86] Black Committee, *Report of the Children and Young Persons Review Group* (Belfast, HMSO, 1979) p 47.

[87] Home Office, *Young Offenders* Cmnd 8045 (London, HMSO, 1980) p 62.

[88] S McCabe and P Treitel, *Juvenile Justice in the United Kingdom: Comparisons and Suggestions for Change* (London, Croom Helm, 1983) p 20. See Ch 6 for further discussion of the court process.

Cautioning or warning an offender is, in contrast, a process during which the police officer speaks directly to the young person and is felt to be a more meaningful and 'real' communication with the offender than the rather remote and ritualistic proceedings of a court, but being less public is less likely to stigmatise as well as to label.

These widely accepted benefits undoubtedly prompted the expansion of the practice of diversion during the 1980s and the preference for this form of minimal intervention. Since then policy makers have not sought to deny these advantages and yet have been less keen to maintain intervention at the pre-trial stages. New Labour youth justice policy, for example, is as concerned with preventing delinquency as practitioners were in the 1980s, but their approach is centred more on court-ordered responses. The tension here is between the clear advantages of early, informal intervention on the one hand and anxiety about net-widening on the other. Whilst it is assumed that net-widening does not occur in the more open and formal arena of the court, the opportunity to draw offenders into the criminal justice net at the more hidden pre-trial stage is thought to be a peril which seriously undermines the appeal of diversion. Indeed, the further the expansion of the practice in the 1980s the greater this concern. In 1986 Pratt noted that while cautioning was

> designed with the intent of delaying the point of entry to the juvenile justice system, it can also be seen as further extending the orbit of delinquency decision-making, helping it reach out to points further away from the juvenile court than before.[89]

As enthusiasm for the opportunities for constructive work with young offenders at this pre-trial stage increases, so too does the temptation to apply it to a greater pool of recipients, including those committing very minor infractions of the law or, even worse, those at risk of offending. By expanding mechanisms for diversion the state expands its capacity to observe, control and manipulate a wider section of the youth population, creating what Stanley Cohen called the 'Punitive city'.[90] The dangers of increasing social control through diversion to informal, non-criminal proceedings has been criticised in Scotland.[91]

The response to fears of net-widening in England and Wales has been to formalise the diversion process, a mechanism which is designed to control the use of diversion and restrict it only to those identifiable offenders whose offending is serious enough to warrant even an informal response. Formalising the practice to prevent inappropriate over-use, however, also serves to increase net-widening. As guidelines were developed to ensure process was administered fairly, previous

---

[89] J Pratt, 'Diversion from the Juvenile Court: A History of Inflation and a Critique of Progress' (1986) 26 *British Journal of Criminology* 212 at 228.

[90] S Cohen, *Visions of Social Control* (Cambridge, Polity Press, 1985).

[91] P Duff, 'The Prosecutor Fine and Social Control: The Introduction of the Fiscal Fine in Scotland' (1993) 33 *British Journal of Criminology* 481.

cautions were recorded and were citable in court, the process became less individ-ualised and tailored to the welfare needs of the offender and police officers had greater confidence to apply the regulated procedure in order to manage a burgeoning crime problem with maximum efficiency. Young offenders were no longer diverted away from the formal towards the informal, but from one formal process to another:

> This entailed a move away from the dispensation of individualised treatment towards the construction of an administrative process which was tailored for the surveillance and notation of the delinquent activities of sections of the youth population as a whole . . . Diversion takes place from a court into a court of another kind, whose hallmark is efficiency rather than formalised justice.[92]

As an officially sanctioned response to offending, cautioning acquired a formal identity and credibility that in its informal guise, it did not possess. First, record-ing incidences of diversion gave the young offender a criminal record, so that they could be more readily identified in future as a repeat offender and could find themselves on the fast-track to court. Previous cautions on a young offender's record should indicate that previous attempts at prevention were ongoing, but could also indicate to a magistrate a propensity for recidivism and thereby prompt an even more formal response. Farrington and Bennett found that magistrates tended to regard previous cautions as equivalent to previous convictions.[93] The statutory schema for diversion enacted in the Crime and Disorder Act 1998 takes this form of net-widening a step forward, formalising a fast-track to prosecution approach as it does not allow for repeat diversion beyond the confines of the rigid hierarchy of reprimands and warnings. In this way net-widening increases but diversion does not so that the net result is an increase in young offenders being sucked into the courts. Second, a formal requirement for the admission of guilt does not necessarily prevent net-widening nor protect the due process rights of the offender. Rather, the concern is that, as it is diversion from court on offer and this may be perceived as a better option than going to court, offenders may feel pres-sured to admit guilt where there is doubt over their criminal responsibility for the offence, or even involvement in it. This problem emerged from Evans and Puech's evaluation of the new warning system:

> Young people and their parents state that they would rather receive a warning than go to court although they clearly see this as the lesser of two evils. They feel under pressure to accept a warning even where there are disputes about the evidence or when the young person does not fully admit the offence . . . The young person may give a different ver-sion of events during a home visit to that recorded in the police summary of the evidence.

---

[92] Pratt above n 88 at pp 224–29.
[93] D Farrington and T Bennett, 'Police Cautioning of Juveniles in London' (1981) 21 *Journal of Criminology* 123.

So the YOT worker is then left trying to deal with an offence or offending behaviour that is denied.[94]

The Politics of Diversion

As net-widening increases, so too does the perception that the problem of youth crime is increasing rather than diminishing. A growing crime problem needs to be managed and the political pressure to prevent crime rates rising out of all proportion is great. It is therefore tempting for policy makers to resort to crime control methods reminiscent of Packer's first model, namely informal, administrative forms of justice which are capable of efficiently processing large numbers of cases. The managerial benefits of a diversion scheme are undoubtedly politically attractive and explain why a Conservative government in the 1980s gave such strong support to a policy which so contradicted their commitment to a more traditionally right-wing law and order policy. Therein lies a further tension for more recent governments who lack the political confidence to depart too far from populist punitiveness and yet who cannot ignore the managerial possibilities of diversion.

Non-prosecution appears unduly lenient and cautioning had acquired a reputation for 'letting offenders off'[95]—a public image that sat uneasily alongside New Labour's pledge to be 'tough on crime, tough on the causes of crime'. We therefore see a hesitant approval of the value of diversion, New Labour claiming that it has merits for first time offenders but that 'it becomes progressively less effective once a pattern of offending sets in.'[96] They cite no evidence to support this theory; the re-offending rate for repeat cautions has never been proven to be any higher than for first cautions. The point of using repeat cautions under the developmental approach in the 1980s was to enable the authorities to identify the hard core persistent offender who faced greater personal difficulties and was unlikely to grow out of crime, without causing undue damage to those whose offending was part of the adolescent phase. Evans reports that repeat cautions were used in many police force areas, finding that where a second offence was different to or occurred some time after the first a further diversion was both appropriate and effective.[97] The government's assertion therefore appears to be driven by politics not criminological data.

---

[94] Evans and Puech above n 32 at pp 800–2.

[95] The Police Federation claimed in 1993 that 'Juveniles are actually laughing at you. They are not taking any notice of you . . . Something has to be done and that something has to be custody because the alternative is to take decisions that will allow them to burgle someone's house and steal someone's car'—reported by P Wynn Davies, 'Police Urge New Approach to Young Offenders' *Independent* (11 February 1993).

[96] Home Office, *Tackling Youth Crime* above n 28 at p 3.

[97] Evans, 'Cautioning' above n 13.

The political dilemma posed by the conflicting attributes of managerialism over populism has contributed to the reluctance to pursue a diversionary strategy in reforming the youth justice process in the 1990s. This can be contrasted with political approaches elsewhere where the commitment to divert has been less diluted by the tensions discussed above. In the Republic of Ireland, for example, a Juvenile Liaison Scheme was established nationally in 1963, providing a formalised diversion programme for young offenders to ensure that the majority of first time offenders avoided a court appearance.[98] By 2001 the Youth Diversion Project was placed on a statutory footing[99], partly to give official recognition to the scheme, but also to fully endorse and encourage its maximum use. Far from concerns about the dangers of diversion, the Irish government have recognised its welfare and developmental potential, and more recently the opportunity to use the programme as a means of implementing a restorative approach to youth crime aimed at involving the victim at the pre-trial stage. This scheme will be discussed in more detail in Chapter 8 below, but for now provides an example of a jurisdiction holding on to the confidence to divert, regardless of its possible demerits or perceived political inexpediency.

---

[98] See further H Burke, C Carney and G Cook, *Young Offenders in Ireland* (Dublin, Turae Press, 1981).

[99] The Children Act 2001 Part 4.

6

Tribunals

An indication of the extent to which young offenders are kept separate from adult criminal justice procedures can be measured in the tribunals in which they are tried and sentenced. Indeed the establishment, or 'birth' of a separate youth justice system in England and Wales has been measured in terms of the establishment of a separate court for dealing with the crimes of the young.[1] However, more than that, the tribunals in which children appear to account for their wrongdoing may also be a measure of the extent to which a youth justice system in any jurisdiction chooses to criminalise troublesome behaviour and to practise a shaming ritual in which society may collectively express their disapproval of a child's misbehaviour. The tribunal may symbolically take the role of stern, but kindly, parent acting as *parens patriae*, mediator in a dispute between the child and the state, in instilling a sense of discipline and morality in the child. The role taken by a tribunal in any system gives us an indication of the wider philosophical approach to youth justice and collective or societal attitude towards the troublesome behaviour of the young.

Whilst there have been a number of changes to the tribunals in this context in England and Wales over the last century, they remain criminal courts, trying and sentencing young people within the framework of the criminal law. At the same time, these courts have statutory welfare responsibilities towards all children involved in court proceedings. The plurality of responsibilities and the ambivalence of purpose of the criminal trial will be explored in relation to the operation of the youth and Crown Courts. The decision to include a discussion of referral orders in this chapter reflects my view of youth offender panels as an 'alternative' to the youth court in formulating a sentence in response to youth crime. Whilst these panels are not technically (or otherwise) a criminal court, they have been assigned the youth court's sentencing function in certain cases, arguably for managerial reasons. The panels will therefore be discussed here as a 'tribunal' although the purposes, and particularly the alleged restorative aspect, of the referral order will be discussed further in Chapter 8. The plurality of ideology is as problematic for the youth offender panel, as it is for the 'real' courts.

---

[1] J Fionda,'Youth and Justice' in J Fionda (ed) *Legal Concepts of Childhood* (Oxford, Hart Publishing, 2001) p 77.

In other jurisdictions, non-criminal alternative tribunals have been established, either as an alternative to a criminal court, approaching troublesome behaviour as symptomatic of a welfare need (suggesting an abolitionist agenda) or to deal with non-serious delinquency (as a form of diversion). The establishment of alternative forms of tribunal may, in part, emerge as a resolution of some of the problems associated with the criminal trial for young offenders and in this sense provide some insight into whether it is the criminal nature of proceedings which is, in itself, problematic. These comparative jurisdictions also provide examples of an ideologically alternative approach to youth crime, where the notion of 'criminality', and all that accompanies that notion as regards blame, punishment and shame, has no meaning since troublesome behaviour is simply not defined in those terms. These systems operate with a more remedial or preventive ideology. The role of tribunals in these systems and the ideological significance of this approach will be explored further in Chapter 10.

The Youth Court

The Development of a Jurisdiction

The first criminal court to deal solely with children was the Juvenile Court, created by the 1908 Children Act. Prior to this Act children were dealt with in the adult courts, although by 1908 many areas had already provided for children to be tried and sentenced in separate sittings of the magistrates' court. The 1908 Act required such separation on a nationwide basis and established an entirely new branch of the magistrates' court. The Juvenile Court originally had jurisdiction over children aged between 7 (at that time the minimum age of criminal responsibility) and 17. As a criminal court it was empowered to try and sentence young offenders for any offence except murder. Only children charged with murder, charged jointly with an adult or over the age of 17 were at that time tried in an adult court. However, the Juvenile Court also held a civil jurisdiction for family law and child protection issues for children within the same age band.

The establishment of the new court was a climax of the new welfare approach to young offenders which had begun to emerge over 50 years earlier, though in a less formal guise.[2] Those sentenced to custody had begun to be held separately from adults as early as 1838 when Parkhurst prison, on the Isle of Wight, opened its doors exclusively to young boys, initially as a holding institution before they were transported overseas. Between 1850 and 1870 Mary Carpenter had campaigned to

---

[2] See further Ch 3.

remove boys from this institution to place them in reformatories and other educational institutions for rehabilitative purposes. Both types of institution were designed to avoid the corrupting influence of mixing young and adult offenders in the same living environment, and separation became a prominent feature of the welfare approach. The 1908 Act extended this feature to the court process. Indeed the Children Act was regarded as one of the first forms of official recognition of the welfare approach as it also placed restrictions on the imprisonment of young offenders under the age of 15. The creation of a separate tribunal mirrored developments across the Atlantic, the first of the American Juvenile Courts having been established in Chicago in 1899. The influence of the 'child savers' in the United States ensured that by 1917 all but three of the States had passed legislation to establish a separate Juvenile Court.[3]

It was not just a perceived need to avoid the corruption of minors by adult defendants during the court process that prompted the establishment of these courts. The welfare ideal extended to granting them special powers to respond to juvenile crime in a more constructive and rehabilitative way, under a more benevolent working ideology. In the United States, Platt notes that:

> The juvenile court system was part of a general movement directed toward removing adolescents from the criminal law process and creating special programs for delinquent, dependent and neglected children. Regarded as 'one of the greatest advances in child welfare that has ever occurred,' the juvenile court was considered 'an integral part of total welfare planning.'[4]

In England and Wales the 1908 Children Act had been shortly preceded by the 1906 Probation of Offenders Act, which established a national probation service and gave the courts the first probation order, providing supervision in the community as an alternative to custody. At the same time the Prevention of Crime Act 1908 provided for the establishment of borstals, at that time educational, reforming institutions for young men aged under 20. In addition, Juvenile Courts were able to dispose of young defendants variously by discharge on a recognisance, committal to the care of a relative, committal to a reformatory, whipping, a fine or, as a last resort, imprisonment for those aged over 14.

In contrast with the American style of Juvenile Court, the English court was very firmly a criminal tribunal. In the United States, emphasis was placed on highly informal proceedings, without rigid adherence to procedural requirements, aimed at alleviating neglect of those who had been, or even were at risk of becoming delinquent. The role of the court was very much that of *parens patriae*, concerned for the welfare of all young people whose lifestyle gave cause for

---

[3] See A Platt, *The Child Savers: The Invention of Delinquency* (Chicago, University of Chicago Press, 1969).

[4] *Ibid* p 10, citing Charles Chute 'Fifty years of the Juvenile Court' (1949) *National Probation and Parole Association Yearbook* 1.

concern, regardless of whether that lifestyle culminated in criminal behaviour or not. Platt, critical of this intrusive aspect of the new courts, describes them thus:

> The juvenile court movement went far beyond a humanitarian concern for the special treatment of adolescents. It brought within the ambit of government control a set of youthful activities that had been previously ignored or handled informally. It was not by accident that the behavior selected for penalizing by the child savers—drinking, begging, roaming the streets, frequenting dance-halls and movies, fighting, sexuality, staying out late at night and incorrigibility—was primarily attributable to the children of lower-class and immigrant families.[5]

The reforming influence of Mary Carpenter's institutions had been aimed at a similar group of young people and their activities. However, the Juvenile Court in England and Wales reserved its criminal jurisdiction for those who had committed a clearly defined criminal offence and operated on more formal due process principles. This came under criticism when the operation of the new court was first reviewed in 1927 by the Malony Committee.[6] This Home Office Committee, charged with a review of the treatment of young offenders in the new juvenile justice system, considered the appropriateness of using criminal proceedings in relation to young people. Having considered the more informal, but wider-ranging, approach of the American courts, they finally concluded that due process and public interest concerns required that the proceedings remain relatively formal and criminalised for the following reasons:

> Two considerations presented themselves strongly to our minds. In the first place it is very important that a young person should have the fullest opportunity of meeting a charge made against him, and it would be difficult for us to suggest a better method than a trial based on the well-tried principles of English law. The young have a strong sense of justice and much harm might be done by any disregard of it . . . Secondly, when the offence is really serious and has been proved it is right that its gravity should be brought home to the offender. We feel considerable doubt whether a change of procedure . . . might not weaken the feelings of respect for the law which it is important to awaken in the minds of the young if they are to realise their duties and responsibilities when they grow older.[7]

The Juvenile's Court's jurisdiction and philosophical approach therefore did not change in 1927, and neither did it change significantly until 1991. Major reforms were proposed in the late 1960s and enacted in the Children and Young Persons Act 1969, but like other major reforms in this legislation, they were never

---

[5] Platt, *The Child Savers* above n 3 at p 138.

[6] Home Office Committee on the Treatment of Young Offenders. For further discussion of this Committee's deliberations and recommendations see A Rutherford, *Growing Out of Crime: The New Era* (Winchester, Waterside Press, 2002) pp 52–55.

[7] Malony Committee, *Report of Departmental Committee on the Treatment of Young Offenders* Cmnd 2831 (London, Home Office, 1927) p 19.

implemented.[8] Just as Scotland were moving to de-criminalise Children's Hearings, at the same time[9] the 1969 legislation proposed to phase out criminal proceedings for young offenders and replace them, where necessary, with care proceedings, Intermediate Treatment and a greater use of the cautioning system. By the time that Act was finally repealed in 1991, the Juvenile Court had not changed a great deal but was about to undergo some apparently minor changes.

In drafting the Criminal Justice Act 1991, the government at that time were envisaging a new sentencing framework for the juvenile court, in common with all other criminal courts. However, in relation specifically to young offenders, section 70 of that Act re-named the court the youth court and the panels of magistrates sitting in the court were re-named youth court panels. Subsequently, official discourse in this area refers to youth justice, youth offending, young offenders and youth crime in line with the new terminology introduced by the 1991 Act. The term 'juvenile' is now considered anachronistic and obsolete. Not only was the term 'juvenile' considered to be old-fashioned in 1991, but the white paper had justified the name change in the following terms:

> The age balance those appearing in criminal cases before the juvenile court is changing. In 1988, nearly 90 per cent were aged 14–16. Increasingly those under 14 are being dealt with without bringing them before a court. If the proposal for a court to hear most cases with defendants aged 17 is implemented, it is estimated that about three-quarters of the defendants appearing before it will be aged 16 or 17. The name of the court should reflect this considerable change in its responsibilities.[10]

The new name was therefore to be more reflective of the 'clientele' of the court which, at that time, was aging. The term 'juvenile' in the field of paediatric medicine does indeed refer to infants and younger children and may in this sense have appeared inappropriate. It is notable, however, that the Children Act 1989, implemented at the same time as the Criminal Justice Act 1991, defines a 'child' as a person under the age of 18.[11] This suggests childhood in these legislative terms extends further in civil law than it does in criminal law. Furthermore it is arguable whether the business of the youth court remains primarily concerned with the offending of older teenagers, given various amendments to criminal procedure and practice discussed elsewhere in this book.

The passage from the white paper quoted above indicates a further amendment to the jurisdiction of the youth court which was ultimately implemented. Section 68 of the Criminal Justice Act 1991 extends that jurisdiction to include 17-year-olds, giving the court powers to try and sentence young offenders aged from 10 to

---

[8] See further A Rutherford, 'A Statute Backfires: The Escalation of Youth Incarceration in England during the 1970s' in J Doig (ed) *Criminal Corrections: Ideals and Realities* (New York, Lexington, 1983).
[9] Social Work (Scotland) Act 1968.
[10] Home Office, *Crime, Justice and Protecting the Public* Cm 965 (London, HMSO, 1990) para 8.30.
[11] Children Act 1989 s 105.

their eighteenth birthday. The inclusion of this group had a significant impact on the youth court's work, since 17-year-olds are a highly criminogenic age group.[12] This amendment would not only have substantially increased the workload of the court, but, more importantly, would have brought this group within the relatively informal procedures and restricted sentencing powers of the youth court.

The Children Act 1989, previously enacted but implemented coincidentally with the Criminal Justice Act 1991, had created a new branch of the magistrates' court, the Family Proceedings Court.[13] This court took over all the civil or 'domestic' proceedings previously dealt with by the Juvenile Court. The effect of this provision was to provide the new youth court with a focused and entirely criminal jurisdiction. Whilst this may make managerial sense and enable the youth court panel to be more carefully selected and trained for a more specialised function, it also renders that panel unable to make sometimes necessary connections between criminal and civil proceedings involving the same child.[14] The Juvenile Court may have overseen the child protection or care proceedings relating to a particular individual as well as dealing with their criminal behaviour and was in a position to link the two. It was in a better position to review a young person's situation more holistically, even without a pre-sentence report, where it was more likely to be aware of difficulties at home or school which had necessitated proceedings in their own right. The youth court panel must now hope that such information is provided in a pre-sentence report or is volunteered by way of mitigation or explanation at the criminal hearing.

New Labour have left the jurisdiction of the youth court relatively untouched, although section 37 of the Crime and Disorder Act 1998 does provide them with an over-arching or 'principal' aim for their sentencing, to prevent crime.[15] The introduction of the referral order in the Youth Justice and Criminal Evidence Act 1999 will also have had an impact on both the sentencing function of the youth court in many cases, as well as in their capacity to bring cases to a speedier conclusion. These provisions will be discussed further below.

The Youth Court in Action

Youth court sittings are characterised by their informality. The rationale, implicit in the initial establishment of the Juvenile Court in 1908, to respond to youth crime in a way that reflects special consideration for the youth of the offender, remains a current theme. A Home Office Circular issued in 1992, to explain the

---

[12] See further Ch 4.
[13] Children Act 1989 s 92.
[14] See further C Ball, 'Youth Justice and the Youth Court: The End of a Separate System?' (1995) 7 *Child and Family Law Quarterly* 196.
[15] The principal aim will be discussed further in Ch 7.

Criminal Justice Act changes, reminded the youth court that the change of name did not imply a change in operational ethos:

> The existence of a separate court for dealing with young people reflects the special consideration that has to be given to them when they are involved in the criminal justice process. The juvenile court is marked out by the special powers it has and the special procedures which govern its operation. Although the powers of the youth court will in some respects be different from those of the juvenile court, the 1991 Act preserves the distinctive features of the juvenile court. This is intended to ensure that young people are dealt with in a way which has proper regard for their youthfulness.[16]

Such 'regard for youthfulness' will include informal proceedings, held in appropriately furnished rooms, and conducted in a manner and in language that is accessible and comprehensible to a young person and their parents. Legal terminology should be avoided where possible, the young person should be addressed directly by their first name and all decisions must be explained, with reasons, in a manner that the young person can understand. Most significantly, youth court sittings are closed to the public and only officers of the court and parties to the case are permitted to attend proceedings. Members of the press may attend although there are restrictions on what they may report.

The youth court, as a branch of the magistrates' court, will usually sit in the same building as the adult court. However, where possible a separate room, preferably with a separate entrance and exit from the adult court will be used. This provides for complete separation from the adult court and prevents any of the 'contamination' between offenders of different ages that prompted the establishment of the court in the first place. Where this was not possible, for many years the youth court was not permitted to sit in a room that had been used for adult hearings unless an interval of at least an hour between proceedings had elapsed. This requirement was dispensed with in 1998[17], apparently to 'reduce inefficiency in the use of court time.'[18] Where the hour's interval is dispensed with, however, separate waiting areas for young defendants must be provided. Whichever room is used, preference should be given to a working environment which avoids, where possible, the imposing and formal furnishings and arrangement of adult court rooms. Raised benches, for example are not ideal and the often august and stately architecture of many courtrooms are thought to be inappropriate surroundings for proceedings involving children.

In 2000 the Home Office and Lord Chancellor's Department reported on a pilot Demonstration Project in five youth courts in Rotherham and Leicestershire. The purposes of the project had included 'providing a Youth Court which is more

---

[16] Home Office, *Criminal Justice Act 1991: Young People and the Youth Court* Circular (27 March 1992).
[17] Crime and Disorder Act 1998 s 47(7).
[18] Home Office, *New Powers for Youth Courts* Circular (November 1998).

open and which commands the confidence of victims and the public; [and] processes which engage young offenders and their parents and focus on the nature of their offending behaviour and how to change it.'[19] In the course of the pilot, the youth courts experimented with, amongst other things, different court layouts. Defendants were asked to remain seated during the proceedings, with their parents sitting next to them, and magistrates were encouraged to sit beneath the raised bench in the well of the court. This practice received a mixed reaction. Whilst magistrates acknowledged that the more prominent position of the parent and the more relaxed seating arrangements for the defendant encouraged greater participation and more effective communication, they were less keen on sitting so close to the defendants. Some reported feeling 'intimidated and threatened' whilst others felt that the more intimate seating arrangements 'undermined the status and significance of a court appearance'.[20] This reveals the tension involved between maintaining the gravity and dignity of the proceedings as a criminal court of law, whilst attempting to facilitate a welfare oriented and constructive discussion of the offender's behaviour and needs.

The youth court panel will consist of three experienced and specially selected magistrates, preferably containing both male and female members. The selection of magistrates to serve in this court should take into account a person's experience or propensity for dealing with young people and youth court magistrates should have had two years' experience of working in the adult criminal court. Persons selected to sit in the youth court must undergo a period of training which will include observation of youth court procedures; training on the relevant law and practice relating to remands, trials and sentencing; criminological discussions on youth crime and the backgrounds of young offenders; and visits to a Young Offenders' Institution. Initial training will be followed by refresher courses and, more recently, a regular appraisal procedure. In common with magistrates in the adult courts, the youth panel are members of the lay judiciary and are not legally qualified. As such, a justices' clerk provides them with legal advice on their powers, procedures, laws relating to sentencing and evidence. This is a system designed to ensure that magistrates do not act ultra vires on the one hand, whilst avoiding any fetter on their independent discretion on the other (although some have questioned the extent to which clerks influence the sentencing decision).[21]

Despite attempts at informality, the youth court remains a criminal court and, in the common law tradition, is founded on the adversarial mode of trial. A prosecuting lawyer from the Crown Prosecution Service (CPS) will present the

---

[19] C Allen *et al*, *Evaluation of the Youth Court Demonstration Project* HORS 214 (London, Home Office, 2000) p v.

[20] Home Office, *The Youth Court 2001—The Changing Culture of the Youth Court: Good Practice Guide* (London, Home Office/Lord Chancellor's Department, 2001) p 9.

[21] Liberty, *Unequal before the Law: Sentencing in Magistrates' Courts in England and Wales 1981–1990* (London, Liberty, 1992).

case for the Crown and the defendant will sit to the right of the prosecutor, facing the Bench. The defendant is entitled to be represented in their defence, although this remains a rarity in the youth court, where there are few contested trials and, despite the availability of State funding for legal representation from the Criminal Defence Service, few young offenders seek legal advice. The young defendant must, however, be accompanied by a parent or guardian if they are under 16.[22] The youth court panel is assisted in the sentencing function by a member of the youth offending team, who, having prepared a pre-sentence report, will be present in court to advise on the offender's rehabilitative needs and how far these can be met through services available locally.

Reforming the Youth Court: Issues and Developments

Despite nearly 100 years of operation, relatively little research has been conducted on the juvenile/youth court and it has been the subject of very little academic comment.[23] Nonetheless a number of critical issues have arisen in relation to the proceedings of the youth court, some of which have been the subject of government attempts at reform. In 1997, the white paper *No More Excuses* outlined some difficulties with the culture and operation of the youth court and proposed changes, the most significant of which was the introduction of referral orders, which will be discussed below. Whilst this new procedure eased some of the administrative burdens from the youth court, the court remained constitutionally and philosophically unchanged. Any inherent problems in the choice of this criminal tribunal as a forum for dealing with youth crime have never been seriously addressed.

Philosophical Issues

It was noted above that in the early days of the juvenile court, successive governments insisted that the tribunal should be, and remain, a criminal court. This inevitably restricts any development of a welfare orientation in the philosophy of the court. As a tribunal it relies upon the prosecution of young people for behaviour which is identified and labelled as a criminal offence, which inherently involves attributing blame or fault and assigning punishment. The youth court remains locked into this criminal philosophy, regardless of attempts, if any, to design more rehabilitative and constructive responses to crime aimed at tackling

---

[22] Section 56 Criminal Justice Act 1991. This *may* also be a requirement where the young person is aged 16 or 17. See further Ch 9.

[23] With the exception of a few academic research studies, all conducted over 20 years ago: A Morris and H Giller, 'The Juvenile Court: The Client's Perspective [1977] Crim LR 198; R Anderson, *Representation in the Juvenile Court* (London, Routledge, 1978); H Parker, M Casburn and D Turnbull, *Receiving Juvenile Justice: Adolescents and State Care and Control* (Oxford, Blackwell, 1981).

the causes of such behaviour. The adversarial nature of English criminal procedure adds to the blame culture of the court. The offender appears *against* the State, and the layout of the courtroom reinforces the imbalance of power between the Bench and the defendant as well as the contested nature of the proceedings. Furthermore, the outcome of such proceedings after an adjudication or admission of guilt will always take the form of a criminal conviction, a sentence and legal sanctions for breach of any order made.

At the same time, since 1933 the youth court has been required to have regard to the welfare of any child appearing before it, as a statutory obligation.[24] Further, individualised justice was a part of the welfare rationale for the original establishment of the court. There is, therefore, a conflict of ideologies which places the youth court in the ambiguous position as guardians of the welfare of the child before it as well as guardians of public safety and the public interest. Their social work role rests uneasily alongside their juridical role, a philosophical conundrum that exists not just in the court setting itself, but is also evident in their sentencing powers and the policy considerations underlying the legal principles they are required to implement. It is a theme that recurs throughout the chapters of this book and is discussed in greater detail elsewhere, but the youth court stands as a symbolic representation of the ideological conflict present throughout youth justice policy between justice and welfare models. John Pratt emphatically argues that the two ideologies 'simply cannot work coherently together'[25] because of their contrasting aims and methods. Rutherford noted that the failure of the 1969 Children and Young Persons Act to make lasting changes to the youth justice system of England and Wales was testimony to the disastrous mixture of the two approaches.[26]

The contrast in approaches becomes clearer with an examination of those jurisdictions where criminal proceedings have been dispensed with entirely. The Scottish Children's Hearings system and the Irish Youth Diversion Project are both jurisdictions in which criminal proceedings exist to deal with only the most serious or persistent offender, the exception rather than the rule. In these jurisdictions issues of proving the requirements of a criminal offence and attributing an appropriate level of blame are superseded by inquiries into the welfare needs of a young offender which prompted the behaviour which has caused concern—they are dealt with 'less for their deeds than for their needs'.[27] The behaviour itself is relevant only in as far as it is symptomatic of wider behavioural or social issues which are not considered to be within the remit of the criminal justice system and are better dealt with within the family or, in extreme cases, by social work author-

---

[24] Section 44 Children and Young Persons Act 1933.

[25] J Pratt, 'Welfare and Justice: Incompatible Philosophies' in F Gale *et al* (eds) *Juvenile Justice: Debating the Issues* (St Leonards, NSW, Allen & Unwin, 1993) p 39.

[26] Rutherford, 'A Statute Backfires' above n 8.

[27] M Hogan, 'Children's Courts: To Be or What to Be?' in F Gale *et al* (eds) above n 25 at p 144.

ities. In those jurisdictions not only is the philosophy and aim of the tribunal clearer, but the outcomes of the decision-making process are focused on a more constructive and informed attempt to prevent crime. Re-offending in these jurisdictions highlights further welfare needs of the offender rather than indicating threat to the innocent public which requires control.

Participation

The power imbalance evident from the adversarial nature of youth court proceedings does little to encourage meaningful communication between the defendant and the Bench, nor to encourage young people and their parents to participate in the decision-making process. The proceedings are legalistic, since formal rules of evidence and procedure must be followed, due process must be observed and this means, ideally, that the young person is represented by a lawyer.[28] There is a danger that an inarticulate teenager may neither understand the process, nor feel sufficiently engaged in it to express themselves. Incomprehensible discussions between professional adults in making important decisions on a young person's future may produce reactions of resigned apathy or resentment and defiance, neither being conducive to the defendant learning from the experience as sentencers might hope they would.[29] Of even greater concern is that a young person's reluctance or inability to speak during any trial in the youth court may be interpreted as an exercise of their 'right' to silence from which the youth court panel may now draw adverse inferences.[30] For the parents of the young offender, for whom the proceedings may be equally baffling, the lack of participatory opportunity may well prompt resentment at having to be there at all. Further, since greater emphasis is now placed by the court on the role of the parent in preventing re-offending, it is even more important that the parent is able to contribute to the discussion about the outcome of the case, which may well involve responsibilities for themselves as well as their child.

The problem of participation has been recognised by policy makers. Proposals for changes to the youth court in the 1997 white paper acknowledged that 'It is vital, when a young offender goes to the youth court, that the process involves the young person and his or her parents directly.'[31] More effective participation for both the defendant and their parent would enhance the reinforcement of their responsibilities and help them to face up to the consequences of the offending

---

[28] See further NACRO, *The Future of the Juvenile Court in England and Wales* (London, NACRO, 1986).

[29] Ido Weijers describes this as part of the 'moral dialogue' in the interaction between the court and the young person—'Requirements for Communication in the Courtroom: A Comparative Perspective on the Youth Court in England/Wales and the Netherlands' (2004) 4 *Youth Justice* 22 at pp 25–26.

[30] Crime and Disorder Act 1998 s35. Adverse inferences may now be drawn from the silence of any young person aged 14 or over.

[31] *No More Excuses* Cm 3809 (London, Home Office, 1997) at p 29.

behaviour, a key theme of the new policies at that time. The government proposed
further training to encourage magistrates to engage parties to the case more effectively; changes to the physical environment of the court, such as sitting around a
table; and the referral order, which would enable the defendant and his parent to
actively negotiate the outcome.

The issue of effective participation was subsequently addressed in the Youth
Court Demonstration Project, from which the Home Office produced a Good
Practice Guide. The focus of this guide is on *engagement* with the defendant,
though not necessarily for a kindly discussion of their welfare needs:

> The intention is not to treat offenders (or families and supporters) to a homily but to
> involve them, so that they are not passive observers; to promote a culture in which they
> expect to be put on the spot, confronted with their offending and required to take
> responsibility for it.[32]

Good practice in this context includes encouraging magistrates to introduce
themselves to the defendant and his parent; to speak directly and plainly to the
defendant at the appropriate level; avoiding legal and technical language, to discuss in a language appropriate for the defendant's maturity and understanding any
proposed sentence to ensure it focuses effectively on preventing further offending.
Such plain speaking with defendants was identified as a training need for many
youth court magistrates and the Judicial Studies Board has been asked to issue a
training package for them on oral and listening skills.[33] Despite the intentions of
the government, implicit in the above quote, the evaluation of the pilot project
suggested that magistrates who embraced the ideal of engagement appeared more
'human' and concerned about the welfare of the young people before them,
although some reported that the discussions were rather banal and some clerks
were concerned at magistrates asking inappropriate questions.[34] Magistrates felt
they were able to sentence more effectively having 'got to the bottom of the offending behaviour' and perceived a greater awareness in defendants as to why they
were in court and the gravity of the situation. The discussions held between magistrates, defendants and their parents did not appear to unduly extend the times of
hearings.

Openness and Shaming

The closed environment of the youth court and the restrictions on press reporting
of cases in any way which may identify a young offender, their victim or their
family are presumed to be part of the welfare ideology of the court and exist for the

[32] Home Office, *The Youth Court 2001* above n 20 at p 7.
[33] To be fair, such skills may not come so naturally to the judiciary in an adversarial system as they
do to judges in an inquisitorial system who are more used to interacting more actively with defendants—see Weijers above n 29 at pp 27–30.
[34] Allen *et al*, *Evaluation of the Youth Court Demonstration Project* above n 19 at p 16.

protection of the defendant and to enhance their potential rehabilitation. This has, however, been a subject of concern for the government:

> There must . . . be more openness in youth court proceedings . . . Justice is best served in an open court where the criminal process can be scrutinised and the offender cannot hide behind a cloak of anonymity.[35]

This may be mistaken for a due process concern on behalf of the defendant—Article 6 of the European Convention on Human Rights[36] requires that court hearings be open to such scrutiny to protect the defendant from arbitrary or partial decision making.[37] The Good Practice Guide reveals, though, that the concern lies more with the public's and the victim's confidence in the youth court process, to which they do not have access. The 1998 British Crime Survey revealed that the public had the least confidence in the youth court system than in any other part of the criminal justice system and that this could be connected to the fact that they also knew least about it.[38] Victims are only usually permitted to attend court if they give evidence and may not observe proceedings. The Home Office favours that both issues be resolved by allowing all victims to attend proceedings if they wish to do so, that reporting restrictions be lifted and that the general public, in some circumstances, be allowed to observe (though they do not specify what those circumstances may be).[39]

Reporting restrictions, introduced in section 49 Children and Young Persons Act 1933, could already be lifted in exceptional circumstances, where the court considered it to be in the public interest to do so. In 1998 the government wished to encourage greater use of this exception:

> The government believes that the youth court should make *full use* of its discretion to lift reporting restrictions in the public interest following conviction. This is particularly important where the offence is a serious one; where the offending is persistent or where it has affected a number of people or the local community; and at the upper age range of the youth court.[40]

A joint Home Office and Lord Chancellor's Department Circular gave guidance to the youth court to this effect in 1998 although the Queen's Bench Divisional Court maintain that 'great caution' should be exercised in this discretion and reminded youth courts of their duty to balance their welfare responsibilities towards the child (particularly under Article 8 of the ECHR) with their duty to the public.[41]

---

[35] *No More Excuses* white paper Cm 3809 above n 31 at p 30.

[36] 'Brought home' to England and Wales in the Human Rights Act 1998.

[37] Although this contrasts with Article 40 of the UN Convention on the Rights of the Child—see further J Fortin, *Children's Rights and the Developing Law* (London, Butterworths, 2003) p 563.

[38] J Mattinson and C Mirlees-Black, *Attitudes to Crime and Criminal Justice: Findings from the 1998 British Crime Survey* HORS 200 (London, Home Office, 2000).

[39] *The Youth Court 2001* above n 20 at p 11.

[40] *No More Excuses* white paper Cm 3809 above n 31 at p 30.

[41] *R v Teesdale and Wear Valley Justices ex p McKerry* (2000) 164 JP 355 (Lord Bingham CJ).

Here again we see the tension inherent in the two responsibilities of the youth court; their welfare and justice roles. The Home Office have clearly suggested that part of the 'new culture' of the youth court should involve a shaming ritual, in which the retributive process of punishment is enhanced by the naming of the offender, encouraging public condemnation of their behaviour. Increasing public awareness of the youth court procedure in this way is likely to increase public fear of youth crime beyond its already irrational extent.[42] It also seriously undermines the welfare requirement of a closed court without any reintegrative benefit for the offender.[43]

The Referral Order and the Youth Offender Panel

The package of reforms undertaken by the new Labour government in the late 1990s included a new procedure aimed at changing the way in which a majority of young offenders are sentenced by the youth court. Part of the rationale behind this new procedure was to amend acknowledged difficulties with the youth court as detailed above, including the problems of lack of participation by the young offender and their parents, a lack of openness in court proceedings and ineffective and unfocused sentencing. Chapter 9 of the Home Office white paper *No More Excuses* set out proposals aimed at reforming the culture as well as the practice of the youth court:

> The purpose of the youth court must change from simply deciding guilt or innocence and then issuing a sentence. In most cases, an offence should trigger a wider enquiry into the circumstances and nature of the offending behaviour, leading to action to change that behaviour. This requires in turn a fundamental change of approach within the youth court system.[44]

However, whilst the youth court was to facilitate this 'wider enquiry' into the troublesome behaviour and design a response to tackle such behaviour, the government were equally concerned that this should not unduly delay proceedings in the court. Delays and backlogs in the criminal system had been criticised in a further consultation paper published in 1997[45] and we were promised not just a fundamental change of approach but 'fast track' justice and greater efficiency in the management of cases in the youth court, at the same time.

---

[42] See further M Hough and J Roberts, *Youth Crime and Youth Justice: Public Opinion in England and Wales* (Bristol, Policy Press, 2004) ch 2.

[43] This is disintegrative rather than reintegrative shaming—see further J Braithwaite, *Crime, Shame and Reintegration* (Cambridge, Cambridge University Press, 1989).

[44] Home Office, *No More Excuses* above n 31 at p 29.

[45] Home Office, *Tackling Delays in the Youth Justice System: A Consultation Paper* (London, Home Office, 1997).

This was to be achieved through the development of the referral order procedure. The objectives of this new procedure were fivefold and aimed to provide:

- Speedier decisions on guilt and innocence, much closer to the date of the offence
  and with less tolerance of adjournments;
- A system which is more open, and which commands the confidence of victims
  and the public;
- Processes which engage young offenders and their parents and focus on the
  nature of their offending behaviour and how to change it;
- A stronger emphasis on using sentencing to prevent future offending; and
- More efficient arrangements for the scheduling and management of cases.[46]

Further, the white paper cited three themes of the new culture of the youth court,
namely restoration, reintegration and responsibility. In addition to tackling and
being tough on the causes of crime, preventing offending and encouraging
offenders to take responsibility for their crimes (as already discussed in the
previous consultation paper) the new procedure was to embrace principles of
restorative justice, which, according to the government's interpretation involved:
'young offenders paying their debt to society, putting their crime behind them and
rejoining the law abiding community'.[47] This interpretation of restorative justice
and the relation between the practice of referral orders and theories of restoration
will be explored further in Chapter 8. However, to summarise, the reforms proposed sought to address problems of delay, participation, ineffectiveness and
inefficiency in the youth court as well as to involve the victim and the public to a
greater extent in proceedings to improve levels of confidence in the system.

The referral order was introduced in Part I of the Youth Justice and Criminal
Evidence Act 1999, though is now governed by sections 16 to 32 of the Powers of
the Criminal Courts (Sentencing) Act 2000 (PCC(S)A). Where a young offender
appears before the youth court for the first time, pleads guilty to their first offence
and that offence is neither so serious that it warrants a custodial penalty nor so
non-serious that it warrants an absolute discharge, the youth court are obliged[48]
to sentence the offender to a referral order lasting between 3 and 12 months. The
order effectively *refers* the young offender to a youth offending panel established
by the local youth offending team (YOT). The panel, consisting of a YOT member
plus two volunteer members from the local community, must meet with the
offender and their parent or other appropriate adult at least three times during the
course of the order. At the first meeting, to which the panel may additionally invite

---

[46] Home Office, *No More Excuses* above n 31 at p 29.

[47] *Ibid* at p 32.

[48] The procedure is compulsory where these criteria are met and the youth court has little discretion. Where the offender is charged with more than one offence on their first appearance in the
youth court and pleads guilty to at least one of them, the referral order may be given but the court has
discretion in such a case (s 17 PCC(S)A).

the victim and another adult 'capable of having a good influence on the offender,[49] the young offender and the panel must negotiate a contract, the principal aim of which is to prevent re-offending by the offender, and the terms of which form the detail of the sentence that the young offender will serve as a response to their offending behaviour. Once agreed the 'contract' is written, signed by the offender and the panel and copies are 'exchanged' between the two parties. There is no requirement that the 'contract' contain any particular term, save that the terms must include action to address the offending behaviour and prevent its reoccurrence, but suggested terms are set out in section 24 PCC(S)A, and broadly reflect the non-custodial sentencing options available to the youth court.[50] The panel must then meet with the offender and their parent or appropriate adult a second time during the course of the order, to assess the offender's progress with complying with the terms and a final time at the end of the order to assess whether the terms have been fully carried out. Failure to comply with the order or further re-offending during the course of the order can result in the offender being referred back to the youth court for re-sentencing. This may also result after the first meeting if the offender fails to agree the terms of a contract with the panel.

There is no doubt that the new procedure fulfils the expectation that it will speed up the justice process, at least as far as the youth court is concerned. The referral order provides the youth court with a quick and convenient way to bring cases where guilt is uncontested to a conclusion by simply referring the offender elsewhere. At the point of sentencing the case is concluded for the youth court unless and until there is any breach of the order or other problem which results in the young offender reappearing. In this way the youth court is better able to reach its performance targets in relation to shortening the time between arrest and sentence.[51] It is, however, a meaningless saving in other terms since the referral order procedure bears its own costs in terms of recruiting and training volunteer members of the panel, utilising the resources of the YOT, arranging and finding premises for meetings, supervising offenders under the contracts and providing the rehabilitation and mediation services required under the terms of the contract. The referral order process is neither fast nor inexpensive for the local authority, which bears these costs. However, since the resource implications are not borne by the youth court the procedure provides at least the image of saving court time.

There is also little doubt that the referral order encourages (or expects) greater participation on the part of the offender and the parent involved in the process. The offender cannot be a passive observer during these meetings and is required

---

[49] Section 22 PCCC(S)A.

[50] They include measures such as a curfew, unpaid work in the community, mediation, reparation, supervision in the community and specified activities to address offending behaviour.

[51] Home Office guidance on the principal aim of the youth justice system suggests this should be halved from 140 to 70 days—see Home Office, *Youth Justice: The Statutory Principal Aim of Preventing Offending by Children and Young People* (London, Home Office, 1998).

to actively discuss the terms of their sentence in the course of negotiating the contract. Such negotiations should also involve the parent and possibly the victim as well, although neither of these participants are parties to the contract. There is some logic behind this new transactional approach whereby the offender agrees to the terms of their sentence, since securing the agreement of the offender in the first place is likely to prevent breach of the contract as well as ensuring a bespoke and therefore more constructive response to the offender's situation and behaviour. However, Wonnacott queries the propriety of negotiated justice for young offenders, suggesting that the contractual symbolism of the procedure masks a traditionally punitive approach which has merely been disguised in more benign, consensual terms.[52] The young offender is indeed in such a weak bargaining position, having little to bargain with and a great deal to lose, that in Wonnacott's view this contractual process would be considered voidable for duress, had it any force in civil law. Young offenders have little choice but to agree to the terms, facing a worse fate in the youth court if they fail to do so.[53] Moreover, the procedure has taken the offender from passive observer and a submissive role in the youth court to an overly active participation in the panel meetings, a leap from one extreme position to another. As has been observed: 'it is quite remarkable that the Government considers children under 18 able to negotiate such a contract without any professional assistance whatsoever, particularly given the reluctance to allow children under 18 to make binding contracts in civil law.'[54] Negotiated justice and the mediated sentence on offer as part of the referral order process requires a degree of articulacy, confidence and self-awareness on the part of offenders, aged as young as 10, which past experience in the youth court has already demonstrated they often do not possess. Whilst the more informal nature of the panel meetings may put an offender at greater ease, they still face a panel of adults, a potentially angry victim, a shamed parent and an official response to their offending behaviour, which falls outside the requirements of proportionality that govern sentences of the youth court. With appropriate training magistrates in the youth court may engage the offender in a discussion of the requirements of a particular sentence, whilst ensuring that due process principles are upheld and the sentence duly reflects the gravity of the offence.[55]

[52] C Wonnacott, 'The Counterfeit Contract: Reform, Pretence and Muddled Principles in the New Referral Order' (1999) 11 *Child and Family Law Quarterly* 271.

[53] Note, however, that upon successful completion of the contract, the referral order is discharged and the offender's record therefore wiped clean. In this way the state offers some consideration in return for compliance in the tradition of a contractual bargain—s 27 PCC(S)A.

[54] J Fionda, 'Youth and Justice' in J Fionda (ed) *Legal Concepts of Childhood* (Oxford, Hart Publishing, 2001) p 93.

[55] Indeed, the evaluation of the piloted referral order projects revealed that over use of the procedure for inappropriately minor offences and disproportionality in the levels of intervention imposed by the contracts were a significant concern—see *Referral Orders: Research into the Issues Raised in the 'Introduction of the Referral Order in the Youth Justice System'* Report produced by Cap Gemini Ernst & Young (London, Youth Justice Board, 2003).

The Crown Court

When the juvenile court was established in 1908, certain children were explicitly excluded from its jurisdiction. Any child charged jointly with an adult was to be tried and sentenced in the adult court.[56] Children charged with murder, as well as those charged with attempted murder, manslaughter and wounding with intent (GBH) were to be tried and sentenced in the adult courts, since the Juvenile Court was not empowered to award sufficient (or any) periods of detention to adequately punish such offences. Therefore, these more serious offenders were excluded from the separate jurisdiction, not necessarily because they did not require the welfare provision of the Juvenile Court, but rather in order to properly restrict the custodial sentencing powers of the new court. The legal position regarding these more serious offenders was clarified in section 53 Children and Young Persons Act 1933. Section 53(1) provided that all children over the minimum age of criminal responsibility, who were charged with murder would automatically be transferred to the Crown Court for trial and sentencing and, having abolished the death penalty for young offenders, the mandatory penalty for murder became detention during Her Majesty's Pleasure. Section 53(2) provided a discretion for the juvenile court to transfer to the Crown Court children, aged over 14, charged with attempted murder, manslaughter and GBH where the magistrates did not feel that their custodial sentencing powers were sufficient to adequately deal with the case. This gave them the option of dealing with such cases themselves where possible and prohibited the use of the adult courts for those aged under 14 unless they were charged jointly with an adult. Conviction of a child in the Crown Court entitled the court to impose a custodial sentence up to the maximum term possible for the offence.

In this way, the separate Juvenile Court was preserved for what was envisaged to be the vast majority of young offenders. Those few exceptional offenders who committed these 'grave' offences against the person were sentenced to protective custody. This was done to protect the public rather more than for punitive reasons and the welfare approach of the juvenile court had to give way to this more important consideration where young people committed acts of serious violence. Both the 1908 and 1933 Acts were greatly concerned with the welfare of all children (whether offenders or not) and the provision of an exception to the use of separate courts must be read in the light of the spirit of those legislative enactments.

By the early 1960s, however, enthusiasm for the welfare ideal was strained, not least as a reaction to social concerns at the time that teenagers, in particular, were developing a social identity as a group and the emerging youth culture was seen as

---

[56] Children Act 1908 s 111(4)

threatening by many.[57] Section 2 of the Criminal Justice Act 1961 made fundamental changes to the discretionary procedures through which children could be tried in the Crown Court. The short list of serious offences against the person, to which this discretion applied, was replaced with a generic group of offences punishable in the case of an adult with 14 years' or more imprisonment. The group, of course, included the previously listed offences, since they all carried maximum sentences of life imprisonment in the case of an adult. However, the new definition brought other offences against the person, including sexual offences such as rape and sexual intercourse with a girl under 13, within the procedure. After this enactment, changes in the criminal law retrospectively brought other *property* offences within the procedure as well, including robbery and aggravated burglary (after the Theft Act 1968); serious forms of criminal damage (after the Criminal Damage Act 1971); and latterly domestic burglary (for which the maximum penalty was increased under the Criminal Justice Act 1991).

These changes have significantly altered the rationale behind the discretion to transfer young offenders to adult courts. Whereas this procedure could previously be justified for the protection of the public, this became rather less convincing after the inclusion of property offences (albeit serious ones). There was no discussion of this provision during the Parliamentary debates on the Bill, so we are unable to ascertain what the government's rationale for the changes might have been. It appears, however, to suggest that, even where the public did not need protection from serious young offenders, they may well wish to see them punished more severely than the juvenile court's powers allowed. The discretion to transfer a young person out of the juvenile court has always carried the potential to be used where magistrates feel that the young person's behaviour indicates a transcendence out of traditional childhood and a moral maturity that needs the firmer hand of the adult court. The extension of the discretion in 1961 made this more possible. An even clearer indication of this intention can be seen in the further amendments made in 1994. The Criminal Justice and Public Order Act of that year not only reduced the age at which this procedure begins to apply (down to 10) but also extended the discretion to offences not covered by the 14-year rule to include indecent assault on a woman and causing death by dangerous driving. These amendments can be read alongside a number of other changes to the youth justice system all aimed at an increasingly punitive approach, particularly towards the younger part of the youth justice age range. This Act followed in the wake of the Bulger murder and enacted a number of policies under the 'Back to Basics' political campaign of the, by then, relatively unpopular Conservative government. These amendments were clearly meant to be punitive and the intention was to encourage magistrates to pass greater numbers of young offenders to the adult courts for lengthy sentences of imprisonment.

---

[57] See further J Muncie, *Youth and Crime* 2nd edn (London, Sage, 2002) ch 5.

The current procedure for transferring a defendant to the Crown Court is contained in sections 90 and 91 of the (PCC(S)A) 2000. This has consolidated the procedure from the previous enactments without change, so the current position is that children aged between 10 and 17 inclusive may be transferred where they are charged with an offence carrying a maximum penalty of 14 years or more in the case of an adult, or if they are charged with one of the exceptions to this rule (indecent assault on a man or a woman or causing death by dangerous driving whether or not under the influence of drink or drugs). Children charged with murder continue to be automatically transferred under section 90. Similarly children jointly charged with an adult will also be tried in the adult courts.

It is not surprising, given that the ambit of the youth court's discretion to transfer a child to the adult courts has widened, that the extent to which the discretion is used has also increased. Figures 6.1 and 6.2 illustrate how, in recent years, this increase has gathered pace significantly.

In 1993 the rate of children sent to the Crown Court trebled. This may largely be explained through the change in the youth court's jurisdiction in 1991 to include 17-year-olds for the first time. This change can into effect in October 1992 and would therefore cause this stark escalatory trend. Seventeen-year-olds are a highly criminogenic group and their offences are likely to be more serious than younger members of the youth justice age range. However, throughout the 1990s and particularly after 1993 the escalatory trend continued at a rapid pace. It is less easy to account for this, except that it coincided with an era in youth justice policy marked by its return to the hard-line, illiberal justice approach of the government

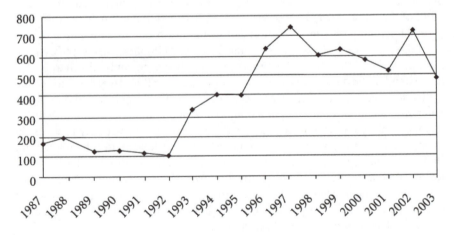

Fig 6.1 *Juveniles sentenced in the Crown Court 1987–2003*
Source: Home Office

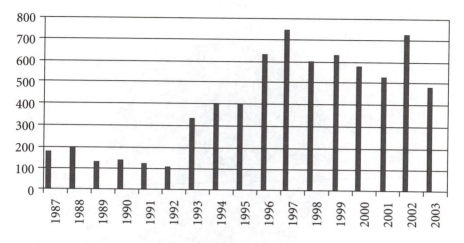

Fig 6.2 *Juveniles sentenced in the Crown Court by 1987–2003*
Source: Home Office

at that time. The extent to which this discretion is used depends on a number of factors: the youth court panel's own ideology and sentencing practice, which determines how they view more serious offenders and the extent to which they are prepared to hold on to them in the youth court; the charging practice of the CPS and the extent to which they use their discretion to use flexible criminal law definitions to charge young offenders with more serious offences; and the rate at which young offenders are committing such serious offences.

We saw in Chapter 4 that there has been an overall decline in youth crime in the last few years. However the rate at which young people are committing serious offences against the person has increased slightly. This may account for a small rise in the use of this discretion, but could not account for the steep escalatory trend that we have witnessed. It is less easy to make any scientific analysis of the other two determining factors in this phenomenon. However, we do know that guidance issued to Crown Prosecutors since 1994 has become less tolerant of youth and more focused on the seriousness of the offence in determining both whether to prosecute and how to use their charging discretion where applicable. Figure 6.3 provides an indication of the offences with which young offenders were charged under section 91 PCC(S)A 2000 in 2003.

A majority of them had committed violent offences against the person and robbery, both criminal law charges where a greater degree of discretion exists for the prosecutor in choosing a charge. For example, the difference between a theft (which, unless charged jointly with an adult would not render the young offender liable to transfer to the Crown Court) and a robbery (which would) may, in some circumstances depend on the view of the degree of force used or threatened in the

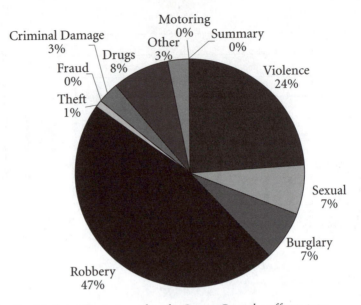

Fɪɢ 6.3 *Juveniles sentenced in the Crown Court by offence type*
Source: Home Office

course of committing the theft. Similarly the Offences Against the Person Act 1861 provides the prosecutor with a discretion, depending on a view of the degree of injury caused to the victim and the defendant's state of mind, to choose from a range of offences which may include causing grievous bodily harm with intent (section 18) or attempted murder (to which section 91 does apply) or causing grievous bodily harm maliciously (section 20) to which it does not. The Annual Reports of the CPS do not provide detailed statistical information on their charging practice. However, their *Code* stipulates that they do seek to find the most appropriate charge to the seriousness of the circumstances of the case, bearing in mind the sentencing powers of the court likely to deal with it.[58] Indeed it is not in their interests to overcharge a defendant where there is a serious risk of failing to secure a conviction before a jury in the Crown Court.

This may lead us to surmise that the youth court has become more ready to use the discretion contained in section 91 than was the case in previous decades. The figures certainly suggest that the discretion is no longer being used for the few highly exceptional cases of very serious offending by young people that it was originally intended for. It is not impossible for the youth court to use the discretion in itself for punitive reasons. The increased willingness of the youth court to use custodial sentences themselves[59] may suggest that they are equally more

[58] *Code for Crown Prosecutors* 5th edn (London, CPS, 2004) para 7.
[59] See Ch 7.

willing to consider that an extended custodial sentence is required for the most serious offences coming before them. Court of Appeal guidance on the use of section 53(2) has certainly changed in emphasis over the last two decades. In 1986 youth court magistrates were discouraged from over-using the procedure and warned to exercise caution. Lord Lane CJ in *R v Fairhurst* suggested that the procedure should only be used where the offence committed was one of 'exceptional gravity' such as armed robbery, serious violence or attempted murder or manslaughter. Further, he advised magistrates to avoid using the procedure simply because of the constraints of their own restricted custodial sentencing powers and that it was inappropriate to send a young offender to the Crown Court simply because 12 months' detention (the maximum sentence available in the juvenile court at the time) was 'a little on the low side'.[60] A sentence of at least double the youth court's powers (that is, 2 years) should be required before the power is used. This guidance needed some updating after the changes made to section 53(2) in the 1994 legislation. Swinton LJ in *R v Wainfur* maintained a cautious tone in the guidance, but with less emphasis on mathematical formulations and struck a slightly more permissive note. The offence must merit a 'substantially greater' sentence than the youth court could offer, but in that case a sentence of 3 years had been rightly imposed under section 53(2).[61] By 1998 Lord Bingham felt that the youth court should feel less constrained and favoured unfettered use of their discretion over the strict formula set out in *Fairhurst*. That formula, he argued, created a

> sentencing no-man's-land in the cases of offenders for whom youth custody was available, between the maximum term of such custody (then 12 months) and a term of 24 months under s. 53($\frac{2}{}$) . . . The object of the Court in laying down this rule in Fairhurst was plainly to discourage sentencers from exceeding the limit of 12 months then applicable to youth custody, so as to give effect to the Parliamentary intention that young offenders should not be confined for lengthy periods unless such confinement was necessary.[62]

We see in Lord Bingham's judgment a move away from such a decarcerative philosophy and a statement that the rule in *Fairhurst* should not be followed since 'it has its own dangers.'[63] Rather than feel obliged to up-tariff or down-tariff offenders within that sentencing no-man's-land, Lord Bingham now suggested that:

> The court should not exceed the 24 month limit for detention in a young offender institution without much careful thought; but if it concludes that a longer sentence, *even if not a much longer sentence*, is called for, then the court should impose whatever it considers the appropriate period of detention under s. 53(2). (emphasis added).[64]

[60] *R v Fairhurst* (1986) 8 Cr App R (S) 346 (Lord Lane CJ) at 350.
[61] *R v Wainfur* [1997] 1 Cr App R (S) 43.
[62] *R v Mills* [1998] 2 Cr App R (S) 128 at 132.
[63] *Ibid.*
[64] *Ibid.*

This more 'licentious' guidance has evidently had effect in enabling the youth court to use section 91 (as it is now) with a greater sense of security and reflects the wider tone of penal policy in this context which has moved from a strongly decarcerative policy during the 1980s[65] to a more expansionist policy in which it is acknowledged in government circles that 'prison works'.[66]

The increased use of Crown Court trial for young offenders has renewed the impetus for those pressure groups that consider that the adult status accorded to such defendants is inappropriate and harmful. In the 1980s both NACRO and the Association for Juvenile Justice expressed serious concern at the increased use of the procedure, the potential for racial discrimination in the discretion of the juvenile court and at the trial conditions that children were subjected to in the Crown Court.[67] Indeed in 1988 NACRO reported that trial in the Crown Court, which is open to the public and makes no allowances for the youth of the offender before it, was 'prolonged and stressful' and one of their researchers revealed that:

> Few of the juveniles I met appeared to have any clear understanding of the court process which they recalled as being frightening and distressing. One interviewee, 12 years old at the time of the hearing, was subjected to a public Crown Court trial lasting seven days. Another aged 14 recalled being scared and having to sit on a special stool because he could not see over the dock.[68]

This scene was mirrored in the trial of Jon Venables and Robert Thompson in Preston Crown Court in 1994 for the murder of James Bulger. Much was made of their diminutive size in an adult courtroom and their childish behaviour, boredom and distress during the proceedings. The mental image of a small child in the overwhelmingly large and austere surroundings of the Crown Court has an *Alice in Wonderland* surrealism and epitomises the antithetical reality behind the section 91 procedure. Children who commit very serious crimes lose the privilege of childhood and are assigned adult status, even though their physical (and possibly mental) capacity simply does not assimilate with that status. They face a double jeopardy in this regard since they have not only offended against the law and society, but against their own social identity. This rests uneasily with international laws on children's rights which seek to protect a child's youthfulness in the criminal process in order to protect their welfare needs. The United Nations Committee on the Rights of the Child firmly oppose adult trials for children and were highly critical of this procedure which they considered to be unjustifiable.[69]

---

[65] The government stated in the 1990 white paper that 'prison is an expensive way of making bad people worse'—*Crime, Justice and Protecting the Public* (London, HMSO, 1990) p 6.

[66] Michael Howard repeated this claim throughout his tenure as Home Secretary.

[67] See *Grave Crimes . . . Grave Doubts* (London, NACRO, 1988); F Gosling 'Against the Tide: The Rise of Orders under Section 53 CYPA 1933' (1988) *AJJUST* 18.

[68] *Grave Crimes . . . Grave Doubts* previous n at p 15.

[69] *Concluding Observations of the Committee on the Rights of the Child: United Kingdom of Great Britain and Northern Ireland* CRC/C/15/Add 188 (Geneva, Centre for Human Rights, 2002) paras 60–62.

The European Court of Human Rights expressed similar concerns in adjudicating on Venables and Thompson's claim that they had not received a fair trial, but were less emphatic in declaring the procedure unlawful. They acknowledged that the two defendants had not had a fair trial, but only in relation to one of their many claims, on the narrow ground that the behaviour of the public during the proceedings was sufficiently rowdy and hostile that the defendants had not had sufficient opportunity to consult with their lawyers.[70]

The outcome of this case does not render the section 91 procedure (or section 90 in their case) unlawful. However, the Home Secretary at the time, Jack Straw, was moved to acknowledge that the 'Bulger' trial had revealed serious problems with the trial of children in the Crown Court and requested that the Lord Chief Justice make a Practice Statement offering guidance to the Crown Court on appropriate measures to be taken to alleviate the trauma and distress suffered by young defendants in that environment and to avoid further Article 6 claims. The Lord Chief Justice duly obliged in 2000:

> The trial process should not expose the young defendant to avoidable intimidation, humiliation or distress. All possible steps should be taken to assist the young defendant to understand and participate in the proceedings. The ordinary trial process should so far as necessary be adapted to meet those ends. Regard should be had to the welfare of the young defendant as required by section 44 of the Children and Young Persons Act 1933.[71]

This statement was followed by suggestions for practical measures that could be taken to adapt the trial process to the needs of children such as the removal of wigs and gowns, frequent breaks to aid the concentration of children, a pre-trial visit for the young defendant to acquaint them with the layout of the court, allowing the young person to sit with his family and using a room without a raised bench if possible. Whilst welcome as an acknowledgement of a child's reduced capacity to withstand an adult trial, these measures merely dress the window of the more significant problem. Not only do they fail to equate with the special measures offered to children who appear as witnesses (though not defendants) under the Youth Justice and Criminal Evidence Act 1999, Part II, but they fail to address the underlying ideological concerns of according children adult status. To remind the Crown Court that they must observe the section 44 welfare principle is a rather incongruous and belated piece of advice. To effectively deny the child a child's status and then to ask the court to be wary of the child's youthfulness makes little sense. It is disappointing that the European Court did not make a more profound statement regarding the ideological danger of the practice of sections 90 and 91.

---

[70] *V v UK; T v UK* (2000) 30 ECHR 121.
[71] Practice Direction, *Trial of Children and Young Persons in the Crown Court* [2000] 1 Cr App R 483.

7

Sentencing

Guiding Sentencers

Sentencing practice had been largely a matter for discretion for juvenile court magistrates until 1991. Aside from setting out the various sentencing options, the government did not greatly intervene in sentencing practice nor prescribe precise guidelines on how these options were to be used. In 1991, however, the government proposed to set out, for the first time, a more rigid sentencing framework to guide magistrates, and to ensure that sentencing policy reflected the goals and values of the government's general criminal justice policy. This process had started, in relation to youth justice in 1982, when the Criminal Justice Act (CJA) of that year had set out restrictive criteria for the use of custodial sentences.[1] In 1988, a further Criminal Justice Act tightened these criteria further to render custody a last resort for only the most serious and dangerous of young offenders.[2] The 1991 Criminal Justice Act developed this model, both for a more prescriptive approach to guiding magistrates and judges, and for seeking to minimise the use made of custody, for both adults and young offenders. The framework they designed borrowed heavily from the wording of the 1988 Act.

The 1991 Act was a product of three years of discussion and drafting of statutory principles, beginning in 1988 with the consultation paper *Punishment, Custody and the Community*.[3] In this paper Douglas Hurd, the Home Secretary of the time, set out his vision for a bifurcated approach to sentencing in which the use of custody was to be minimised in favour of greater use of community penalties. Each type of penalty was to be used in relation to one of two 'tracks' to this sentencing policy. Track A provided for custodial sentences to be available to sentencers where they could justify their use for the most serious or dangerous offenders. To this end, Hurd had ring-fenced £1.5 billion for a large-scale prison

---

[1] Although at this stage the government had been reluctant to do this and the custody criteria were added as amendments during the committee stage of the Bill—see further A Rutherford, *Growing Out of Crime: The New Era* (Winchester, Waterside Press, 2002) pp 17–18. The criteria were set out in CJA 1982 s 1(4).

[2] CJA 1988 s 1(4).

[3] Home Office, *Punishment, Custody and the Community* Cm 424 (London, Home Office, 1988).

building programme. However, realising that building prisons had limited value as a strategy to avoid the severe problem of over-crowding that the government were struggling with at the time, Track A was to be minimally used. Where custody was not seen as essential for retributive and incapacitative purposes, Track B was to be employed in which non-custodial penalties were available and re-designed to be more attractive to sentencers.[4]

The rationale behind this bifurcated approach was two-fold. There is no doubt that managerial concerns about the escalating prison population at the time, and the cost of maintaining a prison estate of increasing size, was a key incentive in seeking to find less costly alternatives. Not only is it widely believed that punishing an offender in the community is less costly than keeping them in prison,[5] but the bill for implementing community penalties, especially in the youth justice arena, falls largely on local government and social work or probation agencies funded at the local level. However, the government at the time was rather surprisingly liberal in its approach to criminal justice policy, despite having used the traditional 'tough-talking' approach to crime as well as other social and economic issues in their election manifestos throughout the 1980s. However, the 1988 consultation paper adopted a decarcerative tone, especially in relation to young offenders, which reflected the developments in practice at that time:

> Punishment in the community would be particularly suitable for young men and women, who are likely to grow out of crime . . . Punishment in the community, with compensation, community service and help to sort out the underlying problems, could well be suitable for these offenders.[6]

Margaret Thatcher was, indeed, appearing 'soft on crime'.[7] That said, the title of the consultation paper, and a consistent theme within it, was *punishment* in the community and a strengthening of community penalties to reflect some retributive element.

After due discussion, a white paper was published in 1990 which set out more formal proposals for a 'coherent framework for the use of financial, community and custodial punishments'.[8] The framework aimed to provide a clear set of objectives to sentencers with a more focused rationale. A lack of guidance on the priorities and weighting of the four traditional theoretical justifications for punishment (rehabilitation, deterrence, retribution and incapacitation) had resulted in what Ashworth described as a 'cafeteria' approach to sentencing[9] in which magistrates

---

[4] The new, 'strengthened', community penalty will be discussed further below.

[5] Although, for an alternative view see J Fionda, 'New Managerialism, Credibility and the Sanitisation of Criminal Justice' in P Green and A Rutherford *Criminal Policy in Transition* (Oxford, Hart Publishing, 2000) pp 120–23.

[6] Home Office, *Punishment, Custody and the Community* above n 3 at pp 15–16.

[7] See R Smith, *Youth Justice: Ideas, Policy, Practice* (Cullompton, Willan, 2003) ch1.

[8] Home Office, *Crime, Justice and Protecting the Public* Cm 965 (London, HMSO, 1990) para 1.15.

[9] A Ashworth, *Sentencing and Criminal Justice* 3rd edn (London, Butterworths, 2000) p 84.

and judges could select a justification from this menu and issue a sentence accordingly. This produced wide inconsistencies because a retributive sentence may differ considerably from a deterrent or rehabilitative one. The proposals put forward in 1990 aimed to move from an 'à la carte' cafeteria to a 'prix fixe' system:

> The aim of the Government's proposals is better justice through a more consistent approach to sentencing, so that convicted criminals get their 'just desserts' [sic!]'[10]

Of the four principles on offer, retribution was clearly the priority—just deserts requiring a proportionate punishment, measured by the seriousness of the offence, providing a response to crime which democratically balanced the expression of collective condemnation for the offence with the avoidance of unduly harsh or barbaric treatment. The government further aimed to reduce crime, through the rehabilitative Track B, as well as to protect the public from more serious offenders through the incapacitative Track A. Deterrence was emphatically rejected as a purpose for punishment:

> Deterrence is a principle with much immediate appeal. Most law abiding citizens understand the reasons why some behaviour is made a criminal offence, and would be deterred by the shame of a criminal conviction or the possibility of a severe penalty. There are doubtless some criminals who carefully calculate the possible gains and risks. But much crime is committed on impulse, given the opportunity presented by an open window or unlocked door, and it is committed by offenders who live from moment to moment; their crimes are as impulsive as the rest of their feckless, sad or pathetic lives. It is unrealistic to construct sentencing arrangements on the assumption that most offenders will weigh up the possibilities in advance and base their conduct on rational calculation. Often they do not.[11]

Here the government listened to criminological data[12] and not populism.

We thus see in the 1991 Criminal Justice Act a framework for sentencing in which proportionality is the leading determinant for sentencing. Sections 1 and 2 directed sentencers to calculate the seriousness of the offence before them[13] and assess a penalty that was commensurate with that level of seriousness. A departure was permitted from that basic principle where the offence was sexual or violent, such offences denoting a degree of dangerousness in the offender, which could prompt a greater than proportionate, incapacitative custodial sentence. This did not go down well with practitioners in the criminal justice field, for a number of widely diverging reasons. The judiciary regarded the Act as too liberal and restrictive of their power

---

[10] Home Office, previous n at para 1.6. The term 'just deserts' is misspelled throughout the white paper, prompting many to refer to it as the pudding theory of justice.

[11] *Ibid* para 2.8.

[12] Ashworth, *Sentencing and Criminal Justice* above n 9 at pp 64–68.

[13] Originally the Act forbade them from even considering previous convictions. This part of the Act was amended by the CJA 1993, after considerable criticism from both the judiciary and the media, who argued that persistence in offending needed to be reflected in the punishment process.

to use custodial sentences.[14] At the same time those in the probation field argued that the Act was punitive in its approach, had inherently damaged the rehabilitative potential of community sentences and allowed too great a discretion on the part of sentencers to use Track A.[15] The contradictory nature of this critique perhaps reflects the dual-purpose or bifurcatory strategy behind the Act.

The 1991 Act was implemented in October 1992. Almost immediately, policy makers[16] and practitioners[17] back tracked from any liberal tone that the Act may have had. A change of government in 1993 and the insecurity of that government in the mid-1990s prompted a more punitive strategy for criminal policy which continued (and arguably stepped up a gear) through to the end of the decade, well after New Labour were elected in 1997.[18] In 2003 New Labour placed their own stamp on the sentencing framework though the far-reaching Criminal Justice Act 2003. The Act was a product of a number of policy documents published between 2000 and 2002. These included the white paper *Criminal Justice: The Way Ahead* in 2001[19] which emphasised the renewed belief in the value of custodial sentences, pledged £689 million for prison building schemes and sought to deal with the increasing crime rates and fear of crime that had been revealed in the 1998 British Crime Survey.[20] Notwithstanding this generous pledge of public funds for the prison system, the government were keen to reduce the costs of dealing with crime elsewhere. In addition to rehabilitation, retribution and incapacitation, that white paper further discussed the need for a greater focus on actuarial justice[21] and the need for entire communities as well as criminal justice professionals to minimise the risk of victimisation. The later white paper *Justice for All*[22] expressed the government's intention to place the victim more centre-stage in the criminal justice process, give greater priority to their needs and interests and restore their confidence in the system.

The principles behind the 1991 Act did not do justice to these new concerns of reparation, risk and managerialism. Consequently the 2003 Act sets out a new and

---

[14] Eg the Lord Chief Justice, Lord Taylor, famously described the Act as an 'ill-fitting straitjacket' in a speech to the Scottish Law Society in March 1993.

[15] See the various perspectives on these arguments in H Rees and E Hall Williams (eds) *Punishment, Custody and the Community: Reflections and Comments on the Green Paper* (London, LSE, 1989). The key pressure groups such as NACRO, the Association for Juvenile Justice and the Howard League also published their own responses to the proposed legislation in 1989.

[16] The strict 'just deserts' principle was diluted in CJA 1993, see above n 13.

[17] In defining seriousness for the purposes of guiding the lower judiciary in the rudiments of the Act, the Court of Appeal resurrected the principle of deterrence (*R v Cunningham* (1993) 14 Cr App R (S) 444) and, it is argued, lowered the threshold of custody—see Ashworth, *Sentencing and Criminal Justice* above n 9 at ch 9).

[18] See further Ch 3.

[19] Cm 5074 (London, TSO, 2001)

[20] J Mattinson and C Mirlees-Black, *Attitudes to Crime and Criminal Justice: Findings from the 1998 British Crime Survey* HORS 200 (London, TSO, 2000).

[21] See further B Hudson, *Justice in the Risk Society* (London, Sage, 2003).

[22] Cm 5563 (London, TSO, 2002).

clearer statement of the values which were to underpin the sentencing process in this new decade. Section 142 of the Act states:

(1) Any court dealing with an offender in respect of his offence must have regard to the following purposes of sentencing—

    (a) the punishment of offenders
    (b) the reduction of crime (including its reduction by deterrence)
    (c) the reform and rehabilitation of offenders
    (d) the protection of the public, and
    (e) the making of reparation by offenders to persons affected by their offences.

This has been described as a return to the à la carte or 'smorgasbord'[23] in the cafeteria of sentencing, since it adds a wider set of considerations for sentencers to select from. These principles are clearly more punishment-oriented than the 1991 Act principles were intended to be and deterrence has made a reappearance.

However, the section specifically excludes the consideration of these principles for the sentencing of offenders aged under 18.[24] This is rather curious since a further consultation paper, *Youth Justice: The Next Steps*[25], set out how the government wanted to set about 'clarify[ing] the purposes of sentencing juveniles'.[26] This was to be achieved by the statutory incorporation of a set of principles, which, though juvenile-specific in relation to parental reposnsibility and age, are broadly similar to the principles outlined in the 2003 Act:

> We now propose a single main sentencing purpose of preventing offending, matching the principal statutory aim of the youth justice system . . . This would be supported by requirements for sentencers also to take into account the extent to which punishment is needed; whether, and if so how, there needs to be public protection because of the seriousness or persistence of the offending; the individual's age and vulnerability; whether there should be a restorative or reparative approach and/or obligations on the young person's parents; and what particular interventions have been tried if the person has been sentenced before and what would be appropriate now.[27]

Furthermore, guidance for sentencers in this specialist field is already contained in the principal aim of the youth justice, and in particular the six objectives which enhance the pursuance of that aim. These will be reviewed below, but, to a large extent, they closely resemble the list of principles set out in the 2003 Act.

---

[23] A von Hirsch and J Roberts, 'Legislating Sentencing Principles: The Provisions of the Criminal Justice Act 2003 Relating to Sentencing Purposes and the Role of Previous Convictions' [2004] Crim LR 639 at 642.

[24] CJA 2003 s 142(2)(a).

[25] London, Home Office, 2003.

[26] *Ibid* para 3.

[27] *Ibid* para 6.

The Statutory Framework

The statutory framework for sentencers in making their choice between financial, community and custodial sentences is now to be found in the 2003 Act. It remains, however, broadly similar to the 1991 framework. Based on the seriousness of the offence, the three tiers of sentence are to be applied to different offence groups, according to a clear hierarchy. This can be represented as a pyramid structure as illustrated in Figure 7.1.

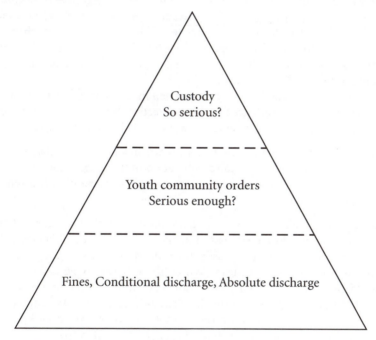

Custody
So serious?

Youth community orders
Serious enough?

Fines, Conditional discharge, Absolute discharge

FIG 7.1 *The Sentencing 'Pyramid'*

Broadly, the less severe the sentence, the more it is designed to be used and so the bottom of the pyramid, containing the fines and discharges, comprises the largest volume of the structure. Community sentences comprise the middle tier and custodial sentences, which should, in theory, be used most restrictively, are placed at the narrowest point of the pyramid. The boundaries between each tier are marked by a 'threshold', governed by the statutory criteria for each type of penalty, which must be satisfied before the sentencer can consider a sentence from the tier above. The sentencer must calculate the seriousness of the offence in order to assess which threshold the offence has passed. The CJA 2003 gives rather more guidance on this than the 1991 legislation did. Section 143 directs the sentencer to issues of the harm involved in the offence, but goes wider than harm actually caused:

(1) In considering the seriousness of any offence, the court must consider the offender's culpability in committing the offence and any harm which the offence caused, *was intended to cause or might foreseeably have caused.* (emphasis added).

In addition, previous convictions are specifically relevant and *must* be counted as an aggravating feature,[28] as must the fact that the offence may have been committed whilst the offender was on bail.[29] The Act also specifies further aggravating factors such as where an offence was motivated by discrimination, whether racial, religious, relating to disability or sexual orientation.[30] Section 166 provides for any mitigating factors to be weighed against these aggravations, and does not specify what those mitigating factors must be.

Once the seriousness of the offence is assessed the sentencer may then ascertain which tier of sentence the offence falls within. Section 148 of the 2003 Act uses the same threshold for community sentences as the 1991 legislation did, namely:

(1) A court must not pass a community sentence on an offender unless it is of the opinion that the offence, or the combination of the offence and one or more offences associated with it, was *serious enough* to warrant such a sentence. (emphasis added).

This reflects the process of 'strengthening' community sentences begun in 1991, in order to make them more credible to sentencers (this will be discussed below). Therefore, unless the offence is reasonably serious, or serious enough, a fine or discharge should be issued instead. Where the offender is aged over 16, this threshold is weakened somewhat by section 151, which allows for a community sentence to be passed where the offender has, since their sixteenth birthday, been previously fined for offences on three or more occasions. In this way the just deserts principle must yield to retribution for persistent offenders.

The threshold for custody is set out in section 152 and is also phrased in similar terms to the 1991 legislation:

(1) The court must not pass a custodial sentence unless it is of the opinion that the offence, or the combination of the offence and one or more offences associated with it, was *so serious* that neither a fine alone nor a community sentence can be justified for the offence.

---

[28] CJA 2003 s 143(2).
[29] CJA 2003 s 143(3).
[30] CJA 2003 ss 145 and 146.

This is designed to reserve custodial sentences for the most serious of offences, and also provides some clarification of the lower threshold—community sentences are appropriate for offences that are serious enough for one, but not so serious that a custodial sentence should be imposed. This threshold, though, is no more water-tight than the lower one, since failure on the part of the young offender to consent to a community order or to a pre-sentence drug test[31] can enable the court to pass a custodial sentence without due regard for the just deserts principle. Young offenders aged under 18, sentenced in the youth court, may then be liable for a detention and training order, but this requires that further criteria be met. These will be discussed below. Where the young offender commits a serious offence and is sentenced to detention in the Crown Court, the provisions of the 2003 Act must work in conjunction with those of the Powers of the Criminal Courts (Sentencing) Act (PCC(S)A) 2000.[32]

Whichever type of sentence is passed, its severity must be commensurate with the seriousness of the offence, maintaining the just deserts approach. In relation to the use of community sentences for young offenders, this means that the requirements of the order must restrict the liberty of the offender to an extent that is proportionate to the gravity of the offence.[33] This does not, though, detract from the courts' responsibility to choose requirements forming part of the sentence which are suitable for the needs of the offender in relation to preventing further offending.[34]

In relation to custodial sentences, however, the government's pledge to implement actuarial justice, mentioned above, is realised in the 2003 Act so that where it is considered necessary, the court may depart from the just deserts approach, with radically strengthened powers to detain for the protection of the public. This will largely apply to the Crown Court, since the youth courts are more restricted in determining the length of custodial sentences. First, section 228 allows for the court to impose a longer than proportionate custodial sentence where the offence committed is violent or sexual, and there is a 'significant' risk to the public of further harm being occasioned by the offender through future offending. The 'specified' violent or sexual offences are exhaustively listed in schedule 15 of the Act and are too numerous to list here (amounting to no fewer than 65 violent offences and 88 sexual offences). The extended period of detention must exceed 12 months, must not exceed the maximum permissible under criminal law for any particular offence in the case of an adult and must also not exceed five years for a violent offence and eight years for a sexual offence.[35] If the court considers that this extended detention is still inadequate for the protection of the public, they may alternatively use their powers under section 226 to impose detention for

---

[31] CJA 2003 s 161(2).
[32] See further Ch 5.
[33] CJA 2003 s 148(3)(b).
[34] CJA 2003 s 148(3)(a).
[35] CJA 2003 ss 228(3) and (4).

life,[36] or an indeterminate period of detention.[37] This provision does not specifically relate to violent or sexual offences, though it is hard to see how such draconian powers could be justified for any of the offences known to criminal law but not included in the lists in Schedule 15.

The 2003 Act provides a framework for selecting a sentence type and the sentence length, but the youth court magistrate must then turn to previous enactments to select a specific order. These are now consolidated in the PCC(S)A 2000 and include a single custodial sentence, the detention and training order, as well as a series of community sentences, now to be referred to as youth community orders. In addition, the youth court is obliged to sentence an offender to a referral order where the young offender is convicted of their first offence and pleads guilty.[38] This requirement, for the first, non-serious, offence only, overrides the provisions of the 2003 Act.

A Principal Principle?

A labyrinthine and complex set of guiding principles and rules emerge from the statutory provisions outlined above. Indeed, the end of the twentieth century and beginning of the twenty-first has been a period in youth justice history marked by extensive change and an excessive degree of guidance which must inevitably detract from the discretion of sentencers, and in the view of most commentators, does not necessarily mean that the youth justice system has embarked on a 'new' journey.[39] Magistrates in the youth court have a tough job to do, navigating their way through this statutory labyrinth and keeping up with new twists and turns added on an almost annual basis. To make matters even more complex, existing provisions from previous administrations remain on the statute books without repeal and need to be considered alongside the new statutory schema. A number of overriding principles govern youth justice policy, and sentencing in particular, but youth court magistrates have been given little advice about which takes priority and whether there is a principal principle.

---

[36] CJA 2003 s 226(2).

[37] CJA 2003 s 226(3).

[38] PCC(S)A 2000 ss 16–32—see further Ch 5.

[39] Commentaries on the Crime and Disorder Act, for example, have included the following pieces, the titles of which concur in their view that the Act contained little that had not been tried before: J Fionda, 'New Labour, Old Hat: Youth Justice and the Crime and Disorder Act 1998' [1999] Crim LR 36; A Morris and L Gelsthorpe, 'Something Old, Something Borrowed, Something Blue, but Something New?: A Comment on the Prospects for Restorative Justice under the Crime and Disorder Act 1998' [2000] Crim LR 18; Smith, *Youth Justice* above n 7 at ch 3 which is entitled 'Old Wine, New Bottles: New Labour and Youth Justice'.

First, as detailed above, the most current statutory framework for sentencing suggests that retribution, just deserts and, where necessary, the protection of the public are key considerations, and the creation of a set of statutory rules for sentencing suggests these principles have to be applied, not least to avoid decisions being made ultra vires and being subject to appeal. Second, the Crime and Disorder Act (CDA) 1998 had set out a principal aim in section 37, namely 'to prevent offending by children and young persons.' This overriding, but rather vague principle, marked an attempt by the incoming government to establish a 'clear focus' for youth justice practitioners in the face of criticism by the Audit Commission, among others, that the youth justice system had been trying to pursue conflicting purposes which rendered it ineffective and wasteful of resources.[40] New Labour had, in opposition in 1996, pledged to 'end the confusion over punishment and welfare at national and local levels'[41] and the principal aim, we assume, was the mechanism for doing so. Lacking as it did, any practical guidance or clarity, the statutory principal aim was discussed and explored further in Home Office guidance, which suggested that the pursuance of six key objectives would enable the aim to be fulfilled. These objectives are set out (in the following order) thus:

- The swift administration of justice so that every young person accused of breaking the law has the matter resolved without delay
- Confronting young offenders with the consequences of their offending, for themselves and their family, their victims and the community and helping them to develop a sense of personal responsibility
- Intervention which tackles the particular factors (personal, family, social, educational or health) that put the young person at risk of offending and which strengthens 'protective factors'
- Punishment proportionate to the seriousness and persistence of the offending
- Encouraging reparation to victims by young offenders
- Re-inforcing the responsibilities of parents[42]

While the framework document sets out further practical advice for sentencers, such as ensuring they have sufficient information in a pre-sentence report to tackle the individual needs of young people, aspiring to consistent and proportionate decision-making and ensuring they are aware of intervention programmes available in their locality, the objectives do little to clarify what any sentence should achieve as a matter of priority and, indeed, may be inherently contradictory. A proportionate sentence which encourages an offender to take responsibility for

[40] Audit Commission, *Misspent Youth . . . Young People and Crime* (London, Audit Commission, 1996).
[41] Labour Party, *Tackling Youth Crime, Reforming Youth Justice* (London, Labour Party, 1996).
[42] Home Office, *Youth Justice: The Statutory Principal Aim of Preventing Offending by Children and Young Persons* a framework document (London, Home Office, 1998).

their offending may, for example, do little to tackle the causes of crime. A sentence which does attempt rehabilitative intervention may not enhance the 'swift' administration of justice.

A third principle, which is often forgotten in this quagmire of guidance, is the welfare principle, enacted in statutory form in section 44 of the Children and Young Persons Act 1933 and never yet repealed.[43] This provides a statement of principle which emphasised the welfare orientation of youth justice and child protection policy at that time:

(1) Every court in dealing with a child or young person who is brought before it, either as . . . an offender or otherwise, shall have regard to the welfare of the child or young person and shall in a proper case take steps for removing him from undesirable surroundings, and for securing that proper provision is made for his education and training.

It is not surprising that, in the current fervour to legislate and to dictate to sentencers, that they omit to consider this rather ancient and 'old-fashioned' principle. However, it is a statutory duty which, significantly, remains in place to counter-balance the more retributive aims of recent enactments. Indeed, on three occasions in recent decades the courts have been reminded of its existence by higher authorities. In 1991, the Home Office issued a Circular to the new youth courts, providing advice on the legislative changes that had recently affected their jurisdiction and practice. This Circular reminded them of their old, as well as new, statutory duties:

> The principle set out in section 44 of the Children and Young Persons Act 1933 that all courts must have regard to the welfare of children and young people who appear before them is accordingly extended to include 17 year olds. As the youth court will deal with almost all court cases involving defendants under 18, this principle will have a particular importance to the youth court.[44]

Over a decade later, in the punitive furore of the mid-1990s, the House of Lords reminded both the courts and the Home Secretary, at that time exercising a quasi-judicial discretion as to whether to order the release of Venables and Thompson, that putting aside condemnation and horror at what any particular offender had done, they must also consider their welfare as children.[45] In their view, even child murderers were children first and murderers second. After Venables and Thompson had taken their appeal to the European Court of Human Rights, and

---

[43] Even the CJA 2003 leaves it intact—sch 37 does not list this section among the many repeals prompted by the new legislation.

[44] Home Office, *Criminal Justice Act 1991: Young People and the Youth Court* Circular (London, Home Office, 1992) para 4.

[45] *R v Secretary of State for the Home Dept ex p Venables and Thompson* [1997] 3 All ER 97 at pp125–26 (Lord Browne-Wilkinson).

won, the Lord Chief Justice issued a practice statement on special arrangements that must be considered during the trial of young children in the Crown Court in order that sensitivity to their youth is not overlooked in the adversarial proceedings of the trial. The practice statement has been discussed in Chapter 6, but it significantly reminded Crown Courts that, although the children before them were being tried in an adult-like fashion, they still have a statutory duty to have 'regard . . . to the welfare of the young defendant as required by section 44 of the Children and Young Persons Act 1933'.[46]

Magistrates are left to juggle with these three 'balls' without a clear sense of their respective weightings and without a sense of priority. The third, welfare, principle, lacks authority and, possibly, appeal in modern times. Further in criminal courts the welfare of the child is not stated to be 'paramount', in the same way that it is in section 1 of the Children Act 1989, guiding the family proceedings court. It is therefore, easy, if they are so minded, for the youth courts to sideline this consideration. This leaves them with two sets of more recent statutory rules to juggle with. We can now review how they have approached this juggling exercise.

Punishment in the Community?

The statutory framework gives a more defined role to community sentences in perpetuating the bifurcation policy developed in the 1990s. They have a much clearer identity and place in the sentencing system than their original manifestation as alternatives to custody, tentatively used by the more liberal-minded sentencers who were troubled by the commitment of young people to custody. Punishment in the community is no longer, technically, an alternative to custody, since the legislative frameworks developed in 1991 and 2003 provide that where custody is appropriate it should be used and where it is not, it should not be used. In this section we will trace the policy behind the transformation of the identity of community penalties and assess the extent to which they remain, in a rather different way, an alternative *form* of custody.

The first seeds of decarcerative thought in relation to young offenders began to germinate at the turn of the nineteenth century. A growing disenchantment with custodial and other incarcerative institutions based on their 'dismal history'[47] of failure to realise their rehabilitative potential crime amongst this group and their capacity to cause further damage to the developmental process, led to consideration of the possibility of avoiding incarceration of offenders and achieving rehabilitative goals by working with the offender in their own community. A nascent

---

[46] Practice Direction, *Trial of Children and Young Persons in the Crown Court* [2000] 1 Cr App R 483.
[47] Rutherford, *Growing Out of Crime* (2002) above n 1 at p 50.

form of the probation service, the Church of England Temperance Society, established in 1876, had already been working with some offenders appearing before the magistrates to keep them out of custody, but their main concern was with persuading drunken offenders towards a life of sobriety and Christian values. In 1907 the Probation of Offenders Act provided for the transformation of this charitable organisation into a court-appointed and organised national probation service whose task was to 'advise, assist and befriend' offenders and to supervise them in the community under the first probation order. The order was primarily used for the under-21s and, as a consequence, the population of young people held in custodial institutions fell dramatically by the 1920s.

The probation service, with a statutory duty founded on welfare principles, found themselves key implementers of the welfare approach in the 1960s. Fines had long since been available as a non-custodial penalty, but further, more constructive, penalties were added to the choice of alternatives for sentencers during this period. The suspended prison sentence was created in the 1967 Criminal Justice Act, followed by the introduction of community service orders and compensation orders in 1972.[48] The 1982 Criminal Justice Act provided further forms of the probation order and an early form of curfew for young offenders. Indeed, as that Act placed restrictions on the use of custody for young offenders, it was all the more important that these non-custodial alternatives were available, and for the minority of young people not cautioned during the developmental era, community sentences enabled magistrates to keep the incarceration of young people to a minimum. Notwithstanding that successive governments had kept community sentencing firmly within their penal agenda during the 1960s and 1970s, however, the use of custodial penalties had continued to rise during that period and this provided evidence that magistrates were reluctant to use them, particularly in relation to adults. In the 1980s, while the imprisonment of young offenders fell considerably, the prison population as a whole reached unprecedented levels and resulted in a severe overcrowding problem.

This problem prompted the Conservative government at that time to re-assess their entire penal strategy and to give thought to mechanisms for reducing the prison population, partly for managerial reasons. In addition to 'back-door' methods such as a comprehensive and generous early release scheme, they focused on how to prevent offenders entering the prison system through the 'front door' and in this respect the work of youth justice practitioners during the 1980s provided some precedent for the rehabilitative effectiveness of non-custodial measures. Any new strategy had to involve providing alternatives that were credible and attractive to sentencers. Concerns that community sentences were too lenient

---

[48] See further J Harding, 'The Development of Community Service: Its Application and Relevance to the Criminal Justice System' in N Tutt (ed) *Alternative Strategies for Coping with Crime* (Oxford, Basil Blackwell, 1978).

and inadequately enforced in practice had to be addressed before they would be routinely and enthusiastically used. The bifurcation policy outlined above, therefore aimed to give community sentences a central role in the new sentencing framework for non-serious offences, but more than that community sentences were to be given a new identity and rationale. The 1988 consultation paper stressed that there was need to reinvent existing community penalties as more rigorous and demanding:

> The Government believes that there is scope for reducing the use of imprisonment by introducing a form of punishment which leaves the offender in the community but has components which embody three elements . . . some deprivation of liberty, action to reduce the risk of offending and recompense to the victim and the public.[49]

In other words, if community penalties could look 'tough' and resemble the custodial penalties that sentencers often preferred, then they might just be inclined to use them, if provided with clear guidance and a full range of non-custodial options.

The proposed philosophical transformation of community penalties met with a uniformly critical response. The Howard League saw no merit in the government's proposals and saw through their apparently 'decarcerative' guise:

> The way forward in reducing reliance on imprisonment is not to be found by transferring the methods or ethos of the prison system into the general community . . . The League is mindful of Professor Nils Christie's warning that the prison could be abolished by making the whole society into something like it.[50]

David Garland further attacked the 'self-contradictory' nature of this policy, arguing that

> For all its progressive suggestions it tends to reinforce the punitive elements of our penal culture. It underlies the current sentencing pattern, but it refuses to challenge or even question this culture of severity. Instead it treats this mentality as a given fact of the world to which governments (and penal practitioners) must somehow adapt.[51]

Not only did the enacted 1991 legislation attribute these punitive characteristics to community penalties, but it also added non-custodial options that were considered to have limited rehabilitative potential such as a new form of the curfew order,[52] reinforced, if necessary, by electronic tagging,[53] which the Howard League

---

[49] Home Office, *Punishment, Custody and the Community* above n 3 at para 3.8.
[50] Howard League, *The Community, Punishment and Custody: The Response of the Howard League for Penal Reform to the Green Paper* (London, Howard League, 1988) at pp 6, 9.
[51] D Garland, 'Critical Reflections on the Green Paper' in H Rees and E Hall Williams (eds) *Punishment, Custody and the Community: Reflections and Comments on the Green Paper* (London, LSE, 1989) p 14.
[52] CJA 1991 s 12.
[53] CJA 1991 s 13.

claimed was 'incompatible with the essential fabric of a free society'.[54] Existing community orders were additionally made subject to National Standards stressing their role in restricting liberty, protecting the public and, if possible, rehabilitating the offender.

Notwithstanding the new punitive philosophy of community sentences, by 1995 Home Secretary Michael Howard perceived that they were still not tough enough and that further work needed to be done:

> It is the view of the Government that the role of community sentences is poorly under-stood and—perhaps as a result—that they have failed to command the confidence of the public despite the greater prominence and extra resources given to the probation service in recent years. Probation supervision is still regarded as a soft option. *Although in many cases, this perception may be misconceived, it must be addressed.*[55] (emphasis added)

This view signified the arrival of punitive populism in youth justice policy, whereby public confidence is a determinant of effectiveness, regardless of criminological data on 'what works'. Howard wished to see community penalties becoming even harsher in order that the public could *see* offenders being punished. His consultation paper therefore proposed changes which included removing the consent requirement to community service orders,[56] greater discretion to determine the content of community orders and enforce compliance, more intensive supervision and, though not specified in the consultation paper, but publicly discussed in publicising the proposals, that 'hard work' in the community should be visible to the public with offenders possibly wearing uniforms.[57] Ironically the new structure for a generic community order comprising a series of orders chosen by the court, bears considerable resemblance to the new structure of community sentencing under the Criminal Justice Act 2003.

Nothing came of Howard's proposals and the Crime (Sentences) Act 1997 left community sentences largely untouched. However, given Tony Blair's pledge, in opposition, to be 'tough on crime, tough on the causes of crime' it was to be expected that community sentences which were suitably 'tough' would be heavily employed in tackling the 'causes of youth crime'. The Crime and Disorder Act 1998 maintained the 1991 sentencing framework but gave the youth court a much wider set of non-custodial options, some providing intervention to tackle specific aetiological factors,[58] others appearing to repeat the *modus operandi* of existing

---

[54] Howard League above n 50 at pp 6–7.

[55] Home Office, *Strengthening Punishment in the Community: A Consultation Document* Cm 2780 (London, HMSO, 1995) para 4.4.

[56] With an ingenious argument that the European Convention on Human Rights Art 4.2 may prohibit the use of forced or compulsory labour, but the exception in relation to labour carried out in connection with detention could be applied here—*ibid* at para 4.20.

[57] See Home Office, 'Strengthening Punishment in the Community: Green Paper' Press Release (15 March 1995).

[58] Such as the Drug Treatment and Testing Order s 61.

penalites.[59] The same punitive ethos was to underpin punishment in the community as Jack Straw stressed that:

> To prevent offending and re-offending by young people, we must stop making excuses for youth crime. Children above the age of criminal responsibility are generally mature enough to be accountable for their actions and the law should recognise this.[60]

Further, the probation order and community service order have been re-named as the community *punishment* order and community *rehabilitation* order,[61] stressing the precise functions of each option. New Labour's contribution to the development of community penalties has therefore been to add more orders into the menu of options providing every conceivable intervention to prevent offending, offered through a re-organised, multi-agency team of professionals, the Youth Offending Team. To clarify the, by now, very muddled set of provisions, the Powers of the Criminal Courts (Sentencing) Act 2000 consolidated the list of community penalties available (with the addition of a couple more in the Criminal Justice and Court Services Act 2000). The Criminal Justice Act 2003 now refers to these penalties as Youth Community Orders[62] and Community Orders[63] and provides for sentencers to choose appropriate orders to form a unified 'community sentence' according to the criteria in section 148.

The Community Orders

In accordance with the aim of legislators in 1991 to create a discrete youth age range for those aged 16 and 17 and who might be considered rather more independent and mature than their younger counterparts,[64] community orders are organised in two distinct groups. First, those which are youth-specific in that they are not available in the sentencing of adults. Second, when young people attain the age of 16, they may be subject to a second group of penalties, which we might call 'adult' community penalties, as they apply to any offender aged over 16. The former group now comprise the 'youth community orders' namely:

• *Supervision order*[65]

This order provides for offenders aged under 18 to be supervised in the community by the YOT or a probation officer. Conditions, such as requirements to reside

---

[59] For example the Action Plan order criticised by Fionda as 'superfluous and unnecessary'—'New Labour, Old Hat: Youth Justice and the Crime and Disorder Act' [1999] Crim LR 36 at 44.

[60] Home Office, *No More Excuses* Cm 3809 (London, TSO, 1997) at p 1.

[61] See Criminal Justice and Court Services Act 2000 ss 43 and 44.

[62] Section 147(2)—where the order is only applicable to offenders aged under 18, or 25 in the case of the attendance centre order.

[63] Section 147(1) where the orders are applicable to offenders aged 16 and over.

[64] This is discussed in Ch 9.

[65] PCC(S)A 2000 s 63.

in particular place, take psychiatric treatment or other therapeutic measures, make reparation or submit to drug treatment and testing[66] can be attached. The order may last for up to three years.

• *Attendance centre order*[67]

This order provides for an offender to be required to attend a centre, run by the police on a Saturday afternoon, for an aggregate of between 12 and 36 hours over a period of weeks. This order, unusually, applies to offenders aged under 25 (the upper age limit having been raised in the 2003 Act) so that, for these limited purposes young adults fall within youth justice measures. However, separate centres are run for those over and those under 18 and the older offenders would be expected to attend for longer periods. Practice varies, but an offender would be required at the centre to participate in directed activities usually involving sport, creative activities or the development of general life skills.

• *Action plan order*[68]

New Labour invented this community order in 1998, providing a three-month period of supervision and action to tackle offending behaviour, set out in a plan drawn up by the YOT and the young offender. The order aims to provide a 'short but intensive and individually tailored response to offending behaviour, so that the causes of that offending as well as the offending itself can be addressed'.[69] Subsequent amendments have made it possible to further require the offender to make reparation as part of this action plan,[70] and to submit to drug testing and treatment.[71]

• *Curfew order*[72]

Strictly speaking this is not a 'youth specific' order since it may be applicable to any offender, young or adult, over the age of 10, although for those aged under 16 the maximum period of curfew allowed is three months. During this time the court may specify a place where the offender must be at certain times, on certain days, taking care not to interfere with a young person's education or work commitments, religious beliefs and family life. Their presence in that place (usually their home) is monitored by a responsible officer, and this may include electronic monitoring, or 'tagging' where this technology is available.

---

[66] An amendment set out in s 279 of the CJA 2003 and applies to offenders aged 14 and over only.
[67] PCC(S)A 2000 s 60.
[68] PCC(S)A 2000 s 69.
[69] Home Office, *Guidance Document: Action Plan Orders* (London, Home Office, 1998) para 2.1. I previously described this as a 'short sharp shock in the community'—J Fionda, 'New Labour, Old Hat' above n 59 at p 44.
[70] PCC(S)A 2000 s 70.
[71] CJA 2003 s 279—applicable to offenders aged over 14.
[72] PCC(S)A 2000 s 37.

• *Exclusion order*[73]

This is another new order introduced by New Labour in 2000, which operates as a 'reverse' curfew order. It requires a person aged over 10 to stay away from a specified place at certain times, on certain days for a period of three months (for those aged under 16); for two years (for those over 16). Although it was possible to issue a curfew order in these terms, rather than as a form of detention in the home, this order is clearly intended to separate exclusion from incapacitation and should be applied to keep offenders away from areas where their offending behaviour takes place.

An offender aged 16 or 17 may also be subject to the youth community orders listed above, or alternatively can graduate to the 'adult' community orders. In the Criminal Justice Act 2003 a standard community order may involve one of a long list of requirements set out in section 177, including:

• Unpaid work in the community (without consent if necessary)[74]
• Activities, rehabilitation programmes or refraining from prohibited activities[75]
• A curfew, exclusion or residence requirement[76]
• Participation in psychiatric, drug or alcohol treatment programmes[77]
• Supervision[78]

The community punishment and community rehabilitation orders have therefore been replaced by specific requirements forming part of the generic community sentence. This gives the court greater discretion in tailoring a community sentence to the individual needs of the offender, always, of course, mindful of proportionality and commensurability.

Welfare Agencies and the Implementation of Community Punishment

Despite their preference for punishment in the community rather than in custody, the Audit Commission formed the view in 1996 that the implementation of community sentences during the 1990s had been problematic.[79] In particular, efforts to prevent re-offending in young people were being made by social workers and the probation service in the criminal justice system, as well as by education and health workers elsewhere, without any real attempt to co-ordinate their work or

---

[73] PCC(S)A 2000 s 40A.
[74] There is no mention of a consent in the detailed discussion of this requirement in s199.
[75] CJA 2003 ss 201, 202, 203.
[76] CJA 2003 ss 204,205, 206.
[77] CJA 2003 ss 207, 209, 212.
[78] CJA 2003 s 213.
[79] Audit Commission, *Misspent youth* above n 40 at p.

even inform each other of the issues they were dealing with. Consequently the Audit Commission felt that that not only rendered rehabilitation work less effective, since it suffered from a lack of coherence, but that this was a waste of resources. It had further become clear during the 1980s that, when welfare agencies worked together in dealing with youth crime, co-ordinated efforts to keep young people out of trouble were more successful.[80] Mindful of these influences, New Labour published a further consultation paper, *New National and Local Focus on Youth Crime*.[81] While *Tackling Youth Crime*[82] set out proposed new legal measures, the second consultation paper addressed how these measures were to be implemented by professionals at the ground level. A new national framework for the management of the youth justice system was to be designed, with clear leadership at the top and a focus on local partnerships at the ground level:

> For too long there has been a lack of clear direction in the youth justice system. The Government will give the necessary leadership—setting out clearly in legislation the aim of the youth justice system and establishing a national body to monitor the delivery of youth justice services and help to raise standards . . . Young offenders often present multiple problems—for example drug or alcohol misuse, problems at school or problems at home. It makes sense for the agencies which deal with each of these issues to come together locally, to address these problems and so reduce the risk of further crime.[83]

The Crime and Disorder Act 1998 subsequently set out this new management structure, creating both the national Youth Justice Board[84] to monitor practice and advise the Home Secretary on good practice in youth justice, and local, multi-agency Youth Offending Teams (YOTs) to provide youth justice services.[85]

It is the responsibility of local government to both establish, and more importantly fund, one or more YOTs in their area. Membership of the YOT must include a representative from each of the following agencies: probation, social services, the police, the health authority and the local education authority, as well as members of any other local agency or group whom the local authority considers appropriate.[86] Their statutory duties are simply stated as 'to co-ordinate the provision of youth justice services for all those in the authority's area who need them',[87] youth justice services being listed in section 38. This will include the provision of rehabilitation programmes, supervising young people on various non-custodial court orders, assessing young people for intervention following a warning, preparing

---

[80] See further Smith, *Youth Justice* above n 7 at pp 11–14.
[81] Home Office (London, Home Office, 1997).
[82] Home Office (London, Home Office, 1997).
[83] Home Office, *No More Excuses* above n 60 pp 26–27.
[84] Section 41. The Board was discussed above in Ch 3.
[85] Section 39.
[86] Government advice on the establishment of YOTs suggests these other agencies may include religious groups, local youth groups, the fire service or, more curiously, the prison service. Home Office, *Inter-Departmental Circular on Establishing Youth Offending Teams* (London, Home Office, 1998) para 11.
[87] CDA 1998 s 39(7).

pre-sentence reports, providing appropriate adult services in the police station, providing bail support and post-release supervision of young people released from custodial institutions. Further enactments since 1998 have added another, weighty, responsibility to establish, train and participate in youth offender panels under the referral order system. The fulfilment of these duties are all monitored by the Youth Justice Board, principally through both periodic inspection by HM Chief Inspector of Probation (as was) and the local Youth Justice Plan, submitted annually by the local authority to the Board, setting out proactive plans for the provision and funding of youth justice services in each area.[88]

Pilot teams were established in 1998 and evaluated, swiftly followed by the creation of teams nationwide. Evaluations of the pilot schemes were enthused by the opportunities that multi-agency working provided for developing 'innovative work' in a new culture of coherent welfare provision.[89] At the same time, however, problems emerged regarding the hurried implementation of a very complex legislative structure, a lack of training, a lack of resources and too heavy a set of duties and responsibilities. Smith suggests that the experience of those who had worked in Juvenile Liaison Bureaux (JLBx) during the 1980s was that, where agencies were drawn together as an organic process, by consent, they were more likely to form constructive partnerships in which they could pool their experience and knowledge, communicate effectively and work together with uniform objectives. This explains why JLBx were established on a rather ad hoc basis, in areas where agencies were prepared to work effectively together. Under the Children Act 1989, where social services have a statutory duty to call upon other local authority departments for assistance and work together with them in alleviating the welfare needs of children,[90] experience in practice was less positive. In some areas, these departments did not get on well, found they had conflicting priorities and resented being forced into partnerships that they felt compromised their ability to carry out their statutory duties.[91] Experiences in Hampshire in the youth justice system in the 1980s, also demonstrated that partnerships between agencies often had to be founded below senior management level where key individuals provided the impetus for forming teams.[92] Smith is similarly sceptical about the enforcement of partnerships in the youth justice system: 'The Northampton initiative perhaps provided grounds for optimistic assumptions that the good working relationships established in one area between agencies at all levels could straightforwardly be replicated elsewhere.'[93] The blunt and dictatorial formalising of a process that

---

[88] CDA 1998, s 40.

[89] Home Office, *Interim Report on Youth Offending Teams* (London, Home Office, 1999).

[90] Children Act 1989 s 17.

[91] See further D Cowan and J Fionda, 'Housing Homeless Families: An Update' (1995) 7 *Child and Family Law Quarterly* 66.

[92] These experiences are recounted by Sue Wade, amongst others, in A Rutherford, *Growing Out of Crime* (2002) above n 1 at pp 20–27.

[93] Smith, *Youth Justice* above n 7 at p 89.

had previously been highly informal, organic and mindful of the necessary sensitivities may yet backfire. Despite these changes, the National Audit Office has continued to suggest that co-ordination in the provision of services to young people is inadequate.[94]

John Pratt had previously asserted that probation practice was gradually being subject to more centralised control, losing their professional discretion and adopting the new ideology of 'corporatism':

> This sociological concept refers to the tendencies to be found in advanced welfare societies whereby the capacity for conflict and disruption is reduced by means of the centralization of policy, increased government intervention, and the co-operation of various professional and interest groups into a collective whole with homogeneous aims and objectives.[95]

The new management structure into which YOTS have been integrated does indeed demonstrate greater government surveillance of practice, via the Youth Justice Board,[96] and changes to sentencing practice in legislation since 1991 have rendered the welfare professional less able to determine best practice in relation to any individual, or, as happened in the 1980s, to develop a progressive working ideology which enabled practitioners to determine policy.[97] Indeed, the working ideology of these welfare agencies has fundamentally changed through changes in their statutory duties since 1991 and, more recently changes to their statutory purpose in 2000. The probation service (now subsumed into the National Offender Management Service, along with the prison service) attained a new set of statutory aims in the Criminal Justice and Court Services Act 2000, section 2, namely to have regard to:

(a) The protection of the public,
(b) The reduction of re-offending,
(c) The proper punishment of offenders
(d) Ensuring offenders' awareness of the effects of crime on the victims of crime and the public
(e) The rehabilitation of offenders.

Many had concluded after 1991, that the occupational culture of the service had already adopted a more punitive tone.[98] The new statutory aims are embedded with a focus on punishment, with rehabilitation appearing bottom of this list of priorities.

---

[94] National Audit Office, *Youth Offending: The Delivery of Community and Custodial Sentences* HC 190 (London, TSO, 2004).
[95] J Pratt, 'Corporatism: The Third Model of Juvenile Justice' (1989) 29 *British Journal of Criminology* 236 at 239.
[96] In theory an independent quango, but with a statutory duty to act 'in accordance with any guidance given' by the Home Secretary—CDA 1998 s 41(7).
[97] See further Ch 3.
[98] See for example M Nellis, 'Probation Values for the 1990s' (1995) 34 *Howard Journal* 19.

Social Control

Changes in the working ideology of the probation service and other welfare agencies mirrors the transformation of punishment in the community in the late twentieth century. The repeal, after almost a century, of the statutory role of 'advise, assist and befriend' signalled the last death knell in the welfare orientation of community sentences. Whilst there remains some attempt to genuinely address welfare needs in the community, the rigorous enforcement procedures and penalties for breach, the movement of discretion in building a rehabilitative response from the professionals to the courts and the new aims of community sentences suggest that social work agencies have acquired a community policing role, administering the increasingly punitive diktats of the courts. Indeed Pitts has suggested that welfare agencies have been deprofessionalised over the last decade and have become the technicians of the court, carrying out their wishes and ensuring that their punitive technologies function appropriately:

> The vacuous rhetoric of correctional 'newspeak' inevitably evokes the image of Postman Pat going about his uncontentious and socially useful job, with a smile on his face and a cheery word for everyone.[99]

This changing role reflects the inherent tension in non-custodial sentencing policy between welfare and justice concerns; the tension that is inevitable while the government attempts to use this set of penalties to be both 'tough on crime' and 'tough on its causes' at the same time. This is, to some extent a problem with the bifurcated policy that the government embarked on in 1991 and that has been evident in the rationale behind New Labour's legislative packages. This is discussed further below.

Trying to achieve multiple aims through this set of provisions may result in the failure to achieve any of them. While Cavadino and Dignan assert that if we must pursue retributive and incapacitative ideals then it is better to do so in the community than in prison,[100] Home Office statistics demonstrate that community sentencing in the last decade has singularly failed to reduce the prison population for young offenders. The first edition of Cavadino and Dignan's book had suggested that the proliferation of non-custodial measures available to the court may serve to widen the net of the youth justice system and expand the state's capacity to socially control young people as a group:

> One of the most significant effects of the 1991 'just deserts' package is its strengthening of the disciplinary and control elements associated with the probation and community service order . . . which is very much in line with the dispersal of discipline theory.[101]

---

[99] J Pitts, 'The End of an Era' (1992) 31 *Howard Journal* 133 at 143.

[100] M Cavadino and J Dignan, *The Penal System: An Introduction* 3rd edn (London, Sage, 2002) pp 149–50.

[101] M Cavadino and J Dignan, *The Penal System: An Introduction* (London, Sage, 1992) p 197.

In conjunction with a more restrictive diversion programme at the pre-trial stage, and an increasing intolerance of 'persistent' or repeat offending, young offenders may even be propelled towards custodial institutions before their welfare needs have been exhaustively met. The difference between community sentencing now and 20 years ago is that whereas repeat offending may once have been regarded as the failure of these mechanisms to fully address the welfare needs of an offender, or allow him opportunity to grow out of crime, it is now perceived as a failure on the part of the offender to take advantage of the privilege of welfare that he has been afforded and he must lose that privilege in 'taking responsibility' for his failure.

The other danger concerns the expansion of social control of young people. The 'dispersal of discipline' theory mentioned in the above quote, refers to the work of both Stanley Cohen and Thomas Mathiesen and their respective critiques of the tendency for penal developments during the twentieth century to extend the state's surveillance of its citizens. Cohen's influential book *Visions of Social Control*[102] describes how the state once confined its methods of social control to specific deviant groups through the use of institutions such as the prison, the reform school and the psychiatric hospital. The more recent development of community penalties, however, has enabled the state to continue to expands its control of deviant groups within the community setting, creating, in effect, the situation where the entire community becomes in itself the new panopticon, a penal institution in which young offenders may be monitored and controlled. The 'punitive city' had been predicted by Michel Foucault:

> [A]t the cross-roads, in the gardens, at the side of the roads being repaired or the bridges built, in workshops open to all, in the depths of mines that may be visited, will be hundreds of tiny theatres of punishment.[103]

Cohen argues that this prediction was realised during the later decades of the twentieth century as decarcerative penal strategies and the development of community corrections both 'widened the net' and 'thinned the mesh' of social control, drawing both offenders and those 'at risk' of offending into a system where ever more intervention was waiting for them. Further, the welfare ideal blurred the distinction between responses to crime and responses to welfare need resulting in social control spreading further beyond identified deviant groups.[104] Mathiesen traces a similar evolution, but argues that social control has gradually extended beyond the individual to entire deviant groups by means of surveillance techniques, designed and justified for the prevention of crime and the protection of us all from victimisation, but once established, equally capable of being used to

---

[102] S Cohen, *Visions of Social Control* (Cambridge, Polity Press, 1985).
[103] M Foucault, *Discipline and Punish: The Birth of the Prison* (London, Allen Lane, 1977) p 113.
[104] S Cohen, 'The Punitive City: Notes on the Dispersal of Social Control' (1979) 3 *Contemporary Crises* 339.

watch us all.[105] He discussed this theory, more recently in relation to the Schengen Convention, a pan-European surveillance system monitoring the movement of persons across national borders, allegedly to facilitate the prevention of international crime and to protect the national and internal security of member states, but in reality watching the movements of large numbers of people travelling through Europe in order to prevent the illegal entry of asylum seekers.[106] 'Panopticism' in forms such as community penalties, allow the few to watch the many. As technology advances and now that the electronic media has proliferated, Mathiesen argues that a process of 'synopticism' allows 'the many to watch the few'.[107] Punishment in the community provides both the hardware (such as tagging and CCTV), and the legitimacy, for extensive control of young people, who are increasingly viewed as a threat.

As social control increases, crime levels do not necessarily retract. Indeed, our perception of crime and the fear thereby generated is likely to increase as members of society are told to be vigilant and share a role policing their own neighbourhood. As fear and anxiety increase, notions of risk are heightened and the need for even greater social control is keenly felt; a vicious circle ensues. Stuart Waiton has demonstrated, through his study of local curfews to restrict the presence of young people in social spaces, that 'safety campaigns' tend to promote fear of youth crime, rather than disarm it, impacting not just on the response of adults to young people as a social group, but also on young people's perception of risk and socialisation: 'by creating fear among children and young people, they are encouraged to avoid all potentially dangerous situations and ultimately grow up ill equipped to cope with life'.[108]

Where socialisation is impeded, so too is the developmental process, which, as we saw in Chapter 4, results in a failure to prevent crime. The hysteria that has emerged in the 'risk society' prevents a meaningful discussion of penal strategies and the rejection of alternative approaches. Mathiesen suggests that for this, we need an 'alternative public space'[109] away from the media and political forums, in which penal strategies can be sensibly discussed and informed by more scientific and ideological discourse. Youth justice policy makers have yet to find this space.

---

[105] T Mathiesen, 'The Future of Control Systems' in D Garland and P Young (eds) *The Power to Punish: Contemporary Penality and Social Analysis* (London, Heinemann, 1983).

[106] T Mathiesen, 'On the Globalisation of Control: Towards an Integrated Surveillance System in Europe' in P Green and A Rutherford (eds) *Criminal Policy in Transition* (Oxford, Hart Publishing, 2000).

[107] See further T Mathiesen, *Silently Silenced* (Winchester, Waterside Press, 2005).

[108] S Waiton, *Scared of the Kids?: Curfews, Crime and the Regulation of Young People* (Sheffield, Sheffield Hallam University Press, 2001) p 110.

[109] Mathiesen, 'On the Globalisation of Control' above n 106 at p 190.

Custody

A dominant theme in youth justice policy, since the very beginnings of a separate youth justice system, has been the incarceration of young people. While the institutions have changed from time to time, some offering education and reform, others punishment and incapacitation, the theme itself has not changed. There have rarely been concerted attempts, at least in policy circles, to decarcerate or even abolish the institutionalisation of children, and the general statistical trend over the course of the twentieth century has been escalatory. However, we have witnessed in previous eras some discussion of the value of imprisonment (or lack of it) and some temporary impetus to reduce the use of custody, sometimes prompted by a conscience behoving policy makers to seek more benevolent alternatives, sometimes by managerial concerns over the expense of expansionism. What is, however, notable in recent years, is a clear expansionist aim but with little discussion in any of the many official discussion papers of how custodial penalties aspire to fulfil the principal aim of the youth justice system.

The notable exceptions to the general incarcerative theme came in 1969 and later in the 1980s. Prior to this, whilst the welfare ideal was in its ascendancy, in practice terms it was assumed that the ideal could be reached through detention in reformatories or penal institutions, notwithstanding the pleas of reformers such as Sir Godfrey Lushington in the late nineteenth century.[110] Reforms throughout the twentieth century saw young people transferred variously between reform schools, industrial schools, borstals, prisons, detention centres and youth custody centres.[111] During the 1960s, policy makers, embracing the welfare ideal were keen to remove all but the most serious and older offenders from the prison system and the 1969 Children and Young Persons Act sought to replace criminal with care proceedings, in which local authority care homes could provide the incapacitative and rehabilitiative benefits that custodial sentences had previously provided. Detention centres and borstals were to be phased out in favour of community alternatives such as Intermediate Treatment. Failure to implement the Act meant that these aims were never realised, but even if they had been, Rutherford argues they did not constitute a wide-scale abolitionist approach. With what he calls 'studied disregard' for developments in Scotland at that time and the focus there on retaining parental responsibility for troublesome behaviour with appropriate social services assistance, the 1969 Act signified

> less a policy of decarceration than a reiteration of the traditional welfare abhorrence of the prison system. In fact the 1969 Act and the preceding discussions and debates failed

---

[110] See further Rutherford, *Growing Out of Crime* above n 1 at pp 43–50.

[111] See further *ibid* ch 3; A Morris and H Giller, *Understanding Juvenile Justice* (London, Croom Helm, 1987) chs 1, 3 and 4 for more detailed analysis of historical developments.

to address directly the issue of institutions. While supporters of the Act sought to end the use of the prison system, regarded as punitive, there was no objection to institutions tied to the care system.[112]

Developments in the 1980s were rather different, because they were founded on principles that departed from the traditional welfare and punishment ideals. Although nothing in government policy and legislation at the time sought to pursue an abolitionist agenda,[113] practitioners at ground level had adopted a working ideology which was fundamentally opposed to any form of institutionalisation. The developmental ideal, based on the notion that a majority of young people would grow out of crime, required that young people be allowed to address their offending behaviour in a natural environment which nurtured that growing-up process. Custody, or any form of institutionalisation, it was claimed, would damage the developmental process and render the developmental institutions of the family and the school powerless to intervene. Probation officers and social workers then began a campaign to divert as many young people out of the criminal justice system at an early stage through cautioning, and, where a young person was prosecuted, to implore magistrates not to use their custodial sentencing powers. Indeed, in some areas magistrates were amongst those practitioners who shared this developmental ideology and were themselves opposed to custodial sentences. As a result, the rate of imprisonment of juveniles fell extensively between 1982 and 1990 from 7100 to 1400 (the juvenile prison population as a whole falling from 1717 in 1980 to 284 in 1990).[114] This period was reminiscent of a concerted, but sometimes surreptitious decarceration of young people in Massachusetts in the 1970s, resulting in the closure of a number of institutions.[115]

We have seen above how the government, at the end of the 1980s, sought to capitalise on this decarcerative trend and implement a sentencing framework that would at least minimise the use of custody, if not end the practice altogether. The discussion papers at this time are riddled with anti-custody statements, though the rationale behind these ranges from managerial concerns over the cost of imprisonment, the incapacity of prisons to rehabilitate and provide reparation:

> Imprisonment restricts offenders' liberty, but it also reduces their responsibility; they are not required to face up to what they have done and the effect on their victim or to make any recompense to the victim or the public.[116]

Whilst the white paper famously declared that prison is 'an expensive way of making bad people worse'[117] it also, as its title suggests, expressed commitment to

[112] Rutherford, *Growing Out of Crime*(2002) above n 1 at p 59.
[113] Although the CJAs of 1982 and 1988 sought to reduce the use made of custody, there were no attempts to eradicate this sentencing possibility entirely.
[114] Home Office, *Criminal Statistics 1989* Cm 1322 (London, HMSO, 1990).
[115] J Miller, *Last One over the Wall* (Columbus, Ohio State University Press, 1991).
[116] Home Office, *Punishment, Custody and the Community* above n 3 at para 1.1.
[117] Home Office, *Crime, Justice and Protecting the Public* above n 8 at para 2.7.

it as a means of incapacitation to protect the public. In this way, the government failed to challenge the futility of custodial penalties to truly tackle the real causes of youth crime in the majority of cases. This ambivalence is reflected in the twin-track approach taken by that legislation, in which imprisonment plays a key role in Track A for 'serious' offenders (however that was to be interpreted). What is notable, however, is that the same government did take a far more emphatic and minimalist approach to institutionalisation in relation to care proceedings in the Children Act 1989. That legislation placed greater restrictions on the use of care orders, preferring no order to be made where that was appropriate, and preferring that parental responsibility remained intact, with support and assistance from social services where necessary. In this sense legislation in civil law was beginning to reflect Scottish practice in relation to young offenders, although the Children Act 1989 worked alongside a criminal justice agenda for offenders south of the border.[118]

At the time that the Criminal Justice Act 1991 was being implemented, the government had already embarked on plans to expand the juvenile prison estate and open it up to younger offenders. On 2 March 1993, the then Home Secretary, Kenneth Clarke, announced to the House of Commons, proposals to create a new custodial order, the secure training order. This announcement was made several months before the murder of James Bulger and it is therefore inappropriate to attribute the government's change of heart in relation to custody for young offenders to that event. This was a political move, responding to a number of media panics over petty, but persistent offending which, the police had complained, the courts were powerless to control within their existing powers, which were:

> insufficient to deal effectively with that comparatively small group of very persistent juvenile offenders whose repeated offending makes them a menace to the community.[119]

Despite vehement criticism from the Howard League, the Association for Youth Justice, the Magistrates' Association and the National Association for Probation Officers, the Home Affairs Committee reluctantly endorsed the government's proposal, subject to minor amendments. However, they were minded to suggest that the government consider a more 'radical' proposal, for intensive supervision in the community for all but the most persistent of offenders, who would be contained in non-prison care institutions with regimes that were 'educational, vocational and therapeutic'.[120] While more benevolent than the government's intentions, the HAC remained loyal to an institution of one sort or another ('They

---

[118] This is discussed further in Ch 10.

[119] HC Debates vol 220, col 139 (2 March 1993).

[120] Home Affairs Committee, *Juvenile offenders* Sixth Report HAC 441–I (London, HMSO, 1993) p lxiv.

would be secure institutions, but not penal institutions'[121]) and therefore fell into the trap experienced by policy makers in 1969.

The government was subject to a barrage of criticism for this proposal. The Howard League denounced the new secure units as 'Child Jails',[122] Allan Levy and Frances Crook suggested this idea flew 'in the face of accepted research, received wisdom and good sense',[123] and Baronness Lucy Faithfull commented that

> The secure training order is a step backwards in penal policy and child care policy, which has been devised by people with no experience of working with difficult and disturbed young people. It will mean sending delinquent young people to 'mini-prisons' which will greatly increase their chances of becoming adult criminals.[124]

The Penal Affairs Consortium alleged that there were few 'persistent offenders' in this age range, and even fewer involved in serious offending, that existing sentencing provisions were in fact adequate to deal with the very small number that were causing concern and that the re-offending rates after custodial sentences for young offenders demonstrated that the new proposal would be unlikely to succeed, concluding that:

> [T]he secure training order is a retrograde and damaging measure which will increase rather than reduce offending by young people and which represents an indefensible misuse of public expenditure.[125]

Nevertheless the Home Office persisted with their plans and the Criminal Justice and Public Order Act 1994 introduced the new order for young offenders aged 12 to 14.[126] For the first time in many decades, imprisonment was to be available again for young people aged under 15. Moreover, the same Act doubled the length of custodial sentences available for those aged over 15 (from one year to two years),[127] and reduced the age at which children could be transferred to the Crown Court for the trial of grave offences to 10.[128]

Michael Howard's conviction that 'prison works' prompted further legislation in 1997, the Crime (Sentences) Act introducing mandatory prison terms for serious and persistent offenders, but this 'two strikes and you're out' policy did not extend to young offenders under 18. When New Labour came into power later that year, discussion of their plans for a radically new youth justice system did not

---

[121] *Ibid* p lxiv.

[122] Howard League, *Child Jails: The Case against Secure Training Orders* (London, Howard League, 1994).

[123] A Levy and F Crook, 'Children's Prisons: Secure Training Centres Considered' (1995) *The Magistrate* 36.

[124] Speaking at a NACRO conference on New Approaches to Juvenile Crime—' "Lock-up" Proposals for Young Offenders Criticised' NACRO Press Release (10 March 1994).

[125] Penal Affairs Consortium, *The Case against the Secure Training Order* (London, Penal Affairs Consortium, 1994).

[126] Section 1.

[127] Section 17.

[128] Section 16—see further Ch 6.

mention custody. However, they were confronted with a hotch-potch of custodial provisions through which youth courts could sentence younger children to secure training units and older youths to Young Offender Institutions, via different legislative powers and for different purposes. The Crime and Disorder Act 1998 tidied these provisions up, by merging them into one, uniform Detention and Training Order, but in the course of doing so, quietly extended the availability of youth court custodial sentences to offenders as young as 10.[129]

Custodial Orders

As the legislation now stands, young people may find themselves imprisoned through one of an increasing number of routes. Indirectly, a young person who either breaches an anti-social behaviour order, or refuses, in the youth court, to consent to a community order, may be sentenced to a period of imprisonment. More explicitly, the youth court may utilise the detention and training order (DTO) and the Crown Court may issue a longer prison sentence under sections 90 and 91 of the PCC(S)A 2000.[130] The DTO enables the youth court to imprison a young person aged 10[131] to 17 inclusive where the relevant criteria are met. First, the offence must be 'so serious' that no other type of penalty can be justified (as required by the Criminal Justice Act 2003, s 152). If that criterion is satisfied, further restrictions apply according to the age of the offender—the younger the offender, the more restrictions placed on a custodial sentence. Those aged 12 to 14 inclusive must, in the opinion of the court, be both persistent and dangerous,[132] whereas those aged between 15 and 17 inclusive merely need to be regarded as persistent.[133] Persistence is not defined in this Act and it is for the court to decide when repeat offending becomes abnormally persistent so that it justifies a custodial penalty. The order must last for an even number of months between 4 and 24, and the permissible lengths of DTOs are set out in section 101 of the PCC(S)A 2000. Oddly, the youth court was not left with discretion to construct a sentence for whatever even number of months it considered appropriate, and sentences of 14, 16, 20 or 22 months are inexplicably prohibited. The sentence length must involve an even number of months because the sentence is divided into two equal periods; the first half served in a custodial institution and the second half in the community under supervision by the YOT.[134] Three types of institution are

---

[129] CDA 1998 s 73.

[130] After the CJA 2003, this may even involve indeterminate custody—s 226. Ss 90 and 91 PCC(S)A 2000 are discussed further in Ch 6.

[131] The use of the DTO for offenders aged 10 and 11 has not yet been implemented.

[132] PCC(S)A 2000 s 100(2)(b).

[133] PCC(S)A 2000 s 100(2)(a).

[134] This format has been borrowed from the original secure training order devised in 1994, but here it is applied to all custodial sentences.

available to hold those young people imprisoned, although placement of the offender is not part of the youth court's discretion and will be decided by the Youth Justice Board. Local authority secure accommodation, which is not part of the prison estate and which is run by social services, may be available for offenders aged up to 16, but is generally used for those aged 12 to 14. These small institutions house both offenders and vulnerable young people placed in care, and focus on intensive one-to-one work with young people to address their behavioural difficulties. Clearly the regime in such institutions is not in any way punitive. However, they are few and far between across England and Wales[135], hold very few young people (between 6 and 40 in each unit) and may refuse to take any particular young offender from the courts. Young people in the same age range may alternatively be allocated to a secure training unit. These units were established as part of the prison estate in 1994, as part of the Home Office's policy outlined above. There are currently only four such units, holding no more than 50 young people at a time. Although run by the prison service, they have a comparatively higher staff/inmate ratio than young offender institutions and aim to provide a more constructive and educational regime. Older offenders will be allocated to a young offender institution (YOI), a more traditional prison environment for young people, with a much higher capacity to hold larger numbers. As the prison population for young people increases, any overspill from the first two types of unit is likely to be absorbed by the YOI estate, which also holds young people aged up to 21.

Critique

The use of any form of custodial penalty for children and young people has been subjected to unremitting and fervent critique for many years. The criticisms fall into two categories; first, that the imprisonment of young people does little to either prevent them re-offending nor to address their behavioural problems. The second, more principled, objection, is that it is unethical and abusive to imprison young people, and experience in England and Wales in the last few decades reveals custodial regimes that are so dire, that that abuse is unjustifiable and a breach of the child's human rights. Re-offending rates calculated after young people leave custodial institutions suggest that prison does little, in a direct sense, to 'prevent offending by children and young people'.[136] Since estimates of between 75 and 95

---

[135] The House of Commons Public Accounts Committee also noted, with disapproval, that detention in a local authority secure home was far more expensive than detention in a penal institution (presumably because of the intensive one-to-one treatment offered there—see Public Accounts Committee, *Youth Offending: The Delivery of Community and Custodial Sentences* 40th Report of Session 2003–04, HC 307 (London, TSO, 2004) Evidence p 2, qu 7.

[136] The principal aim of the youth justice system, discussed above.

per cent of young people re-offend after varying periods following a custodial sentence, the experience of detention may even prompt further offending behaviour. It was this argument that underpinned the Labour Party's opposition to the creation of secure training units in 1994, claiming that they would be 'schools of crime',[137] a view from which they have clearly departed in recent years.

A recent study of young people's own perceptions of their experiences in custody, conducted by HM Chief Inspector of Prisons, revealed a lack of education, purposeful activity and assistance with resettlement after release which may explain the high re-offending rates. Many young people surveyed had drug and alcohol problems that were not addressed while they were in prison. Further, whilst most of them believed that finding employment after release was most likely to prevent them from re-offending, only 32 per cent of the boys and 44 per cent of the girls consider that they had done something in custody that would help them to find employment, and many who were about to be released considered that they still needed further help with resettlement.[138] These findings reflect the ongoing criticism in numerous inspection reports of individual YOIs in recent years, that education and vocational training provision is woefully inadequate.[139]

These inspection reports have been equally, if not more, critical of the conditions in which young people are held, the regimes in operation and the negative experiences of young people in the care of the prison service. So much so that Sir David Ramsbotham, a former Chief Inspector, declared that 'I do not believe that children under 18 should be held in prison',[140] strong words that he has continued to stand by after his retirement.[141] This view was formed after numerous visits to YOIs in which suicide, bullying, unhygienic and dangerous conditions, insufficient health and psychiatric care and profound inactivity were found to be rife.[142] Feltham YOI in west London, the largest YOI in England and Wales, has been subject to a very public media criticism, particularly of their inability to prevent suicides and suicide attempts.[143] The experiences of young people, reported in the study mentioned above, bear witness to these problems, reporting that they

---

[137] The Labour Party, *Partners against Crime: Labour's New Approach to Tackling Crime and Creating Safer Communities* (London, Labour Party, 1994).

[138] Her Majesty's Inspectorate of Prisons, *Juveniles in Custody* (London, TSO, 2004).

[139] Many of these reports can be found at <http://www.homeoffice.gov.uk/justice/prisons/insprisons.index.html> (9 June 2005).

[140] Her Majesty's Inspectorate of Prisons, *Young Prisoners: A Thematic Review by HM Chief Inspector of Prisons for England and Wales* (London, TSO, 1997) p 6.

[141] D Ramsbotham, *Prison-gate: The Shocking State of Britain's Prisons and the Need for Visionary Change* (London, Free Press, 2003) particularly ch 10. Sir David was a former senior officer in the British Army, appointed to this role by Michael Howard in 1995, presumably to inject a more robust perception of the rightful role of the prison in punishing offenders. This agenda failed dramatically as he immediately gained for himself a reputation as one of the most critical Chief Inspectors to date.

[142] A thorough reading of many of the reports of these visits prompted one of my students, in dismay, to write of the three 'Bs' which depict life in a YOI: 'boredom, bullying and buggery'!

[143] See for example S Ferguson, ' "This Place is Doing My Head In" ' *Independent* (13 March 1989).

had been bullied and insulted by staff, assaulted by other inmates, had inadequate access to washing facilities and few opportunities for association with other inmates.[144] Penal pressure groups, such as the Prison Reform Trust, the Children's Society and the Howard League, have also campaigned vociferously for the ending of the imprisonment of young people.[145] The Howard League have consistently asserted the view that the excessive use of imprisonment for children and the appalling conditions in which they are held constitute a breach of the United Kingdom's international human rights obligations, a view which has been confirmed by the United Nation's Committee on the Rights of the Child who have been highly critical of the UK government's expansionist policies and inappropriate regimes.[146]

This discussion inevitably leads us to question why we continue to imprison young people. It must be clear to the government that it not only fails in achieving their own 'principal aim' for youth justice, but it renders them liable to extreme criticism, and possibly litigation under their own Human Rights Act 1998. Custody for this age group indeed defies any sensible rational or ideological justification. It is therefore not surprising that the current government have been so reticent to discuss it publicly in relation to their wider youth justice agenda. They claim that the public (or adults at least) support the use of imprisonment for serious young offenders[147], though this may tell us more about the phrasing of questions put to the public, rather than their considered views about value of this penalty.[148] The reason for the continued use of imprisonment, must therefore be political; it serves the purposes of a government to whom popular appeal is more important than achieving long-term reductions on the crime figures. Both Fionda[149] and Pratt[150] have discussed ways in which imprisonment may hold some political value to policy makers. It remains within the discretion of the sentences, however, to implement their own 'politics of redress' should they be so inclined.[151]

[144] HM Inspectorate of Prisons, *Juveniles in Custody* above n 138.

[145] See eg, B Goldson, *Vulnerable Inside: Children in Secure and Penal Settings* (London, The Children's Society, 2002); Howard League, *Sentenced to Fail—Out of Sight, Out of Mind: Compounding the Problems of Children in Prison* (London, Howard League, 1998).

[146] UN Committee on the Rights of the Child, *Concluding Observations of the Committee on the Rights of the Child: United Kingdom of Great Britain and Northern Ireland* CRC/C/15/Add 188 (Geneva, Centre for Human Rights, 2002) paras 50–62.

[147] See Home Office, *Stopping Youth Crime—Tell Us What You think: Summary of Responses from Children and Young People and the Government Response* (London, Home Office, 2004).

[148] *Ibid.* The views of respondents to questions concerning the use of custody, length of sentences etc were variable according to the questions asked.

[149] Fionda, 'New Managerialism and the Sanitisation of Justice' above n 5 pp 118–23.

[150] J Pratt, *Punishment and Civilization* (London, Sage, 2002).

[151] See W de Haan, *The Politics of Redress: Crime, Punishment and Penal Abolition* (London, Unwin Hyman, 1990).

Sentencing Policy

The discussion above indicates that sentencing policy in relation to both punishment in the community and in custodial institutions has been unremittingly expansionist over the past 10 years. The picture is of more young people being sentenced, to more available orders, involving more intervention. It is a far cry from the minimalist approach of the 1980s and, what is more, emerges from a policy developed in the late 1980s by a government which wanted to minimise the use made of prison and encourage youth justice practitioners to divert young offenders where possible. Of course, subsequent governments have abandoned the liberal approach of Douglas Hurd and his predecessors, and we have more recently witnessed a resurgence of punitive populism. However, the framework within which the more expansive policies were to be implemented was set in 1991. The bifurcated nature of the sentencing framework rendered it ambiguous enough to be used for either a minimalist or more interventionist policy, according to political whim. It is therefore not surprising that any intention to minimalise the use of imprisonment, in particular, failed and that bifurcation resulted in proliferation.

The twin tracks of the bifurcated policy were never given equal emphasis either in the policy discussion or in the sentencing framework. Track A was already a high-speed inter-city track, given a £1.5 billion fuel booster to fund its expansion. It was also more widely publicised, as promises to protect a fearful public from violence and harm[152] were more warmly received in the media and popular discourse than a commitment to the long-term rehabilitation of offenders and the distant creation of a safer community. Track B, on the other hand, resembled the slow, unreliable and decrepit track on which progress faltered at faulty signals and which was in need of investment, repair and re-organisation. The £15 million invested in Intermediate Treatment not only paled in comparison with the investment in Track A, but had long since been spent and the pot never replenished. JK Galbraith has noted how, in the socio-economic climate that Margaret Thatcher created, Track B is less likely to command public and media support, given that its objectives are long term and it involves the 'contented' moral majority consenting to spend Treasury funds on what appears to be the privilege of welfare:

> [S]hort-run public inaction, even if held to be alarming as to consequence, is always preferred to the protective long-run action. The reason is readily evident. The long run may not arrive; that is the frequent and comfortable belief. More decisively important, the cost of today's action falls or could fall on the favoured community; taxes could be increased. The benefits in the longer run may well be for others to enjoy.[153]

---

[152] Note the title of the 1990 white paper: *Crime, Justice, and Protecting the Public.* Protecting the public became a more prominent theme in the 1990 paper than it had been in the 1988 green paper.

[153] JK Galbraith, *The Culture of Contentment* (London, Penguin, 1992) p 20.

Politicians who embark on a twin-track approach are therefore more likely to utilise Track A when speaking publicly to announce and discuss their criminal policy, while Track B remains in the comparatively quiet realm of the academics, welfare workers and back benchers.

The resultant sentencing framework left ambiguities in the dividing line between the two tracks, which enabled the judiciary, and succeeding governments to manipulate it. It was mentioned above that the only restraints on Track A are the 'politics of bad conscience' that de Haan discusses in relation to reductionism in Dutch penal policy throughout the twentieth century.[154] Whereas in the Netherlands the ideological commitment of the Utrecht School, which tutored a future generation of prosecutors, judges and politicians, to minimal use of short prison sentences, England and Wales have lacked a unified conscience which mitigates against the imprisonment of young people. Rather, the lack of intellectual integrity in penal policy

> leaves the judiciary prey to every populist tremor, so that it sometimes seems as if a single banner headline in the *Sun* carries more weight than the combined findings of the Home Office's own redoubtable Research and Planning Unit.[155]

This has justified continued high levels of expenditure and expansion of the prison estate.

The discussion of community sentencing above reveals that this area has been subject to expansionist policy as well. Track B has received the investment and repair that it needed to catch up with Track A. However, the expansion in community sentences has supplemented rather than supplanted expansion in custodial sentencing, resulting in a divergence of the tracks.

Each track now hurtles with gathering speed in different directions, towards oblivion. The 2003 legislation, in which New Labour put their stamp on sentencing policy, has not radically altered the progress of this divergence except to add perhaps greater emphasis on Track A, boosting its speed a little more. Youth justice policy witnessed significant growths in custodial sentencing and the social control of young people immediately after both the 1969 Children and Young Persons Act and the 1991 Criminal Justice Act, both of which had liberal foundations. Either New Labour are blind to the lessons that history can teach us, or these historical processes are exactly what they are aiming to repeat.

---

[154] de Haan, *The Politics of Redress* above n 151.

[155] D Downes, *Contrasts in Tolerance:Post-war Penal policy in the Netherlands and England and Wales* (Oxford, Clarendon Press, 1988) pp 203–4.

8

Restorative Justice

Recent concern over the plight of victims in the criminal justice process, and their alleged secondary victimisation, has led scholars and policy makers to consider alternative approaches to youth justice which are thought to be less harmful. Restorative justice has been developed in many jurisdictions, as a response to youth crime, which is aimed at providing a form of justice based on a conflict resolution model rather than a retributive one. The theory behind restorative justice, however, has informed practice in these jurisdictions to a greater or lesser extent, and this chapter examines both the theory and practice in England and Wales and elsewhere. In theory, restorative justice seeks to reduce social exclusion through its integrative approach, protecting the needs and interests of both the victim and the marginalised offender, and re-balancing their social position as an outcome to their conflict. However, in practice there is a danger that restorative justice is misunderstood and that undue focus on the plight of victims induces a response to youth crime that is more punitive and hateful, fuelled by an emotional empathy for the victim's suffering. In this chapter, both the theory of restorative justice and its application in practice are critically assessed.

Restorative Justice in Theory

Restorative justice, as developed in academic discourse, fundamentally differs in focus from traditional retributive systems of justice. The former rely on defining certain behaviours as crime in accordance with definitions prescribed by the state. A criminal justice system is then assigned the task of attributing guilt for that behaviour where it corresponds with such definitions and imposing sanctions. In England and Wales this task will be performed through an adversarial contest between the offender and the state. Where sanctions are imposed by the state it is commonly assumed that they will reflect at least one of the four traditional theories of punishment: retribution, deterrence, incapacitation or rehabilitation. These theories are principally focused on two of the three parties in the triumvirate of interests affected by the criminal behaviour, namely the state (or community) and the offender. They are criticised for ignoring the needs and interests of the victim. In one way or another they seek to punish the offending behaviour and prevent it from recurring and in this way retributive justice may be said to be 'backward-looking and grounded in the past'.[1]

Restorative justice theory emerges from critique of these retributive systems of justice and perceptions of the failure of the latter to either prevent crime or offer an inclusive approach for the victim. The failure of traditional forms of justice fall into three broad themes. First, the objectives underlying traditional penal sanctions are ineffective and counter-productive. Rehabilitation, as an aim of criminal sanctions, has been largely marginalised in official discourse in recent years, prompting academic commentators to refer to the collapse of the rehabilitative ideal:

> There was pressure for an increase in the use of indeterminate custody so that offenders could be let out when, and not before, they had been successfully 'treated'. Judges and magistrates were advised to avoid passing very short prison sentences, because these would not allow sufficient time for rehabilitative treatment . . . This ideal is now in the process of evaporating. A succession of negative research reports has suggested that different types of treatment make little or no difference to subsequent reconviction rates.[2]

In relation to young offenders, the collapse of the welfare ideal has been similarly noted as its unduly interventionist approach was thought to be more damaging than effective, increased the parameters of social control and was replaced, at least briefly, by a more minimalist approach.[3] In recent years, rehabilitation or 'tackling the causes of crime, has re-emerged but firmly within a strategy of retribution. Hence New Labour's pledge to be 'tough on the causes of crime'. A wealth of empirical evidence suggests that deterrent approaches to punishment are ineffective in so far as they attribute undue conscious pre-meditation on the part of offenders and ignore the often opportunistic nature of much offending.[4] So much so that the government even rejected its utility as a theme of penal policy in 1990.[5] More recently governments have found the principles of retribution and incapacitation more attractive, politically and pragmatically, arguing that the former serves to protect citizens in an increasingly risk-oriented society[6] and the latter inspires public confidence in the strength of governments to 'do something' about

---

[1] C Cunneen and R White, *Juvenile Justice: Youth and Crime in Australia* (Melbourne, Oxford University Press, 2002) p 361.

[2] See eg A Bottoms, 'An Introduction to the Coming Crisis' in A Bottoms and R Preston *The Coming Penal Crisis* (Edinburgh, Scottish Academic Press, 1980) p 12.

[3] See further Ch 3; A Rutherford, *Growing Out of Crime: The New Era* (Winchester, Waterside Press, 2002) ch 3.

[4] See further A Ashworth, *Sentencing and Criminal Justice* 3rd edn (London, Butterworths, 2000) pp 64–68.

[5] Home Office, *Crime, Justice and Protecting the Public* white paper Cm 965 (London, HMSO, 1990) para 2.8—'It is unrealistic to construct sentencing arrangements on the assumption that most offenders will weigh up the possibilities in advance and base their conduct on rational calculation.'

[6] See B Hudson, *Justice in the Risk Society* (London, Sage, 2003).

crime. The result has been what Garland describes a 'culture of control' and a strategy of 'punitive segregation' in criminal justice policy in the late twentieth century.[7] Proponents of an alternative approach claim that such a socially exclusive crime control policy is marked, at best, by its ineffectiveness in reducing crime levels and, even worse, may cause such damage to societal relations and offenders' behaviour that it may actually increase crime. Incapacitation, for example, can only ever provide temporary protection to society and without further constructive intervention merely temporally displaces offending behaviour.

A second, related criticism of retributive systems is that they further exclude offenders from a society in which they are already disenfranchised by social deprivation.[8] This serves only to increase the likelihood of offending behaviour. In Chapter 4 we saw how the alienation of young people, delinquent labelling and the creation of cultural conflict in society provide aetiological explanations for youth crime. Johnstone also suggests that the depiction of young offenders as 'some kind of external threat, as people who are different from ourselves and who do not belong in our society and against whom we need to raise physical defences' has done little to enable citizens to *feel* protected by these supposedly protective penal measures and that 'we are investing more in alarms, locks, closed circuit television and other security hardware in the hope that they will protect us from criminals'.[9] Far from achieving this aim, instilling a siege mentality in a community enhances the social alienation of young people and the vicious circle begins to spiral.

Third, and perhaps most significantly in the support of restorative justice, is the argument that traditional retributive systems ignore the needs and interests of victims. The resurrection of restorative justice in the late twentieth century is often attributed to a seminal article by Norwegian scholar Nils Christie who explains eruditely how the victim is marginalised in modern penal systems:

> The key element in a criminal proceeding is that the proceeding is converted from something between the concrete parties into a conflict between one of the parties and the state. First, the parties are being *represented*. Secondly, the one party that is represented by the state, namely the victim, is so thoroughly represented that she or he for most of the proceedings is pushed completely out of the arena, reduced to triggerer-off of the whole thing. She or he is a sort of double loser; first *vis-à-vis* the offender, but secondly and often in a more crippling manner by being denied rights to full participation in what might have been one of the more important ritual encounters in life. The victim has lost the case to the state.[10]

---

[7] D Garland, *The Culture of Control* (Oxford, Oxford University Press, 2001).

[8] See P Carlen, 'Youth Justice? Arguments for Holism and Democracy in Responses to Crime' in P Green and A Rutherford *Criminal Policy in Transition* (Oxford, Hart Publishing, 2000). This view will be discussed further below.

[9] G Johnstone, *Restorative Justice: Ideals, Values and Debates* (Cullompton, Willan, 2002) p 10.

[10] N Christie, 'Conflicts as Property' (1977) 17 *British Journal of Criminology* 1 at 3.

In this way Christie argues that the state, as a 'professional thief' steals the conflict that rightfully belongs to the victim by denying them the opportunity to participate in it. This is a deliberate and unashamed theft, which the state commits in the name of a wider crime reduction strategy and to maintain the public interest in justice. In practice, many have criticised a process that has been dubbed the 'secondary victimsation' of crime victims, whereby the state's treatment of them is so unethical, traumatic and unjust that it can be equated with the effects of the original offence committed against them.[11] Having exhausted their utility in providing reports of an offence and statements of evidence to the police, victims are then often ignored in the various decisions made about the progress of the case, not informed of the outcome of these decisions, not officially represented at court[12], often not actually present at court, especially where there is no trial, and neither consulted nor acknowledged in the sentencing process. Proponents of the restorative approach argue that any attempt to deal with offending behaviour must restore, as far as possible, equality between the parties and maintain equal respect for all involved. As Dworkin has stated:

> Government must treat those whom it governs with concern, that is, as human beings who are capable of suffering and frustration, and with respect, that is, as human beings capable of forming and acting on intelligent conceptions of how their lives should be lived. Government must not only treat people with concern and respect, but with equal concern and respect.[13]

So too must the criminal justice system recognise that the victim is equally entitled to consideration in a process that is ordinarily heavily offender oriented and this is achieved by the application of the restorative philosophy. This is particularly ironic since developments in the criminal law in England and Wales have moved from focus on crimes against the interests of the institutional community or public morality (such as the decriminalisation of homosexuality) towards enactments aimed at preventing harm to individuals (such as the development of the semi-criminal anti-social behaviour legislation). Indeed research on the police response to assault conducted by Cretney *et al* revealed that 'the police do not respond to 'crime'; they respond to 'complaints against the aggrieved'.[14] As the criminal law makes this progression, it could be argued that the criminal justice system should follow suit and should cease to focus on merely meting out punishment to an offender for retributive purposes in favour of redressing the harm caused to an individual victim.

---

[11] See eg J Morgan and L Zedner, *Child Victims: Crime, Impact and Criminal Justice* (Oxford, Clarendon Press, 1992).

[12] Barbara Mills, as former Director of Public Prosecutions, had always famously asserted that the CPS was not a Victims Prosecution Service.

[13] R Dworkin, *Taking Rights Seriously* (London, Duckworth, 1981) pp 272–73.

[14] A Cretney, G Davis, C Clarkson and J Shepherd, 'Criminalizing Assault: Failure of the "Offence against Society" Model' (1994) 34 *British Journal of Criminology* 15.

The failure of retributive justice has created a vacuum in which more effective and constructive alternative forms of justice have been sought. This has prompted a renewed interest in the notion of restoration to be found in other legal cultures as well as in the civil law of many Western societies. This system of justice takes a wholly different perspective of offending behaviour, whereby crime produces a conflict between individuals. The perpetrator has deprived the victim of their rights and caused them to suffer some form of loss, whether physical or emotional. The resulting imbalance of the respective positions of the victim and the perpetrator results in a conflict between them. The behaviour is therefore defined in relational terms rather than in terms of legal definitions of crime:

> [R]estorative justice rests on the principle that crime, like any other social problem, represents a disjuncture between the aims, aspirations, needs, feelings, and behaviour of different individuals and social groups, including society as a whole. Crime is a relationship problem that therefore should be approached in a rational problem-solving way.[15]

The purpose of a system of justice based on the restorative ideal seeks to restore the balance between the parties and to solve the conflict situation that has arisen. Attempts to label the behaviour a 'crime' and the perpetrator an 'offender' are largely irrelevant in a system which does not seek to formally punish the former for the sake of punishment. The central concern is to identify the source and impact of the conflict on each party and to negotiate a solution which puts right the harm caused and seeks to repair broken relationships with a view to preventing a recurrence of the behaviour.

A perception of wrongdoing in these terms is not new. The civil law approach to disputes over property, contractual rights or the commission of a tortious wrong similarly regards the dispute in relational terms and adopts a dispute resolution approach that is, in the main, restorative rather than punitive. In civil law, damages compensate for loss rather than express collective disapproval of the harm caused. Since the boundary between civil and other harmful actions are artificially constructed by the state and constantly changing, it is argued that crime is not necessarily fundamentally different in nature to other wrongs and that a restorative approach to crime is not ideologically incongruous.

The cultural roots of restorative justice are also thought to be borrowed from ancient tribal or religious customs in which wrongdoing prompts a process of shame, repentance, forgiveness and reintegration. Howard Zehr traces a biblical precedent for this approach to sin in Christian doctrine. His attempts to define restorative justice draw on biblical references and he argues that the state (in whatever guise) under a restorative system resembles the stern but kindly deity, who, according to Psalm 103:

---

[15] T Marshall, 'Grassroots Initiatives towards Restorative Justice: The New Paradigm?' in A Duff, S Marshall, RE Dobash and RP Dobash (eds) *Penal Theory and Practice: Tradition and Innovation in Criminal Justice* (Manchester, Manchester University Press, 1994) at p 255.

> [I]s tender and compassionate
> Slow to anger, most loving;
> His indignation does not last forever,
> His resentment exists a short time only;
> He never treats us, never punishes us,
> As our guilt and our sins deserve.[16]

The roots of the restorative approach are also thought to originate in tribal systems of justice such as in traditional Maori culture in New Zealand. The customary approach to dealing with wrongdoing in such cultures often involves entire communities coming together to resolve disputes in a community meeting place (or *murae* in Maori custom). These are not formal proceedings but rather reflect a conference in which representations may be made by all interested parties in the presence of the local community and its leader. In this way the dispute can be discussed by all and a solution reached which promotes community harmony, the restoration of peace and equal respect for all community members. Far from this informal process being a form of private vengeance, it is a collective approach which aims to maximise community cohesion, ensures that no member of the community is deliberately excluded and that the perpetrator of the wrongdoing can be shamed but ultimately reintegrated into that community. An alternative, secular, view of restorative justice is Braithwaite's republican theory of justice.[17] The aim of this theoretical approach is to maximise personal liberty or 'dominion' and a justice system based on this theory seeks to restore 'dominion' that has been denied though the perpetration of the crime. Crime is a denial of the personal liberty of the victim as well as damaging to the dominion of the community as a whole. As each criminal act promotes fear of crime and potential victimisation, the dominion of each member of the community is diminished and community cohesion suffers. Republican theories of justice therefore proscribe a restorative approach to dealing with crime, in order to achieve the aims of recognition, recompense and reassurance. The offender must recognise their threat or damage to the dominion of others, that dominion must be restored and collectively the community needs to be reassured that their dominion is no longer under threat. As seen above, retributive systems do little to achieve any of these aims.

The pursuit of the restorative ideal therefore requires what Zehr describes as a different 'lens'; not just a minor alteration in procedure but a wholly different perspective on wrongdoing and the role of any attempt to resolve disputes. In the new system of justice the victim's interests are of more paramount importance, though not at the expense of the perpetrator's interests. Rather it is the state whose role

---

[16] Psalm 103 cited in H Zehr, *Changing Lens: A New Focus for Crime and Justice* (Scottdale, PA, Herald Press, 1990) p 1.

[17] J Braithwaite and P Pettit, *Not Just Deserts: A Republican Theory of Justice* (Oxford, Clarendon Press, 1990).

must subside. There are two essential, but equally significant, facets to a restorative justice, first a centralisation of the victim's position in the conflict and second, the reintegration of the perpetrator with whatever rehabilitative action that may require. In practice the implementation of these facets requires a fundamental reassessment of justice procedures which fall outside the boundaries of a criminal justice system and involves the removal of familiar processes and ideologies. The entire rationale behind the justice system needs to change from some form of offender-oriented aim to punish to what Martin Wright describes as the aim of 'creating a just society, one that is as fulfilling and rewarding as possible for all its citizens'.[18]

For the victim, a restorative justice system needs to offer much more than material compensation or reparation as a ancillary to punishment. Material compensation may be necessary as part of the restorative process but Christie argues that respect for victims requires, at the very least, participation in the justice process:

> Material compensation is not what I have in mind with the formulation of 'conflicts as property'. It is the conflict itself that represents the most interesting property taken away, not the goods originally taken away from the victim, or given back to him. In our types of society, conflicts are more scarce than property. And they are immensely more valuable . . . The victim is a particularly heavy loser in this situation. Not only has he suffered, lost materially or become hurt, physically or otherwise. And not only does the state take the compensation. But above all he has lost participation in his own case. It is the Crown that comes into the spotlight, not the victim.[19]

Wright envisages a system where mediation and conferencing replace the traditional adversarial trial, so that the victim reappears in the 'spotlight' that Christie referred to.[20] Mediation involves discussion, rather than establishing guilt and the outcome of the discussion focuses on the interests of the parties not the interests of the public. The outcomes of each mediation may be different, heavier or lighter, constructive or reparative. The key difference is that the focus is on the process and procedural fairness and not on achieving uniformity of outcome. Providing the process is ethical, sympathetic to all parties and avoids any harm to anyone involved then the outcome will be fair, properly negotiated and based on notions of forgiveness and understanding.

For the perpetrator there are rehabilitative benefits to the process which seek to prevent the behaviour recurring (which is in the interests of both parties) and to reintegrate him into the community, thereby preventing the social exclusion often associated with retributive systems.[21] Christie envisaged that the 'pain' of

---

[18] M Wright, *Justice for Victims and Offenders: A Restorative Response to Crime* (Winchester, Waterside Press, 1996) p 140.

[19] Christie, 'Conflicts as Property' above n 10 at p 7.

[20] Wright, *Justice for Victims and Offenders* above n 18 at p 141.

[21] See further J Young, *The Exclusive Society: Social Exclusion, Crime and Difference in Late Modernity* (London, Sage, 1999).

punishment need not necessarily involve the infliction of material loss or loss of liberty as traditional methods of punishment dictate:

> Compensatory justice presupposes that compensation can be given. The offender must be able to give something back. But criminals are most often poor people. They have nothing to give . . . We let the poor pay with the only commodity that is close to being equally distributed in society: time. Time is taken away to create pain. But time could be used for compensatory purposes if we so wished. It is an organisational problem, not an impossibility.[22]

Christie is therefore suggesting that with a little imagination we can create a justice system that enables the perpetrator to offer something back to the victim and to the community without exacerbating the social inequality that so often exists between identified offenders and the rest of society, and which so often results in their social exclusion or 'social death'.[23] Braithwaite takes this argument a step further and suggests that in the process of shaming an offender and expressing collective approbation of their behaviour, a restorative justice ritual may take steps to alleviate that social exclusion:

> The crucial distinction is between shaming that is reintegrative and shaming that is disintegrative (stigmatisation). Reintegrative shaming means that expressions of community disapproval, which may range from mild rebuke to degradation ceremonies, are followed by gestures of reacceptance into the community of law-abiding citizens. These gestures of reacceptance will vary from a simple smile expressing forgiveness and love to quite formal ceremonies to decertify the offender as deviant. Disintegrative shaming (stigmatisation) in contrast, divides the community by creating a class of outcasts.[24]

The suggestion here is that all the constructive benefits of retributive justice (rehabilitation, shaming, condemnation) can be achieved in a restorative system, but in an inclusive rather than exclusive way.

Restorative Justice in Practice

There was a resurgence of interest in restoration in youth justice policy in the late twentieth century, principally emerging from concern at the plight of victims and their secondary victimisation. This was a gradual process. During the 1960s and 1970s in England and Wales we witnessed a growth in state compensation initiatives through the establishment of Victim Support Centres, the Criminal Injuries

---

[22] N Christie, *Limits to Pain* (Oxford, Martin Robertson, 1982) p 95.
[23] See further A Rutherford, 'Criminal Policy and the Eliminative Ideal' (1997) 31 *Social Policy and Administration* 116.
[24] J Braithwaite, *Crime, Shame and Reintegration* (Cambridge, Cambridge University Press, 1989) p 55.

Compensation Board, the increased use and priority of compensation orders over more punitive sanctions and the potential for supervisory and probationary facilities to be used for compensatory or reparative purposes. During the 1980s the plight of victims of sexual offences was particularly highlighted,[25] together with their insensitive and often unethical treatment by the criminal justice system. This, together with a growing rights-oriented social policy and the creation of the Citizen's Charter,[26] prompted a justice movement calling for greater rights for victims of crime, including their right to be heard, to be informed, to be supported and protected by the law enforcement agencies, to receive compensation and reparation and, above all, to receive recognition and respect.[27]

By 1997 New Labour were keen to inject the restorative ideal (as they saw it) into their new youth justice system. They commissioned a report into the treatment of victims in the criminal justice system which highlighted the imbalance between the status, interests and protection of the victim and offender in the justice process, and suggested that a more victim-centred policy might alleviate these problems of inequality.[28] Crawford and Newburn noted that the plethora of consultation documents on youth justice produced by the Home Office discussed this concern:

> The influence of communitarian thinking was very visible in the Home Office's consultation documents published immediately after the 1997 General Election. Restorative justice, it appeared, was an idea whose time had come.[29]

That said, the themes of *Tackling Youth Crime* did not specifically reflect the aims and objectives of restorative justice. Rather they were focused on the offender taking responsibility for their actions, preventing future offending and being tough on youth crime and its causes.[30] The reparation order was proposed in this paper but within the theme of offender's taking responsibility:

---

[25] See eg J Morgan and L Zedner, 'The Victims Charter: A New Deal for Child Victims?' (1992)32 *Howard Journal* 294; L Blom-Cooper, 'Legal Lessons from Cleveland' (1988) *New Law Journal* 492; R Mawby 'The Victimization of Juveniles: A Comparative Study' (1979) 16 *Journal of Research in Crime and Delinquency* 275.

[26] A Victim's Charter was drafted in 1990 as a subsidiary document to the Citizen's Charter. Whilst not offering rights to victims, it is a symbolic statement of the standard of treatment that all victims of crime can expect from the criminal justice system.

[27] See eg, Liberty, *The Rights of Victims: A Manifesto for Better Treatment of Victims in the Criminal Justice System* (London, Liberty, 2003) which calls for legally enforceable rights for victims, the establishment of a Commissioner for Victims and further action to eliminate disrespect and ill-treatment of victims by the criminal justice system.

[28] Home Office, *Speaking Up for Justice: Report of the Interdepartmental Group on the Treatment of Vulnerable or Intimidated Witnesses in the Criminal Justice System* (London, Home Office, 1998).

[29] A Crawford and T Newburn, *Youth Offending and Restorative Justice: Implementing Reform in Youth Justice* (Cullompton, Willan, 2003) p 17.

[30] Home Office, *Tackling Youth Crime: A Consultation Paper* (London, Home Office, 1997) see pp 2–3.

The reparation order will help to show young offenders the harm which they have done to their victims and their communities, and will enable courts to impose punishments which make some amends to the victim.[31]

It was not until the white paper *No More Excuses* was published that the government made a slightly firmer statement of their commitment to the restorative ideal of this new form of justice. Restoration was one of the 'three R's' which formed the thematic approach of the proposed legislation (the others being reintegration and responsibility). However, even here the focus on restorative justice was heavily subsumed under punitive rhetoric and managerial concerns about delay in the youth justice system.[32] Nowhere in these papers is the language of repairing relationships, enhancing community cohesion or resolving conflict that is to be found in the theoretical discourse in this area. It was not until 2003 that the Home Office began to talk in these terms, in a further consultation paper specifically focused on restorative justice. This paper will be discussed more fully below.

Despite their punitive rhetoric, through the Crime and Disorder Act 1998 and Youth Justice and Criminal Evidence Act 1999, New Labour have laid claim to a restorative strategy in enacting provisions aimed at giving victims a greater participation and central role in youth justice proceedings. Some of these provisions, such as the referral order and the reparation order are more fundamentally designed to implement the restorative ideal. Others such as changes to the supervision order, the new warnings procedure and the proposals for changes to the youth court add a restorative 'flavour' to existing retributive sanctions. However, one overriding statement of commitment to the restorative approach can be found in the new statutory 'principal aim' of the youth justice system. Section 37 of the Crime and Disorder Act 1998 establishes a unified and central goal for all youth justice practitioners to aim for, namely that of 'preventing offending by children and young persons'. This may appear very offender oriented, but for the purposes of clarification of this rather vague aim, the Home Office issued guidance which sets out a further six objectives to be pursued in reaching for the overall principal aim. Objective number five is 'encouraging reparation to victims by young offenders'.[33] However, the guidance goes on to stress that reparation 'gives the young person the opportunity to take responsibility for, and control of, his or her behaviour and to make a new start'.

---

[31] *Ibid* p 8.

[32] The only mention of victims in this paper appears at p 1, again under the heading of 'taking responsibility'—see Home Office, *No More Excuses: A New Approach to Tackling Youth Crime in England and Wales* Cm 3809 (London, TSO, 1997).

[33] Home Office, *Youth Justice: The Statutory Principal Aim of Preventing Offending by Children and Young Persons* (London, Home Office, 1998) p 8; also available at <http://www.homeoffice.gov.uk/docs/youjust.html> (9 June 2005).

The Referral Order

The referral order[34] appears to mimic the Children's Hearings system of Scotland, in its informal approach to a negotiated outcome and dialogue between the offender, his family and the victim. New Labour had previously endorsed the Scottish system and proposed its adoption in this country.[35] However, once in power they lacked the courage to practice as they had preached and the referral order process falls rather short of the Scottish system in a number of ways. Similarly, it is proudly boasted as a shining example of the implementation of restorative justice in the government's developing strategy in this area.[36] However, it also falls short of the restorative justice ideal in a number of ways.

Central to the claim that the referral order process is restorative, is the fact that victims may be invited to the youth offending panels' (YOPs) meetings with the offender and his family. The meetings provide an informal and non-criminal arena in which, if handled carefully, a process of mediation can occur and the victim certainly has the opportunity to participate in the proceedings and discuss the offence with the offender. Furthermore, the contractual outcome of the meetings may involve reparation to the victim or the community and the opportunity to arrange further mediation sessions with the victim.[37] Since the victim is not formally represented in the youth court, and is unlikely to be present at all where there is no trial, there is undoubtedly more opportunity for victim participation and an appreciation of the victim's interests in YOP meetings than in the court and the outcomes may well be more restorative than the sentencing powers of the youth court allow.

Notwithstanding these benefits, appraisal of the procedure has been distinctly lukewarm. Caroline Ball notes that the coercive nature of the proceedings renders the restorative potential of them rather defunct. It was indeed noted above that the coercion of retributive justice appears antithetical to notions of restoration. The comparative models which influenced the design of the referral order, she claims, are based on 'voluntary co-operation, not coercion'.[38] The problem in Ball's view lies in the inappropriate adoption of comparative ideas without regard for legal culture and ideology, resulting in:

> [T]he hazards of 'cherry picking' research findings and attractive elements from other systems without recognising that they can only work as a whole, properly resourced, package.[39]

---

[34] The referral order process is discussed further in Ch 6.

[35] Labour Party, *A Safer Britain* a shadow 'white paper' (Labour Party, London, 1990) 21.

[36] Home Office, *Restorative Justice—The Government's Strategy: A Consultation Document on the Government's Strategy on Restorative Justice* (London, Home Office, 2003) p 15.

[37] Section 23(2) Powers of the Criminal Courts (Sentencing) Act (PCC(S)A) 2000.

[38] C Ball, 'The Youth Justice and Criminal Evidence Act 1999 Part I: A Significant Move towards Restorative Justice or a Recipe for Unintended Consequences?' [2000] Crim LR 211 at 215.

[39] *Ibid* at 216.

This cherry picking has resulted in a lack of holism in the approach to restorative justice and an attempt to implement restorative values alongside retributive ones, combining two incompatible approaches.

Evaluations of the referral order in practice reveal a further problem. One of the key findings of the Youth Justice Board funded evaluation of the piloted referral order found a disappointingly low level of victim participation in YOP meetings. Whilst the researchers reported that 'Possibly the most encouraging result to date is the fact that within a year youth offender panels appear to have established themselves as deliberative and participatory forums in which to address a young person's offending behaviour',[40] this forum evidently did not include the victim as often as envisaged to be truly restorative. The final report of the evaluation suggests that this was due to a lack of resourcing (YOT members of the panels had insufficient time to devote to 'the sensitive nature of victim-led work' which requires 'patience, time and skill, following up letters with phone calls, visits and repeat visits'[41]) as well as a lack of identifiable victims and a reluctance on the part of victims to be involved. Those that were involved reported a high level of satisfaction in the process, particularly in the sense that they had their say and were informed of the outcome of the case. The impact on their fear of crime was mixed, some reporting that 'I didn't have any more trouble, I know he won't have a go at me when I see him in the street' while others reported that 'I was worried if I asked for something, he might come back at me later on, I was worried for my wife.'[42] Reducing fear of crime is a key objective of restorative justice and both practitioners and policy-makers acknowledge the sensitivity that needs to be practised in facilitating participation of an already fearful victim in a meeting with their offender. However, Home Office guidance on implementing the referral order is rather negative in its advice on involving victims, focusing on circumstances where victim participation is inappropriate or inadvisable rather than offering advice on the communication skills required to facilitate their involvement.[43] Of course, victim involvement can never be enforced or compulsory, but proper resourcing of the process (including allowing for the process to be slow) and mediation training for the practitioners involved could improve the rate of participation. The practice in England and Wales has prompted Crawford and Newburn to note that:

> The low level of victim attendance suggests that on most occasions youth offender panels are only ever 'mostly restorative' . . . as they involve only two of the three key stakeholders: victim offender and community.[44]

[40] Home Office, *The Introduction of Referral Orders into the Youth Justice System: 2nd Interim Evaluation Report* (London, Home Office, 2001) para 11.

[41] Youth Justice Board, *Referral Orders: Research into the Issues Raised in 'The Introduction of the Referral Orders into the Youth Justice System'* (London, Youth Justice Board, 2003) p 41.

[42] *Ibid* p 42.

[43] Home Office, *The Referral Order: Draft Guidance to Youth Offending Teams* (London, Home Office, 1999) paras 3.23–3.30.

[44] Crawford and Newburn, *Youth Offending* above n 29 at p 241.

What the Home Office have singularly failed to do with the referral order is to divorce it from criminal proceedings and offer it as an alternative in all cases, regardless of offence seriousness or offender persistence. As it stands, it is only possible to implement restorative justice in this context where sentencing guidance for the youth court allows for the referral order route to be taken. For a victim it is rather coincidental whether they are victimised by an offender who is eligible for a referral order, so that the process is dictated by offender-focused criteria, and does not embrace the change of 'lens' suggested by Zehr. Restorative justice, in its true format, needs to involve more than inviting the victim along to participate in a retributive process. The 'spirit' (as opposed to the 'letter') of restorative justice can be more clearly seen in the procedures of other jurisdictions which loosely reflect the referral order but are more widely available outside the retributive criminal process. These will be discussed below.

The Reparation Order

A major part of New Labour's flagship legislation on youth justice was to provide a greater range of orders to the youth court in their efforts to hold the young offender responsible for their behaviour and to tackle the causes of youth crime. The reparation order was a new departure for the youth justice system in providing a penalty which enabled the young persons to make reparation to their victim or the community at large, thereby taking the restorative ideal in England and Wales a step further than merely requiring the offender to pay financial compensation to an identified victim. This new requirement, however, is proposed in *Tackling Youth Crime* as a means of holding a young offender accountable for their actions in a section which borrows heavily from classical criminology and its retributive approach: 'Young people who commit crime must face up to the consequences of their actions for themselves and for others and must take responsibility for their actions.'[45] Yet this particular sanction, as the name suggests, looks towards giving something back to the person who has lost or been harmed by the behaviour, thereby restoring some of the imbalance in the positions of victim and offender (although this assumes that the offender has in some way gained from the behaviour). At best, therefore, the reparation represents a curious mixture of restorative and retributive principles.

The order was enacted in sections 67 and 68 of the Crime and Disorder Act 1998, though it is now consolidated into sections 73 to 75 of the Powers of the Criminal Courts (Sentencing) Act 2000. The reparation order is not a community sentence in the sense that it does not have to be applied within the confines of the sentencing framework established in the Criminal Justice Act 1991, and therefore

---

[45] Home Office, *Tackling Youth Crime* above n 30 at p 2.

justified on the basis that the offence is serious enough to warrant such an order.[46] Rather it takes the form of an order ancillary to a community sentence or other non-custodial order. The order requires the young offender[47] to make any reparation specified by the court to either the victim or the community at large. That reparation may take any form other than the payment of money, which remains the purpose of a compensation order. Indeed, the Home Office envisaged that the distinctive feature of the reparation order was to give the offender the opportunity to repay or repair 'in kind' any harm caused, suggesting that this may involve writing a letter, making an apology, weeding a garden, collecting litter or doing other work to help the community.[48] In making the order, court is reminded to take into account the victim's views[49] and reparation should not be ordered without the explicit consent of any individual victim.[50] Whilst it was originally proposed that consideration of a reparation order would be compulsory in relevant cases, the court having to give reasons for failing to make such an order, ultimately the legislation was phrased in more discretionary terms and the court 'may' order reparation where the relevant criteria are met and it is thought to be appropriate to do so. The reparative idea was further implemented through amendments to the supervision order. Section 71 of the Crime and Disorder Act 1998 inserted the requirement to make reparation to the victim or the community into the list of possible conditions of the supervision order.[51]

The reparation order has, in common with the referral order, a coercive element as it is *ordered*, rather than facilitated, by the court. Again this smacks of mixing the retributive and restorative approaches in a combination that has doubtful utility. The focus of a reparation order is on a reparative *outcome* rather than a restorative *process*. The victim may be given something in return for their suffering but is not involved in the process in any way except for a brief canvassing of their views and consent to the reparation being made. Morris and Gelsthorpe note the contrast between this order and restorative procedures elsewhere:

> This . . . is a very limited version of the kind of involvement which proponents of restorative justice advocate. Victims in restorative justice practices elsewhere have . . . the right to be present and to give their views on appropriate outcomes and, in some jurisdictions have a veto on whether or not the matter should be dealt with through the courts rather than through restorative processes.[52]

[46] Criminal Justice Act 1991 s 6. This requirement is now superseded by a similar requirement in s 148 of the Criminal Justice Act 2003.
[47] The order specifically only applies to young offenders—s 73(1) PCC(S)A.
[48] Home Office, *Tackling Youth Crime* above n 30 at p 8.
[49] Section 73(5) PCC(S)A.
[50] Section 74(1) PCC(S)A.
[51] Now consolidated in Sch 6, cl 3(2)(d) PCC(S)A.
[52] A Morris and L Gelsthorpe, 'Something Old, Something Borrowed, Something Blue, but Something New?: A Comment on the Prospects for Restorative Justice under the Crime and Disorder Act 1998' [2000] Crim LR 18 at 28.

Far from offering an 'alternative' process to formal court proceedings, the reparation order simply provides a hint of the reparative in an otherwise retributive system.

Reprimands and Warnings

The statutory enactment of a diversion system in the Crime and Disorder Act 1998 provided a further opportunity for the development of restorative practices. Whilst the reprimand for first time, minor offenders offered no more than the old caution in diverting offenders away from court, the new statutory warning allowed for diversion to a rehabilitative form of intervention, reminiscent of the old 'caution plus'. A warning issued by a police officer is followed by referral to the Youth Offending Team(YOT) for assessment of the potential appropriateness of further action. The form of the further action is a matter for the professional discretion of the YOT, but feasibly may include offering the offender and the victim the chance to meet in mediation proceedings or offering the offender the opportunity to make reparation.[53] Under the more informal 'caution plus' procedure, the Thames Valley police had developed a pioneering mediation programme for young offenders in the 1980s. This involved referring all offenders who had been cautioned to a mediation process. Where appropriate the police would chair face-to-face meetings between the offender and victim for discussion of the offence and its consequences. The process was modelled on the Australian family group conferencing arrangements and was inspired by Braithwaite's vision of restorative justice.[54] The 'plus' element of the statutory warning procedure is run by the YOT, but where arrangements for these conferences exist locally there is no reason why they cannot form an integral part of the warning procedure. The problem remains, however, that the new statutory diversion system is now firmly embedded into a rigid framework for processing offenders and is much less flexible and far more retributive than its more informal predecessor.[55] Moreover any diversion process 'operates at the margins of the criminal justice system rather than as integral to it since it deals with offenders involved in the relatively low level offending which the police and others believe does not require to be dealt with in court'. Rather than providing an alternative to criminal justice procedures, therefore, this form of restorative justice, where it is used, tinkers at the margins of the process and does not address the potential of the restorative approach as a radical new departure for youth justice.

---

[53] See further J Dignan, 'The Crime and Disorder Act and the Prospects for Restorative Justice' [1999] Crim LR 48.

[54] See further R Young and B Goold, 'Restorative Police Cautioning in Aylesbury: From Degrading to Reintegrative Shaming Ceremonies?' [1999] Crim LR 126,

[55] See further Ch 5.

The Youth Justice Board has provided extensive funding[56] for restorative projects to be used in relation to both the reparation order and the warnings procedure. The projects included family group conferencing, mediation meetings, reparation to the victim and to the community and victim awareness training for offenders. The evaluation of these projects acknowledges that only the family group conferencing was truly restorative (in that it most closely resembled restorative justice theory) and yet this was the least commonly provided programme, community reparation accounting for 36 per cent of the projects, victim awareness 21 per cent, mediation 13 per cent, reparation to the victim 19 per cent and an apology 40 per cent.[57] Further projects where the offender actually met the victim, as opposed to merely offering reparation or a written apology, enjoyed lower reconviction rates after 12 months (41.6 per cent compared with 42.1 per cent for victim awareness projects and 47.3 per cent for community reparation schemes).[58]

Overall the evaluation was positive in terms of successful completion of the requirements by the offender, reconviction rates which were slightly lower than for non-restorative interventions and in terms of the victim's satisfaction with the process. However, these projects suffered from the same problem as referral orders with a disappointing level of participation by the victim in schemes where their presence was required. While 53 per cent of victims participated to some extent, in many cases this involved little more than giving consent to their views on the offence being communicated to the offender by a police officer or YOT worker. Only a minority of them met the offender in some form of mediation. This was attributed to the ambiguity of the legislation governing these projects as well as a lack of expertise in handling communication with the victim and a lack of time, particularly in the context of short-term court orders, to properly facilitate meetings. This latter factor particularly highlights the problems associated with combining a just deserts, retributive approach to sentencing, with its requirement of proportionality, with a restorative justice approach that often cannot work within the restrictive confines of a proportionate sentence.

Comparative Perspectives

Restorative justice practices were developed in other jurisdictions much earlier than in England and Wales. Indeed, international practice in this area has informed the development of practices and strategies in this country. Though

---

[56] £13.3 million was spent developing 46 projects nationwide between 1998 and 2004—see further A Wilcox and C Hoyle, *Restorative Justice Projects: The National Evaluation of the Youth Justice Board's Restorative Justice Projects* (London, Youth Justice Board, 2004).
[57] *Ibid* p 20.
[58] *Ibid* p 21.

most often associated with the use of family group conferences (FGCs) in Australia and New Zealand, restorative practice has taken a variety of forms. In some jurisdictions diversion from formal court processes, usually at the pre-trial stage, may involve diversion to a mediation or reparation scheme informed by this theoretical model. The Thames Valley mediation process, developed as an element of caution plus in the 1980s, was modelled on similar practices in Australia, particularly the police diversion programme initiated in Wagga Wagga in New South Wales.[59] Elsewhere, restorative justice may involve circle sentencing, a practice developed in Canada amongst First Nation people. The circle consists of the parties to a dispute and their various social supporters, led by a facilitator or circle 'keeper'. Whilst the purpose of the circle is to discuss the offending behaviour, its consequences and a way forward to reparative and reintegrative action, these circles differ from conferences or other mediation procedures in that they are more ritualistic, perhaps, for example, involving a 'talking stick' or other ritual practices to ensure the circle is emotionally inclusive and not broken. The outcome of such circles aims not just to restore the particular harm caused by a single incident, but also to address more structural conflicts within a community.[60] The Community Peace Programme in South Africa provides a similar example of a peace building and problem resolution approach to community issues, including victimisation.[61] Two particular examples will be discussed here to illustrate attempts to place restorative justice fully in the criminal justice agenda.

Family Group Conferencing in New Zealand

By the early 1980s, criminal policy makers in New Zealand faced a growing dissatisfaction with traditional, adversarial forms of youth justice. Not only were existing practices seen as ineffective in reducing youth crime, but there was increasing concern at the marginalisation of certain groups of young people through these practices, in particular Maori youth. This concern was heightened by the need, under the Treaty of Waitangi, to ensure the Maori community both self-determination and inclusion in all aspects of New Zealand social policy. A process of research and consultation was begun to find an alternative which avoided discrimination against marginalised groups, worked towards greater inclusion of Maori culture and values in responding to crime and which avoided

---

[59] See further D Moore and T O'Connell, 'Family Conferencing in Wagga Wagga: A Communitarian Model of Justice' in C Alder and J Wundersitz (eds) *Family Conferencing and Juvenile Justice: The Way Forward or Misplaced Optimism?* (Canberra, Australian Institute of Criminology, 1994).

[60] See further B Stuart, 'Circle Sentencing: Turning Swords into Ploughshares' in B Galway and J Hudson (eds) *Restorative Justice: International Perspectives* (Monesy, NY, Criminal Justice Press, 1996).

[61] See further Crawford and Newburn, *Youth Offending* above n 29 at pp 35–36.

the growing paternalism of the state and its professionals which had been a feature of welfare-based legislation.[62] Subsequent legislation was passed in 1989, implementing a restorative ideal but not before an extensive period of public discussion, consultation, research and careful drafting over a period of no less than five years. The Children, Young Persons and Their Families Act 1989 gave statutory form to the conferencing procedure, focusing emphatically on the family:

> It placed primary responsibility with extended families for making decisions about what was to be done with their children and young people who had come to official notice. Families were to have the assistance of the police . . . the child protection service . . . and any others the family wished to be present at the meeting. Family decisions were to be made using a process not previously encountered in statute called the family group conference.[63]

The Act also seeks to achieve 'responsible reconciliation':

> [A] positive, growing process where the strength is derived from the interaction of victim, offender and family in a supportive environment. It is a 'responsible' process in that those most directly affected take responsibility for what has happened and for what is to happen.[64]

The Act provides for a routine diversion from court, as all young people charged with an offence are automatically referred to a family group conference, unless the offence is extremely serious and the FGC procedure is thought to be inappropriate. Around 95 per cent of all cases are, however, referred. The offender and his family supporters attend the conference, and the victim and their supporters are invited to attend. The meetings are held in private without officials present and the negotiated outcomes and decisions made in the conference are only later discussed with a Youth Justice Co-ordinator, after agreement has been reached between the parties. It is then their task to liaise with the prosecuting authorities to discuss non-prosecution and an acceptance of the agreement for future action agreed between the parties. If no agreement is reached in the conference, the matter will be referred to the youth court, although the tenets of the discussion in the conference will be made available to the court so that they are aware of what alternatives were considered. As a statutory procedure, FGCs are governed by the principles enshrined in the legislation. These include proportionality, to ensure the agreed intervention is not unduly severe, determinacy and specificity, and equality of treatment as far as possible between classes of offence. The professionals in this system offer a monitoring role to ensure these principles are upheld, without

---

[62] See further M Doolan, 'Youth Justice: Legislation and Practice' in B Brown and F McElrea (eds) *The Youth Court in New Zealand: A New Model of Justice* (Auckland, Legal Research Foundation, 1993).

[63] I Hassall, 'Origin and Development of Family Group Conferences' in J Hudson *et al* (eds) *Family Group Conferences: Perspectives on Policy & Practice* (Leichhardt, NSW, The Federation Press, 1996) p 18.

[64] F McElrea, 'A New Model of Justice' in B Brown and F McElrea (eds) above n 62 at pp 13–14.

controlling or taking over the conference proceedings themselves. The Act also specifically asserts a commitment to maximum diversion and the avoidance of formal intervention where possible, and minimalism in response to petty and minor offending.

Maxwell and Morris, among others, have extensively evaluated the operation of FGCs in practice.[65] It is difficult to measure the success of restorative justice practices using criteria usually reserved for more retributive responses, since the two approaches conflict in their aims and objectives. However, their research has prompted a generally positive regard for the process; the extent of diversion of young people from the court has substantially increased, without evidence of undue net-widening and the outcomes of the conferences provided challenging and 'active' intervention for young people which appropriately held them responsible for their behaviour. Levels of participation by members of offenders' families is high and they recorded high levels of satisfaction with the process.[66] Levels of victim participation were not as high as they could have been, and, despite this often being a result of poor social work practice (not being invited in good time to attend or being given insufficient information and guidance on attendance), resulted in Maxwell and Morris commenting that 'Overall, as a system of restorative justice, family group conferences are not always successful.'[67] A majority of victims who did participate were pleased with the process: 'The meeting with the offender was described as a cathartic experience: negative feelings about the offence and the offender could be released.'[68] The opportunity to participate in determining the outcome of their case was also welcomed. There were, however a minority who were less impressed, particularly where they were unhappy with the outcome of the meeting, where the offender's remorse was not felt to be genuine,[69] or where they were not kept informed of events after the meeting.

A further problem with this form of restorative practice, was the tendency of the procedure to be coercive, to fail to adequately respond to the welfare needs of the young people involved, and to fail to prevent social exclusion:

> [A]lthough family group conferences could transcend tokenism and embody a Maori process, they often failed to respond to the spirit of Maori or to enable outcomes to be reached which were in accord with Maori philosophies and values.[70]

---

[65] See, eg, A Morris and G Maxwell, 'Juvenile Justice in New Zealand: A New Paradigm?' (1993) 26 *Australian and New Zealand Journal of Criminology* 72.

[66] G Maxwell and A Morris, 'Research on Family Group Conferences with Young Offenders in New Zealand' in J Hudson *et al* (eds) *Family Group Conferences: Perspectives on Policy & Practice* (Leichhardt, NSW, The Federation Press, 1996).

[67] *Ibid* p 100.

[68] *Ibid*.

[69] A problem with reparation proceedings also identified in England in relation to restorative diversion. See G Davis, J Boucherat and D Watson, 'Reparation in the Service of Diversion: The Subordination of a Good Idea' (1988) 27 *Howard Journal* 127.

[70] Maxwell and Morris, 'Research on Family Group Conferences' above n 66 at p 95.

In some cases responses were harsh, culturally specific and ineffective in referring young people to interventions and services required to prevent further offending. Indeed, in relation to Australian FGCs, Blagg argues that the entire process of holding meetings, in locations specified by professionals and run in a manner akin to other 'conferences', while based on the Aboriginal notion of reconciliation, are inappropriate for a cultural group whose lifestyle is highly transient. The meetings represent a Westernised appropriation of a cultural tradition which is then re-imposed on that cultural group:

> They are not in the *marae* or long houses or *wigwams* waiting to have meetings. Aboriginal ceremony involves an emphasis not on place as much as on *movement*, the ritual passages along the 'song lines' and dreaming tracks, replenishing their links with kin groups, sacred sites and 'country' . . . Processes intended to involve Australia's aboriginal people in the criminal justice system must go in train with processes designed to free them from its destructive devices.[71]

This is unlikely, in Blagg's view, to improve the prospects for reconciliation of these young people in their communities. Cunneen and White also note discriminatory practices and a lack of referrals to a discretionary form of conferencing in Australia.[72] In this sense the marginalized groups of youths that the restorative ideal seeks to reintegrate appear to be experiencing further exclusion.

The Youth Diversion Project in the Republic of Ireland

Policy makers in the Republic of Ireland have also undergone a process of re-thinking their approach to youth crime and were, themselves, influenced by the New Zealand and Australian experiences in making their choices. A similarly long period of consultation and discussion has produced a root and branch re-design of the youth justice system for the first time since the Children Act 1908, which shaped the establishment of a separate justice system for juveniles in Ireland as well as in England and Wales. A draft Children Bill was presented to Parliament in 1996, but policy makers were unhappy with it and continued to give careful thought to its terms, while examining the practices of overseas jurisdictions for a number of years, until the Children Act 2001 was finally enacted.

The Act, heralded as 'enlightened, enduring and forward thinking',[73] is founded on a number of principles including minimal criminalisation of children, the use of welfare and non-criminal alternatives where possible, and restorative justice as

---

[71] H Blagg, 'A Just Measure of Shame? Aboriginal Youth and Conferencing in Australia' (1997) 37 *British Journal of Criminology* 481at 497.

[72] Cunneen and White above n 1 at p 172.

[73] Irish Minister for Justice, Mr O'Donoghue, commenting during the second reading of the Bill: Dáil Éireann Debates vol 517 cols 32–33 (1999).

the underlying rationale for a comprehensive diversion programme. Policy makers were mindful not to directly transplant the New Zealand experience into a system whose legal and cultural heritage was different in many ways. However, they were keen to embrace the notions of participation by offenders, families and victims in the decision-making process, the informality of conference proceedings compared with the youth court and the possibilities this offers for providing welfare services to offenders and their families without the coercion of a court order. The Act provides two forms of conferencing, Family Welfare Conferences for non-offending children with identified welfare needs, and a diversion programme for young offenders, a statutory form of a diversion practice that had been developed in Ireland by the Garda during the 1990s.

The diversion programme is available to all young people (aged between 12—the new minimum age of criminal responsibility after 2001—and 18) who commit offences and who 'accept responsibility for [their] criminal behaviour.'[74] The statutory criteria set out in section 23 of the Children Act, however, emphasise that this acceptance of responsibility may only be evident after the young person has consulted with their family and possibly a lawyer, thereby seeking to avoid allegations that the Garda coerce offenders into accepting guilt for the purposes of diversion. The young person must consent to a caution being given by the Garda[75] before referral to a conference takes place. The referral is made to a juvenile liaison officer who must prepare a report for the Director of the Programme to ascertain whether the case is appropriate for a conference or whether no further action should be taken. In this way there is a gate keeping process to minimise net-widening. If the Director is satisfied that it is in the best interests of the child and not inconsistent with the interests of society and the victim (whose views must be sought) then the caution may be given and a conference arranged. The caution is informal and given by a Garda officer, in the presence of the victim where they choose to attend, and this can provide an opportunity for informal mediation and the offer of an oral apology to the victim.[76]

The functions of the conference are set out in section 29 of the legislation:

(a) to bring together the child in respect of whom the conference is being held, his or her parents or guardian, such other family members, relatives and other persons as appropriate and the facilitator with a view to

    (i) establishing why the child became involved in the behaviour that gave rise to his or her admission to the Programme,

---

[74] Children Act 2001 s 18.

[75] Section 23(c) specifies, however, that refusal to consent to a caution, where the child is placed under undue pressure not to consent by their parent or another person, may not negate referral to a conference.

[76] Children Act 2001 s 26.

(ii) discussing how the parents or guardian, family members, relatives or any other person could help prevent the child from becoming involved in further such behaviour, and

(iii) where appropriate, reviewing the child's behaviour since his admission to the Programme;

(b) as appropriate . . . to mediate between the child and the victim;

(c) to formulate an action plan for the child; and

(d) to uphold the concerns of the victim and have due regard to his or her interests.

The emphasis on the family is similar to that found in New Zealand, and in these conferences, as opposed to English referral orders, the extended family and other persons with close ties to the family can take part in developing a strategy to prevent further offending. The victim may also bring supporters from their family or other social networks, and the meeting may be attended by a relevant professional such as a health worker, school representative or (strangely) a Garda officer. Any action plan must be agreed unanimously by all parties at the meeting, although the same contractual symbolism is applied to this plan as to the referral order. However, here all parties participate in the agreement and therefore the views of the victim can be more than merely canvassed. Failure to reach an agreement does not invalidate the proceedings of the conference and does not result in referral to the youth court. Admission to the Programme is a form of non-prosecution, no criminal conviction results and the proceedings are entirely confidential.

The Programme began its operation on May 2002, since when 64 Programmes have been established throughout the Republic of Ireland, with a government investment of over €5 million. The Programmes are subject to ongoing evaluation, little of which has been published to date. In their previous non-statutory form, some Garda diversion projects were evaluated. Those were criticised for net-widening and drawing young people 'at risk' of offending into the margins of the criminal process, as well as for an ad hoc organisation and lack of legitimacy.[77] These issues have been addressed in the legislation and, once evaluated, it will be possible to ascertain the extent to which these problems persist and whether the Irish practice shares the difficulties identified in New Zealand.

Discussion

Attempts to put restorative justice ideals into practice, both in England and Wales and in other jurisdictions have been subject to criticism and allegations of failure.

---

[77] M Bowden and L Higgins, *The Impact and Effectiveness of Garda Special Projects: Final Report* (Dublin, Children's Research Centre, 2000).

The enthusiasm for restorative practices even in jurisdictions like Australia is beginning to wane as they are subject to both ideological and pragmatic criticism.[78] In England and Wales, the critique of restorative justice has been largely focused on the failure of the government's strategy and commitment to the ideal, but the supposition has largely been that the ideal, if implemented properly is ideologically sound. There are however, fundamental difficulties with importing restorative notions into the youth justice system. As the welfare/justice debate has run its course and policy makers and commentators search for a viable alternative approach in the philosophical vacuum that has been created, there is a danger in pursuing this particular ideal, without full appreciation of its difficulties, its cultural heritage and its potential to exacerbate the perception of young offenders as 'devils'.

Conflicting Principles

The discussion of restorative justice in England and Wales above, demonstrates a key problem in the government's strategy; that is their attempt to insert restorative aims into an inherently retributive and increasingly punitive youth justice system. Some consider this to be a mission doomed to failure, which 'so perverts [restorative justice's] underlying rationale as to strip it of much of its original appeal'.[79] It is further argued here that the half-hearted attempt at 'cherry-picking'[80] from various penal theories is indicative of the government's strategy not only failing to take a holistic approach to alternatives, but, more importantly, a deliberate misrepresentation of the true meaning of restorative justice. New Labour have adopted their own definition of this conceptual approach, which reflects little in the theoretical discourse set out above. Their 2003 consultation paper justifies their restorative strategy in these terms:

> The government is committed to placing victims' needs at the centre of the Criminal Justice System. We also want a system that encourages responsibility, so that offenders face up to what they've done and make amends. And we want the wider community to be involved in finding positive solutions to crime and anti-social behaviour . . . Restorative justice is not a soft option. Many offenders find it hard to face up to the real impact of their crime. For victims, restorative justice may not be about forgiveness, but a desire to tell the offender how the crime has affected them and their family, or getting information that only the offender can give.[81]

Restorative justice, it appears, can only be politically acceptable if it is tough. The tone of this statement is punitive and confrontational, rather than reparative and

---

[78] See, eg, Cunneen and White above n 1 at pp 375–83; Blagg, above n 71.
[79] L Zedner, 'Reparation and Retribution: Are they Reconcilable?' (1994) 57 MLR 228 at 250.
[80] Ball above n 38.
[81] Home Office, *Restorative Justice—The Government's Strategy* above n 36 at pp 4–5.

reintegrative. Further, the use of capital letters in the first sentence denotes the central position of a *criminal justice* system in which restorative justice may play some role alongside other goals and values. Whilst restorative justice elsewhere aims to shift the balance of power in the response to crime, giving the victim a greater share of that power, it is the state's role that subsides so that, in Christie's vision, the offender and victim take a central position in their own conflict. In England and Wales the victim's more central role appears to be at the expense of the offender's position and greater awareness and sensitivity to the victim's inter-ests becomes another stick with which to beat offenders. Where a victim's needs dictate the nature of the response to the offending behaviour, welfare concerns about the young person's needs and interests are marginalised.

Many supporters of restorative justice claim that it can only work where it is entirely divorced from retributive principles and preferably from any criminalised procedure. Walgrave argues that the values central to a retributive system will inherently be compromised by a restorative approach. The government's attempts to employ aspects of both systems produces a 'cocktail' which is:

> [A] miscellaneous profusion, an odd assortment of good intentions, opportunism and clear visions. It is an uncontrolled growth which may at times conflict with fundamental principles which govern the function of justice in a democratic state. Especially two qualities of correct legal procedure are threatened: due process and proportionality.[82]

The pursuit of meretricious new ideas without careful consideration of their ide-ological roots produces politically fashionable criminal policy which, in the long term, may lack efficacy:

> Governments do not let themselves be guided by scientific options or data. Governments use criminology, like a menu from which they choose à la carte what fits best into their political and electoral options . . . They pay lip-service to criminological options, like restorative justice, without really implementing the concepts behind the words.[83]

Ethnocentricity

This is not only a problem of prioritising political expediency over meaningful attempts to reduce crime, but it also suggests a degree of ethnocentricity on the part of governments in transplanting comparative ideas into the furrowed ground of Western penal systems with an expectation that not only will they grow in such retributive soil, but that they will flourish in this superior environment. Blagg

---

[82] L Walgrave, 'Restorative Juvenile Justice: A Way to Restore Justice in Western European Systems?' in S Asquith (ed) *Children and Young People in Conflict with the Law* (London, Jessica Kingsley, 1996) p 189.

[83] L Walgrave, 'Criminology, Criminal Policy and Democracy' (1998/99) *Criminal Justice Matters* Winter, 23–4.

accuses Australian governments of what he calls 'orientalism' in respect of borrowing the conferencing approach from Maori culture:

> It imposes a westernized interpretation of Maori justice reform, denuding the process of its history, context and internal structures of meaning and 'representing' it as simply regional, albeit exotic, variation on a universal theme . . . [they] have likewise attempted to identify globally applicable values, structures and norms.[84]

An innate sense that retributive justice is the superior and universally acclaimed paradigm, prevents governments from adopting the 'different lens' though which to view the problem of crime that Zehr claims is necessary for restorative justice to be successful.[85]

Without an unflinching commitment to such a different lens, the government in England and Wales have been unable to successfully pursue the strategy that they proudly propose in their consultation paper. It is not only an unshaken belief in retributivism that dilutes this commitment, but also their attraction to its managerial and populist merits:

> When used as diversion from court, as it is in a number of other countries, restorative justice frees up court time for cases that really need it, such as serious and complex cases, or those where the accused pleads not guilty. These cases can proceed faster, giving more effective administration of justice.[86]

Restorative justice is perceived not only as cheaper and faster than court proceedings, but, New Labour claim, it inspires greater confidence in the criminal justice system especially where it involves a shaming process for the offender which is more visible to the victim and the wider community.[87] Where restorative procedures aim to do little more than further label and stigmatise offenders, thereby enhancing their social alienation, it is little wonder that practical experience demonstrates that victims are reluctant to participate in these procedures and that they may increase their fears of crime. A functional rather than philosophical perception of the restorative ideal is therefore counter-productive.

Social Exclusion

Restorative justice may be counter-productive in another sense. Theorists have argued that it involves the perception of crime in relational terms, focusing on the problem as arising from tensions in social relationships. Far more than merely repairing the damage caused by the offending behaviour or compensating for loss, restorative justice seeks to repair broken relationships and enhance social

---

[84] Blagg above n 71 at p 484.
[85] Zehr, *Changing Lens* above n 16.
[86] Home Office, *Restorative Justice—The Government's Strategy* above n 36 at p 10.
[87] *Ibid* p 5.

cohesion. Braithwaite insists that it is, or should be, a socially inclusive practice which reintegrates the offender in to the community and should never involve shaming which socially excludes. In this way the practice involves the entire community taking responsibility for all its citizens, treating them with equal respect and concern. It is argued, however, that this fails to take account of the process of modernity and the inherent inequalities that exist in communities that render any attempt to restore equality and balance between its members bound to fail. Carlen[88] argues the process may even exacerbate the social deprivation and exclusion faced by young people when applied to youth crime. Restorative justice needs to be implemented in the setting of a strongly cohesive community which is both willing and able to accept offending members back into its fold. The idealised goal is to *restore* equality between citizens of this community. If that equality did not exist in the first place then restorative justice faces an enormous challenge to create it, let alone restore it. Further, it is argued that reintegration into a community that is inherently fragmented and in which youth are an increasingly disenfranchised and marginalised social group poses even greater challenges.

In 1977 Christie recognised stumbling blocks or 'rolling stones' which mitigated against the implementation of his restorative vision. These included 'a lack of neighbourhoods':

> Much of our trouble stems from killed neighbourhoods or killed local communities. How can we then thrust towards neighbourhoods a task that presupposes they are highly alive?[89]

Carlen similarly argues that post-industrial societies, in which youth unemployment, educational under-achievement and homelessness are rife, provides an environment in which it is not 'feasible' to think in terms of *restoring* equality:

> The fundamental problem of feasibility behind the notion of restorative justice is the implicit assumption that, prior to the offence, the needs and assets for the victim and offender are usually in a relation of symmetry to each other and that, therefore, the restorative process can once more bring them into balance. Not so. Many young offenders are not in a position to restore *anything* to their victims, and, in such cases, attractive as it may be to yearn for a system of justice which satisfies the 'just deserts' of victim and offender in one single process, reparation for the victim will have to remain a state obligation.[90]

The impotence of a process of restorative *justice*, responding to individual incidences of harmful behaviour, can do little to create, rather than restore, social equality. For this, Carlen argues, we need a more 'holistic' approach to crime which incorporates a wider social intervention to alleviate the divisive and exclusionary effects of modernity.

---

[88] Carlen, 'Youth Justice?' above n 8.
[89] Christie, 'Conflicts as Property' above n 10 at p 12.
[90] Carlen, 'Youth Justice?' above n 8 at p 73.

Even if restoration of equality were possible, modern communities lack the cohesive structure and collective motivation to reintegrate young offenders. Cunneen and White stress that the pre-requisites for a restorative justice policy are solidarity within a society to include to socially weak members and community empowerment to actively enhance 'the welfare and prospects of collectivities, of which individuals are integral members.'[91] Again Carlen refutes the feasibility of this in the late twentieth century England and Wales where social and economic policy have consistently marginalised youth as a social group. Governments have

> produced 'high anxiety' societies, wherein young people are too often being placed under surveillance as 'threats', rather than being cherished as 'assets'; and where 'uncertainty', rather than being seen as an inevitable part of human existence, is wielded as a sinister political weapon to keep citizens in awe of the market.[92]

Not only are communities fearful and suspicious of youth, but they are increasingly being encouraged to actively police those who epitomise and project their fears and intolerance. Far from the active participation in reintegration that Cunneen and White describe above, communities in England and Wales are encouraged to actively participate in the state's strategy to exclude, in a process that Garland describes as 'responsibilization'.[93] This can be most clearly seen in the strategy to combat anti-social behaviour, discussed in Chapter 10, but is also evident in the government's restorative justice strategy:

> Restorative justice . . . gives rights to victims and challenges offenders, communities and victims to take part in building a better future. And, by helping citizens to resolve conflicts between themselves it forms a key part of this government's emphasis on civil renewal, empowering ordinary people to tackle problems at a local level.[94]

Both Braithwaite and Walgrave argue that an adequately cohesive society, in which young people are as much stakeholders as anyone else, is possible to envisage. For Braithwaite, it is already a reality, as he claims that complex urban societies are founded on a series of interdependencies, bonds and relationships which render them even more cohesive than the traditional village communities from which the restorative ideal was borrowed:

> The contemporary city dweller may have a set of colleagues at work, in her trade union, among members of his golf club, among drinking associates whom he meets at the same pub, among members of a professional association, the parents and citizens' committee for her daughter's school, not to mention a geographically extended family.[95]

---

[91] Cunneen and White, *Juvenile Justice* above n 1 at p 379.
[92] Carlen, 'Youth Justice?' above n 8 at p 65.
[93] D Garland, 'The Limits of the Sovereign State: Strategies of Crime Control in Contemporary Society' (1996) 36 *British Journal of Criminology* 445.
[94] Home Office, *Restorative Justice—The Government's Strategy* above n 36 at p 9.
[95] J Braithwaite, 'Shame and Modernity' (1993) 33 *British Journal of Criminology* 1 at 13.

While Braithwaite glibly suggests these social networks 'have spread throughout the class structure', what he describes here is a rather utopian, middle-class, urban community of adults and presupposes inclusion in these various clubs and associations. The evidence presented in Chapter 4 suggests that young people who offend rarely belong to these sorts of networks; they are more likely to be members of dysfunctional or unattached families, educationally disaffected and, when old enough, unemployed. For Walgrave, the interdependent community is still a vision, but one which he believes is achievable given 'a change in social ethics and a different ideology of society. That means a society governed with the aims of individual and collective emancipation, in which autonomy and solidarity are not seen as diametrically opposed, but as mutually reinforcing principles.'[96]

The Role of the State

Perhaps then, these pragmatic issues can be overridden, though this is easier said than done, and is perhaps more than a restorative justice system can achieve. Christie suggests it only requires some imagination and courage to radically alter our perceptions of what we can achieve through our response to crime.[97] However, there are more ideological concerns with restorative justice which question whether, as a model, it provides a suitable paradigm. Ashworth, for example, denies that it is appropriate or advisable to marginalise the role of the state in conflicts involving criminal behaviour. Whilst not averse to arguments calling for greater respect and more sensitive treatment of victims, for Ashworth the ideological danger of restorative justice is that it removes the function of the state as guardian of human rights, protecting the offender from arbitrary 'justice'. The state has responsibilities for ensuring that our response to crime avoids vengeance and unethical or inconsistent practices.

> The State can and should do this in a way that shows respect for the offender as a rational citizen (e.g. by conforming to human rights) and which adopts a fair and consistent approach to the task . . . The victim's view should no more be relevant to this than the personal view of any other individual. The rule of law, embodied in the Convention and other human rights documents, requires decisions to be taken by an independent and impartial tribunal according to settled rules announced beforehand . . . it would be an abdication of the State's responsibility to allow such individual feelings to influence the sentence.[98]

---

[96] L Walgrave, 'Restorative Justice for Juveniles: Just a Technique or a Fully Fledged Alternative?' (1995) 34 *Howard Journal* 228 at 245.
[97] Christie, *Limits to Pain* above n 22 at p 95.
[98] A Ashworth and M Redmayne, *The Criminal Process* 3rd edn (Oxford, Oxford University Press, 2005) p 50.

Christie had argued that it is this assertion of responsibility that has caused conflicts to be 'stolen' from the parties who rightfully own them in the first place. In his view there are 'too many professionals' working within the State's apparatus for controlling crime and this has proliferated the theft of conflicts to serve the interests of those professionals, albeit justified for 'honourable reasons . . . to do with the state's need for conflict reduction and certainly also its wishes for the protection of the victim'.[99] Maxwell and Morris further claim that, given state involvement in restorative justice practices in New Zealand, their responsibility is not abrogated and that their interests are served by the professionals representing them in implementing the ideal. They suggest that this may not be a good thing, since family group conferencing may be seen as an extension of state social control 'making families instruments of the state in this task.'[100] They nevertheless assert that the restorative approach, even with state involvement, gives participants a greater voice than retributive systems and the outcomes are therefore more satisfactory for their consultative nature.

It is a difficult dilemma. There is no doubt that human rights concerns are of increasing importance in protecting the offender's interests and liberties from abuse by the state and the victim, and Ashworth's arguments reveal the potential that individualised justice has to produce unjust, inequitable and uncontrolled outcomes. These arguments represent different perspectives on controlling outcomes and who is being protected from whom. Ashworth's human rights view seeks to control those outcomes to protect the offender from the state and the victim, whereas the restorative justice model seeks to control outcomes to protect the offender and the victim from the state. It is a subtle shift in partnerships in the triumvirate of parties concerned with reducing crime. For Carlen, however, criminal justice policy needs to take a step away from this triumvirate and the balance of power within it and to focus instead on a more constructive, or 'holistic' approach to alleviating the causes of criminal behaviour which have arisen from the failure of wider social and economic policy to prevent social injustice:

> In any fully holistic sentencing programme, notions of censure and regulatory social intervention should be separated from those of incapacitative punishment and reparation, and the ideal in cases involving young people would be to redress the wrong done to the crime victim and to *address* any adverse social circumstances, such as unemployment or homelessness, which might make the offender more crime or arrest-prone in the future.[101]

It is argued here and throughout this book, that a holistic policy for tackling criminal behaviour needs to be a social policy devoid of notions of offending and definitions of crime, which serve only to label young people as 'devils' or 'angels'.

---

[99] Christie, 'Conflicts as Property' above n 10 at pp 3–4.
[100] Maxwell and Morris, 'Research on Family Group Conferences' above n 66 at p 94.
[101] Carlen, 'Youth Justice?' above n 8 at p 76.

This falls outside the remit of the criminal justice system. Restorative justice may enable us to embark on such a path, if properly implemented. What is clear is that retributive systems of punishment fail to do this and restorative justice at last provides a more constructive move away from that. However, in Chapter 10 I discuss how we may take a further step on this path, as we look to develop alternative approaches which are less blinded by the criminal label, and guided by perceptions of social need.

9

Parents, Schools and Youth Crime

Introduction

Parental responsibility can be considered from two different perspectives. Policy makers have recognised the aetiological link between young people's criminal behaviour and their family and educational situations, and youth justice policy in the last two decades has targeted these areas in seeking to prevent crime. Legislation on youth justice will inevitably contain provisions aimed at ensuring that the child attends school and that the parents properly supervise and control a child out of school hours. The emphasis in this area of policy tends to be forced social control and punitive sanctions where youth crime provides evidence that such social control has failed. The implicit message from policy makers is that schools and parents must share the responsibility for youth crime where they have failed in their respective roles, and the punishment of parents reflects the condemnation that accompanies the punishment of their children. The criminal justice system carries the responsibility of reinforcing standards of acceptable behaviour not only by young people but by their parents as well. Indeed the principal aim[1] of the youth justice system incorporates 'reinforcing parental responsibility' as a key objective to be pursued in preventing offending by young people.[2]

However, alternatively the school, the family and other community networks may be seen as informal discipline networks capable of fulfilling the role of a 'justice system' themselves. Rutherford's developmental model of youth justice[3] takes the latter approach and recognises the crime prevention potential of such informal networks, provided they are enabled to 'hold on' to their own young people in trouble. The developmental approach places such central importance on these informal discipline networks that intervention by the criminal justice system

---

[1] Section 37 Crime and Disorder Act 1998.

[2] Home Office, *Youth Justice: The Statutory Principal Aim of Preventing Offending by Children and Young People* (London, Home Office, 1998) p. 8; also available at <http://www.homeoffice.gov.uk/docs/youjust.html> (9 June 2005).

[3] A Rutherford, *Growing Out of Crime: The New Era* (Waterside Press, Winchester, 2002) pp 29–30. This model is discussed further in Ch 3 of this book.

ideally becomes the exception rather than the rule. The model's criminological foundation draws from evidence that most young people grow out of their offending behaviour and therefore the consequential crime prevention approach would be to encourage the growing-up process and ease the transition between childhood and adulthood, particularly during the adolescent years. The consequent policy approach to youth crime therefore involves minimal intervention by the criminal justice authorities, whose *modus operandi*, it is claimed, inevitably hinders that growing-up process. Indeed, such is the abolitionist stance of proponents of this approach that, ironically, it may be the criminal process itself which exacerbates youth crime in its very attempt to prevent it. Not only does a criminal conviction imposed on a young person in this transitional stage hinder the development of key desistance criteria[4] but in weakening the influence of the informal networks[5] or even separating the young person from them altogether, reduces the level of support for young people necessary in their healthy and expeditious growing-up process. Criminal justice procedures, whether based on punitive or welfare ideals, tend to interfere in the family's and the school's capacity to support, and incarcerative or other residential responses to crime may irreparably damage the essential relationships between the young person and these networks and thus exacerbate youth crime.

The focus of a youth crime prevention policy under this model, therefore, is to relinquish the crime prevention role to these networks and to encourage the support required for the developmental process:

> The . . . emphasis implied by the developmental approach seeks to strengthen intervention by homes and schools to enable these institutions to deal directly with the problem, to hold on to young people and, thereby, to avoid or limit formal intervention.[6]

In practice this means formal criminal justice intervention should avoid separation of the young person from their home or school where possible and otherwise should take the form of diversion to or referral back to these networks. Hence the substantial rise in cautioning of young people during the 1980s when the developmental model was most clearly seen in youth justice practice. The state's function becomes one of trusting these networks in their crime prevention role and supporting them where necessary to heighten their effectiveness.

In this chapter both approaches to the responsibilities of parents and schools will be assessed. Aetiological research on youth crime has revealed links between these networks and youth crime and provide the substantive evidence for crime prevention policies targeted at these areas of a young person's life. This rhetoric

---

[4] According to Graham and Bowling these include taking up employment on leaving education and becoming financially independent. J Graham and B Bowling, *Young People and Crime* HORS 145 (London, Home Office, 1995) ch 5

[5] Rutherford calls these the developmental institutions.

[6] Rutherford, *Growing Out of Crime* (2002) above n 3 at p 30.

may be compared with the realities of the policies targeted at the same areas in legislation and policy discussions on youth crime.

Parental Responsibility

The 'Scientific' Rhetoric

There is a general consensus amongst psychologists, criminologists and popular discourse that children are products moulded and shaped by parental influence. For example, Hirschi's social control theory, discussed in Chapter 4, identifies the family, and parental attachment, in particular, as a primary social control mechanism preventing young people from following the 'natural' urge to indulge in delinquent behaviour. Edwin Sutherland also suggested, in his differential association theory, that delinquent behaviour, in common with other behavioural traits, are socially learned, particularly from parental role models.[7] It is therefore not surprising that there is also a general consensus that youth crime is symptomatic of the parenting role having been carried out 'badly' or in a dysfunctional way, the suggestion being that successful parents do not produce young offenders. A consistent theme of criminological research on youth crime has therefore been family relationships and parenting styles in order to investigate exactly what has gone wrong in the young offender's home to cultivate criminal behaviour. As early as 1925 Cyril Burt identified the family as an influence over young people's offending behaviour in *The Young Delinquent*.[8]

This theme is strongly present in more recent research on the aetiology of youth crime. Graham and Bowling, in 1995, found a strong correlation between parental behaviour and youth crime in their self-report study.[9] Young people in that study were questioned about their experiences at home including their social class, their family size, structure, and relationships, parental supervision and family involvement with the police. The most significant results emerged in relation to parental supervision and parental attachment. Parental supervision, measured in terms of the extent to which parents were aware of what their children were doing and both where they were and who they were with when out with their friends, appears highly influential in the onset of offending. Whilst 32 per cent of males (and 14 per cent of females) who were closely supervised admitted to offending, the respective offending rates for those who were not closely supervised were much higher;

---

[7] E Sutherland, *Principles of Criminology* (Philadelphia, Lippincott, 1939).

[8] C Burt, *The Young Delinquent* (London, University of London Press, 1925).

[9] Graham and Bowling above n 4 at ch 4

53 per cent of males (and 30 per cent of females).[10] As regards parental attachment, those who had bad relationships with either parent were generally twice as likely to offend. Those who were strongly attached to their parents produced an offending rate of only 42 per cent whereas the offending rate for those less attached was 70 per cent overall.

Interestingly, family structure and size in themselves did not appear to affect the onset of offending. Offending rates were marginally higher for those young males who lived with one natural and one step parent (57 per cent) and lower for those who lived with both natural parents (42 per cent). Single parent families produced an overall offending rate of 49 per cent. Those young males with only one sibling demonstrated the highest offending rate of 46 per cent compared with 18 per cent where there were no siblings, 22 per cent where there were two siblings and 14 per cenr where there were more than 3 siblings. These figures would suggest that large families and single parent or step families are not significantly more criminogenic than smaller families where both natural parents live together. Neither does social class (often anecdotally associated with larger families and single parenthood) appear significantly to affect criminal behaviour as there were few differences between the offending rates of young people from different socio-economic groups.[11]

The findings of this study place more emphasis on the *quality* of parents' behaviour rather than the *quantity or status* of parents living in the family home. Of course, social class, poverty and the single parent status of some families may be influential to the extent that they affect these qualitative measures of parental behaviour. A single parent may have a lower income and fewer opportunities for supervision than two parents. However, their relationship with their child is equally important and there is no reason why this relationship should be more problematic in the case of a single parent. To this end, Graham and Bowling's study was able to dispel a popular urban myth that single parent families (and single mothers in particular) may be blamed for rising youth crime rates and that two parents are necessarily better than one in this context. In the face of this evidence right realists such as Charles Murray can no longer confidently assert:

Adolescence and testosterone are a destructive combination, and the only antidote is a civilising process that begins in infancy and is completed by marriage. I am arguing that the civilising process *cannot* occur in communities where the two-parent family is not the norm.[12]

Graham and Bowling's study also provided substantive quantitative data which served to confirm the findings of previous, respected, academic research.

---

[10] *Ibid* Table 4.1, p 34.
[11] *Ibid* p 33.
[12] C Murray, *Underclass: The Crisis Deepens* in R Lister (ed) *Charles Murray and the Underclass: The Developing Debate* (London, Institute for Economic Affairs, 1996) p 121.

Farrington and West's Cambridge study concluded that young people whose domestic life included 'harsh and erratic discipline', poor supervision and neglect, parental separation and delinquent parents were more likely to offend.[13] Similar findings emerge from studies by Riley and Shaw,[14] Rutter and Giller,[15] and Power *et al.*[16] This has been further compounded by ongoing Home Office research in the form of later self-report studies such as the Youth Lifestyles Survey[17] and the Crime and Justice Survey 2003[18]. The former study found similar correlations between family lifestyles and offending rates to Graham and Bowling. Those under poor supervision were three times more likely to offend than those who were well supervised and weak attachments to parents resulted in young people being 50 per cent more likely to offend than those enjoying a better relationship with their parents.[19] Indeed, the authors of that study noted how fractious relationships between young people and their parents produce a vortex in which crime becomes both a symptom and cause of worsening attachments:

> Research has shown how hostile, anti-social behaviour from children elicits a negative response from their parents and other adults and so offenders and their parents can become locked into a cycle into which their relationship gradually deteriorates.[20]

The early findings of the Home Office Crime and Justice Survey reveal 'risk factors' associated with anti-social behaviour as well as crime. This study questioned young people about the extent to which their parents argue and fight (with them and each other), praise and listen, treat the young person fairly and want to know where they are. Negative parental relationships based on these factors accounted for a high level of anti-social behaviour.[21] So too did a relaxed attitude on the part of parents towards certain types of behaviour, investigated through questions asked about how a young person's parent would feel about them starting a fight, using graffiti, skipping school and smoking cannabis. Parents with more relaxed attitudes towards such behaviour produced higher rates of anti-social behaviour in their children.

[13] See D Farrington, 'Developmental and Risk-focused Prevention' in M Maguire *et al* (eds) *Oxford Handbook of Criminology* 3rd edn (Oxford, Oxford University Press, 2002).

[14] D Riley and M Shaw, *Parental Supervision and Juvenile Delinquency* HORS 83 (London, HMSO, 1985)

[15] M Rutter and H Giller, *Juvenile Delinquency: Trends and Perspectives* (Harmondsworth, Penguin, 1983).

[16] M Power *et al*, 'Delinquency and the Family' (1974) 4 *British Journal of Social Work* 13. For further discussion see M Rutter, H Giller and A Hagell, *Anti-Social Behaviour by Young People* (Cambridge, Cambridge University Press, 1998).

[17] C. Flood-Page *et al*, *Youth Crime: Findings from the 1998/99 Youth Lifestyles Survey* HORS 209 (London, Home Office, 2000).

[18] T Budd, C Sharpe and P Mayhew, *Offending in England and Wales: First Results from the 2003 Crime and Justice Survey* HORS 275 (Home Office, London, 2005).

[19] Flood-Page *et al* above n 17 at Table 3.1 p 34

[20] *Ibid* p 34.

[21] R Hayward and C Sharp, *Young People, Crime and Anti-Social Behaviour: Findings from the 2003 Crime and Justice Survey* Home Office Findings no 245 (London, Home Office, 2005).

We can conclude from this wealth of empirical research that crime prevention policies would do well to focus on aspects of a young person's family life. However, care needs to be taken in devising appropriate policies in this regard. Utting *et al* warn against fixing aspects of family life that are not broken: 'In the search for practical ways to prevent children from growing into criminals, there is little advantage to be gained from focusing policy on the *structure* of families.'[22] On the strength of the evidence set out above, exacerbating the prejudice against single parent families or those from socially or economically disadvantaged groups, is unlikely to assist in preventing crime if such factors do not influence the onset of offending. Utting's research focuses rather more on the above findings in seeking a more constructive response to family problems and provides a useful and systematic rhetoric for policy makers.

Utting *et al* suggest a three-tiered approach to tackling parental responsibility to crime. It is noteworthy that none of their suggested policies fall within the remit of the Home Office or criminal justice agencies. Rather they suggest an agenda for wider social policy aimed at encouraging more positive parental relationships with children, enabling greater supervision and more consistent discipline. This agenda consists of the state provision of services on three levels, each aimed at providing support for the parental role, alleviating disadvantage and dysfunction among families and encouraging effective parenting skills. The three tiers suggest provision at different levels, the overall aim being that as many services as possible are not targeted at individual families but used on a voluntary basis. This proposes to avoid any stigma attached to the need to use such services and any labelling of families as having 'failed'. Only the final tier of services are targeted at particularly problematic family situations where more intensive state intervention may be necessary.

The first tier comprises universal services available to all families. These services may include a coherent package of parent education, building on, but extending further than, the current provision of post-natal assistance with newborn children by health authorities. Utting *et al* favour a more comprehensive parent education which recognises that 'it is illogical and unreasonable to expect parents to cope instinctively with the modern day stresses of raising children'[23] and which extends beyond infancy to other stages of a child's development. This recognises the lack of general provision to all parents of guidance on how to provide coherent discipline, supervision and care of children of all ages up to (and possibly beyond) the age of adolescence, regardless of family circumstances. Education on this level, it is argued, fosters confident child-rearing as well as equipping all parents in skills necessary to avoid many behavioural problems in later childhood which may develop into criminal behaviour.

---

[22] D Utting, J Bright and C Henricson, *Crime and the Family: Improving Child-rearing and Preventing Delinquency* (London, Family Policy Studies Centre, 1993).
[23] *Ibid* p 29.

The second tier comprises neighbourhood services, targeted at areas where youth crime is higher than average and where social disadvantage may be more pronounced. At this level, however, services are still not targeted at individual families. Services such as open access family centres, family therapy, play groups, parenting discussion groups and respite care for parents under stress should, according to Utting *et al*, be available to those families that recognise their own difficulties and acknowledge a need for them. Such services provide support and advice to parents experiencing difficulty in relating to their children, managing their children's behaviour and providing discipline and control.

The final tier comprises family preservation services for individual families identified by the police or social work authorities as 'at risk' in terms of criminal behaviour or abuse (although the services should still be offered to parents on a consensual basis). Here the stigma may be greater, but the family problems are also more acute and require a more focused and targeted response from professional groups. These services may be therapeutic or more practical, but extend beyond neighbourhood services into the homes of the minority of most disadvantaged families who are unable to cope without such support. The Children Act 1989 provides services of this type where children are considered by social services departments to be 'in need'.[24]

Many of the services in the second and third tiers of this policy agenda may already be provided in some areas although this may be on an ad hoc basis and, in the case of neighbourhood services, very often courtesy of voluntary and charitable organisations. Family preservation services, as mentioned above, may be available from state-funded organisations but only where the highest level of 'need' is identified and often such 'need' is defined on a resource-led basis, which may exclude many other marginalised and disadvantaged families.[25] The Audit Commission lamented that 'Despite the preventive philosophy built into the Children Act 1989, social services departments have found it difficult to move from a reactive social policing role, which focuses on child protection cases, towards more proactive work that supports families.'[26] There is no precedent for universal and comprehensive education of parents in this country. The ideal agenda set out here presupposes that the state would resource services at all three levels. Whilst this may appear overly Utopian and politically unjustifiable in the post-Thatcher era,[27] Utting *et al* claimed in 1993 that the costs of pursuing a crime

---

[24] Children Act 1989 s 10. The approach of the Children Act 1989 to crime prevention is discussed more fully in Ch 10.

[25] See further D Cowan, *Homelessness: The (In)Appropriate Applicant* (Aldershot, Ashgate, 1998) ch 4, where he argues that there is a moral or judgmental allocation of resources to families in many areas.

[26] Audit Commission, *Misspent Youth . . . Young People and Crime* (London, TSO, 1996).

[27] See JK Galbraith *The Culture of Contentment* (Penguin, London, 1992) which discusses how Thatcher's economic policy bred a contented, well-off middle class whose self-interest precludes costly State welfare support for the more disadvantaged.

prevention policy ex post facto through the criminal justice system far outweigh the costs of this more proactive strategy.[28] Since 1998, the principal aim of the youth justice system[29] and the crime prevention duties imposed on local authorities and their crime prevention partners through the Crime and Disorder Act,[30] would support this proactive and wide-ranging agenda as a more cost-effective approach.[31]

The Political Rhetoric

Much of the research outlined above has been Home Office commissioned and funded with a view to inform policy making in this area. Indeed, policy makers in the past few decades have clearly recognised the links between parenting behaviour and youth crime and have sought to embrace parental responsibility in their discussion of youth justice policy. One of the first explicit articulations of the importance of the family was expressed by the Black Committee in Northern Ireland in 1979:

> The family is the first and most basic institution in our society for developing a child's potential . . . It is within the family that the child experiences love, attention, care, supervision, discipline, conflict, neglect, stress or abuse depending on parental and family characteristics and circumstances . . . Society must seek to develop and provide the environment, resources and opportunities through which families can become more competent to deal with their own problems.[32]

A decade later on the other side of the Irish Sea, the Home Office echoed a similar sentiment in their white paper *Crime, Justice and Protecting the Public*.[33] John Patten, a junior Home Office Minister in 1989 had previously suggested the creation of a new offence of 'failure to prevent child crime'.[34] In proposing legislation to reform the youth justice process, later to become the Criminal Justice Act 1991, Douglas Hurd, as Home Secretary, acknowledged what we now know to be a critical influence on the onset of youth crime:

> Crime prevention begins at home . . . when effective family control is lacking, children are more likely to grow up without self-discipline and a sense of concern for others. They are more likely to commit crimes. Loving authority is critical in a child's development.[35]

---

[28] Utting *et al*, above n 22, at pp 67–75.
[29] Section 37 Crime and Disorder Act 1998.
[30] Sections 5 and 6.
[31] The Audit Commission embraced this view in their critique of the cost effectiveness of the youth justice system in 1996—see *Misspent Youth* above n 26.
[32] Black Committee, *Report of the Children and Young Persons Review Group* (HMSO, Belfast, 1979)
[33] Home Office, *Crime, Justice and Protecting the Public* Cm 965 (HMSO, London, 1990).
[34] John Patten in a letter to the UK Federation of Business and Professional Women. The proposal was abandoned in the light of criticism of the proposal from various interested pressure groups.
[35] Home Office, *Crime Justice and Protecting the Public* above n 33 at p 40.

However, the government's approach to encouraging this loving authority stopped short of Patten's earlier dogmatic suggestion and focused instead on 'reminding parents of their responsibilities',[36] particularly in relation to younger children where 'the responsibility must be placed squarely on the parents to help their children keep out of trouble and to deal with the consequences if they get into trouble'[37] whilst acknowledging that 'Some parents will need help.'[38] The Children Act 1989, implemented concomitantly with the Criminal Justice Act 1991, was designed to provide this help.

In Opposition at this time, the Labour Party's interpretation of the proposals set out in the white paper nevertheless sensed a move towards a more authoritarian approach and was highly critical of any suggestion that parents should be punished for their failure to prevent their children's criminal behaviour:

> We take the issue of parental responsibility and parental involvement very seriously. But we are convinced by those experts in the study of juvenile crime who argue that any proposals to prosecute parents for the actions of their children are, at best, ineffectual and, at worst, likely to be counterproductive and increase the likelihood of family breakdown.[39]

This sentiment was echoed by the Magistrates' Association who believed the provisions would contribute to youth homelessness as despairing parents would relinquish all parental responsibility for older teenagers,[40] as well as other opponents of the parental responsibility provisions in the legislation such as Lord Henderson who envisaged that clause 48 of the Bill (later section 57 CJA 1991) 'cannot make things better. [They] can introduce resentment and stress into an already stressful situation.'[41] At this time, the Labour Party's favoured agenda was a move to a de-criminalised procedure for parental involvement in proceedings mirroring the Scottish Children's Hearings system. The resulting provisions, passed in the CJA 1991, are discussed below.

By the end of the Conservative government's last term of office their rhetoric on parental responsibility took on a more controlling and punitive tone. In a consultation paper published in March 1997[42] Michael Howard claimed that enough support had been offered to struggling parents and yet:

---

[36] Home Office, *Crime Justice and Protecting the Public* above n 33 at p 40.
[37] *Ibid.*
[38] *Ibid.*
[39] Labour Party, *A Safer Britain* a shadow 'white paper' (London, Labour Party, 1990) p 21.
[40] Editorial, (1991) 46/11 *The Magistrate.*
[41] HL Debates vol 528, col 98 (1990–1).
[42] Home Office, *Preventing Children Offending: A Consultation Document* Cm 3566 (London, TSO, 1997). This paper was published very shortly before the general election was announced and the proposals had no hope of being enacted before Parliament was dissolved. The paper can therefore only be read as a steer on the direction that youth policy was to take if the government retained power after the election—see further Ch 3.

[T]he government notes with concern that a small minority of parents not only fail to exercise adequate control over their children but also fail to respond to the support that is offered. Their children may continue to behave in a way suggesting that they are likely to offend, or may actually commit an offence.[43]

The language of failure in relation to parental responsibility had arrived in the political rhetoric, as had the language of control, since Howard proposed a new Parental Control Order, breach of which would be a criminal offence. For the time being, the political 'ping pong' between the government and (by now) New Labour in opposition continued. New Labour's numerous discussion documents published in the early 1990s focused on parenting as a recurrent theme, but their stance was still broadly supportive:

The roots of criminal and delinquent behaviour are planted in childhood. Research has shown that parental supervision and discipline is key to its prevention. Despite the difficulty of parenting, little attention is given to helping people acquire the necessary skills to cope with bringing up children in today's world. We believe there needs to be a wider discussion of parental responsibilities and public policies which would assist successful parenting. New strategies are needed for preparing people for parenthood, for resolving the conflicts between work and parenting, and for coping with parenting danger zones such as children in need and those in public care.[44]

It was only later, after their election victory in 1997, that New Labour's discussion of this subject began to reflect that of the previous administration and embraced the notion of parental punishment and control. The brief discussion of the proposed parenting order in *Tackling Youth Crime* is rather more reminiscent of Michael Howard's pre-election statements than of their own: 'Parents who wilfully neglect the[ir] responsibilities should be answerable to the courts.'[45] By the time the white paper was published this view was expressed in the authoritarian language of enforcement, parental responsibility being discussed under the general heading of 'Reinforcing responsibility.'[46] Both documents cited the research of Graham and Bowling but neither referred to chapter 7 of that report in which the authors firmly support the agenda for reform set out by Utting *et al.*

We can conclude from this that the 'scientific' rhetoric is at odds with much of the 'political' rhetoric on parental responsibility. Whilst the former attempts to make sense of the influence that parents may have on the onset of youth offending, and places the emphasis on attachment between parents and children as well as the level of parental supervision and discipline, the latter tends to produce

---

[43] *Ibid* p 23.

[44] J Straw and J Anderson, *Parenting: A Discussion Paper* (London, Labour Party, 1996)

[45] *Tackling Youth Crime: A Consultation Paper* (London, Home Office, 1997) p 9.

[46] *No More Excuses: A New Approach to Tackling Youth Crime in England and Wales* Cm 3809 (London, TSO, 1997) ch 4. Note also that within the broad principal aim of the youth justice system under s 37 CDA 1998 'reinforcing' parental responsibility is a key objective—see Home Office, *Youth Justice* above n 2.

policies which aim to use the sledgehammer of criminal sanctions to force parents not to fail in taking control of their children. Cursory readings of the research may well produce stereotypical responses and a prejudicial approach. However, political influences appear to take over once the discussion of youth crime reaches official levels.

Successive Home Office and opposition papers quote the research in depth and recognise the importance of the parental role in preventing crime, but when translated into firm proposals the political rhetoric and consequent reality (or legislation) are much more draconian. Note New Labour's swift U-turn between their opposition and government statements on this issue. It is easy to pledge support to parents in opposition, less easy in government where they are more politically comfortable with the language of punishment and control.

The Reality

The reality of parental responsibility in the youth justice context can be found in a series of legislative provisions in which the courts impose obligations on the parents[47] of convicted young offenders. Parental responsibility provisions have now largely been consolidated under the Powers of the Criminal Courts (Sentencing) Act 2000 (PCC(S)A 2000) although they were originally enacted in the Criminal Justice Act 1991 (CJA 1991). Others remain where initially enacted, in the Crime and Disorder Act 1998 (CDA 1998) and the Anti-Social Behaviour Act 2003 (ASBA 2003).

The CJA 1991 set out a revolutionary new framework for sentencing, but, as the 1990 white paper illustrated, part of this new framework in the youth court was to include duties on parents to involve them in the response to their children's offending behaviour. At this time, in view of the approach being taken by the legislature in the Children Act 1989 implemented at the same time as the CJA, and in view of the recent House of Lords decision in *Gillick v West Norfolk and Wisbech AHA*,[48] the Home Office recognised that parental responsibility for children may diminish as the child attains greater maturity and the capacity to take responsibility for aspects of their own life, including their criminal behaviour. They therefore favoured a discretionary approach to parental responsibility where the child is aged 16 or 17:

> Some flexibility will be necessary in the way that the courts involve the parents of young offenders in this age group. Some 16 and 17 year olds will be fully independent of their parents. Some may be married with family responsibilities of their own . . . In dealing

---

[47] For the purposes of simplicity reference is made throughout this chapter to parents but the legislation, of course, also applies to legal guardians, other adults with legal parental responsibility for a child and, where a child is in care, the local authority with legal responsibility for them.

[48] [1986] AC 112.

with young offenders of this age, courts should not be required to involve parents . . . when their children are living away from home, but they should have a power to do so when they consider it necessary. But when the young people are living in their parents' home and still in full-time education, then their parents must be involved as they would be with younger juveniles.[49]

Therefore sections 56, 57 and 58 of the CJA 1991 provided the youth court with a *duty* to impose the obligations contained therein on parents of children aged under 16, but a discretionary *power* to do so where the child is aged 16 or 17.

Section 56 of the Act reinforced a parent's obligation to attend court where their child was subject to proceedings. This had previously been a possibility under the Children and Young Persons Act 1963 where the juvenile court was able (though not obliged) to require parents to attend court. The duty to attend was restated in 1991 in more compulsory terms. It was clearly necessary to restate this duty given the new bindovers that were to be imposed on parents in a later section of the Act. Such bindovers could hardly be imposed upon parents who were not there. The usual justification for compulsory attendance however, is less pragmatic and it is claimed that forced attendance at court, at the very least makes parents aware of the criminal behaviour of their children, but also should act symbolically to remind them of their responsibility and influence over their children's behaviour. Few would argue with this view, but forced attendance during working hours may result in further stress and conflict for a busy parent. This requirement might be seen as more reasonable if the youth court was available to sit outside of working hours, in the evenings and at weekends, in order to reduce the burden on working parents. Despite the fact that there is precedent for this in other jurisdictions, such as in Scotland[50], this flexibility has not been embraced.

The responsibility of parents to pay financial penalties imposed on a young offender was also restated[51] in section 57 of the CJA 1991. This means that where a child is fined for their criminal behaviour or where a compensation order is made, the parents are legally responsible for ensuring that the penalty is paid, with full consequent liability for non-payment (which ultimately could result in imprisonment). The youth court may avoid their duty to impose the financial penalty directly on a parent of a child aged under 16 where they consider it 'unreasonable' to do so. Home Office Circular 3/1983 had given them further guidance on this and suggested that they should have regard to means of the child themselves and whether it may be more appropriate to direct the penalty on the child. However, they are further guided to the particular circumstances of the

---

[49] Home Office, *Crime Justice and Protecting the Public* above n 33 at p 44.

[50] The Children's Hearings Panels regularly meet outside of office hours. Notably, the meetings of a Youth Offending Panel under the referral order procedure may also take place in the evenings and at weekends. See further Ch 6.

[51] The court was *able* (but not under a duty) to require parents to pay fines under Children and Young Persons Act 1933.

relationship between parents and child and consider to what extent the parent's neglect of their duties contributed to the offence, suggesting that responsibility for a financial penalty may be an indirect way of punishing a parent for such neglect. Whilst parental responsibility in its wider context involves financial responsibility for the child, this more punitive, financial responsibility risked exacerbating family conflict and disadvantage in family homes where, according to the research set out above, there were already likely to have been attachment difficulties.

The third element of parental responsibility in the 1991 legislation was the creation of the new parental bindover. It was principally this section which prompted the fears of the Magistrates' Association and others outlined above. Under section 58 the youth court must (or can where the child is 16 or 17) require the parent to enter into a recognisance of up to £1000 to take proper care or exercise proper control over their child. This is, in effect, a suspended fine, where the recognisance must be paid only if the youth court receives evidence that the parent has failed to meet the requirements of the order. The parents are means tested before the level of the recognisance is set. A parent may refuse to enter into the recognisance, but the youth court then has the discretion to fine a parent up to £1000 for that refusal.[52] Consent to such an order may clearly, therefore, not be a matter of free choice for the parent. This provision was further amended in the Criminal Justice and Public Order Act 1994, so that a parent may now be bound over additionally to ensure that a child complies with the requirements of any community penalty imposed on them.[53]

Aside from the extra financial pressure this bindover may impose on a parent, the ambiguous and vague nature of the recognisance is a matter of concern. What does it mean to take proper care of a child? Or to exercise proper control? The use of the word 'proper' suggests a normative standard of child care which may not be shared by many. Of equal concern is the dictatorial nature of the order, in the absence of support mechanisms. The offending behaviour of the child, which has resulted in the court appearance for both them and their parent, is already symptomatic of a failure to take proper care or exercise proper control over the child. To blindly reassert the parent's responsibilities without acknowledgement of difficulties a parent may be having in executing them, or without the offer of any support, re-emphasises the focus on failure and the punishment thereof. A leading article in *The Times* went so far as to say:

> This is the kind of [provision] that makes perfect sense to middle class Ministers, who generally leave the taming of adolescence to their children's boarding schools. For, say, the single mother in Brixton, struggling against odds to keep a young person on track, they represent only a threat.[54]

[52] Section 58(2)(b).
[53] Sch 10 para 50.
[54] *The Times* (10 November 1990).

The provision fails to appreciate the best efforts of 'parents who have genuinely but unsuccessfully tried to improve their children's behaviour. Such parents are often at their wits' end to know how to control their children and prevent them from offending.'[55] The more sympathetic and reassuring rhetoric of the white paper preceding the Act is not reflected in this provision.[56]

New Labour were rather more honest about their approach to parental responsibility in acknowledging a punitive approach.[57] Ironically, the resultant provision in the CDA 1998 is rather more supportive! Section 8 of that Act imposes a further[58] duty on the court to address parental responsibility in the form of the parenting order. This order *must*[59] be imposed on a parent of a child aged under 16 where that child is subject to a child safety order, an anti-social behaviour order or sex offender order, is convicted of an offence or where the parent is convicted of an offence for failing to ensure a child attends school.[60] The court must further be of the opinion that the order is desirable in the interests of preventing further offending, anti-social behaviour or other behaviour resulting in one of the above orders. Once justified, the order must firstly contain any requirements of the parent that the courts see fit over a period up to a year and, secondly, a requirement to attend parenting classes on a weekly basis for up to three months.[61] Section 9 of the Act seeks to avoid potential breaches of the European Convention on Human Rights by requiring the court to consider carefully the likely effect of this order on the rest of the family as well as any possible interference with the parent's religious beliefs and work or educational commitments.

The first part of the order is deliberately vaguely described in the Act, although the Home Office has provided guidance on the type of requirements that may be appropriate in individual cases. These may include ensuring the child attends school, ensuring the child attends extra-curricular activities or homework clubs, ensuring the child avoids contact with disruptive peers, avoids certain areas without supervision (such as shopping centres) and ensuring the child spends

---

[55] Penal Affairs Consortium, *Parental Responsibility, Youth Crime and the Criminal Law* (London, Penal Affairs Consortium, 1995).

[56] Indeed Mark Drakeford noted that, in practice, the imposition of these legislative duties resulted in resentment on the part of parents and 'embitterment and erosion of productive family functioning'—'Parents of Young People in Trouble' (1996) 35 *Howard Journal* 242 at 254.

[57] See the discussion of *Tackling Youth Crime* above n 45 and *No More Excuses* above n 46.

[58] The provisions of the CJA 1991 ss 56–58 have not been repealed and the parenting order supplements them.

[59] Reasons must be given where the court chooses not to impose a parenting order—s 9(1).

[60] The relevant offences are contained in ss 443 and 444 Education Act 1996 and are discussed in more detail below.

[61] Section 8(4). A subsequent amendment in the Anti-Social Behaviour Act 2003 s 18, provides for these parenting classes to be offered on a residential basis where that is deemed to be more appropriate, subject, of course to the necessary avoidance of interference in family life.

more time at home in the evenings, with proper supervision.[62] The requirement
of parenting classes is demonstrative of a more supportive approach. Whilst these
classes may fall under Utting *et al*'s category of family preservation services, since
they are targeted at families proven to be in difficulties, they are an attempt to
provide some guidance and assistance to parents in carrying out their parenting
role. Assuming such classes avoid cultural and class bias in their guidance, this
provision makes some positive steps towards a more empathetic approach and a
recognition of the need for assistance in some families.

Nevertheless there are still punitive aspects to these orders. Firstly breach of a
parenting order is a criminal offence punishable by fine in the youth court.[63] This
breach provision sends out a further threatening message to parents that further
failure to carry out their responsibilities will be punished. Given the difficulties
inherent in the parenting role, especially in relation to adolescents, it is likely that
many such orders will be 'breached' until any support mechanisms offered have
their full effect.[64] However, the legislation does not countenance tolerance of
further failure and provides a 'one strike and you're out' approach. Moreover,
the parenting order has developed a new identity as a 'punishment' for breach of
the slightly more informal parenting contract, introduced in the Anti-Social
Behaviour Act 2003.

Such contracts are made between parents and the relevant authorities where the
child's problematic behaviour falls short of criminal offending. Contracts made
with a local education authority (LEA) where a child is excluded from, or truants
from, school will be discussed below. 'Contracts'[65] may also be made between a
parent and a youth offending team (YOT) where a child has engaged in *or is likely
to engage in* anti-social or criminal behaviour under section 25 of the 2003 Act.
These contractual agreements are not compulsory and may be seen as a preliminary attempt at addressing parental difficulties before a more compulsive order is
deemed necessary, although, inevitably their informality means that the youth
court is not involved in the negotiations of such a contract and there may be due
process concerns in this regard. However, under section 26 of the 2003 Act the
YOT may apply to the magistrates' court for a parenting order and section 27
further explains that this may be necessary where a parent refuses to enter into
such a contract or breaches the conditions of one. Further perusal of the complex
statutory provisions in this area reveals that the Criminal Justice Act 2003 makes a
parenting order a penalty for breach of a parent's obligation to attend the meet-

---

[62] *Parenting Orders and Contracts for Criminal Conduct and Anti-Social Behaviour: Guidance* Joint
Home Office/Department of Constitutional Affairs/Youth Justice Board Circular (London, Home
Office, 2004).

[63] Section 9(7).

[64] These parenting difficulties are discussed above.

[65] Section 25(7) points out that breach of such a 'contract' does not give rise to liability in contract
or tort law; hence my use of inverted commas here.

ings of a youth offending panel under the referral order procedure.[66] Where a parenting order is imposed as a breach of subsidiary obligations on parents, we return to our original position in section 9 of the CDA 1998 where breach of the parenting order is a criminal offence. This circuitous journey inevitably brings us to a destination where failure (albeit persistent failure) in carrying out parental responsibilities effectively becomes a criminal offence. This is precisely what John Patten sought to achieve in 1989 and, more importantly, what the Labour Party criticised the government for in 1990 in opposing the proposals for the CJA 1991, which appear tame in comparison with the parenting order. The effective criminalisation of parents through these procedures raises due process concerns under Article 6 of the European Convention on Human Rights. Parents subject to criminal sanctions in the youth court are punished for very vaguely defined behaviour and face those sanctions on evidence falling below the criminal burden of proof.[67]

Schools and Youth Crime

Introduction

A similar dichotomous analysis of the role of the school in preventing youth crime can be taken. Policy makers have again recognised the research evidence (discussed below) which suggests there is a link between school attendance and performance and the onset of criminal behaviour. Schools share in the responsibility to prevent crime, since they exert a great deal of influence over a child through a large part of the day; indeed going to school is a child's 'job'. It is presumed that the influence of schools, in the education they provide, is a positive one, where the child learns academically, morally and socially. Legislation has not ignored this influence and seeks to ensure the child attends school so that this positive influence may have its full effect. The emphasis of legislation in this area is on attendance, treating truancy as a problem consisting of absence from school. Criminal justice legislation, quite rightly, does not touch upon the qualitative issues involved in the child's experience in school once they pass through the school gates. We must look to education policy and legislation for that. The criminal justice system does, however, seek to assign responsibility for non-attendance and here the emphasis is again punitive and the responsibility lies, to a large extent,

---

[66] Section 324 CJA 2003.

[67] See further N Stone, 'Legal Commentary: "Parenting Orders", "Warnings and Reprimands" and "Age at Time of Offence"—Human Rights Considerations' (2003) 3 *Youth Justice* 112.

with the parent and the child. The school does not feature in the youth justice system's principal aim, or in its key objectives, in preventing offending.

The alternative approach, again advocated by Rutherford,[68] is to embrace the discipline system already in operation in schools as a non-criminal forum in which to deal with pupils' troublesome behaviour. More importantly, the school has a pastoral role in relation to its pupils which may enable them to proactively prevent offending behaviour:

> The incorporative school will do what it can to hold on to disruptive, delinquent or truanting pupils because it regards them in positive terms. It believes that the school should not fail its pupils, and that it has something of value to offer. Furthermore, it enjoys the confidence of the police and courts. Schools not only differ in the behaviour of their pupils but in the determination and the ability of the school to prevent or reduce contact between their pupils and criminal justice.[69]

Policies emanating from the Home Office and departments of education, which seek to employ the criminal justice system to deal with truancy and youth crime, reduce the capacity of the school to 'hold on' to their pupils in the way Rutherford suggests. A developmental policy in this context, however, again requires non-exclusionary measures, support for the school's pastoral role and trust in them to realise their crime prevention potential.

The Rhetoric

Research evidence overwhelmingly suggests that there is a strong correlation between truancy and youth crime, both of which, according to Graham and Bowling's study,[70] tend to begin at the same age. That study found that 67 per cent of those young males who had truanted from school admitted offences, whereas only 38 per cent of non-truants offended. (For females the respective proportions were 36 per cent of truants and 15 per cent of non-truants.)[71] The Youth Lifestyles survey 1998/99 and the Crime and Justice Survey 2003 produced similar results. In the former study, the more persistent the truant, the higher the offending rates. For example, amongst males aged 12 to 16, 47 per cent of those who had truanted more than once a month reported offending behaviour, compared with 13 per cent of those who truanted less often and only 10 per cent of non-truants.[72] The Crime and Justice Survey 2003 noted that truancy was a 'high risk' characteristic since 62 per cent of truants in their study admitted to offending and/or anti-social behaviour. The Social Exclusion Unit, established by Prime Minister Tony Blair in

---

[68] Rutherford, *Growing Out of Crime* (2002) above n 3 at ch 5.
[69] Ibid p 101.
[70] Graham and Bowling above n 4 at p 40.
[71] Ibid Table 4.2, p 40
[72] Flood-Page *et al* above n17 at p 36.

1998, addressed truancy in one of their first reports. Their review of statistics found that in London, 5 per cent of all known offences were committed by children during school hours, suggesting that the offenders must have been truanting at the time of committing the offences.[73]

Since absence from school is closely associated with offending behaviour, it is not surprising that those children excluded from school, whether permanently or temporarily, also report high offending rates. The starkest statistics were found by Graham and Bowling; 98 per cent of their male respondents who were permanently excluded from school reported offending compared with 47 per cent of those not permanently excluded. The respective figures for temporarily excluded were 75 per cent compared with 20 per cent not temporarily excluded.[74] The Youth Lifestyles Survey reported that pupils excluded were more than twice as likely to offend.[75] Independent research has reported a 450 per cent rise in rates of school exclusions in recent years[76] and the Social Exclusion Unit report that 'Truancy and school exclusion have reached a crisis point.'[77] Given the link between these factors and the onset of offending we may expect a rise in youth offending as a result, although truancy figures quoted in government circles have been found to be as inaccurate as official offending figures.[78]

The link between education and offending goes beyond issues of attendance, however. The child's experience of school and the extent to which they enjoy school, do well and achieve good results, can be significant factors in preventing crime. Whilst a majority of young people surveyed in self-report studies claimed to enjoy school (75 per cent in the Youth Lifestyles Survey liked school)[79] Graham and Bowling found that detachment from school was a significant indicator of offending behaviour in young females especially.[80] The Youth Lifestyles Survey revealed that 'disaffected' young people of both sexes were more than twice as likely to offend. Among males aged 12 to 16, 22 per cent of children disaffected by their school experience offended compared with 10 per cent who enjoyed school. For females the respective figures were 10 per cent and 3 per cent. The Crime and Justice Survey asked respondents about their school environment and those who complained of poor teaching quality and a lack of clear rules, amongst other problems, also reported a 50 per cent offending rate.[81] Young people whose

---

[73] Social Exclusion Unit, *Truancy and Social Exclusion* (London, Social Exclusion Unit, 1998) p 3.

[74] Graham and Bowling above n 4 Table 4.2, p 40.

[75] Flood-Page *et al* above n 17 at p 38.

[76] C Parsons, 'Permanent Exclusions from Schools in England: Trends, Causes and Responses' (1996) 10 *Children and Society* 177–86. See also R Smith, *No Lessons Learnt: A Survey of School Exclusions* (London, The Children's Society, 1998).

[77] Social Exclusion Unit above n 73 at p 2.

[78] J Pratt, 'Folk-lore and Fact in Truancy Research' (1982) 22 *British Journal of Criminology* 336.

[79] Flood-Page *et al* above n 17 at p 36.

[80] Graham and Bowling above n 4 at ch 4.

[81] Hayward and Sharpe, *Young People, Crime and Anti-Social Behaviour* above n 21 at p 4.

educational performance was below average also reported higher offending rates in each of these surveys. Again the Youth Lifestyles Survey presents the clearest data on this, reporting that young males were three times as likely to offend where their school achievements were below rather than above average (and females were twice as likely to offend). Interestingly, young people who were bullied at school reported similar offending rates to those who were not. However, those who bullied others were significantly more likely to be offenders (although we cannot tell from this data whether their offending behaviour was linked to the bullying or other forms of assault).[82]

We can therefore conclude that in preventing crime it is crucially important that young people attend school, and in particular are not prevented from attending school through exclusion. Moreover, once at school, the child's experience needs to be a positive one. The results of the surveys set out below, replicate the conclusions of earlier research conducted by Michael Power in the 1960s[83] and Michael Rutter in the 1970s.[84] Both pieces of research found differences in delinquency rates in secondary schools which could not be explained by the schools' catchment areas, size or the ages of the pupils attending. Whilst Power's research was ultimately blocked by the National Union of Teachers before he could establish firm conclusions, Rutter attributed the differences in delinquency rates to the differences in organisation and discipline methods in schools. John Graham's review of the empirical research in this area led him to conclude:

> Schools which are likely to have high rates of delinquency among pupils are those which, inadvertently or otherwise, segregate pupils according to academic ability, concentrate on academic success at the expense of practical and social skills . . . [and] permanently exclude those who persistently fail to attend school.[85]

Indeed, Reynolds and Jones' have also suggested that the school may in itself be a criminogenic institution where the organisational ethos and discipline practices of a school may be so ineffective that this in itself causes disaffection and thus causes criminal behaviour:

> Faced by an irrelevant curriculum, hostile teachers, a lack of payoff from effort and the experience of failure, the child will begin to dissociate himself from the school.[86]

Observations by these researchers found that 'delinquent schools' share some common features, including streaming pupils by ability, high rates of corporal

---

[82] Flood-Page *et al* above n 17 at p 39.

[83] M Power, 'Delinquent Schools' (1967) 10 *New Society* 542.

[84] M Rutter *et al, Fifteen Thousand Hours: Secondary Schools and Their Effects on Children* (London, Open Books, 1979).

[85] J Graham, *Crime Prevention Strategies in Europe and North America* Helsinki Institute for Crime Prevention and Control; Paper no 18, (Helsinki, HEUNI, 1990) p 23.

[86] D Reynolds and D Jones, 'Education and the Prevention of Juvenile Delinquency' in N Tutt (ed) *Alternative Strategies for Coping with Crime* (Oxford, Basil Blackwell, 1978) p 34.

punishment,[87] high staff turnover, and an authoritarian school climate. Moreover, they were able to apply criminological theory to the school setting as a micro society and found evidence of labelling of pupils as troublemakers or deviant by teachers as well as cultural conflict between working-class children and schools operating on white, middle-class values:

> [D]elinquency results from blockages upon the attainment of highly valued success goals. The educational system and the teachers that staff it may, because of their middle class assumptions as to what constitutes the 'good pupil', deny working class pupils status within the schools because these pupils have not been socialized to fulfil the status requirements of middle class society and its schools.[88]

According to these interactionist, sub-cultural, labelling and strain theories the ineffective school is more likely to amplify deviance than to prevent it. Crime prevention policies founded solely on truancy and school exclusion (that is, on absence from school) are missing the point. Once a child is physically in the school building, the problems do not cease. Indeed Reynolds and Jones argue that this is where they may begin.

Utting *et al* concur in this assertion that, far from being a preventive institution, an ineffective school may contribute to delinquency. In their view, the key characteristics of an ineffective schools are: the categorisation of pupils who behave badly or who truant as deviants, inadequate or failures; the abrogation of responsibility for the troublesome behaviour and welfare of such 'failures'; and the tendency to reject such pupils and place them in the hands of outside agencies such as the police or social services.[89] Conversely, effective schools avoid such labelling through a more integrative ethos where pupils of all abilities are offered a sense of achievement and opportunities to participate in all activities regardless of their background. Positive relationships between teachers and their pupils as well as parents are also important. Graham and Bowling again cited this view as a policy strategy in response to their aetiological findings, stressing the need to 'strengthen schools' as well as reduce truancy and exclusion.[90]

The Reality

Educational problems and their relationship with youth crime receive scant attention in the consultation and white papers published by the government in late

---

[87] This research, published in 1978, is clearly outdated in this respect since corporal punishment is now banned in all state schools. However, what is still relevant is the fact that these schools resorted to a punishment ethos in dealing with delinquent behaviour, which they found to be ineffective in improving behaviour: Reynolds and Jones previous n at p 40.

[88] Reynolds and Jones above n 86 at p 32.

[89] Utting *et al* above n 22 at ch 4.

[90] Graham and Bowling above n 4 at p 88.

1997. Indeed, since truancy is not in itself a criminal offence in England and Wales, criminal justice legislation is bereft of provision in this area before 1998, education policy being left to welfare and other specialised legislation.[91] Reference is made in *Tackling Youth Crime* to the research evidence on truancy and its aetiological correlation with offending, though no mention is made of the more qualitative issue of detachment from school. This paper promises nothing more concrete than a vague proposal to provide 'action to raise educational standards and combat the problems of truancy and school exclusion'.[92] The white paper *No More Excuses* focuses rather more on parenting, drug misuse and alcohol consumption in its chapter on tackling the causes of crime.[93] The resulting Crime and Disorder Act 1998, however, did introduce the topic of truancy into criminal justice legislation through section 16: the removal of truants to designated premises. This section gives the police the opportunity to effectively implement a temporary 'operation truancy' in their area and for a specified time to remove a child, believed to be truanting[94] from a public place and take them to 'designated premises'. Home Office guidance on the implementation of this provision suggests that such premises would usually mean the school which the child is absent from, but may also include the offices of an education welfare officer. Designated premises must not include a police station, since the guidance reminds practitioners that 'children who truant from school are not committing a crime'.[95] This temporary 'operation' must be deemed necessary on consultation with the LEA and the YOT, based on evidence of increased levels of truancy in an area or a perception of so-called crime 'hot spots' where children are offending during school hours.

The power conferred in section 16 is akin to an emergency provision to be used where the truancy problem is acute across an area in general. It complements the Department for Education and Skills' introduction of National Truancy Sweeps in 2002, where a nationwide operation for police and education welfare officers to pick up truants is sanctioned.[96] Aside from literally placing them back into the physical environs of the school, these powers do not tackle truancy problems in individuals. Policy in relation to individuals may be found in a combination of criminal justice and welfare legislation which aims to work with parents as well as young people in improving attendance rates at school. In relation to the young persons themselves, sentencing options provide a window of opportunity to tackle truancy in those who have already offended. Discretion in framing the require-

---

[91] Including successive Education Acts since 1944 and the Children Act 1989.

[92] *Tackling Youth Crime* above n 45 at p 4.

[93] *No More Excuses* above n 46 at ch 3.

[94] That is, absent from school without lawful authority under the Education Act 1996 s 444, where the child is of compulsory school age.

[95] Home Office, *Power for the Police to Remove Truants: A Guidance Document* (London, Home Office, 1998) p 5; also available at <http://www.homeoffice.gov.uk/docs/truancy.html> (2005) p 5.

[96] See further Department for Education and Skills, *Guidance on Truancy Sweeps* (London, DfES, 2002).

ments of some community penalties (such as an action plan or supervision order) will allow the youth court to impose a requirement to attend school on a regular basis as one of a number of conditions of the order.[97] This may, though, be frustrated by the failure of YOTs to address educational disaffection in pre-sentence reports to the youth court,[98] which limits its capacity to identify and tackle this welfare need during the sentencing process. Similarly, the referral order process[99] results in a negotiated 'contract' for action to address the offending behaviour, the terms of which may include attendance at school. For non-offenders, the anti-social behaviour order (the terms of which are highly discretionary)[100] often contains restrictions on the young person's activities, but also may require attendance at school. All of these options share common enforcement procedures in the sense that the YOT will monitor compliance with these conditions, and breach results in criminal sanctions. So, whilst truancy remains a non-criminal form of deviance, in these diverse ways criminal sanctions can be imposed on specific young people who fail to attend school.

It remains the position in law, however, that parents are ultimately responsible for ensuring that their child receives education on a regular basis whilst they are aged under 16.[101] Therefore much of the policy in this area has focused on that parental responsibility, either in providing support for parents in carrying it out or, more recently, by imposing sanctions for failure to do so. The Children Act 1989, section 36, created the Education Supervision Order which embraced the supportive approach and sought to end the draconian practice of using civil care proceedings where parents persistently failed or refused to send their child to school.[102] Where a child is of compulsory school age and is not receiving 'efficient full-time education', rather than removing them from their home, this order leaves parental responsibility intact, whilst placing them under the supervision of the LEA. Schedule 3, part III, requires that authority to 'advise, assist and befriend' the child and the parents in order to 'secure that [the child] is properly educated'.[103] In this way, primary legal responsibility for the child's education is passed to the LEA but is carried out in partnership with the parents and, as with all provisions of the Children Act 1989, in accordance with the child's wishes and feelings. The language of these provisions is conciliatory and the Education Supervision Order is designed to prevent the need for criminal proceedings to be brought against parents under the Education Act 1996, section 444.

---

[97] See further Ch 7.
[98] See C Ball and J Connolly, 'Educationally Disaffected Young Offenders: Youth Court and Agency Responses to Truancy and School Exclusion' (2000) 40 *British Journal of Criminology* 594.
[99] See further Ch 6.
[100] See further Ch 10.
[101] Education Act 1996 s 444.
[102] See eg *Re S (A Minor) (Care Order: Education)* [1978] QB 120.
[103] Children Act 1989 sch 3, para 12.

In a similar conciliatory vein, the Anti-Social Behaviour Act 2003 (ASBA 2003) creates a parenting contract which can be made between a parent and an LEA where a child has been truanting or has been temporarily or permanently excluded.[104] Under such a contract the parent agrees to comply with requirements aimed at ensuring the child receives education and the LEA agrees to provide any support necessary. Breach of this contract on the part of the parent may result in them being subject to a parenting order.[105] Breach of the contract on the part of the LEA is not provided for in the Act. Whilst these provisions largely replicate those of the Children Act 1989, but in a less welfare-oriented context, they do provide a series of more constructive and intermediary steps to be taken before prosecution is resorted to. The ASBA 2003 goes on to provide for a fixed penalty system of 'on the spot fines' for parents in cases of truancy.[106] Under this procedure the LEA (in the guise of a teacher, head teacher, or other 'authorised officer')[107] may issue a fixed penalty notice requiring the parent to pay a fine as a punishment for an offence under section 444 of the Education Act 1996. This may be seen as a further step to avoid prosecution and court proceedings for such an offence. However, it is rather odd that the government chose the fixed penalty model as a framework for this procedure since the section 444 offence usually relates to a *persistent* failure to ensure a child receives education, whereas fixed penalty notices are traditionally used in respect of single incidences of minor infractions of the law, such as motoring offences. Of particular concern is the fact that under section 23(6) of the ASBA 2003, the LEA is entitled to use income from such fines 'for the purposes of any of its functions'. No other fixed penalty scheme allows those who levy such fines to exercise their powers as a profit-making exercise. Aside from the due process concerns that this may give rise to, it provides an incentive to the LEA to increase the application of the section 444 offence, rather than to avoid it.

The trump card wielded by LEAs in combating truancy is to prosecute the parent under section 444 of the Education Act 1996. Section 444(1) contains a strict liability offence framed simply in the following terms: 'If a child of compulsory school age who is a registered pupil at a school fails to attend regularly at the school, his parent is guilty of an offence' (punishable by fine). The Criminal Justice and Court Services Act (CJCSA) 2000 creates a new, more serious offence, of knowing that the child is not regularly attending the school and, without reasonable justification, failing to 'cause' the child to attend school.[108] The latter offence is punishable with a fine or imprisonment of up to 3 months or both. Prosecution is intended as last resort for parents who have refused or been

---

[104] Anti-Social Behaviour Act 2003 s 19.
[105] ASBA 2003 s 21.
[106] ASBA 2003 s 23.
[107] Section 23(6).
[108] Section 72 CJCSA 2000 which creates a new section 444(A) Education Act 1996.

unable to co-operate with previous attempts at partnership with the LEA or school. Indeed it is unlikely to achieve constructive results in relation to school attendance, especially where a parent may be imprisoned for the more serious offence. Before criminal proceedings are invoked, Department for Education and Skills (DfES) guidance requires schools to engage the LEA and Education Welfare Officer in attempting to resolve issues which are preventing attendance.[109] However the same guidance introduces a Fast Track to Prosecution for this offence which allows only four weeks in which to attempt the partnership approach before a summons is issued and the case is reviewed for court proceedings. The rationale behind the Fast Track is partly to allow for speedy early intervention in problematic cases, but also to achieve more managerial aims of consistency and efficiency in the prosecution process. Adding a sense of urgency to the threat of prosecution may also enhance its deterrent effect. Indeed, an evaluation of the Fast Track procedure piloted in 12 LEAs reported a positive outcome in terms of greater co-operation between parents and LEAs as well as better attendance rates, especially where non-attendance was a relatively new and emerging problem. The evaluation was rather less positive in relation to cases where non-attendance had been persistent over a period of time and where there were 'deeply entrenched' behavioural, social and family problems:

> Some LEAs did use the Fast Track for these types of cases in order to move them quickly to court. In this context Fast Track could be considered effective based on its procedural efficiencies.[110]

The outcome of this set of legal provisions to combat truancy may result in the use of the blunt instrument of the criminal law and a consequent, though indirect, criminalisation of truancy for both parents and children. Wardhaugh found that in assessing truancy problems in individual cases, truants tended to be categorised either as 'school phobic' or as 'morally endangered or delinquent' truants. Even at the conciliatory or partnership phase (before prosecution was considered) education welfare officers tended to view the latter as 'more culpable than the "fearful" variety' and 'were far more likely to be processed through the court system'.[111] That court system may begin with the imposition of an Education Supervision Order, but breach of that prompts further, more punitive, court proceedings. The problem, in Wardhaugh's view, lies in

---

[109] Department for Educations and Skills, *Ensuring Regular School Attendance: Guidance on the Legal Measures available to Secure Regular School Attendance* (London, DfES, 2003).

[110] K Halsey *et al*, *Evaluation of Fast Track to Prosecution for School Non-Attendance* Research Report 567 (London, National Foundation for Educational Research, 2004).

[111] J Wardhaugh, 'Criminalising Truancy' in T Booth (ed) *Juvenile Justice in the New Europe* (Sheffield, Joint Unit for Social Services Research, 1991) p 137.

a dual legal approach to truancy . . . with the punishment orientation of the 1944 Education Act [as amended by the Education Act 1996] co-existing alongside the more welfare-oriented philosophy of the Children Act 1989.[112]

A similar pattern in relation to educational difficulties emerges to that found in relation to parental or family difficulties in the home, as discussed above. Both are identified as welfare needs and the rhetoric and research evidence, oft-quoted at official levels, reveals their influence over youth crime. However, political expediency tends to pre-empt resort to punitive sanctions which, in the field of education, uses a simplistic understanding of truancy as absence from school and targets enforcement of the requirement to attend in both parents and young people.

Conclusion: 'Holding On'?

Policy in relation to tackling the parental influence over youth crime, and the important educational factors such as truancy and school exclusion which are linked to it, has been posited firmly within the criminal justice arena. The policy outlined above is characterised by its compulsion and coercion, rather than co-operation and support. Whilst it is widely recognised in policy circles that the family and the school have an important role to play in tackling youth crime, the emphasis in recent decades has been on forcing young people and their parents to address problems within their relationships or problems with attendance at school, with or without assistance from the state. Parental responsibility in particular is therefore as much a focus of criminal justice legislation as the young people responsible for the offending behaviour themselves. Parents are not trusted to carry out their developmental role without such coercion, and the plethora of orders relating to parents of young offenders is testimony to that lack of trust.

The tone of policy in this area is at odds with the research rhetoric on parental influence, which militates against punishment for failure and in favour of a more supportive and facilitative approach. Graham and Bowling and a number of others have concluded their discussions of parental responsibility for youth crime by suggesting a wider social policy, which seeks to improve fractious relationships and supervision opportunities as a means of directly tackling the *qualitative* features of family dysfunction which influence offending behaviour. This is a more subtle approach than using the blunt instrument of the criminal law. NACRO have persistently argued that a partnership approach between parents and the state is likely to be more conducive to preventing crime than an authoritarian or dictatorial approach:

---

[112] Ibid p 141.

[B]ringing up children is not always an easy task and if parents are to be encouraged to play a full role in limiting their children's delinquent behaviour it is important that they are given as much support as possible during such periods of difficult behaviour. They also need to be involved as fully as possible in decisions about official responses to their child's offending, if they are to exercise parental responsibility as fully as possible.[113]

Such support is less likely to be forthcoming from criminal justice legislation that has a greater focus on punishing offending behaviour, and is more appropriate to non-criminal legislation on welfare which addresses wider needs of families and children in the context of social policy.

In relation to education and youth crime, policy is also becoming increasingly intolerant of non-attendance and coercive in ensuring a child's presence at school. In this regard we also see an anti-partnership approach, which seeks to coerce parents into compliance with their statutory responsibilities for the education of their children and has engaged the school as an informal policing organisation to regulate and monitor this compliance. In this environment the relationship between schools and parents in problematic cases has shifted to one of police/policed. Education policy and the publication of league tables to highlight the attainment of performance targets within each school have also altered the relationship between schools as service providers and parents as 'clients'. In this way a conflict arises between the school's duty towards the state and their identified performance targets and their potential to carry out a pastoral role in relation to the children within their care. This tends to preclude schools and parents taking a partnership approach in ensuring any child not only attends school, but performs to the best of their ability and is nurtured to realise their potential. Parents and schools pitched against one another may not be inclined to work together in ensuring that the education provided to their children is 'effective' in the sense that Utting *et al* used the word in the discussion above. Further, a school facing the shame of failure in league tables where their pupils are misbehaved, playing truant or facing difficulties at home may be less likely to embrace their pastoral role and more likely to eject troublesome pupils passing them on to another agency, such as the police or social services, to deal with.

Parents vilified for their failure to prevent offending by their own children may therefore also be labelled as 'devils' through this coercive approach. Both the school and the state are in the position, as a result of further legislative duties imposed on parents, to pass the buck to parents for their own failure of social policy and educational provision. Parental failure to control children and ensure that they are effectively educated, like youth crime, is saddled with the label of 'crime' and addressed through censure and sanction. An alternative, more constructive, approach, however, is more likely to be achieved in a statutory or informal

---

[113] NACRO, *Partnership with Parents in Dealing with Young Offenders* Young Offenders Committee; Policy Paper 4 (London, NACRO, 1994) p 4.

environment where the threat of sanctions for failure is not present and where failure is not branded as a form of stigma for struggling parents. The developmental approach advocated by Rutherford calls for more child-centred practice, in which the key focus is on encouraging young people to mature and grow out of crime as a natural process, which cannot be forced or accelerated. It is argued in the next chapter that existing provision in the Children Act 1989 provides for a more co-operative approach between the parents and the state, recognising that failure is not a social 'offence' but a signal for the need for greater assistance and support.

Part III
Alternatives

10

Alternatives

Crime is not a 'thing'. Crime is a concept applicable in certain situations where it is possible and in the interests of one or several parties to apply it. We can create crime by creating systems that ask for the word. We can extinguish crime by creating the opposite types of systems.[1]

We saw in Chapter 4 how Nils Christie, in this statement, provides a way forward for policy makers genuinely seeking to reduce youth crime. It is an unusual way forward, since it involves 'extinguishing' the problem through some form of decriminalisation. The youth crime problem rests upon perceptions of teenage behaviour as 'crime' and so the criminal justice system is utilised to find a solution to it. As criminal justice measures increase, more and more young people whose behaviour is troublesome are brought into the criminal justice system to be either punished or rehabilitated using these measures, and so more and more young people are labelled as offenders. In this way, the more the youth justice system provides mechanisms to tackle teenage behaviour, the greater this crime problem will become. As the youth crime problem self-perpetuates through the use of the criminal justice system, the perception of youth crime as a problem intensifies, policy makers create further mechanisms in response and again the youth crime problem escalates. And so the vortex of criminalisation sucks larger and larger numbers of young people into the system.

The alternative of decriminalisation, however, is not just a numbers game in substantive criminal law, whereby swathes of criminal activity are removed from the crime statistics by changes to the definitions of offences. Decriminalisation can also involve changes in how we perceive behaviour and how we, as a society, choose to respond to it. Youthful behaviour is commonly perceived as problematic, harmful and immature and often falls within the technical definitions set out in the criminal law. In some jurisdictions such behaviour is perceived as a criminal problem and those criminal law definitions are used wherever possible; in others it is perceived more as a social problem. Youthful misbehaviour may be tolerated to a certain extent as an inevitable product of immaturity and adolescence, but if it exceeds some limit of acceptability, it may be perceived as symptomatic of deeper underlying problems which go beyond the norm for adolescence and

[1] N Christie *Limits to Pain* (Oxford, Martin Robertson, 1982) at p 74.

which need to be addressed. Beyond normality, authorities may intervene; otherwise, discipline and establishing boundaries are within the realm of parental responsibility and nurturing. The difference between the two types of jurisdiction is in the degree to which troublesome behaviour of young people is viewed with tolerance and a sense of normality. In the former the problem of misbehaviour is defined as youth crime and in terms of youth justice, and state intervention in relation to both the young person and their parents is maximised. In the latter the terminology of youth *justice* and youth *crime* are irrelevant and intervention is minimal.

A central question for both policy makers and society therefore involves making a choice between the criminal and non-criminal approach to the behaviour of young people. This book has examined the approach in England and Wales in which the choice to opt for a criminal system has been a long-standing one. Even in 1930s as the juvenile court was developing, policy makers rejected idea of removing young offenders from the criminal process, albeit for the most benevolent of reasons. In the 1960s, as Scotland was decriminalising their response to youth crime, the English government proposed a similar approach in 1965 but, in the face of opposition, rejected the decriminalisation route and sought merely to reduce the impact of criminal proceedings on young people as far as possible, leaving the youth justice system intact. At both times the youth justice process was seen as a portal through which social welfare provision could be offered. In this chapter we examine examples of where a different choice has been made, to abandon the criminal law and use civil proceedings or non-legal measures, where troublesome behaviour is perceived as especially problematic. These are alternative *systems*; as opposed to decriminalisation through raising the minimum age of criminal responsibility which was discussed in Chapter 2.

There is however, a further choice, between tolerance and zero tolerance. I have included in this chapter a discussion of the anti-social behaviour legislation as a non-criminal alternative to criminal justice procedures, albeit with a diametrically different approach to other non-criminal approaches in Scotland, and in English civil law. The anti-social behaviour legislation provides a form of decriminalisation which widens, rather than diminishes (or abolishes) the criminal justice net.

England and Wales

Crime, Disorder and Zero Tolerance

A feature of recent criminal justice policy in England and Wales is the focus, not just on criminal activity, but also on a more nebulous concept of 'disorder'.

Disorder is a wider term, which may encompass petty offending, but which also refers to behaviour among young people which, for various reasons, falls short of criminal offending. This may be because the children committing it are below the minimum age of criminal responsibility and their actions cannot technically constitute a criminal offence, or it may include behaviour by older youths which falls outside criminal definition but is considered nuisance behaviour, which in aggregate and persistent form, is viewed as harmful and distressing to the community as a whole. The government has felt that this wider form of deviance causes unease and social anxiety and requires an authoritative response.

The concern about disorder was originally confined to nuisance neighbours whose noisy, anti-social and abusive behaviour could disrupt neighbourhoods and destroy the 'quiet life' of a community. In a paper of that name, the Labour Party, in opposition, used case examples to demonstrate how families who 'act so selfishly as effectively to terrorise the neighbourhood' were a serious social problem which governments, in developing only criminal policy, had failed to address.[2] In targeting families, it was hoped that children indulging in such behaviour could be tackled through holding their parents and their family to account for their anti-social behaviour. They therefore proposed a series of measures to include a community safety order involving curfews, restraints on specified behaviour and requirements to desist from activities such as making threats, racial harassment, making noise and other forms of abuse. Upon election in 1997, when the new Labour government began to discuss reforms to the youth justice system, they did not confine their discussion to criminal acts and began to consider how to tackle more general disorderly conduct among young people.

The 1997 consultation paper *Tackling Youth Crime* sought to prevent young people from 'slipping into' crime by tackling disorderly behaviour which, in young children, was viewed as symptomatic of a propensity to graduate to more serious criminal behaviour. The paper depicts a miserable picture of very young children running amok through the estates on which they live:

> Unsupervised young children gathered in public places at night can cause real alarm and misery to local communities and can encourage one another into anti-social and criminal habits.[3]

A series of measures was therefore proposed, aimed at 'nipping crime in the bud' among the under 10-year-olds, whose wayward behaviour was thought to be reminiscent of the Dickensian waifs and mobs of wild, licentious rascals that Mary Carpenter and the American 'child savers'[4] had sought to rescue in the nineteenth century.[5]

---

[2] Labour Party, *A Quiet Life: Tough Action on Criminal Neighbours* (London, Labour Party, 1995) p 1.
[3] Home Office, *Tackling Youth Crime: A Consultation Paper* (London, Home Office, 1997) para 113.
[4] See further A Platt, *The Child Savers: The Invention of Delinquency* (Chicago, Chicago University Press, 1969).
[5] See further Ch 3.

By 1997, firm legislative proposals were set out providing for the community safety order to be available in respect of young people aged over 10 individually, rather than collectively within their families.[6] Jack Straw, in designing this order, was influenced by the 'broken windows' theory, developed in the US by right realist commentators James Q Wilson and George Kelling.[7] In this theory, Wilson and Kelling trace the breakdown in social and moral order in a neighbourhood to decay and physical degeneration of an area, depicted by broken windows, litter and graffiti. Residents of such neighbourhoods cease to take pride in their immediate environment, and fearful of the petty offending and disorder that begins to invade the area, lock their doors and place bars on their windows. Left unchecked by community surveillance, that petty offending and disorder is allowed to burgeon, followed by increasingly serious levels of crime:

> [A] stable neighbourhood of families who care for their homes, mind each others' children, and confidently frown on unwanted intruders can change, in a few years or even a few months, to an inhospitable and frightening jungle.[8]

This community degeneration requires a proactive and intense strategy of zero-tolerance policing to clear the 'intruders' from the area before physical and moral re-generation of the neighbourhood can begin and the broken windows can be repaired. However, as the problem begins, not with serious crime, but with persistent petty disorder on the margins of the criminal law, Wilson and Kelling argue that strict criminal law definitions may need to be dispensed with in order to implement the zero-tolerance policing strategy.[9] This requires using civil law measures through which precise criminal definitions of behaviour need not trouble the police and the courts in holding young people to account for misdemeanours and troublesome behaviour, which may, in any event, be excluded from the criminal law.

The new Labour government, mindful that many communities in Britain were plagued by the 'broken windows' syndrome, were anxious to develop mechanisms through which they could tackle intolerable behaviour committed by young people. Tony Blair, shadow Home Secretary at the time, had commented that the Bulger murder provided a signal to society that moral decay had set in, and the solution

---

[6] Home Office, *Community Safety Order: A Consultation Paper* (London, Home Office, 1997) para 23.

[7] The theory was first expounded in the article 'Broken Windows: The Police and Neighbourhood Safety' (1982) 249 *Atlantic Monthly* 29.

[8] *Ibid* at pp 31–32.

[9] For further discussion of this aspect of their theory see A Rutherford and M Telford, 'Criminal Policy without Crime: An Anglo-American Journey of Exploration' unpublished paper presented to the Annual Meeting of the American Society of Criminology (18 November 2000).

must come from a rediscovery of a sense of direction as a country and most of all from being unafraid to start talking again about the values and principles we believe in and what they mean for us, not just as individuals but as a community. If the value of what is right and wrong is not learnt and then taught then the result is simply moral chaos which engulfs us all.[10]

His successor in this post, Jack Straw, claimed to know only too well what misery could be experienced in these decaying neighbourhoods, having been brought up on a housing estate in Essex.[11] He visited New York in the summer of 1995, and witnessed Mayor Giuliano's apparently successful policy of zero-tolerance policing, which had cleared the streets of Manhattan of undesirable characters and rendered them much safer. As a result, the Crime and Disorder Act 1998 included a number of civil law measures aimed at children and young people whose behaviour fell short of offending, but nevertheless required an authoritarian response.

Controlling Children Under 10

A theme of the 1997 consultation paper *Tackling Youth Crime* was intervention to prevent young children from turning to crime before their troublesome behaviour led them into a life of crime:

> Stepping in before habits have become ingrained and before a child has started to identify him- or herself as an offender will often be more effective than waiting until that child ends up in court. The Government believes that more should be done to help protect young children from being drawn into crime. Children under ten (i.e. below the minimum age of criminal responsibility in England and Wales) need help to change their bad behaviour just as much as older children.[12]

It was therefore thought to be in the child's own interests for criminal justice agencies to intervene at this very early stage, before they had criminal law authority to do so, in the name of preventing the development of criminal behaviour. For the first time, the government was therefore proposing measures to target those under the minimum age of criminal responsibility, but this had to be done by giving criminal justice agencies civil law powers.

Curfews

The Crime and Disorder Act 1998 provided local authorities with the opportunity to apply to the Home Secretary for permission to operate a general local curfew in

[10] Tony Blair speaking to the Wellingborough Labour Party 19 February 1993, cited in A Rutherford, 'An Elephant on the Doorstep: Criminal Policy without Crime in New Labour's Britain' in P Green and A Rutherford *Criminal Policy in Transition* (Oxford, Hart Publishing, 2000) p 36.

[11] J Turner, 'Talking Shock Tactics' *Guardian* (26 May 1998), in which Jack Straw is quoted in conversation with an 18-year-old known offender.

[12] Home Office, *Tackling Youth Crime* above n 3 at paras 98–99.

their area for children under 10.[13] Applications to the Home Secretary must follow 'discussion and dialogue' at a local level between the local authority, the police and local residents,[14] and a perception that disorder among this age group, particularly at night, requires this temporary, emergency solution. Once permission is granted, the local authority may, for one month, impose a ban on children under 10 being in public places between 9 pm and 6 am, unless accompanied by an adult. Local residents must be given prominent notice of the curfew, and children found to breach it may be apprehended by the police and taken home (or to some other place of safety if it is believed that the child would suffer harm at home). This is not a power of arrest and breach of a curfew cannot be a criminal offence for children under 10. However, those apprehended for breach are reported to the local authority, who may take further steps to intervene in the form of a child safety order. Home Office guidance suggests that the curfew should be used minimally as an emergency measure, and should be used to enhance other strategies to combat disorder in a local area.

Child Safety Orders

Whereas the local curfew seeks to use the broad brush to target all children under 10 in a local area, the child safety order applies to a particularly troublesome individual. Section 11 of the Crime and Disorder Act 1998 provides the magistrates' court with a power to impose a child safety order on a child under 10 where specified criteria are met. These criteria include the contravention of a local curfew, or anti-social behaviour committed by the child, but also behaviour committed by the child which would constitute a criminal offence if the child were over10. For a period of three months (or 12 months in exceptional circumstances) the child is placed under the supervision of a social worker or member of the local youth offending team (YOT) and must participate in any intervention deemed necessary to prevent the behaviour recurring. The parent of the child must also be subject to a parenting order[15] and is required by the court to take appropriate care and control of the child as well as fulfilling other conditions, as deemed necessary. The order is founded in civil law as the child is under age for criminal justice purposes, and breach of the order cannot be a criminal offence. Breach can result either in further conditions being attached to the original order, or in care proceedings being taken under the Children Act 1989.

The government has justified this under-age intervention by stating that the 'youth justice system is only part of a wider crime reduction strategy'.[16] However, in the past this crime prevention role has been taken by social services and other

---

[13] CDA 1998 s 14.

[14] Home Office, *Guidance Document: Local Child Curfews* (London, Home Office, 1998) para 2.6.

[15] See further Ch 9.

[16] Home Office, *Guidance Document: Child Safety Orders* (London, Home Office, 1998) para 2.1.

welfare agencies without the intervention of the youth justice system. Indeed, the Children Act 1989 had already made provision for both a proactive crime prevention strategy on the part of social workers, as well as reactive powers to prevent troublesome behaviour in young people by offering advice, assistance, and, if absolutely necessary, some intervention. These provisions are discussed further below. The child safety order, therefore, merely provides further intervention powers, but, significantly, involving the youth justice agencies. The behaviour of the child which, as part of the statutory criteria, may prompt an order is clearly offending behaviour and anti-social behaviour (although they cannot be described as such because the child is under 10). This demonstrates that the order represents an attempt to circumvent the minimum age of criminal responsibility and the minimum age permissible for the imposition of an anti-social behaviour order (ASBO). To have achieved this explicitly, by reducing the minimum age and applying the ASBO to the under 10s, may have stirred up a 'political hornet's nest'.[17] The child safety order, however, reaches the same end in a more surreptitious way. Furthermore, the use of care proceedings, as a response to breach, suspiciously resembles the resurrection of the criminal care order which had been repealed by the Children Act 1989.

The Anti-Social Behaviour Order

For young people over the age of 10, a further new order was created in the Crime and Disorder Act 1998 to combat persistent disorderly behaviour, the anti-social behaviour order (ASBO). However, in legal terms it is a civil, rather than criminal, order for a number of reasons. Wilson and Kelling's 'broken windows' theory, discussed above, suggests a civil law solution to disorder, because much of this behaviour sits at the margins of the criminal law. To require the courts to prove the precise requirements of a criminal offence, according to the criminal burden of proof (beyond reasonable doubt) may hamper their ability to assign legal responsibility for the behaviour and take steps to punish it or prevent its recurrence. Similarly, the police may be powerless to *arrest* suspects for troublesome behaviour where it consists of single incidences of very petty acts such as harassment, shouting, spitting or menacing behaviour. These acts may not, in themselves, be criminal offences, or may be too petty to warrant the full police response of arrest and charge, let alone prosecution.

Existing criminal and civil law in 1998 did provide the police and the courts with measures to prevent this sort of behaviour in some circumstances. In relation to harassment, for example, the Protection from Harassment Act 1997 had

---

[17] J Fionda, 'New Labour, Old Hat: Youth Justice and the Crime and Disorder Act' [1999] Crim LR 36 at 45.

criminalised behaviour known as 'stalking' and in civil law victims of such behaviour could obtain court orders to prevent further molestation or interference. Further, a variety of public order offences existed under the Public Order Act 1986, giving the police powers to disperse rowdy groups of people in public places and arrest suspects for disorderly conduct. However, all of these powers presented problems which the ASBO procedure sought to overcome. First, existing laws required action on the part of victims or witnesses to report an incident to the police or the courts and give evidence to prove that intervention was necessary. However, where the problem behaviour consists of harassment, or is committed by a well-known local family or individual whose bullying reputation is feared, victims may be too anxious of reprisals to take action themselves. Furthermore, the sort of general nuisance behaviour that the ASBO sought to tackle, may not involve individual victims, but 'is directed at a community rather than an individual or family, or where the behaviour is anti-social but not necessarily harassing'.[18]

Second, in *A Quiet Life,* the Labour Party had recognised, as had Wilson and Kelling in 1982, that current criminal law is designed to deal with single specific incidences of harmful behaviour, and that anti-social behaviour often takes a more generic form:

> To use a medical analogy, the criminal justice system tends to treat the commission of a crime as an acute, rather than a chronic condition. The system is therefore at its least effective where the offending is chronic and persistent, where the separation of the incidents may lack forensic worth, where it is the aggregate impact of criminal behaviour which makes it intolerable and where the whole is much worse than the sum of its parts.[19]

A solution was therefore sought which could abandon the requirement for the label of 'crime' to be applied to identified offending acts and which could attempt to tackle more 'general feelings of anxiety, dissatisfaction and irritation'[20] caused by individuals within a community.

The result was a legislative proposal that was deliberately vague in defining the type of behaviour which would prompt official intervention. Rutherford describes the new law as 'criminal policy without crime', the offending behaviour being 'an elephant on the doorstep'; incapable of precise definition, but recognisable by us all once we see it.[21] The government preferred to call it 'sub-criminal law.'[22] Section 1 of the Crime and Disorder Act 1998 enacted the ASBO, a hybrid quasi-

---

[18] Home Office, *Community Safety Order* above n 6 at para 3.

[19] Labour Party, *A Quiet Life* above n 2 at p 6.

[20] R van Swaaningen, *Critical Criminology: Visions from Europe* (London, Sage, 1997) p 213.

[21] Rutherford, 'An Elephant on the Doorstep' above n 10 The original use of the 'elephant' analogy was used by Lawton LJ in *Bradbourn* [1985] 7 Cr App R 181 at 183, in describing the custody threshold in sentencing cases—see Rutherford fn 58.

[22] A phrase used by Home Office Minister, Alun Michael, in the Commons debates on the Crime and Disorder Bill—HC Standing Committee B (28 April 1998) col 37.

criminal order targeting behaviour which causes 'harassment, alarm or distress to one or more persons not of the same household as himself'. The interpretation of this vague definition therefore relies on the perception of the recipients of the behaviour or witnesses to it. The civil order may be imposed on a young person over the age of 10, who, on a balance of probabilities, has been proven to behave in this anti-social manner, and where the order is necessary to prevent recurrence of it. The local authority or the police apply for the order from the magistrates' court, thereby protecting the anonymity of the victims and saving them from the trauma of having to give evidence in court.[23] Once subject to an ASBO, a young person must, for a period of at least two years, be subject to whatever restrictions on their behaviour the court deems necessary to prevent the behaviour recurring. The hybrid nature of the order is revealed by the penalties for breach, which is an indictable criminal offence punishable by a maximum prison term of five years. Subsequent amendments now provide for a young person to be additionally subject to an individual support order in conjunction with an ASBO, which goes beyond restrictions on their behaviour and requires them to participate in specified activities, under supervision of the YOT or a social worker, breach of which is a further criminal offence punishable with a fine.[24]

Notwithstanding these very wide, controlling powers, the government were prompted in 2003 to extend the courts' powers further in an effort to 'stamp out . . . vandalism, litter or yobbish behaviour', this time citing the broken windows theory more explicitly:

> We have seen the way communities spiral downwards once windows get broken and are not fixed, graffiti spreads and stays there, cars are left abandoned, streets get grimier and dirtier, youths hang around street corners intimidating the elderly. The result: crime increases, fear goes up and people feel trapped.[25]

Further legislation was enacted, in the form of the Anti-Social Behaviour Act 2003, providing a tougher set of powers 'forcing people not to behave anti-socially'.[26] The new legislation targets more specific forms of anti-social behaviour, committed by people across the socio-economic spectrum, including nuisance behaviour by tenants, noisy commercial premises, possession of firearms (real or imitation) in public, and high hedges on domestic properties. However, some of the

---

[23] Although this procedure inherently means that applicant authority must rely on hearsay evidence to prove the behaviour. Although hearsay evidence is usually inadmissible in criminal proceedings, the courts have declared that ASBO proceedings are civil and therefore Article 6 concerns that the rule against hearsay should apply are irrelevant—see further *R (McCann & Others v Manchester Crown Court* [2002] UKHL 39 and comment by S MacDonald, 'The Nature of the Anti-Social Behaviour Order' (2003) 66 MLR 630.

[24] Criminal Justice Act 2003 s 322.

[25] Home Office, *Respect and Responsibility: Taking a Stand against Anti-Social Behaviour* Cm 5778 (London, TSO, 2003) see Ministerial Forward by David Blunkett, Home Secretary.

[26] *Ibid.*

provisions go further in targeting behaviour specifically committed by young people, often without any consequent harm. Section 30 of the 2003 Act, for example, allows the police to disperse groups of two or more people of any age whose presence in a public area causes intimidation, harassment, alarm or distress to members of the public. Section 30(6) goes further in relation to young people aged under 16, who may be 'removed' from public places by a police officer between 9 pm and 6 am, regardless of whether they cause any distress or harm to others. This power effectively prohibits any form of gathering or 'hanging around' in public, a very typical behavioural trait of adolescents. There is an assumption that the mere presence of young people in public, in groups of two or more, is anti-social, whether or not someone complains about their behaviour. Our intolerance of young people as a social group has now been explicitly expressed in this provision.

Discussion

Critics of the Crime and Disorder Act 1998 feared that the vague definition of anti-social behaviour, gave the state powers to restrict the behaviour of any type of individual who was considered to be irritating, odd or distasteful:

> Playing a CD player too loud, failing to control noisy children, uttering supposedly defamatory utterances, are only a few examples of behaviour that might qualify. Essentially any conduct that displeases neighbours could be deemed 'anti-social' . . . there is no protection for the defendant against the squeamishness, oversensitivity or intolerance of her neighbours.[27]

Indeed, some of the most vociferous criticisms of the legislation came from the Conservative benches in the House of Commons debates on the Bill who were concerned that all manner of individuals, could, through no fault of their own, become subject to this intolerance:

> We must be careful . . . not to create a system of law that discriminates against eccentric people. I mean people who are loosely described as 'a nuisance': people who raise eyebrows. We should be tolerant of people whose lives are somewhat different from the lives that we would like to lead.[28]

These fears have, in practice, been realised and nowhere more so than in relation to young people. The ASBO has been used as an instrument of intolerance for behaviour such as throwing toys at a car, looking through the windows of flats on an estate, playing football in the street, the disruption of science classes at a school and showing off tattoos.[29] Pressure groups concerned with children and mental

---

[27] A Ashworth *et al*, 'Overtaking on the Right' (1995) 145 *New Law Journal* 1501.
[28] Edward Garnier MP HC Debates vol 310 col 436 (8 April 1998).
[29] Numerous examples are listed on the website <http://www.statewatch.org> (9 June 2005).

health issues are particularly concerned that ASBOs are being used to curb behaviour in a draconian manner, where it is a manifestation of a mental disorder such as autism or attention deficit hyperactivity disorder.[30]

There is a danger that this policy will culminate in the 'quasi-criminalisation' of the normal behaviour of children. Children can be irritating and anti-social, since their immaturity may prompt behaviour which is loud, boisterous, aggressive or simply annoying. In an adult-centric world this behaviour may be increasingly intolerable and misunderstood. Children with a mental disorder are particularly vulnerable as their behaviour may be especially misunderstood and perceived as odd. The anti-social behaviour legislation now provides a legal mechanism which allows members of the public not just to voice disapproval or hatred of young people, but to take strong legal action against it, so that these provisions could result in the further demonisation of young people and further exclusion of this group from the mainstream of conventional society. There is no requirement for an ASBO to provide constructive action to be taken in preventing further disruptive behaviour[31] and most conditions attached to the order have, in practice, been prohibitive rather than facilitative. Further, since ASBOs can only really be enforced by the surveillance of the local community, in ensuring that a young person is not where they should not be, or doing something they are banned from doing, the local authority has no choice but to publicise the order and name the young individual subject to it. In some areas this takes the form of reporting the order in the local press or delivering leaflets to residents in an area informing them of the restrictions contained in the order and details of the recipient. Since this departs from the usual restrictions on naming young offenders subject to criminal proceedings under section 49 of the Children and Young Persons Act 1933, the Serious Organised Crime and Police Act (SOCPA) 2005 specifically excludes that restriction from ASBO proceedings.[32] This provides for exactly the sort of disintegrative shaming process that Braithwaite condemned in his work on restorative justice.[33] It is disintegrative, rather than reintegrative, shaming because it does nothing constructive for the individual to ensure their reintegration into the community, but serves to alert a mistrusting community to their misbehaviour and places them under the surveillance of their neighbours.

In this way, the government has achieved the engagement of members of society in a crime-fighting partnership, having acknowledged that it is beyond the

---

[30] Eg, the National Autistic Society have offered advice to YOTs in spotting behaviour associated with autism in order to avoid the use of ASBOs, after a young boy was given an order after repeatedly trampolining in his garden and making strange noises—see further <http://www.nas.org.uk> (9 June 2005).

[31] Except where an individual support order is issued (as described above) and where the parent of a young person under an ASBO is required to control their children's behaviour more effectively.

[32] SOCPA 2005 s 141.

[33] J Braithwaite, *Crime, Shame and Reintegration* (Cambridge, Cambridge University Press, 1989). See further Ch 8.

capability of the state to carry out the policing role alone. This is what Garland termed the 'responsibilization strategy'.[34] As young people are increasingly policed by their own community and under constant surveillance and suspicion from them, Garland argues that we develop a 'criminology of the other' in which:

> [O]ffenders are treated as a different species of threatening, violent individuals for whom we can have no sympathy and for whom there is no effective help. The only practical and rational response to such types is to have them 'taken out of circulation' for the protection of the public.[35]

Since, in the civil law context of anti-social behaviour, the option of taking the 'offender' out of circulation by placing them into institutions such as the prison is out of the question, they are instead eradicated to the margins of conventional society, from where they are unable to participate as full members of society. Rutherford describes this as the 'eliminative ideal':

> Put bluntly, the eliminative ideal strives to solve present and emerging problems by getting rid of troublesome and disagreeable people with methods which are lawful and widely supported . . . it is a social rather than physical death which is imposed through the enforced removal to a place from where there is little, if any, prospect of return . . . members of society conceive of the socially dead as being bereft of some essential human attributes and undeserving of essential social, civil and legal protections. Furthermore they are treated in a manner that denies them the possibility of receiving social honour, which is a requisite for becoming a recognised and full member of a social community.[36]

As society sweeps its 'devils' under its own carpet, it can begin to repair its broken windows and rebuild a community bereft of undesirable elements. In 1993 the government appointed a panel of experts from business, science, government and elsewhere, collectively known as Foresight, to look ahead to the future consequences of government policy in a number of areas. In 2000 they published a consultation paper considering ways in which new technologies and policies might provide opportunities to prevent crime reaching crisis levels. As part of this paper we are presented with a scenario representing society in 2020 in which their suggested crime prevention policies have been implemented.[37] Brightlands is envisaged as a heavily protected, walled community which is patrolled by both wardens and CCTV, and as residents of the expensive housing in this community are carefully screened, crime within it is eradicated. Outside the walled city, crime is rife, as a prison population of over 200,000 fails to deter, and the poorer people

---

[34] D Garland, 'The Limits of the Sovereign State: Strategies of Crime Control in Contemporary Society' (1996) 36 *British Journal of Criminology* 445.

[35] *Ibid* p 461.

[36] A Rutherford, 'Criminal Justice and the Eliminative Ideal' (1997) 31 *Social Policy and Administration* 116 at 116.

[37] Foresight, *Just around the Corner: A Consultation Document* (London, Department of Trade and Industry, 2000).

who cannot afford the luxury of patrolled housing, are forced to live in 'open housing land' where technological surveillance is less pervading. Residents of Brightlands feel vulnerable and frightened when forced to venture out of their secure environment into the crime-ridden 'ghetto' outside. The government's response to the consultation paper, published nine months later, behoved a crime prevention policy based on the greater use of surveillance (preferably electronic) to remove opportunities for crime.[38] However, what we can learn from the Brightlands scenario is a vision of society where the ASBO legislation is taken to its logical conclusion. The residents of Brightlands are the stakeholders in conventional society and live in an environment which may be clinical, heavily watched and dull, but is crime-and-disorder-free, since it is bereft of the undesirable underclass, including young people, who have been banished to the ghetto, from where they can only victimise each other. The post zero-tolerance society can live their 'quiet life' in peace, unaffected by all that irritates, provided society's 'devils' remain outside the mainstream community.

Scotland

Children's Hearings in Context

The 1908 Children Act, which established the first juvenile court in England and Wales, had equal legal force north of the border in Scotland. However, implementation of the new court was rather more problematic in Scotland. Not only did they not have a suitable court structure, run by magistrates, from which to establish a separate juvenile branch, but there was some reluctance among both practitioners and policy makers in Scotland to be required to 'adopt' English policy on youth crime and change an existing system which, in Scotland at least, was not so problematic. The summary sheriff court, staffed by a single professional sheriff, was thought to be perfectly adequate in dealing with young offenders and the lay magistracy of England was culturally anathema to Scottish legal tradition. Imposing this format of juvenile courts in Scotland, therefore required a great deal more administrative, cultural and organisational change than it did in England and progress in the implementation of the 1908 Act and the later Children and Young Persons Act 1931[39] was very slow and reluctant.[40] Despite pressure from

---

[38] Foresight, *Turning the Corner* (London, Department of Trade and Industry, 2000).
[39] Whilst the 1908 Act had created the institution of the juvenile court, the later Act in 1931 specified its constitution as comprising a panel of three, specially selected and trained, justices of the peace.
[40] See further D Cowperthwaite, *The Emergence of the Scottish Children's Hearings System* (Southampton, Institute of Criminal Justice, 1988).

the Scottish Office who felt obliged to implement legislation from the English sovereign Parliament, little was achieved in practice over several decades as either world events (the Second World War) or other policy priorities took precedence over this issue.

Since no real progress was achieved in establishing an English-style youth justice process in Scotland, the way was still clear in the 1960s to develop a radical alternative. By this time there had been further policy developments in England as the Ingleby Committee had recommended raising the minimum age of criminal responsibility, though it endorsed the structure and jurisdiction of the juvenile court. By the early 1960s the Scottish Office, mindful of the lack of progress so far in implementing the English agenda, called for an independent enquiry into the development of youth justice issues in Scotland. By the mid-1960s, policy north of the border had taken a very different track to that in England, culminating in the diverse pieces of legislation: the Children and Young Persons Act 1969 and the Social Work (Scotland) Act 1968. The independent enquiry in Scotland was carried out by Lord Kilbrandon whose 1964 report[41] reflected an unusually unanimous set of proposals of a committee whose members were drawn from varied backgrounds including social services, healthcare professions, the legal profession and the judiciary as well as local government and the police.

The report contained a blue-print for juvenile panels, which later became Children's Hearings Panels in the 1968 legislation. The key focus of the proposals was on informal measures in preference to formal proceedings, the abandonment of the use of criminal courts for dealing with youth crime and an emphasis on the welfare of the child. As a majority of young people plead guilty in the criminal courts, the real function of them is to deal with the aftermath of offending behaviour. In the very few cases where guilt is contested the criminal courts provide a further function of adjudicating on the facts of the case. It was therefore the view of the Kilbrandon Committee that the larger function of the criminal courts could more effectively be performed by a non-criminal panel—not even a non-criminal court, since the difference between a criminal and civil court was 'little more than a change of nomenclature'.[42] The proposed new panel would be entirely divorced from court proceedings, staffed by volunteers and not judges, and concerned only with the issue of whether compulsory care measures would be necessary in any individual case. Dispensing with legal procedures as a response to youth crime, would also enable the repeal of the minimum age of criminal responsibility, since criminal responsibility under the new system would be irrelevant. The Committee had, in any event, concluded that the minimum age was a nonsense:

---

[41] Scottish Office, *Children and Young Persons: Scotland* (Kilbrandon Report) Cmnd 2306 (Edinburgh, HMSO, 1964).
[42] *Ibid* para 69.

[I]t enshrines a proposition which is not necessarily true [regarding the capacity of children to commit crimes]. It is because the proposition may or may not be true, and because it is considered expedient that the law should provide that matters are to be regulated on the basis of the universal truth of the proposition that the questioning of the truth of the proposition is for practical purposes prohibited.[43]

The Committee adopted the policy view[44] that the minimum age merely served to protect children from the criminal process. Without a criminal process to protect them from, there was no need to keep a minimum age. Further abandoning criminal procedures enabled the system to avoid the conflict between welfare and punishment approaches which the Committee felt were 'incompatible or militate against each other'.[45] Unlike English policy makers in framing the 1969 Children and Young Persons Act, the Committee chose to commit themselves to the welfare approach to the exclusion of the punishment model.

The Kilbrandon Report was published and used as a framework for the white paper *Social Work and the Community*.[46] The proposals for the Children's Hearings system were packaged within a wider re-organisation of social services department and the delivery of their services to the community. Unlike the English white paper published in 1965, the Scottish white paper received a positive response from the media, the judiciary and politicians. Cowperthwaite quotes from a ministerial memo summarising the media response:

> Despite the possibility of a line that the [Kilbrandon] report was proposing 'letting young thugs off', there was a remarkable and complete absence of criticism in the press reception of the Report.[47]

This warm reception prevented the necessity for compromise in drafting a Bill to present to Parliament. Indeed there were few objections during the legislative process, many criticisms relating more to the re-organisation of the work of social services, others tackling aspects of the Children's Hearings system, but not so convincingly that amendments to the Bill were required. The Bill had a relatively easy ride through the Parliamentary process and was enacted in 1968, implemented in 1971.

The Provisions

Scotland has therefore operated a non-criminal procedure for dealing with the majority of young offenders, largely uninterrupted. The procedure was subject to

---

[43] *Ibid* para 62.
[44] See Ch 2.
[45] Kilbrandon Report above n 41 at para 54.
[46] Scottish Office, *Social Work and the Community: Proposals for Reorganising Local Authority Services in Scotland* Cmnd 3065, (Edinburgh, HMSO, 1966).
[47] See D Cowperthwaite above n 40 at p 28.

a major review in 1990[48] and some amendments were made to the procedure when the 1968 Act was repealed and re-enacted in the Children (Scotland) Act 1995. The legislative procedure creates a Children's Hearings system for children (under 16[49]) deemed to be in need of compulsory supervision measures.[50] Children believed to be in need of such supervision can be referred, by a civil or criminal court, the police or social services, to the Principal Reporter who acts as a 'gatekeeper' for the hearings panels. The Reporter must decide whether the grounds for a referral to a panel have been met. These are set out in section 52(2) and are summarised as follows:

(a) the child is beyond of the control of any relevant person;[51]
(b) the child is falling into bad associations or is exposed to moral danger
(c) the child is likely to suffer unnecessarily or his health or development is likely to be seriously impaired due to lack of parental care;
(d) the child has been physically or sexually abused;
(e) the child has failed to attend school regularly;
(f) the child has committed an offence;
(g) the child has misused alcohol or drugs or has misused a volatile substance by deliberately inhaling it;
(h) the child is in local authority care and is need of special supervision measures.

Where one or more of these grounds are met, and the child is deemed in need of compulsory supervision measures, the Reporter may refer the child and the person taking parental responsibility for them to a Children's Hearing Panel.[52] The panel consists of three lay volunteers, who will hold meetings comprising the child, the 'relevant person' with parental responsibility and a representative for either of these parties, which may include a lawyer (although no legal aid is available in Scotland for representation in a Children's Hearing[53]). The media may attend but there are heavy restrictions on the reporting of cases.[54] Otherwise the

---

[48] Scottish Office, *Review of Child Care Law in Scotland* (Edinburgh, HMSO, 1990).

[49] Schemes for including 16- and 17-year-old children in the hearings process are currently being piloted.

[50] C(S)A 1995 s 52, defined as measures taken for the protection, guidance, treatment or control of the child. Previously called compulsory 'care' measures, the new phrase clarifies the fact that this does not necessarily mean taking the child *into* care and away from their parents, but may include state intervention to assist the parents in caring for the child. There are however emergency child protection measures for those deemed to be in immediate need of care under ss 57–62.

[51] The 1995 Act avoids the terminology of 'parent' or 'guardian' and uses the term any relevant person, meaning any person with parental responsibility for the child, whether in law or in fact—s 93.

[52] C(S)A 1995 s 65.

[53] C(S)A 1995 s 92.

[54] C(S)A 1995 ss 43 and 44. The ban on publishing anything which may identify the child, their address or their school is, in Norrie's view, stronger than the reporting restrictions on youth court proceedings in England and Wales, breach of them is a criminal offence and they may only be dispensed with on the authority of the Sheriff, the Court of Sessions or the Secretary of State, where it is in the interests of justice to do so. See further K Norrie, *Children's Hearings in Scotland* (Edinburgh, W. Green, 1997) pp 58–60.

hearings are private and not open to the public. Indeed, while both the child and the 'relevant person' have both a right and an obligation to attend, the panel may exclude the 'relevant person' and the media from parts of the proceedings in order to allow the child to express their views freely and the presence of the relevant person at that time may cause distress.[55]

After a preliminary business meeting involving the Reporter and the panel, the panel will begin the process of discussing the welfare needs of the child in a hearing. The discussions during the proceedings are designed to be as informal as possible, though adhering to procedural rules for due process reasons, and their overriding purpose is to investigate issues which may deem compulsory measures necessary. The panel does not constitute a court of law and punishment for misdeeds is not relevant. If the panel are convinced that compulsory measures of supervision are necessary, they may impose on the child a supervision requirement, for as long as is considered necessary to safeguard the child's welfare, with conditions which may include medical treatment, limited contact with certain persons or residence in a particular place, including secure local authority accommodation for his own or the public's protection.[56] The child has a right of appeal to the Sheriff against the panel's decision,[57] and the supervision requirement must, in any case, be kept under review and may be terminated or amended as necessary.

Throughout these procedures the overriding and paramount principle is the welfare of the child, and all decisions must be made in the interests of safeguarding that welfare, giving due regard to the child's own wishes as appropriate.[58] This goes further than the welfare principle in the Children Act 1989 in England and Wales, since it explicitly requires allowing a child opportunity to openly express their views where they wish to do so. As a non-criminal tribunal, the children's hearings panel makes no distinction between a child referred as a response to criminal offending and a child referred for some other welfare need. Indeed, the criminal behaviour is viewed as symptomatic of need:

> [I]t is assumed that a child who has committed an offence, though culpable, is just as much in need of protection, guidance, treatment and control as the child against whom an offence has been committed. The commission of an offence by a child calls, in other words, for a caring response rather than a punitive response, just as the neglect of a child calls for a caring response.[59]

Further, the child in need is regarded as part of a family unit, those with parental responsibility are fully involved in the response to the child's needs and the panel's

[55] C(S)A 1995 s 46.
[56] C(S)A 1995 s 70.
[57] C(S)A 1995 s 51.
[58] C(S)A 1995 s 16.
[59] Norrie, *Children's Hearings in Scotland* above n 54 at p 2.

decision pays due regard to the entire circumstances of the child's home environment, rather than focusing on the child's behaviour itself.

Discussion

A remarkable feature of the Scottish Children's Hearings system is the enduring commitment of policy makers and practitioners to the principles underlying the original enactment. The child-focused approach has withstood changes to the political climate in neighbouring jurisdictions, such as England and Wales, and maintained a disregard for media hysteria over youth crime, and a European trend towards challenges to the liberal consensus and the adoption of more authoritarian approaches. Responses to a Scottish Executive consultation paper, *Getting It Right for Every Child*, overwhelmingly supported a continuation of this child-focused approach and expressed no wish to move away from a central objective of dealing with the needs of children.[60] However, some weaknesses are being perceived in the strength of this commitment which may pose threats to its continued endurance. The 2004 consultation revealed that 'a substantial proportion' of respondents wished to see further objectives added to the welfare and needs-focused principles, including action to combat poor parenting, the protection and acknowledgement of victim's rights and an emphasis on restorative justice, emphasis of the child's responsibility and accountability for their actions, and some degree of 'punishment'.[61] The Scottish Executive response rejected suggestions that offending children should be excluded from the hearings process and re-asserted the integrated approach to children in need, for whatever reason:

> [U]nacceptable behaviour and offending is addressed first and foremost through the Hearings system and children should only be dealt with through the criminal justice system in exceptional circumstances.[62]

That said, Lockyer and Stone have noted the emerging 'threat of disintegration' between approaches to offending and non-offending children:

> It has long been the practice to classify cases for statistical purposes by grounds for referral, and there is a growing inclination to speak of 'child-protection cases', 'child-abuse cases', 'young offenders' and 'delinquents' as separate types of case. The tendency to talk about 'child-protection procedures' or 'protection work', as distinct from 'working with offenders' is increasingly accepted in social work practice, which parallels a popular idealised dichotomy of 'innocent' children who need protection and 'undeserving' youth from which society needs protection.[63]

---

[60] See R Stevenson and R Brotchie, *Getting It Right for Every Child: Report on the Responses to Phase One Consultation on the Review of the Children's Hearings System* (Edinburgh, Scottish Executive, 2004) p 5.

[61] *Ibid* p 6.

[62] *Ibid* p 7.

[63] A Lockyer and F Stone, *Juvenile Justice in Scotland: Twenty-five Years of the Welfare Approach* (Edinburgh, T & T Clark, 1998) p 259.

The separation, explicit or implicit, of children into categories of offenders and non-offenders was supposed to have ended with the enactment of the hearings system, which sought to focus on their person and not the behaviour, and look forward not back. There were anxieties about this when the original Social Work (Scotland) Bill was presented to Parliament in the 1960s, when critics of the Bill suggested that ignoring the offending act and focusing on whether the child needed compulsory measures, resulted in a 'gap' in provision, in which petty offending which was not symptomatic of an underlying problem, would not be addressed formally at all, since a hearing would be unnecessary and the Sheriff's residual power to try cases in a criminal court would be an over-elaborate response.

It would appear that anxiety about this 'gap' has not diminished and reflects an increasing anxiety in more recent times, north and south of the border, about 'doing nothing' in response to minor offending. The minimalist approach to youth justice in England and Wales in the 1980s was rejected for similar reasons. It is argued here that the key vulnerability of the hearings system in the face of media and political pressure to 'get tough' or resort to restorative, victim-centred approaches,[64] is the failure in both 1968 and 1995 to eradicate the criminal justice mechanisms for dealing with youth crime, which though rarely used in Scotland, have been left intact. The residual power to prosecute where it is thought necessary and the retention of a minimum age of criminal responsibility[65] have ensured that the 'hardware' of the youth justice system remains in place and the threat lies in the fact that, in the event of a change in political whim, the hardware could be re-programmed. Heightened awareness of both persistent minor offending (much of which may fall into the 'gap') and anti-social behaviour[66] poses a threat that youth justice measures will be resurrected, and since the hearings procedure has always been a form of diversion from the Sheriff court (albeit used in the great majority of cases), that diversionary policy can be reversed.

The extension of the anti-social behaviour order to Scottish children may pose a particular threat. In 1998 the Crime and Disorder Act provided for the ASBO to apply only to people aged over 16, so that any interference with the Children's Hearings system was impossible. Since 2004, the ASBO now applies to children aged over 12 and breach of an ASBO is a criminal offence. As with any other offence, it remains a possibility that the young perpetrator can be referred to the Children's Hearings system in place of a prosecution. Indeed, anti-social behaviour is now a ground for referral.[67] However, section 10 of the Antisocial

---

[64] See further Ch 8 where it is argued that these may mean one and the same thing.

[65] It was noted above that the Kilbrandon Report suggested repealing this as it was unnecessary and flawed, but, perhaps by historical accident, it was never actually repealed in the subsequent legislation.

[66] Scotland has not escaped the ASBO, which now can be used for any person over the age of 12; Antisocial Behaviour etc (Scotland) Act 2004s 4.

[67] Antisocial Behaviour etc (Scotland) Act 2004 s 12.

Behaviour etc (Scotland) Act 2004 places an express prohibition on the detention of children who breach an ASBO, which rather presumes that criminal proceedings will be brought against them, since detention would never be a possible outcome of a Children's Hearing. The tone of official reaction to young people's troublesome behaviour has also become less tolerant. In May 2003 Scotland's First Minister, Jack McConnell, announced a 'tough talking crusade' on youth crime. In a speech to ACPO Scotland he claimed that there had been 'a growing crisis in confidence' in the existing legal measures and that:

> We have to change this. We need to address the years of decline in respect for the legal system. We need to set a tone that criminal and anti-social behaviour quite simply will not be tolerated in any community in Scotland, and we need to tell our young people there is a difference between right and wrong.[68]

This English-style rhetoric suggests that a change in political climate is imminent, notwithstanding the rather more objective and restrained tone of the Scottish Executive's 2004 review. Moreover, persistent criticisms of the hearings system, that it lacks resources,[69] does not engage children in a full participatory role,[70] that there are human rights and due process difficulties with it,[71] and that it has not been subject to sufficient independent research, has prompted Janice McGhee *et al* to suggest that the system is vulnerable to political pressure to move away from the welfare approach:

> The lack of baseline information against which to measure the performance of the hearings system leaves it vulnerable to political influence and pressure. The principles which Kilbrandon fought for at a time when juvenile crime was rising seem to [us] to be as relevant today. The current desire to remove young offenders from child-care decision making to a justice model risks stepping back into failed past experiments rather than addressing the social and family conditions which may contribute towards offending behaviour.[72]

The Children Act 1989: A Way Forward?

The discussion of the comparative examples of Scotland in this chapter and Belgium in Chapter 5, demonstrate that notwithstanding benevolent commitment

---

[68] Reported in *Scotsman* (30 May 2003).

[69] See Lockyer and Stone, *Juvenile Justice* above n 63 at pp 263–64.

[70] See A Griffiths and R Frances Kandel, 'Working towards Consensus: Children's Hearings in Scotland' in P Foley *et al Children in Society: Contemporary Theory, Policy and Practice* (Basingstoke, Palgrave, 2001).

[71] See Norrie, *Children's Hearings in Scotland* above n 54 at p 4.

[72] See J McGhee *et al*, 'Children's Hearings and Children in Trouble' in S Asquith (ed) *Children and Young People in Conflict with the Law* (London, Jessica Kingsley, 1996) p 70.

to welfare or developmental ideals, in practice there may be problems where decriminalisation is not absolute and complete. In Belgium the system of decriminalisation involves simply not using a criminal justice process which is in place for young offenders. What is often confused for a minimum age of criminal responsibility set at 18, is, in reality, a form of diversion whereby criminal proceedings are started against children, but almost always result in a finding of 'not guilty' and diversion to welfare agencies. The Scottish Children's Hearings system also left the underlying criminal justice procedure for children intact. The welfare ideal may have been embedded in rhetoric and practice for many decades in both jurisdictions, but both are having to defend that ideal against increasing critique from the political right and the vulnerability of the diversionary measures has become alarming.

These examples do show us, however, that it is possible to contemplate a non-criminal alternative, which, unlike the ASBO procedure, does not seek to punish. This has been achieved in the recent past where policy makers have been so minded, albeit in criminal justice systems founded on different legal cultures to that of England and Wales. Comparative experience shows us that avoidance of the criminal label for young people is not so outlandish. In England and Wales it may be considered an unusual suggestion where the youth justice system is becoming ever more punitive. However, alongside the punitive youth justice system we already have a viable alternative, which, without the creation of any major 'new' procedure or legislative scheme, could be utilised to tackle troublesome behaviour in young people. The Children Act 1989, which encompasses the spirit of the original Scottish legislation, can be applied in the same way, providing a child-centred approach without segregating the offenders from the non-offenders.

The 1989 Act in Context

Towards the end of the 1980s the government sought to codify a large volume of statutory public law provisions relating to children, their families and the state. An equally large volume of case law had developed in this area and the entire public law relating to children needed to be reviewed and set out in a more systematic set of provisions.[73] The Law Commission had been working on a codification of this area for some time, and their work culminated in a report on child custody and guardianship which formed the basis of the government's proposals on this subject, and ultimately Parts I and II of the Children Act.[74] At the same time the

---

[73] The law reform process had, in fact, begun in 1984, with the publication of the House of Commons Social Services Committee report *Children in Care* (London, HMSO, 1984). The impetus had been continued a year later with the inter-departmental report: Department of Health, *Review of Child Care Law* (London, HMSO, 1985).

[74] Law Commission, *Guardianship and Custody* (LC 172) (London, HMSO, 1988).

House of Lords decision in *Gillick v West Norfolk and Wisbech AHA* in 1986[75] had been influential on practice in family law, and the principles the House of Lords had expounded there, concerning the extent of parental responsibility and children's participation in decisions relating to their welfare, formed a key underlying principle of the new legislation.

In addition to these concerns for law reform and development of statutory principles, the Act was prompted by more urgent calls for reform to child protection procedures, the deficiencies of which had been highlighted in a number of recent tragic cases. The death of Jasmine Beckford prompted a highly critical enquiry of the practice of social workers in the London Borough of Brent, in which Sir Louis Blom-Cooper suggested that firmer guidance was necessary in cases such as these where social workers had not used their statutory powers coercively enough to prevent children from dying at the hands of their abusers.[76] Conversely, Lord Justice Butler-Sloss's official enquiry report into the child abuse scandal in Cleveland had been highly critical of social work practice in that area which had been over-zealous.[77] In that report, Butler-Sloss took the opportunity to comment on the proposals that the government had already published on the reform of child law and emphasised the need for urgent law reform in relation to child protection.

The publication of proposals for reform in the white paper *The Law on Child Care and Family Services*[78] coincided with developments in international law on the rights of the child. The UN Convention on the Rights of the Child was being drafted at the same time as the legislation in England and Wales, and the Children Act 1989 provided an opportunity to ensure that domestic law in relation to the child and the family was consistent with both European and wider international human rights obligations of the state. This would involve giving a more central role to children's rights and the participation of children in initiating, or voicing their views on, proceedings concerning their own welfare. At the same time, however, as we have seen in the context of youth justice reform, the government at that time, led by Margaret Thatcher, had managerial concerns which lay under their unusually liberal approach to legal issues. The Children Act 1989 provided an opportunity to reform procedures in this area and offer clearer guidance and statutory duties for social workers with a view to preventing the need for court proceedings and thereby cutting costs. Increasing parental responsibility could diminish the role of the state in protecting the welfare of the child, and reduce the number of children subject to wardship and care proceedings in the courts.

---

[75] [1986] AC 112.

[76] Brent, London Borough of, *A Child in Trust* (London, London Borough of Brent, 1985).

[77] Butler-Sloss, LJ, *Report of the Inquiry into Child Abuse in Cleveland 1987* Cm 412 (London, HMSO, 1988).

[78] DHSS Cm 62 (London, HMSO, 1987).

Themes

The Children Act 1989, which resulted from the various agendas for law reform set out above, is a wide-ranging codification of both the public and private law relating to children. It does, however, have a number of themes which provide a set of underlying principles for practice in this area. A central theme concerns *partnership* between institutions and individuals who collectively have responsibility for the welfare and development of children, including the parents, schools, social services and other local authority departments. The Act provides an earlier example of inter-agency collaboration in ensuring that the welfare needs of children are met, and also provides a rather different perspective to the youth justice system on the responsibilities of parents for bringing up their children. First, the emphasis lies in the parents being the first and most important institution for ensuring that the welfare of the child is protected. The language of the Act moves from the language of parental 'rights' and 'duties' to 'responsibilities' for children, so that children are seen less as a possession of their parents, and, in line with the decision in *Gillick*, as children mature, there is room for them to take over the responsibility for themselves from their parents. Further, the change in language denotes a shift in the relationship between the state and the parents, moving away from the conflict between 'them' and 'us' and towards a partnership in which parents can receive assistance from the state in carrying out their responsibilities without losing overall parental responsibility. The offer of assistance in this context comes without stigmatising labels of failure and without punitive strings attached. Government guidance on implementing the Act stressed this non-stigmatising approach:

> The development of a working relationship with parents is usually the most effective route to providing supplementary or substitute care for their children. Measures which antagonise, alienate, undermine or marginalize parents are counter-productive. For example, taking compulsory measures over children can all too easily have this effect though such action may be necessary in order to provide protection.[79]

The final sentence of that statement indicates a second theme in the Act; that of minimalism. In common with the developmental approach to youth justice, the Act reinforces the family as the most effective and important environment in which to bring up a child, and removing the child should be a last resort used only where the home is likely to induce harm or suffering in the child. The preference is, in most cases, for leaving the family intact, but offering assistance where it is required. More than that, however, the Act firmly states that even intervention to assist should be carefully restricted to cases where it is absolutely necessary.

[79] Department of Health, *Principles and Practice in Regulations and Guidance* (London, HMSO, 1990) p 8.

Section 1 of the Act sets out the key statutory principles for intervention by the state. The welfare of the child is the paramount principle, but section 1(5) reminds practitioners that the welfare of the child may be best served in some cases by not intervening at all:

> (5) Where a court is considering whether or not to make one or more orders under this Act with respect to a child, it shall not make the order or any of the orders unless it considers that doing so would be better for the child than making no order at all.

The provisions of the Act discussed below, will also show how social workers' statutory duties include proactive duties to prevent the need for court proceedings and state intervention to become necessary at all, so that prevention is preferred where possible over intervention. Where it is necessary to intervene, particularly in relation to urgent child protection, the drafters of the Act took on board lessons from the Beckford case and care proceedings remain available, with clear statutory guidelines on their use and a statutory principle in section 1(2) that 'any delay in determining the question [of child welfare] is likely to prejudice the welfare of the child'.

A third theme of the Act is the move away from regarding children as 'objects of concern' and towards regarding them as participants in proceedings and decision making, where they possess sufficient maturity to do so. The Act creates rights for children 'in need', including the right to initiate proceedings on their own behalf and the right to representation through a guardian ad litem in court.[80] Decisions made by the court are to be child-centred, a principle enforced by the paramountcy of the child's welfare in section 1, but also by 'checklist' provided in section 1(3) of further factors for the court to consider in making a decision:

(a) the ascertainable wishes and feelings of the child concerned (considered in the light of his age and understanding);
(b) his physical, emotional and educational needs;
(c) the likely effect on him of any change in his circumstances;
(d) his age, sex, background and any characteristics of his which the court considers relevant;
(e) any harm which he has suffered or is at risk of suffering;
(f) how capable each of his parents is of meeting his needs;
(g) the range of powers available to the court.

In this checklist, the parents and the state take a back seat and the primary considerations are focused on the child himself, including his own views and wishes. This is reiterated in section 22(4) in which the child's wishes must be taken into account before social services offer assistance to a child in need.

---

[80] CA 1989 s 41(4).

Provisions

It was mentioned above that the 1989 Act is wide ranging and contains no fewer than 108 sections and 15 schedules. It is therefore not proposed here to review the entire Act, but rather to examine the provisions that could be effectively used in respect of children who offend, in order to reduce the possibility of re-offending and address the welfare concerns that aetiological research suggests prompts offending behaviour. First, section 17 of the Act provides a general duty on the part of a local authority to 'safeguard and promote the welfare of children within their area who are in need'. This is both a proactive and reactive duty in theory; in practice, social services will respond to requests for assistance under this section as and when they are made by a child or his parents.[81] A definition of a child who is 'in need' is provided in section 17(10) as follows:

(a) he is unlikely to achieve or maintain, or to have the opportunity of achieving or maintaining, a reasonable standard of health or development without the provision for him of services by the local authority; or
(b) his health or development is likely to be significantly impaired or further impaired, without the provision for him of such services; or
(c) he is disabled [which includes suffering from a mental disorder].

In this context a child's development means 'physical, intellectual, emotional, social or behavioural development'.[82] Therefore, providing offending behaviour is viewed as a symptom of impaired behavioural, emotional or social development, an offending child may be perceived as 'in need' for these purposes. Given that a large proportion of young offenders experience emotional difficulties with their parents,[83] and, to some extent, socio-economic disadvantage, and misuse of alcohol and drugs, this is not an unreasonable perception. Where offending behaviour is simply a product of immaturity and adolescence, and where no significant underlying problem exists, the minimal approach of the Children Act behoves non-intervention by the state and a reliance on parents to fulfil their developmental responsibilities. Where there are deeper problems, section 17 requires the local authority to provide whatever assistance is required to alleviate need, whether that assistance is financial, material or other forms of support. This duty falls largely on social services, but the Act does specify a degree of inter-departmental collaboration where an alternative local authority department has the skills or resources required.[84]

---

[81] See further D Cowan, *Homelessness: The (In)Appropriate Applicant* (Aldershot, Ashgate, 1998) ch 4.
[82] CA 1989 s 17(11).
[83] See further Ch 4.
[84] See s 27.

In relation to educational difficulties, section 36 creates an education supervision order, under which:

> A court may only make an education supervision order if it is satisfied that the child concerned is of compulsory school age and is not being properly educated.

The order requires the local authority, again in partnership with the parents, to take steps to ensure that the child regularly attends school (or another form of full-time education) and can include a partnership approach between social services, the local education authority and the parents to supervise attendance at school and make arrangements for any special educational needs that may be necessary. This order has been discussed in chapter 9 in the light of other parental responsibilities in relation to education, but it is noted that the Children Act order is non-coercive and designed to be facilitative and assisting to parents rather than punitive, the focus here being on the educational welfare of the child rather than any failure on the part of the parents.

Where parental responsibility breaks down and the child is beyond the control of the parent, or likely to suffer further harm within the family, the Children Act does provide for the extreme measure of allowing the state to take over that parental responsibility through care proceedings. In the spirit of minimalism within the Act, the criteria for this more heavy form of state intervention is restrictive and set out in section 31(2) stating that an order may only be made where the child is 'suffering or likely to suffer significant harm', attributable to insufficient parental care or to the child being beyond parental control. Any concern that the most dangerous, persistent or serious offender in this age range would be free to continue to cause harm to others under a decriminalised system may be alleviated through the courts' powers to make a civil supervision order, under which the parental control of the child is supervised by social services, or a care order, under which the child is removed to a local authority care home. If necessary, the child may be removed to a *secure* local authority care home, for either their own or the public's protection. We saw in Chapter 7 how local authority secure accommodation can be used for young offenders sentenced to a custodial order, but who are considered to be too young to be held in a young offender institution. Under the Children Act 1989, exactly the same result is produced, but by a very different measure. The family proceedings court, under section 31 may make the order, but only where it is, primarily, in the interests of the child to do so, and secondarily where it may be in the interests of the parents or others to do so. It is significant that, for example, Venables and Thompson were detained in local authority secure accommodation, after their criminal trial in the Crown Court. Had the Children Act 1989 been utilised instead of criminal proceedings, they would probably still have been detained in the same institution, but via civil proceedings which were more mindful of their welfare.

Finally, schedule 2 of the Children Act 1989 provides for a proactive duty on the local authority to reduce the need for any type of court proceedings involving a child, including care and criminal proceedings:

> Every local authority shall take reasonable steps designed. . . (b) to encourage children within their area not to commit criminal offences; and (c) to avoid the need for children within their area to be placed in secure accommodation.[85]

Further, paragraph 8 of the same schedule, requires the local authority to proactively provide services such as advice, guidance and counselling, occupational, social, cultural or recreational activities, home help and assistance to enable the child and his family to have a holiday, all in the name of preventing 'need' and family or behavioural difficulties arising. These proactive duties already existed long before the Crime and Disorder Act 1998 placed further proactive crime prevention duties on local authorities and youth offending teams. The Children Act duties, however, focus on crime prevention as part of the protection of the welfare of children and their families, rather than on the need to protect society from victimisation; thereby effectively seeking to lock the stable door *before* the horse has bolted.

Potential

All that is required to implement this very different approach to youth crime is an altered perception of young people's behaviour and a commitment to abandon notions of criminal law. We have seen how this can be achieved using existing legislation, though changing the perceptions of a society is rather more difficult. The problem of youth crime has a constructive and meaningful solution already in place, but it is often ignored in the concern to separate the 'devils' from the 'angels' using criminal procedures for the former and these civil procedures for the latter. They even have, since 1991, separate courts to deal with their respective legal issues. The separation of the jurisdictions of the old juvenile court, into the youth court for criminal matters and the family proceedings court for civil matters drove a wedge between the two legal systems, but it is not impenetrable. What is required to penetrate that dividing line is a preparedness to view offending behaviour as symptomatic of welfare need rather than the adoption of a classicist, and therefore punitive, view that the child is inherently bad and chooses to express their evil nature in harming others. The 'devils' and 'angels' may, of course, be the same people, as research demonstrates that not only are young people more often the victims of crime than the perpetrators of it[86] but also that children who are abused

---

[85] Sch 2, para 7.
[86] See J Hartless *et al* 'More Sinned Against than Sinning: A Study of Young Teenagers' Experience of Crime' (1995) 35 *British Journal of Criminology* 114.

share background characteristics (including difficulties in parenting styles) with children who offend.[87]

The Children Act 1989 has not been as effective in reducing 'need' in children nor the need for child protection intervention, as had been hoped. Social services departments received insufficient extra resources to implement the proactive spirit of the Act and intervention has tended to be resource and demand led. However, recent reforms to the youth justice system, and the general widening of the youth justice net, have required significant levels of resources to be injected into criminal proceedings and interventions.[88] Resources diverted from the youth justice system to this civil alternative would enable social services and the local authority to take further steps in utilising the 1989 Act in the spirit in which it was intended, rather than taking the resource-led approach that they have taken. Resource issues are rather easier to deal with than other stumbling blocks to this significant change. What is required here is more than a diversion of funds and a change in the law, but a fundamental change in attitude among policy makers and the society which they govern. This is rather more difficult as youth justice policy is increasingly shaped by the forces of the media, public opinion and political marketability. In this context, resort to decriminalised, welfare-based provision appears rather old-fashioned, naively liberal and socially and politically unpalatable.

What is therefore required to reverse that political climate is a renewed focus on the reality of the youth crime problem rather than the rhetoric. The voice of the media and public opinion needs to be silenced, or at least reduced in volume so that beyond the hysteria we find a place of peace to engage in meaningful discussion, based on ideology and principle, of how youth crime can be most effectively handled. Thomas Mathiesen believes it is entirely possible to achieve what he calls a return to 'communicative rationality' and an alternative public discourse on youth crime:

> [P]olitical trends are not irreversible but depend on people's experience with the policies at hand. The movement to the political right which many Western countries experience today, may therefore change once again. A political re-orientation on the part of coming generations would today be of the greatest importance for the question of penal policy.[89]

This is more than whimsical wishful thinking. Historical examples illustrate how such political agendas from a relatively ensconced and stable regime can radically change, sometimes in a short time. Mathieson for example, cites the abolition of slavery and the fall of the Roman Empire as examples. He also places great faith in

---

[87] Department of Health, *Child Protection: Messages from Research* (London, HMSO, 1995).

[88] Eg, upon establishment the Youth Justice Board were given £80 million to spend on piloting new forms of intervention and evaluating the results. Further investment has been made in the custodial estate for young offenders as the prison population for this age range has continued to increase.

[89] T Mathiesen, *Contemporary Penal Policy: A Study in Moral Panics* unpublished lecture presented to the Annual Meeting of the Howard League for Penal Reform (25 November 1992). See also T Mathiesen, *Silently Silenced* (Winchester, Waterside Press, 2005).

the possibility of the collective voice of grass roots movements, practitioners, liberal thinkers and intellectuals as well as writers and academics to forcefully present alternative discourses to create a 'network of opinion and information crossing formal and informal borderlines between segments of the relevant administrative and political systems'.[90] Providing this alternative discourse is not 'silently silenced' there is an opportunity for it to join that of the media and the politicians and to inform developments in youth justice policy.

---

[90] Mathiesen, *Silently Silenced* previous n at p 107.

11

Conclusion

The preceding chapters have demonstrated how youth justice policy and practice in England and Wales is not only expanding but reflects a political shift to the right and an increasingly interventionist and controlling approach. While government policy discussions in recent years have asserted a confident sense of 'what works' in reducing youth crime, the legislation and practice which emerges from those discussions is characterised by a widening chasm between rhetoric and reality, between ideology and politics. It is underpinned by anything but confidence, rather by an anxiety to try as many identifiable mechanisms as possible to try and control a social phenomenon that appears to be out of control. In this final chapter some of the recurrent themes which emerge from the previous chapters will be examined more closely to assess how expansion has resulted from a concern to reduce crime and how the labelling of young people as devils and angels has prompted their wider social control and social exclusion.

In Chapter 2, the discussion of our social constructions of childhood and youth revealed an adult-centric, and therefore inherently negative, perception of the behaviour of young people. The rejection of the concept of *doli incapax*, and its gradual abolition for children over 10, signalled a social perception that children are anything but 'incapable of evil'. Indeed, our fear of the capacity of children for evil deeds, whether borne from a projection of adults' fear of their own internal lack of control or from their fear for their dominant position in contemporary society and confusion over how to treat children, has resulted in a demonisation of young people whose behaviour falls short of our expectations of childhood innocence. The bacchanalian nature of childhood, understood only from an adult-centric perspective, rather than from a tribal or anthropological, child-centred perspective, results in the assignation of the label 'devil' to those young people whom we fear the most. Once labelled as devils, only criminal definitions of their behaviour, and a criminal justice response, will provide the security yearned for to ease our anxiety. We therefore see young people's behaviour defined in criminal terms, and, increasingly, the failure of their parents to control their behaviour, as discussed in Chapter 9, is also criminalised. In Chapter 10 we saw how the nebulous concept of 'delinquency' has undergone a renaissance through the creation of a category of anti-social behaviour, falling short of criminal definitions, but attaining a quasi-criminal status.

Traditionally criminal definitions, in Hulsman's view, have been used to denote extraordinary or exceptional events requiring a response using the special measures of the penal system, as opposed to more informal responses that other systems may provide, for less alarming social problems:

> We are inclined to consider 'criminal events' as exceptional, events which differ to an important extent from other events which are not defined as criminal . . . Criminals are—in this view—a special category of people, and the exceptional nature of criminal conduct, and/or of the criminal, justify the special nature of the reaction against it . . . events are transformed, reconstructed, reduced in order to fit the definition of a criminal offence, quite apart from the original meaning that those directly involved bestowed on the event.[1]

In this way 'devils' are labelled as deviant, as a heinous group of 'others', in need of greater social control. Chapters 4 and 6 have shown how both the criminal definitions assigned to young people's behaviour are enduring and expanding, and how attempts to redefine their conduct, or at least respond to it through non-criminal measures, have been resisted over the decades since the juvenile court was established. Indeed, the tendency to transfer greater numbers of young people to the adult criminal court has reinforced the labelling of young people as 'criminal' and capable of adult-like evil.

The label of 'devil' emphasises the underlying fear of these exceptional events and exceptionally unruly people. In this social environment, even young people themselves recognise the anxiety they cause to conventional, adult society: 'They see you as a danger, a threat. Fuck knows why. Because you've got nothing and they've got something? That's probably it.'[2] A distinctive feature of youth justice policy in the late twentieth and early twenty-first centuries is the extent to which it is dominated by the politics of fear. Governments increasingly refer to public opinion and media perceptions of young people, in place of ideology. Successive chapters of this book have revealed how the 'rhetoric' of youth crime is often divorced from the theoretical and statistical 'reality' of the problem. This is unsurprising when public opinion and media perceptions form the basis of policy, since these perspectives on the problem will inevitably be dramatised and spectacular, informed as they are from a distance from the problem. Media perceptions, designed to entertain rather than inform, will inevitably focus on the truly exceptional, the most salacious and the most shocking for commercial purposes.[3] They will also tend towards dichotomous, stereotypical and banal analysis, since detail and depth in discussions not only make for dull reading but also fail to satisfy

---

[1] L Hulsman, 'Penal Reform in the Netherlands: Part I—Bringing the Criminal Justice System under Control' (1981) 20 *Howard Journal* 150 at 152.
[2] A young homeless man quoted in P Carlen, *Jigsaw: A Political Criminology of Youth Homelessness* (Milton Keynes, Open University Press, 1996) p 121.
[3] S Chibnall, *Law and Order News* (London, Tavistock, 1977).

consumers who seek evidence of trauma to justify their anxieties.[4] Glassner's study of cultural fears in the United States concluded that: 'The success of a scare depends not only on how well it is expressed but also on how well it expresses deeper cultural anxieties.'[5] This produces a warped and irrational picture of youth crime. Public opinion may be similarly irrational or divorced from reality since it is most often formed by those most distant from the events under discussion:

> The reaction of the indirect participants should be understood not so much as taking a firm position in respect to a real event but rather as vicarious participation in the drama of criminal law. In that drama the roles are clearly defined, and the reactions do nothing more than reflect the Manichean structure of the drama. One chooses a side as one supports Feijenoord or Ajax (football teams) or is for St Michael and against Lucifer.[6]

The public who are not directly victimised are therefore the audience of the unfolding drama, supporting the devils or the angels depending on their levels of anxiety or their political stance. Victims of crime tend, according to surveys of their views, to take a more rational, less punitive and more constructive view.[7]

From a distance it is easier to demand punishment for youth crime. Distance from the reality impedes the empathy for the participants that comes from proximity to the problem. Those that come into contact with the young people actually involved, take a more empathetic and considerate approach. The discussion in Chapter 3 of who makes youth justice policy revealed that practitioners at the ground level, dealing with young people more directly, often take a more measured approach and, less influenced by fear, have shown a stronger commitment to minimal intervention and more constructive responses. Nils Christie has described how the 'meeting in the mountains' in Norway, to which experts, policy makers and some offenders themselves are invited, provides ideological and rational discussions of crime in a 'joint moral community' which benefits from the proximity to the problem and distance from hysteria and hype:

> We are forced into some degree of proximity. The situation does not lend itself to complete distortion. Pictures of monsters do not thrive under such conditions . . . a general effect of all these meeting places has probably been to establish some kind of informal minimum standard for what is considered decent in the name of punishment, and valid for all human beings . . . concerning their validity for *all* people, let me suggest here, as a minimum, this has something to do with imaginative power, the capacity to see oneself in the other person's situation. In the contrasting situation, with the offender seen as another breed, a non-person, a thing, there are no limits to possible atrocities.[8]

---

[4] A Young, *Imagining Crime* (London, Sage, 1996) ch 5.

[5] B Glassner, *The Culture of Fear* (New York, Perseus Books, 1999) p 208.

[6] Hulsman above n 1 at p 158.

[7] See further N Walker and M Hough (eds) *Public Attitudes to Sentencing: Surveys from Five Countries* (Aldershot, Gower, 1988).

[8] N Christie, *Crime Control as Industry* (London, Routledge, 2000) p 43.

Lacking in such proximity, youth justice policy influenced by public opinion and the media, as well as political expediency which is dependent on both, focuses on the young person as the 'other' and on the youth crime problem as divorced from its social context. Governments concerned not to deviate too far from public opinion tend to design youth justice policy which focuses on the wrong questions, asking how they can provide *more* criminal measures to tackle a problem entrenched in the criminal law, rather than looking at the holistic nature of the problem and asking whether there are wider social problems which need to be addressed outside the criminal system in order to reduce crime. Chapter 7 discussed the increasing influence of actuarial justice on sentencing policy for young people and in Chapter 8 we saw how more conciliatory, reintegrative approaches to youth justice policy, aimed at minimising social exclusion and allaying irrational fears, have been mutated into an opportunity for victims' (presumed) hatred and mistrust to be voiced and for that to prompt further social control and punishment. The state 'theft' of conflicts from those most directly involved in them ensures that youth justice policy reflects the interests of the system itself and the wider agenda of the public, which perpetuate a punitive response:

> [P]rison figures are not created by crime, but by cultural/political decisions. They are based on decisions on what sort of society we want to be part of.[9]

Youth justice policy founded on the politics of fear has produced an expansion of intervention for a number of reasons. First, policy makers lacking the confidence to commit to a specific ideology and concerned with slavishly embracing public opinion have developed ambiguous policies marked by their bifurcatory approach. Chapters 5 and 7 illustrated how governments have expressed their philosophical indecision through attempts to implement a number of agendas contemporaneously, often with less emphasis on the more unpopular, liberal models. Whereas historically youth justice policy has been marked by the 'pendulum swing' between commitments to extreme models at either end of the political and criminological spectrum, in more recent years we have witnessed the pendulum spiralling between a number of points on that spectrum at the same time. The disparate measures that are implemented attempt some diversion and rehabilitation to address the welfare needs of a young offender, but almost always revert to the more familiar and secure punishment or justice approach when a more liberal approach is thought to fail, or is politically unpalatable to the critics. Governments that have recognised the 'limits of the sovereign state'[10] in combating crime, appear to be trying any policy idea that springs to mind in an effort to cover every eventuality and to please everybody.

---

[9] *Ibid* p 53.
[10] D Garland, 'The Limits of the Sovereign State: Strategies of Crime Control in Contemporary Society' (1996) 36 *British Journal of Criminology* 445.

Second, the persistent labelling of young people as devils, results in an expansion in their social exclusion and control. Chapter 4 examined the criminological analysis of labelling by the likes of Howard Becker and Stanley Cohen and assessed how criminal labels create a marginalised group of 'outsiders'. Pfohl has argued that there is some social utility in the use of the criminal label to divert 'trouble' from a society, since the notion of trouble, packaged neatly within the individual identified as the trouble-maker, can be banished in the process of exiling that individual from conventional society:

> In the act of labelling someone a criminal, we attend to a person while disattending to the conflictual situations out of which that person has been ritualistically wrenched. We reduce the problem of trouble to the problem of the troublemaker, the problem of crime to the 'criminal'.[11]

In this way we need not be troubled about our own responsibility for problems which arise within our communities, nor our influence over them; we may simply eradicate the 'others' from 'us' and reinforce our social identity and the moral consensus of the majority:

> The majesty of the law is the dominance of the group over the individual, and the paraphernalia of the criminal law serves not only to exile the rebellious individual from the group, but also to awaken in law abiding members of society the inhibitions which make rebellion impossible. The formulation of these is the basis for criminal law.[12]

Social exclusion of the devils, therefore, serves to impose greater controls over their behaviour, as well as to reinforce the dominant cultural norms in society which have created a sub-culture out of that group of devils. In recent decades the process has gone further in utilising the mechanisms and institutions of conventional society to assist in the policing of that sub-culture. Through a process which Garland calls 'responsibilization', mistrust and suspicion of the sub-culture is embraced to encourage us all to indulge in surveillance of our own communities and to facilitate the banishment of trouble:

> The recurring message of this approach is that the state alone is not, and cannot effectively be, responsible for preventing and controlling crime. Property owners, residents, retailers, manufacturers, town planners, school authorities, transport managers, employers, parents and individual citizens——all of these must be persuaded to change their practices in order to reduce criminal opportunities and increase informal controls.[13]

Throughout this book we have seen how parents (Chapter 9), victims (Chapter 8), local authority partnerships (Chapter 7) and individual citizens through the

---

[11] S Pfohl, 'Labelling Criminals' in H Ross (ed) *Law and Deviance* (Beverly Hills, Sage, 1981) p 91.
[12] G Mead, 'The Psychology of Punitive Justice' (1918) 23 *American Journal of Sociology* 577 at 591.
[13] Garland, 'The Limits of the Sovereign State' above n 10 at p 453.

anti-social behaviour legislation (Chapter 10) are now fully recruited to the criminal justice corporation.

Commitment to the criminal justice system as an instrument of social exclusion is therefore heightened through the responsibilisation process, since the state does not relinquish its governance over crime, but engages others to offer assistance in carrying it out. However, we saw in Chapter 4 that not only does the labelling of individuals exacerbate their propensity to offend through altering their self-concept,[14] but also, on a more structural level, can manufacture further deviance through the identification of those outcast from the mainstream of society. The labelling of the 'other' serves to enhance suspicion of young people's behaviour at the margins of the criminal law, rather than quell it, which prompts further mistrust, greater anxiety and a greater will to control. A controlling youth justice policy, therefore, produces a vicious circle of exclusion, suspicion, more control, further exclusion and so on. As the vicious circle perpetuates, the criminal justice system expands and new means of intervention are invented. Dobash *et al* also report that excessive contact between young people and the police generates 'ignorance and suspicion' on the part of young people towards the police and a negative spiral in their relationships with these authorities,[15] which will further heighten antagonism and the labelling process.

The criminal justice process is ineffective and damaging as a mechanism for responding to youth crime. Carlen was cited in Chapter 9, as lamenting the lack of a holistic approach of criminal policy to the problem, focusing too much on the deeds of the individual rather than on the socio-economic and undemocratic forces which lie at the aetiological roots of that behaviour.[16] We have also seen in Chapter 5 on diversion and Chapter 7 on sentencing, how formalised criminal processes have a tendency to widen the net of social control and, once established and accepted as effective, draw their raw material from a wider group of young people. The focus on criminal justice procedures in youth justice policy since the 1980s has also marginalised the role of informal institutions, particularly what Rutherford calls the 'developmental institutions' which may be especially well placed and well qualified to deal with the real (as opposed to rhetorical) causes of youth crime without causing further damage to the developmental process. Hulsman argues that the criminal justice process tends to focus on the very small and the 'mega-institutions' of society, namely the individual offender and the state apparatus for punishment. This excludes the 'intermediate institutions':

[14] See further E Lemert, *Human Deviance, Social Problems and Social Control* (Englewood Cliffs, NJ, Prentice-Hall, 1967); D Farrington 'The Effects of Public Labelling' (1977) 17 *British Journal of Criminology* 112.

[15] R Dobash *et al*, 'Ignorance and Suspicion: Young People and Criminal Justice in Scotland and Germany' (1990) 30 *British Journal of Criminology* 306.

[16] P Carlen, 'Youth Justice? Arguments for Holism and Democracy in Responses to Crime' in P Green and A Rutherford (eds) *Criminal Policy in Transition* (Oxford, Hart Publishing, 2000).

Very little attention is paid to the basic elements in society, namely intermediate institutions; that is to say, small local groups in which face-to-face contact between the members is possible. Examples are: the family, the neighbourhood, the setting in which one works, a group of friends, a youth club . . . emphasis on the small and large units, must necessarily lead to alienation and the collapse of social order. It therefore suggests that the State must provide support to intermediate institutions and that the control of conflict and mediation must be left to them as much as possible.[17]

The approach to parental responsibility and engaging schools in combating truancy and school exclusion has become increasingly punitive and parental responsibility, in particular, has become a focus for increased state punishment, rather than an alternative to it. In creating the politics of fear and addressing the presumed anxieties of the public towards young people, the government has become less willing to trust the developmental institutions and more blind to alternative approaches outside of the criminal justice system.

Alternative approaches do, however, exist although discussion of them is less common than it used to be and they are often dismissed as naïve, dangerous and impossible. They are, it is argued, neither naïve nor impossible, but require confidence and trust in developmental institutions and informal processes and an abandonment of criminal definitions which obfuscate the reality of the youth crime problem. A theme of Nils Christie's many writings on penal policy is the reinforcement of the message that we do not need criminal definitions as a starting point for tackling anti-social or harmful behaviour in any society. His latest work summarises this position:

Acts are not, they become; their meanings are created as they occur. To classify and evaluate are core activities for human beings. The world comes to us as we constitute it. Crime is thus a product of cultural, social and mental processes. For all acts, including those seen as unwanted, there are dozens of possible alternatives to their understanding: bad, evil, misplaced honour, youth bravado, political heroism—or crime. The 'same' acts can thus be met within several parallel systems as judicial, psychiatric, pedagogical, theological.[18]

Criminal definitions and perceptions of behaviour as crime are therefore social and policy constructs and not universal truths. It is not impossible to view troublesome behaviour in a different way and deal with it in a different context. Chapter 10 revealed how this has been Scottish practice for over 30 years.

Neither is it impossible, though perhaps politically risky, to approach youth crime in a way which integrates the reality of the problem with the social context in which it occurs, especially where aetiological evidence tells us it is a largely a temporary and non-threatening problem associated with lack of attachment to parents and schools and a lack of social control and supervision by those institu-

---

[17] Hulsman above n 1 at p 155.
[18] N Christie, *A Suitable Amount of Crime* (London, Routledge, 2004) p 10.

tions. It is therefore conceivable, perhaps even sensible, to make these institutions a starting point in tackling young people's troublesome behaviour, using informal intervention where possible and placing trust in parents, the family, schools and the community to deal with the young people that they are already responsible for. The 1980s gave us a snapshot of how a more minimal and informal approach might be more effective than the rather more punitive, interventionist, controlling method of dealing with youth crime which is currently in operation, and which the chapters of this book have shown to be inherently flawed.

In advocating this alternative approach, I am not advocating doing nothing; neither am I denying the harm, pain and loss caused by youth crime to those who are victimised by it. Rather I am suggesting seeking an approach which may involve doing a great deal, but in a less visible and formal arena, in a way which causes less 'pain' or 'suffering'[19] to both the young person and their victim. In Chapter 10 it was suggested that formal intervention, where necessary, can avoid the use of the criminal justice apparatus and can either provide support to the developmental institutions or offer more expert, professional guidance and supervision through the Children Act 1989. This is not so radical; the legislation already seeks to do just that, but at present in relation to young people deemed to be 'in need' as a result of their circumstances and who therefore fall in to the category of 'angels'. The 'devils' currently processed in the criminal system, may well be the same young people, but the persistence of these labels has perpetuated a dual-system of welfare and punishment and precludes the 'joined up', more integrated or 'holistic' approach. Since criminal events do not differ in any real sense from other exceptional social phenomena, according to Christie and Hulsman, there is a justification for dealing with them in similar ways:

> Some of these have a legal character, such as the civil law system; others do not, such as the medical system, the social work system, the education system and several of the intermediate institutions mentioned previously.[20]

Historical and comparative experience has taught us, however, that in order to eradicate the tendency to label and divide the devils from the angels, we need to engage in more than a process of reduction of the use of criminal measures; rather we need to make more radical changes to our perception of young people's behaviour, place greater trust in ground level professionals and entrench the non-criminal approach, so that commitment to a non-criminal alternative cannot be weakened as the political whim changes. The cause and effect relationship between public opinion and responses to youth crime can be reversed so that these

---

[19] Nils Christie has described the process of punishment as the infliction of pain (in *Limits to Pain* (Oxford, Martin Robinson, 1982) and Hulsman describes it as causing 'suffering' in 'Penal Reform in the Netherlands' above n 1 at p 156.

[20] L Hulsman, 'Penal Reform in the Netherlands: Part II—Criteria for Deciding on Alternatives to Imprisonment' (1982) 21 *Howard Journal* 35 at 36.

responses can inform rhetoric rather than reacting to it. A proposal is set out in Chapter 10 to make greater use of the English Children Act 1989 as an alternative, non-criminal way forward.

Ideally, this would involve, as a pre-requisite, the abolition of criminal methods for dealing with youth crime, making it harder to reverse the policy without major new legislation. 'Abolition' is a word uttered in academic discourse on criminal policy these days only by the very brave few. For some it is considered too risky, politically unpalatable and possibly prompts an alternative that is considered even worse. Mathiesen argues that the abolitionists are being 'silently silenced' as academic discourse is increasingly sidelined by populist discourse, media analysis and political zeal.[21] It does involve policy makers taking risks, with their political fortunes as well as with the youth crime problem. It does involve sacrificing the due process procedures, proportionate responses and the expression of collective sentiments through deterrence, retribution and incapacitation that Beccaria had proclaimed were fair and just in his classical model of punishment. Doing less in the formal sense, and offering more informal discretion to experts where necessary, requires us to accept that the discretion may not be subject to formal controls and minimises the monitoring role of the state. However, since the alternative proposed here involves measured minimalism and is rooted in benevolent intention, it is argued that there is less to fear from the alternative than the expanding 'punitive rhetoric'[22] of the current system. Churchill's declaration to the House of Commons in 1910 that 'the mood and temper of the public in regard to the treatment of crime and criminals is one of the most unfailing tests of the civilization of any country' has often been quoted in the context of youth justice.[23] If he was right, the deepening punitive rhetoric of contemporary youth justice policy paints a grave and depressing picture of how we, as a society, choose to treat our young citizens.

---

[21] See further T Mathiesen, *Silently Silenced* (Winchester, Waterside Press, 2005).

[22] See further I Brownlee, 'New Labour—New Penology? Punitive Rhetoric and the Limits of Managerialsim in Criminal Justice Policy' (1998) 25 *Journal of Law and Society* 313.

[23] HC Debates vol 19 cols 1353–54 (1910), quoted, for example, by A Rutherford in 'The Mood and Temper of Penal Policy: Curious Happenings in England during the 1980s' (1989) 27 *Youth and Policy* 27.

BIBLIOGRAPHY

Abrams, D and Hogg, M (eds) *Social Identity Theory: Constructive and Critical Advances* (London, Harvester Wheatsheaf, 1990).

Alder, C and Wundersitz, J, *Family Conferencing and Juvenile Justice: The Way Forward or Misplaced Optimism?* (Canberra, Australian Institute for Criminology, 1994).

Allen, C, Crow, I and Cavadino, M, *Evaluation of the Youth Court Demonstration Project* HORS 214 (London, Home Office, 2000).

Allen, R, 'Parental Responsibility for Juvenile Offenders' in T Booth (ed) *Juvenile Justice in the New Europe* (Sheffield, Joint Unit for Social Services Research, 1991).

—— 'Out of Jail: The Reduction in the Use of Penal Custody for Male Juveniles 1981–88' (1991) 30 *Howard Journal* 30.

Anderson, R, *Representation in the Juvenile Court* (London, Routledge, 1978).

Ariés, P, *Centuries of Childhood* (London, Cape, 1973).

Ashworth, A, 'The "Public Interest" Element in Prosecutions' [1987] Crim LR 595.

—— *Sentencing and Criminal Justice* 3rd edn (London, Butterworths, 2000).

—— and Fionda, J, 'Prosecution, Accountability and the Public Interest: The New CPS Code' [1994] Crim LR 894.

—— Gardner, J, Morgan, R, Smith, ATH, von Hirsch, A and Wasik, M, 'Overtaking on the Right' (1995) 145 *New Law Journal* 1501.

—— Gibson, B, Cavadino, P, Rutherford, A and Harding, J, *The Youth Court* (Winchester, Waterside Press, 1992).

—— and Redmayne, M, *The Criminal Process* 3rd edn (Oxford, Oxford University Press, 2005).

Asquith, S (ed) *Children and Young People in Conflict with the Law* (London, Jessica Kingsley, 1996).

Audit Commission, *Misspent Youth . . . Young People and Crime* (London, TSO, 1996).

—— *Youth Justice 2004: A Review of the Reformed Youth Justice System* (London, TSO, 2004).

Aye Maung, N, *Young People, Victimisation and the Police* HORS 140 (London, TSO, 1995).

Bainham, A, Day Sclater, S and Richards, M (eds) *What is a Parent?: A Socio-Legal Analysis* (Oxford, Hart Publishing, 1999).

Ball, C, 'Youth Justice and the Youth Court: The End of a Separate System?' (1995) 7 *Child and Family Law Quarterly* 196.

—— 'The Youth Justice and Criminal Evidence Act 1999 Part I: A Significant Move towards Restorative Justice or a Recipe for Unintended Consequences?' [2000] Crim LR 211.

—— and Connolly, J, 'Educationally Disaffected Young Offenders: Youth Court and Agency Responses to Truancy and Social Exclusion' (2000) 40 *British Journal of Criminology*, 594.

Bandalli, S, 'Abolition of the Presumption of *doli incapax* and the Criminalisation of Children' (1998) 37 *Howard Journal* 114.

Beccaria, C, *On Crimes and Punishments* (1764; reprinted Cambridge, Cambridge University Press, 1995).

Becker, H, *Outsiders: Studies in the Sociology of Deviance* (New York, Free Press, 1963).

Bell, A, Hodgson, M and Pragnell, S, 'Diverting Children and Young People from Crime and the Criminal Justice System' in B Goldson (ed) *Youth Justice: Contemporary Policy and Practice* (Aldershot, Ashgate, 1999).

Bennett, T, 'The Social Distribution of Criminal Labels' (1979) 19 *British Journal of Criminology* 134.

Bentham, J, *An Introduction to the Principles of Morals and Legislation* reprinted (London, Athlone Press, 1970).

Black Committee, *Report of the Children and Young Persons Review Group* (Belfast, HMSO, 1979).

Blagg, H, 'A Just Measure of Shame? Aboriginal Youth and Conferencing in Australia' (1997) 37 *British Journal of Criminology* 481.

Blom-Cooper, L, 'Legal Lessons from Cleveland' (1988) *New Law Journal* 492.

Booth, T (ed) *Juvenile Justice in the New Europe* (Sheffield, Joint Unit for Social Services Research, 1996).

Bottoms, A, 'An Introduction to the Coming Crisis' in A Bottoms and R Preston (eds) *The Coming Penal Crisis* (Edinburgh, Scottish Academic Press, 1980).

—— and Preston, R (eds) *The Coming Penal Crisis* (Edinburgh, Scottish Academic Press, 1980).

Bowden, M and Higgins, L, *The Impact and Effectiveness of Garda Special Projects: Final Report* (Dublin, Children's Research Centre, 2000).

Box, S, *Power, Crime, and Mystification* (London, Routledge, 1983).

Braithwaite, J, *Crime, Shame and Reintegration* (Cambridge, Cambridge University Press, 1989).

—— 'Shame and Modernity' (1993) 33 *British Journal of Criminology* 1.

—— and Pettit, P, *Not Just Deserts: A Republican Theory of Justice* (Oxford, Clarendon Press, 1990).

Brent, London Borough of, *A Child in Trust* (London, London Borough of Brent, 1985).

Brown, B, and McElrea, F (eds) *The Youth Court in New Zealand: A New Model of Justice* (Auckland, Legal Research Foundation, 1993).

Brown, S, *Understanding Youth and Crime: Listening to Youth?* (Milton Keynes, Open University Press, 1998).

Brownlee, I, 'New Labour—New Penology? Punitive Rhetoric and the Limits of Managerialism in Criminal Justice Policy' (1998) 25 *Journal of Law and Society* 313.

Buckingham, D, 'Television and the Definition of Childhood' in B Mayall (ed) *Children's Childhood* (London, Falmer Press, 1994).

Budd, T, Sharpe, C and Mayhew, P, *Offending in England and Wales: First Results from the 2003 Crime and Justice Survey* HORS 275 (London, Home Office, 2005).

Burke, H, Carney, C and Cook, G, *Young Offenders in Ireland* (Dublin, Turae Press, 1981).

Burt, C, *The Young Delinquent* (London, University of London Press, 1925).

Butler-Sloss, LJ, *Report of the Inquiry into Child Abuse in Cleveland in 1987* Cm 412 (London, HMSO, 1988).

Carlen, P, *Jigsaw: A Political Criminology of Youth Homelessness* (Milton Keynes, Open University Press, 1996).

—— 'Youth Justice? Arguments for Holism and Democracy in Responses to Crime' in P Green and A Rutherford (eds) *Criminal Policy in Transition* (Oxford, Hart Publishing, 2000).

Carpenter, M, *Reformatory Schools, for the Children of the Perishing and Dangerous Classes and for Juvenile Offenders* (London, Gilpin, 1851).

—— *Juvenile Delinquents: Their Condition and Treatment* (London, Cash, 1853).

Cavadino, M, 'Persistent Young Offenders' (1994) 6 *Journal of Child Law* 2.

—— and Dignan, J, *The Penal System: An Introduction* (London, Sage, 1992).

—— *The Penal System: An Introduction* 3rd edn (London, Sage, 2002).

Cavadino, P, 'Goodbye, *doli*, Must We Leave You?' (1997) 9 *Child and Family Law Quarterly* 165.

Cavenagh, W, *The Child and the Court* (London, Gollancz, 1959).

Chibnall, S, *Law and Order News* (London, Tavistock, 1977).

Christiaens, J, 'A History of Belgium's Child Protection Act 1912: The Redefinition of the Juvenile Offender and His Punishment' (1999) 7 *European Journal of Crime, Criminal Law and Criminal Justice* 5.

Christie, N, 'Conflicts as Property' (1977) 17 *British Journal of Criminology* 1.

—— *Limits to Pain* (Oxford, Martin Robertson, 1982).

—— *Crime Control as Industry* (London, Routledge, 2000).

—— *A Suitable Amount of Crime* (London, Routledge, 2004).

Chute, C, 'Fifty Years of the Juvenile Courts' (1949) *National Probation and Parole Association Yearbook* 1.

Cloward, R and Ohlin, L, *Delinquency and Opportunity: A Theory of Delinquent Gangs* (London, Routledge, 1961).

Cohen, A, *Delinquent Boys: The Culture of the Gang* (Chicago, Chicago University Press, 1955).

Cohen, S, *Folk Devils and Moral Panics: The Creation of the Mods and Rockers* (London, MacGibbon and Kee, 1972).

—— 'The Punitive City: Notes on the Dispersal of Control' (1979) 3 *Contemporary Crises* 339.

—— *Visions of Social Control* (Cambridge, Polity Press, 1985).

Coleman, C, and Moynihan, J, *Understanding Crime Data* (Milton Keynes, Open University Press, 1996).

Council of Europe, *Youth Policy in the Netherlands* (Strasbourg, Council of Europe, 2000).

Covington, C and Giller, H, *Hampshire Constabulary Youth Help Scheme: Report of Research Findings* (Winchester, Hampshire County Council, 1985).

Cowan, D, *Homelessness: The (In)Appropriate Applicant* (Aldershot, Ashgate, 1998).

—— and Fionda, J, 'Housing Homeless Families: An Update' (1995) 7 *Child and Family Law Quarterly* 66.

Cowperthwaite, D, *The Emergence of the Scottish Children's Hearings System* (Southampton, Institute of Criminal Justice, 1988).

Crawford, A and Newburn, T, *Youth Offending and Restorative Justice: Implementing Reform in Youth Justice* (Cullompton, Willan, 2003).

Cretney, A, Davis, G, Clarkson, C and Shepherd, J, 'Criminalizing Assault: Failure of the "Offence against Society" Model' (1994) 34 *British Journal of Criminology* 15.

Cromer, G, ' "Children from Good Homes": Moral Panics about Middle-Class Delinquency' (2004) 44 *British Journal of Criminology* 391.

Crown Prosecution Service, *Code for Crown Prosecutors* (London, CPS, 1986).
—— *Code for Crown Prosecutors* (London, CPS, 1990).
—— *Evidence to the Royal Commission* (London, CPS, 1991).
—— *Code for Crown Prosecutors* (London, CPS, 1994).
—— *Code for Crown Prosecutors* (London, CPS, 2000).
—— *Code for Crown Prosecutors* (London, CPS, 2004).
Cunneen, C and White, R, *Juvenile Justice: Youth and Crime in Australia* (Melbourne, Oxford University Press, 2002).
Cunningham, H, *Children and Childhood in Western Society since 1500* (London, Longman, 1995).
Dallos, R and McLaughlin, E (eds) *Social Problems and the Family* (London, Sage, 1993).
Davin, A, 'What is a Child?' in A Fletcher and S Hussey (eds) *Childhood in Question: Children, Parents and the State* (Manchester, Manchester University Press, 1999).
Davis, G, Boucherat, J and Watson, D, 'Reparation in the Service of Diversion: The Subordination of a Good Idea' (1988) 27 *Howard Journal* 127.
Daw, R, 'A Response' [1994] Crim LR 904.
Dencik, L, 'Growing Up in the Postmodern Age' (1989) 32 *Acta Sociologica* 155.
Department for Education and Skills, *Guidance for Truancy Sweeps* (London, DfES, 2002).
—— *Ensuring Regular School Attendance: Guidance on the Legal Measures Available to Secure Regular School Attendance* (London, DfES, 2003).
Department of Health, *Review of Child Care Law* (London, HMSO, 1985).
—— *Principles and Practice in Regulations and Guidance* (London, HMSO, 1990).
—— *Child Protection: Messages from Research* (London, HMSO, 1995).
DHSS, *The Law on Child Care and Family Services* Cm 62 (London, HMSO, 1987).
Dignan, J, 'The Crime and Disorder Act and the Prospects for Restorative Justice' [1999] Crim LR 48.
Dobash, RP, Dobash, RE, Ballintyne, S, Schumann, K, Kaulitzki, R and Guth, H-W, 'Ignorance and Suspicion: Young People and Criminal Justice in Scotland and Germany' (1990) 30 *British Journal of Criminology* 306.
Doig, J (ed) *Criminal Corrections: Ideals and Realities* (New York, Lexington, 1983).
Doolan, M, 'Youth Justice: Legislation and Practice' in B Brown and F McElrea (eds) *The Youth Court in New Zealand: A New Model of Justice* (Auckland, Legal Research Foundation, 1993).
Downes, D, *Contrasts in Tolerance: Post-war Penal policy in the Netherlands and England and Wales* (Oxford, Clarendon Press, 1988).
Drakeford, M, 'Parents of Young People in Trouble' (1996) 35 *Howard Journal* 242.
Duff, A, Marshall, S, Dobash, RE and Dobash, RP (eds) *Penal Theory and Practice: Tradition and Innovation in Criminal Justice* (Manchester, Manchester University Press, 1994).
Duff, P, 'The Prosecutor Fine and Social Control: The Introduction of the Fiscal Fine in Scotland' (1993) 33 *British Journal of Criminology* 481.
Durkheim, E, *The Division of Labour in Society* (New York, Macmillan, 1933).
—— *Suicide* (London, Routledge, 1952).
Dworkin, R, *Taking Rights Seriously* (London, Duckworth, 1981).
Dyer, C, 'Judges Close Child Crime Loophole' *Guardian* (30 April 1994).
East, K, and Campbell, S, *Aspects of Crime: Young Offenders 1999* (London, Home Office, 1999).

Evans, R, 'Cautioning: Counting the Cost of Retrenchment' [1994] Crim LR 566.

—— and Puech, K, 'Reprimands and Warnings: Populist Punitiveness or Restorative Justice?' [2001] Crim LR 794.

—— and Wilkinson, C, 'Variations in Police Cautioning Policy in England and Wales' (1990) 29 *Howard Journal* 155.

Faktablad Ministry of Culture *On Their Terms* (Stockholm, Ministry of Culture, 1999).

Farrington, D, 'The Effects of Public Labelling' (1977) 17 *British Journal of Criminology* 112.

—— 'Developmental and Risk-focused Prevention' in M Maguire, R Morgan and R Reiner (eds) *The Oxford Handbook of Criminology* 3rd edn (Oxford, Oxford University Press, 2002).

——and Bennett, T, 'Police Cautioning of Juveniles in London' (1981) 21 *British Journal of Criminology* 123.

Ferguson, S, ' "This Place is Doing My Head In" ' *Independent* (13 March 1989).

Field, S and Thomas, P, *Justice and Efficiency? The Royal Commission on Criminal Justice* (Oxford, Blackwell Publishers, 1994).

Fionda, J, *Public Prosecutors and Discretion: A Comparative Study* (Oxford, Oxford University Press, 1995).

—— 'The Age of Innocence?: The Concept of Childhood in the Punishment of Young Offenders' (1998) 10 *Child and Family Law Quarterly* 77.

—— 'New Labour, Old Hat: Youth Justice and the Crime and Disorder Act' [1999] Crim LR 36.

—— 'New Managerialism, Credibility and the Sanitisation of Justice' in P Green and A Rutherford (eds) *Criminal Policy in Transition* (Oxford, Hart Publishing, 2000).

—— *Legal Concepts of Childhood* (Oxford, Hart Publishing, 2001).

—— 'Youth and Justice' in J Fionda (ed) *Legal Concepts of Childhood* (Oxford, Hart Publishing, 2001).

Fisher, C and Mawby, R, 'Juvenile Delinquency and Police Discretion in an Inner-City Area' (1982) 22 *British Journal of Criminology* 63.

Fitzgerald, M, *Ethnic Minorities in the Criminal Justice System* Royal Commission on Criminal Justice Research Paper no 20 (London, HMSO, 1992).

Fletcher, A and Hussey, S (eds) *Childhood in Question: Children, Parents and the State* (Manchester, Manchester University Press, 1999).

Flood-Page, C, Campbell, S, Harrington, V and Miller, J, *Youth Crime: Findings from the 1998/99 Youth Lifestyles Survey* HORS 209 (London, Home Office, 2000).

Foley, P, Roche, J and Tucker, S, *Children in Society: Contemporary Theory, Policy and Practice* (Basingstoke, Palgrave, 2001).

Foresight, *Just around the Corner: A Consultation Document* (London, Department for Trade and Industry, 2000).

—— *Turning the Corner* (London, Department for Trade and Industry, 2000).

Fortin, J, *Children's Rights and the Developing Law* 2nd edn (London, Butterworths, 2003).

Foucault, M, *Discipline and Punish: The Birth of the Prison* (London, Allen Lane, 1977).

Franklin, B and Petley, J, 'Killing the Age of Innocence: Newspaper Reporting of the Death of James Bulger' in J Pilcher and S Wagg (eds) *Thatcher's Children: Politics, Childhood and Society in the 1980s and 1990s* (London, Falmer Press, 1996).

Freeman, M, 'The James Bulger Tragedy: Childish Innocence and the Construction of Guilt' in A McGillivray (ed) *Governing Childhood* (Aldershot, Dartmouth, 1997).

Galbraith, JK, *The Culture of Contentment* (London, Penguin, 1992).

Gale, F, Naffine, N and Wundersitz, J, *Juvenile Justice: Debating the Issues* (St Leonards, NSW, Allen & Unwin, 1993).

Galway, B and Hudson, J (eds) *Restorative Justice: International Perspectives* (Monesy, NY, Criminal Justice Press, 1996).

Garland, D, 'Critical Reflections on the Green Paper' in H Rees and E Hall Williams (eds) *Punishment, Custody and the Community: Reflections and Comments on the Green Paper* (London, LSE, 1989).

——'The Limits of the Sovereign State: Strategies of Crime Control in Contemporary Society' (1996) 36 *British Journal of Criminology* 445.

—— *The Culture of Control* (Oxford, Oxford University Press, 2001).

—— and Young, P (eds) *The Power to Punish: Contemporary Penality and Social Analysis* (London, Heinemann, 1983).

Gelsthorpe, L, 'Youth Crime and Parental Responsibility' in A Bainham, S Day Sclater and M Richards (eds) *What is a Parent?: A Socio-Legal Analysis* (Oxford, Hart Publishing, 1999).

—— and Giller, H, 'More Justice for Juveniles: Does More Mean Better?' [1990] Crim LR 153.

Gibb, F, 'High Court Throws Out "Age Rule" Escape for Child Criminals' *The Times* (30 April 1994).

Glassner, B, *The Culture of Fear* (New York, Perseus Books, 1999).

Golding, W, *Lord of the Flies* (London, Faber, 1954).

Goldson, B (ed) *Youth Justice: Contemporary Policy and Practice* (Aldershot, Ashgate, 1999).

—— 'The Demonization of Children: From the Symbolic to the Institutional' in P Foley, J Roche and S Tucker (eds) *Children in Society: Contemporary Theory, Policy and Practice* (Basingstoke, Palgrave, 2001).

—— *Vulnerable Inside: Children in Secure and Penal Settings* (London, The Children's Society, 2002).

——, Lavalette, M and McKechnie, J *Children, Welfare and the State* (London, Sage, 2002).

Gosling, F, 'Against the Tide: The Rise of Orders under Section 53 CYPA 1933' (1988) *AJJUST* 18.

Graham, J, *Crime Prevention Strategies in Europe and North America* Helsinki Institute for Crime Prevention and Control; Paper no 18 (Helsinki, HEUNI, 1990).

—— and Bowling, B, *Young People and Crime* HORS 145 (London, Home Office, 1995).

Green, P and Rutherford, A (eds) *Criminal Policy in Transition* (Oxford, Hart Publishing, 2000).

Griffiths, A and Frances Kandel, R, 'Working towards Consensus: Children's Hearings in Scotland' in P Foley, J Roche and S Tucker (eds) *Children in Society: Contemporary Theory, Policy and Practice* (Basingstoke, Palgrave, 2001).

Haan, W de, *The Politics of Redress: Crime, Punishment and Penal Abolition* (London, Unwin Hyman, 1990).

Hagell, A and Newburn, T, *Persistent Young Offenders* (London, Policy Studies Institute, 1994).

Haines, K and Drakeford, M, *Young People and Youth Justice* (Basingstoke, Macmillan, 1998).

Halsey, K, Bedford, N, Atkinson, M, White, R and Kinder, K, *Evaluation of Fast Track to Prosecution for School Non-Attendance* Research Report 567 (London, National Foundation for Education Research, 2004).

Harding, J, 'The Development of Community Service: Its Application and Relevance to the Criminal Justice System' in N Tutt (ed) *Alternative Strategies for Coping with Crime* (Oxford, Basil Blackwell, 1978).

Hartless, J, Ditton, J, Nair, G and Phillips, S 'More Sinned Against than Sinning: A Study of Young Teenagers' Experience of Crime' (1995) 35 *British Journal of Criminology* 114.

Hassall, I, 'Origin and Development of Family Group Conferences' in J Hudson, A Morris, G Maxwell and B Galway (eds) *Family Group Conferences: Perspectives on Policy and Practice* (Leichhardt, NSW, The Federation Press, 1996).

Hayward, R and Sharpe, C, *Young People, Crime and Anti-Social Behaviour: Findings from the 2003 Crime and Justice Survey* Home Office Findings no 245 (London, TSO, 2005).

Hendrick, H, 'Constructions and Reconstructions of British Childhood: An Interpretive Survey, 1800 to Present' in J Muncie, G Hughes and E McLaughlin (eds) *Youth Justice: Critical Readings* (London, Sage, 2002).

Her Majesty's Inspectorate of Prisons, *Young Prisoners: A Thematic Review by HM Chief Inspector of Prisons for England and Wales* (London, TSO, 1997).

—— *Juveniles in Custody* (London, TSO, 2004).

Heywood, C, *A History of Childhood* (Cambridge, Polity Press, 2001).

Hilson, C, 'Discretion to Prosecute and Judicial Review' [1993] Crim LR 739.

von Hirsch, A and Roberts, J, 'Legislating Sentencing Principles: The Provisions of the Criminal Justice Act 2003 Relating to Sentencing Purposes and the Role of Previous Convictions' [2004] Crim LR 639.

Hirschi, T, *Causes of Delinquency* (Berkeley, University of California Press, 1967).

Hogan, M, 'Children's Courts: To Be or What to Be?' in F Gale, N Naffine and J Wundersitz *Juvenile Justice: Debating the Issues* (St Leonards, NSW, Allen & Unwin, 1993).

Home Affairs Committee, *Juvenile Offenders* Sixth Report HAC 441–I (London, HMSO, 1993).

Home Office, *The Child, The Family and the Young Offender* Cmnd 2742 (London, HMSO, 1965).

—— *Children in Trouble* Cmnd 3601 (London, HMSO, 1968).

—— *Young Offenders* Cmnd 8045 (London, HMSO, 1980).

—— 'The Cautioning of Offenders' Circular 14/1985 (London, Home Office, 1985).

—— *Punishment, Custody and The Community* Cm 424 (London, HMSO, 1988).

—— *Crime, Justice and Protecting the Public* Cm 965 (London, HMSO, 1990).

——*Safer Communities: The Local Delivery of Crime Prevention through the Partnership Approach* (Morgan Report) (London, Home Office, 1991).

—— 'Criminal Justice Act 1991: Young People and the Youth Court' Circular (London, Home Office, 1992).

—— *Strengthening Punishment in the Community: A Consultation Paper* Cm 2780 (London, HMSO, 1995).

—— *Community Safety Order A Consultation Paper* (London, Home Office, 1997).

—— *Getting to Grips with Crime* (London, Home Office, 1997).

—— *New National and Local Focus on Youth Crime* (London, Home Office, 1997).

—— *No More Excuses: A New Approach to Tackling Youth Crime in England and Wales* Cm 3809 (London, TSO, 1997).

—— *Preventing Children Offending: A Consultation Document* Cm 3566 (London, TSO, 1997).

Home Office, *Review of the Delay in the Criminal Justice System: A Report* (Narey Report) (London, Home Office, 1997).

—— *Tackling Youth Crime: A Consultation Paper* (London, Home Office, 1997).

—— *Tackling Delays in the Youth Justice System: A Consultation Paper* (London, Home Office, 1997).

—— *Final Report of the Youth Justice Task Force* (London, Home Office, 1998).

—— *Guidance Document: Action Plan Orders* (London, Home Office, 1998).

—— *Guidance Document: Child Safety Orders* (London, Home Office, 1998)

—— *Guidance Document: Local Child Curfews* (London, Home Office, 1998).

—— *Inter-Departmental Circular on Establishing Youth Offending Teams* (London, Home Office, 1998).

—— *Power for the Police to Remove Truants: A Guidance Document* (London, Home Office, 1998).

—— *Speaking Up for Justice: Report of the Interdepartmental Group on the Treatment of Vulnerable or Intimidated Witnesses in the Criminal Justice System* (London, Home Office, 1998).

—— *Youth Justice: The Statutory Principal Aim of Preventing Offending by Children and Young People* (London, Home Office, 1998); also available at <http://www.homeoffice.gov.uk/docs/youjust.html>.

—— *New Powers for the Youth Court* Circular (London, Home Office, 1998).

—— *Interim Report on Youth Offending Teams* (London, Home Office, 1999).

—— *The Referral Order: Draft Guidance to Youth Offending Teams* (London, Home Office, 1999).

—— *Criminal Justice: The Way Ahead* Cm 5074 (London, TSO, 2001).

——*Final Warning Scheme: Further Guidance for the Police and Youth Offending Teams* (London, Home Office, 2001).

—— *The Introduction of Referral Orders into the Youth Justice System: 2nd Interim Evaluation Report* (London, Home Office, 2001).

—— *The Youth Court 2001—The Changing Culture of the Youth Court: Good Practice Guide* (London, Home Office/LCD, 2001).

—— *Justice for All* Cm 5563 (London, TSO, 2002).

—— *Got Something to Say about Youth Crime?—So Say It* (London, Home Office, 2003).

—— *Respect and Responsibility: Taking a Stand against Anti-Social Behaviour* Cm 5778 (London, TSO, 2003).

—— *Restorative Justice—The Government's Strategy: A Consultation Document on the Government's Strategy on Restorative Justice* (London, Home Office, 2003).

—— *Youth Justice: The Next Steps* (London, Home Office, 2003).

—— *Parenting Orders and Contracts for Criminal Conduct and Anti-Social Behaviour: Guidance* Joint Home Office, Department for Constitutional Affairs/Youth Justice Board Circular (London, Home Office, 2004).

—— *Stopping Youth Crime—Tell Us What You Think: Summary of Responses from Children and Young People and the Government Response* (London, Home Office, 2004).

Hough, M and Roberts, J, *Youth Crime and Youth Justice: Public Opinion in England and Wales* (Bristol, Policy Press, 2004).

House of Commons Social Services Committee, *Children in Care* (London, HMSO, 1984).

Howard League, *The Community, Punishment and Custody: The Response of the Howard League for Penal Reform to the Green Paper* (London, Howard League, 1988).
—— *Child Jails: The Case against Secure Training Orders* (London, Howard League, 1994).
—— *Sentenced to Fail—Out of Sight, Out of Mind: Compounding the Problems of Children in Prison* (London, Howard League, 1998).
Hudson, B, *Justice in the Risk Society* (London, Sage, 2003).
Hudson, J, Morris, A, Maxwell, G and Galway, B (eds) *Family Group Conferences: Perspectives on Policy and Practice* (Leichhardt, NSW, The Federation Press, 1996).
Hulsman, L, 'Penal Reform in the Netherlands: Part I—Bringing the Criminal Justice System under Control' (1981) 20 *Howard Journal* 150.
—— 'Penal Reform in the Netherlands: Part II—Criteria for Deciding on Alternatives to Imprisonment' (1982) 21 *Howard Journal* 35.
James, A and Prout, A, *Constructing and Reconstructing Childhood* (London, Falmer Press, 1990).
Jenkins, S, 'Criminal Conspiracies' *The Times* (1 December 1999).
Jenks, C (ed) *The Sociology of Childhood: Essential Readings* (London, Batsford, 1982).
—— *Childhood* (London, Routledge, 1996).
—— 'Sociological Perspectives and Media Representations of Childhood' in J Fionda (ed) *Legal Concepts of Childhood* (Oxford, Hart Publishing, 2001).
Johnstone, G, *Restorative Justice: Ideals, Values and Debates* (Cullompton, Willan, 2002).
King, M, *A Better World for Children: Explanations in Morality and Authority* (London, Routledge, 1997).
Labour Party, *Protecting Our People* (London, Labour Party, 1988).
—— *A Safer Britain* (London, Labour Party, 1990).
—— *Tackling the Causes of Crime: Labour's Crime Prevention Policy for the 1990s* (London, Labour Party, 1991).
—— *Partners against Crime: Labour's New Approach to Tackling Crime and Creating Safer Communities* (London, Labour Party, 1994).
—— *A Quiet Life: Tough Action on Criminal Neighbours* (London, Labour Party, 1995)
—— *Safer Communities, Safer Britain: Labour's Proposals for Tough Action on Crime* (London, Labour Party, 1995).
—— *Tackling Youth Crime, Reforming Youth Justice* (London, Labour Party, 1996).
Landau, F and Nathan, G, 'Selecting Delinquents for Cautioning in the London Metropolis Area' (1983) 23 *British Journal of Criminology* 128.
Lavalette, M and Cunningham, S, 'The Sociology of Childhood' in B Goldson, M Lavalettte and J McKechnie *Children, Welfare and the State* (London, Sage, 2002).
Law Commission, *Guardianship and Custody* LC 172 (London, HMSO, 1988).
Lee, N, *Childhood and Society: Growing Up in an Age of Uncertainty* (Milton Keynes, Open University Press, 2001).
Lemert, E, *Human Deviance, Social Problems and Social Control* (Englewood Cliffs, NJ, Prentice-Hall, 1967).
Levy, A and Crook, F, 'Children's Prisons: Secure Training Centres Considered' (1995) *The Magistrate* 36.
Liberty, *Unequal before the Law: Sentencing in Magistrates' Courts in England and Wales 1981–1990* (London, Liberty, 1992).

Liberty, *The Rights of Victims: A Manifesto for Better Treatment of Victims in the Criminal Justice System* (London, Liberty, 2003).

Lister, R (ed) *Charles Murray and the Underclass: The Developing Debate* (London, Institute for Economic Affairs, 1996).

Lockyer, A and Stone, F, *Juvenile Justice in Scotland: Twenty-five Years of the Welfare Approach* (Edinburgh, T &T Clark, 1998).

MacDonald, S, 'The Nature of Anti-Social Behaviour' (2003) 66 MLR 630.

Maguire, M, Morgan, R and Reiner, R (eds) *The Oxford Handbook of Criminology* 3rd edn (Oxford, Oxford University Press, 2002).

Malony Committee, *Report of the Departmental Committee on the Treatment of Young Offenders* Cmnd 2831 (London, HMSO, 1927).

Mansfield, G and Peay, J, *The Director of Public Prosecutions: Principles and Practices for the Crown Prosecutor* (London, Tavistock, 1987).

Marshall, T, 'Grass Roots Initiatives towards Restorative Justice: The New Paradigm?' in A Duff, S Marshall, RE Dobash and RP Dobash (eds) *Penal Theory and Practice: Tradition and Innovation in Criminal Justice* (Manchester, Manchester University Press, 1994).

Mathiesen, T, 'The Future of Control Systems' in D Garland and P Young (eds) *The Power to Punish: Contemporary Penality and Social Analysis* (London, Heinemann, 1983).

—— 'Contemporary Penal Policy: A Study in Moral Panics' Lecture at the Annual Meeting of the Howard League (25 November 1992) (unpublished).

—— 'On the Globalisation of Control: Towards an Integrated Surveillance System in Europe' in P Green and A Rutherford (eds) *Criminal Policy in Transition* (Oxford, Hart Publishing, 2000).

—— *Silently Silenced* (Winchester, Waterside Press, 2005).

Mattinson, J and Mirlees-Black, C, *Attitudes to Crime and Criminal Justice: Findings from the 1998 British Crime Survey* HORS 200 (London, TSO, 2000).

Matza, D, *Delinquency and Drift* (New York, John Wiley & Sons, 1964).

Mawby, R, 'The Victimization of Juveniles: A Comparative Study' (1979) 16 *Journal of Research in Crime and Delinquency* 275.

Mayall, B (ed) *Children's Childhood* (London, Falmer Press, 1994).

Maxwell, G and Morris, A, 'Research on Family Group Conferences with Young Offenders in New Zealand' in J Hudson, A Morris, G Maxwell and B Galway (eds) *Family Group Conferences: Perspectives on Policy and Practice* (Leichhardt, NSW, The Federation Press, 1996).

McCabe, S and Treitel, P, *Juvenile Justice in the United Kingdom: Comparisons and Suggestions for Change* (London, Croom Helm, 1983).

McConville, M, Sanders, A and Leng, R, *The Case for the Prosecution: Police Suspects and the Construction of Crime* (London, Routledge, 1991).

McElrea, F, 'A New Model of Justice' in B Brown and F McElrea (eds) *The Youth Court in New Zealand: A New Model of Justice* (Auckland, Legal Research Foundation, 1993).

McGhee, J, Waterhouse, L and Whyte, B, 'Children's Hearings and Children in Trouble' in S Asquith (ed) *Children and Young People in Conflict with the Law* (London, Jessica Kingsley, 1996).

McGillivray, A (ed) *Governing Childhood* (Aldershot, Dartmouth, 1997).

McLaughlin, E and Muncie, J, 'Juvenile Delinquency' in R Dallos and E McLaughlin (eds) *Social Problems and the Family* (London, Sage, 1993).

McWilliams, W, 'Probation, Pragmatism and Policy' (1987) 26 *Howard Journal* 97.

Mead, G, 'The Psychology of Punitive Justice' (1918) 23 *American Journal of Sociology* 577.

Merton, R, 'Social Structure and Anomie' (1938) 3 *American Sociological Review* 672.

Michael, A, *Getting a Grip on Youth Crime* (London, Labour Party, 1993).

Miller, J, *Last One over the Wall* (Columbus, Ohio State University Press, 1991).

Morgan, J and Zedner, L, *Child Victims: Crime, Impact and Criminal Justice* (Oxford, Clarendon Press, 1992).

—— 'The Victims' Charter: A New Deal for Child Victims' (1992) 32 *Howard Journal* 294.

Moore, D and O'Connell, T, 'Family Conferencing in Wagga Wagga: A Communitarian Model of Justice' in C Alder and J Wundersitz *Family Conferencing and Juvenile Justice: The Way Forward or Misplaced Optimism?* (Canberra, Australian Institute for Criminology, 1994).

Morris, A and Gelsthorpe, L, 'Something Old, Something Borrowed, Something Blue, but Something New? A Comment on the Prospects for Restorative Justice under the Crime and Disorder Act 1998' [2000] Crim LR 18.

—— and Giller, H, 'The Juvenile Court: The Client's Perspective' [1977] Crim LR 198.

—— and Giller, H, *Understanding Juvenile Justice* (London, Croom Helm, 1987).

—— and Maxwell, G, 'Juvenile Justice in New Zealand: A New Paradigm?' (1993) 26 *Australian and New Zealand Journal of Criminology* 72.

Mott, J, 'Police Decisions for Dealing with Juvenile Offenders' (1983) 23 *British Journal of Criminology* 249.

Muncie, J, 'The Construction and Deconstruction of Crime' in J Muncie and E McLaughlin (eds) *The Problem of Crime* 2nd edn (London, Sage, 2001).

—— *Youth and Crime* 2nd edn (London, Sage, 2004).

—— Hughes, G and McLaughlin, E (eds) *Youth Justice: Critical Readings* (London, Sage, 2002).

Murray, C, 'Underclass: The Crisis Deepens' in R Lister (ed) *Charles Murray and the Underclass: The Developing Debate* (London, Institute for Economic Affairs, 1996).

NACRO, *The Future of the Juvenile Court in England and Wales* (London, NACRO, 1986).

—— *Grave Crimes . . . Grave Doubts* (London, NACRO, 1988).

—— *The Home Office Circular on the Cautioning of Offenders: Implications for Juvenile Justice* Briefing Paper (London, NACRO, 1990).

—— *Partnership with Parents in Dealing with Young Offenders* Young Offenders Committee; Policy Paper 4 (London, NACRO, 1994).

National Audit Office, *Youth Offending: The Delivery of Community and Custodial Sentences* HC 190 (London, TSO, 2004).

Nellis, M, 'Probation Values for the 1990s' (1995) 34 *Howard Journal* 19.

Newburn, T, 'Young People, Crime and Youth Justice' in M Maguire, R Morgan and R Reiner (eds) *The Oxford Handbook of Criminology* 3rd edn (Oxford, Oxford University Press, 2002).

Noaks, L, Levi, M and Maguire, M (eds) *Contemporary Issues in Criminology* (Cardiff, University of Wales Press, 1995).

Norrie, K, *Children's Hearings in Scotland* (Edinburgh, W Green, 1997).

Oakley, A, 'Women and Children First and Last: Parallels and Differences between Women's and Children's Studies' in B Mayall (ed) *Children's Childhood* (London, Falmer Press, 1994).

Office for National Statistics, *Census 2001: National Report for England and Wales* (London, TSO, 2003).

O'Neill, O, 'Children's Rights and Children's Lives' (1988) 98 *Ethics* 445.

Packer, H, *The Limits of the Criminal Sanction* (Stanford, Stanford University Press, 1969).

Parker, H, Casburn, M and Turnbull, D, *Receiving Juvenile Justice: Adolescents and State Care and Control* (Oxford, Blackwell, 1981).

Parsons, C, 'Permanent Exclusions from Schools in England: Trends, Causes and Responses' (1996) 10 *Children and Society* 177.

Pearson, G, *Hooligans: A History of Respectable Fears* (Basingstoke, Macmillan, 1983).

Penal Affairs Consortium, *The Case against the Secure Training Order* (London, Penal Affairs Consortium, 1994).

Penal Affairs Consortium, *Parental Responsibility, Youth Crime and the Criminal Law* (London, Penal Affairs Consortium, 1995).

Pfohl, S, 'Labelling Criminals' in H Ross (ed) *Law and Deviance* (Beverly Hills, Sage, 1981).

Piaget, J, *The Psychology of the Child* (London, Routledge, 1973).

Pilcher, J and Wagg, S, *Thatcher's Children: Politics, Childhood and Society in the 1980s and 1990s* (London, Falmer Press, 1996).

Pitts, J, 'The End of an Era' (1992) 31 *Howard Journal* 133.

Platt, A, *The Child Savers: The Invention of Delinquency* (Chicago, Chicago University Press, 1969).

Postman, N, *The Disappearance of Childhood* (London, Vintage, 1982).

—— *Amusing Ourselves to Death* (London, Methuen, 1987).

—— *Technopoly* (London, Vintage, 1993).

Power, M, 'Delinquent Schools' (1967) 10 *New Society* 542.

——, Ash, P and Schoenberg, E, 'Delinquency and the Family' (1974) 4 *British Journal of Social Work* 13.

Pratt, J, 'Folk-lore and Fact in Truancy Research' (1982) 22 *British Journal of Criminology* 336.

—— 'Diversion from the Juvenile Court: A History of Inflation and a Critique of Progress' (1986) 26 *British Journal of Criminology* 212.

—— 'Corporatism: The Third Model of Juvenile Justice' (1989) 29 *British Journal of Criminology* 236.

—— 'Welfare and Justice: Incompatible Philosophies' in F Gale, N Naffine and J Wundersitz *Juvenile Justice: Debating the Issues* (St Leonards, NSW, Allen & Unwin, 1993).

—— *Punishment and Civilization* (London, Sage, 2002).

Public Accounts Committee, *Youth Offending: The Delivery of Community and Custodial Sentences* 40th Report of Session 2003–04, HC 307 (London, TSO, 2004).

Quinney, R, *The Social Reality of Crime* (Boston, Little Brown, 1970).

Radzinowicz, L and Hood, R, *The Emergence of Penal Policy* (Oxford, Oxford University Press, 1990).

Ramsbotham, D, *Prison-gate: The Shocking State of Britain's Prisons and the Need for Visionary Change* (London, Free Press, 2003).

Rawnsley, A, *Servants of the People: The Inside Story of New Labour* (London, Penguin, 2001).

Rees, H and Hall Williams, E (eds) *Punishment, Custody and the Community: Reflections and Comments on the Green Paper* (London, LSE, 1989).

Reynolds, D and Jones, D, 'Education and the Prevention of Juvenile Delinquency' in N Tutt (ed) *Alternative Strategies for Coping with Crime* (Oxford, Basil Blackwell, 1978).

Riley, D and Shaw, M, *Parental Supervision and Juvenile Delinquency* HORS 83 (London, HMSO, 1985).

Ross, H (ed) *Law and Deviance* (Beverly Hills, Sage, 1981).

Royal Commission on Criminal Justice, *Report* Cm 2263 (London, HMSO, 1993).

Royal Commission on Criminal Procedure, *Police Cautioning* Memorandum no VI, Evidence no 240 (London, HMSO, 1979).

Rutherford, A, 'A Statute Backfires: The Escalation of Youth Incarceration in England during the 1970s' in J Doig (ed) *Criminal Corrections: Ideals and Realities* (Massachusetts, Lexington, 1983).

—— *Growing Out of Crime* (London, Penguin, 1986).

—— 'The Mood and Temper of Penal Policy' (1989) 27 *Youth and Policy* 27.

—— 'Criminal Justice and the Eliminative Ideal' (1997) 31 *Social Policy and Administration* 116.

—— 'An Elephant on the Doorstep: Criminal Policy without Crime in New Labour's Britain' in P Green and A Rutherford (eds) *Criminal Policy in Transition* (Oxford, Hart Publishing, 2000).

—— *Growing Out of Crime: The New Era* (Winchester, Waterside Press, 2002).

—— and M Telford 'Criminal Policy without Crime: An Anglo-American Journey of Exploration' Paper presented to the Annual Meeting of the American Society of Criminology (18 November 2000).

Rutter, M, *Fifteen Thousand Hours: Secondary Schools and their Effects on Children* (London, Open Books, 1979).

—— and Giller, H, *Juvenile Delinquency: Trends and Perspectives* (Harmondsworth, Penguin, 1983).

——, Giller, H and Hagell, A, *Anti-Social Behaviour by Young People* (Cambridge, Cambridge University Press, 1998).

Sanders, A, 'The Limits to Diversion from Prosecution' (1988) 28 *British Journal of Criminology* 513.

Scottish Executive, *Getting it Right for Every Child* (Edinburgh, Scottish Executive, 2004).

Scottish Law Commission, *Discussion Paper on the Age of Criminal Responsibility* Discussion Paper no 115 (Edinburgh, TSO, 2001).

Scottish Office, *Children and Young Persons: Scotland* (Kilbrandon report) Cmnd 2306 (Edinburgh, HMSO, 1964).

—— *Social Work and the Community: Proposals for Reorganising Local Authority Services in Scotland* Cmnd 3065 (Edinburgh, HMSO, 1966).

—— *Review of Child Care Law in Scotland* (Edinburgh, HMSO, 1990).

Simmons, J, *Review of Crime Statistics: A Discussion Document* (London, Home Office, 2000).

—— and Dodd, T, *Crime in England and Wales 2002/2003* (London, Home Office, 2003).

Smart, C, Neale, B and Wade, A, *The Changing Experiences of Childhood: Families and Divorce* (Cambridge, Polity Press, 2001).

Smith, R, *No Lessons Learnt: A Survey of School Exclusions* (London, The Children's Society, 1998).

—— *Youth Justice: Ideas, Policy, Practice* (Cullompton, Willan, 2003).

Social Exclusion Unit, *Truancy and Social Exclusion* (London, Social Exclusion Unit, 1998).

Stainton Rogers, W, Harvey, D and Ash, E (eds) *Child Abuse and Neglect* (Milton Keynes, Open University Press, 1989).

Stevenson, R and Brotchie, R, *Getting it Right for Every Child: Report on the Responses to Phase One Consultation on the Review of the Children's Hearings System* (Edinburgh, Scottish Executive, 2004).

Stone, N, 'Legal Commentary: "Parenting Orders", "Warnings and Reprimands" and "Age at Time of Offence"—Human Rights Considerations' (2003) 3 *Youth Justice* 112.

Straw, J and Anderson, J, *Parenting: A Discussion Paper* (London, Labour Party, 1996).

Stuart, B, 'Circle Sentencing: Turning Swords into Ploughshares' in B Galway and J Hudson (eds) *Restorative Justice: International Perspectives* (Monesy, NY, Criminal Justice Press, 1996).

Sutherland, E, *Principles of Criminology* (Philadelphia, Lippincott, 1939).

Swaaningen, R van, *Critical Criminology: Visions from Europe* (London, Sage, 1997).

—— 'Back to the "Iron Cage": The Example of the Dutch Probation Service' in P Green and A Rutherford (eds) *Criminal Policy in Transition* (Oxford, Hart Publishing, 2000).

Turner, J, 'Talking Shock Tactics' *Guardian* (26 May 1998).

Tutt, N (ed) *Alternative Strategies for Coping with Crime* (Oxford, Basil Blackwell, 1978).

—— 'A Decade of Policy' (1981) 21 *British Journal of Criminology* 246.

United Nations Committee in the Rights of the Child, *Concluding Observations of the Committee on the Rights of the Child: United Kingdom of Great Britain and Northern Ireland* CRC/C/15/Add 188 (Geneva, Centre for Human Rights, 2002).

Utting, D, Bright, J and Henricson, C, *Crime and the Family: Improving Child-rearing and Preventing Delinquency* (London, Family Policy Studies Centre, 1993).

Vold, G, *Theoretical Criminology* (New York, Oxford University Press, 1958).

Waiton, S, *Scared of the Kids?: Curfews, Crime and the Regulation of Young People* (Sheffield, Sheffield Hallam University Press, 2001).

Walgrave, L, 'Restorative Justice for Juvenile: Just a Technique or a Fully Fledged Alternative?' (1995) 34 *Howard Journal* 228.

—— 'Restorative Juvenile Justice: A Way to Restore Justice in Western European Systems?' in S Asquith (ed) *Children and Young People in Conflict with the Law* (London, Jessica Kingsley, 1996).

—— 'Criminology, Criminal Policy and Democracy' (1998/89) Winter *Criminal Justice Matters* 23.

Walker, N and Hough, M, *Public Attitudes to Sentencing: Surveys from Five Countries* (Aldershot, Gower, 1988).

Wardhaugh, J, 'Criminalising Truancy' in T Booth (ed) *Juvenile Justice in the New Europe* (Sheffield, Joint Unit for Social Services Research, 1991).

Warner, M, *Managing Monsters: Six Myths of Our Time* The Reith Lectures 1994 (London, Vintage, 1994).

Weijers, I, 'Requirements for Communication in the Courtroom: A Comparative Perspective on the Youth Court in England/Wales and the Netherlands' (2004) 4 *Youth Justice* 22.

Wilcox, A and Hoyle, C, *Restorative Justice Projects: The National Evaluation of the Youth Justice Board's Restorative Justice Projects* (London, Youth Justice Board, 2004).

Wilkins, L, *Social Policy, Action and Research: Studies in Deviance* (London, Tavistock, 1964).

Williams, G, 'The Criminal Responsibility of Children' [1954] Crim LR 493.

Wilson, JQ and Kelling, G, 'Broken Windows: The Police and Neighbourhood Safety' (1982) 249 *The Atlantic Monthly* 29.

Wonnacott, C, 'The Counterfeit Contract: Reform, Pretence and Muddled Principles in the New Referral Order' (1999) 11 *Child and Family Law Quarterly* 271.

Wright, M, *Justice for Victims and Offenders: A Restorative Response to Crime* (Winchester, Waterside Press, 1996).

Wynn Davies, P, 'Police Urge New Approach to Young Offenders' *Independent* (11 February 1993).

Young, A, *Imagining Crime* (London, Sage, 1996).

Young, J, *The Exclusive Society: Social Exclusion, Crime and Difference in Late Modernity* (London, Sage, 1999).

Young, R and Goold, B, 'Restorative Police Cautioning in Aylesbury: From Degrading to Reintegrative Shaming Ceremonies' [1999] Crim LR 126.

Youth Justice Board, *Referral Orders: Research into the Issues Raised in 'the Introduction of the Referral Order in the Youth Justice System'* Report produced by Cap Gemini, Ernst & Young (London, Youth Justice Board, 2003).

Zedner, L, 'Reparation and Retribution: Are They Reconcilable?' (1994) 57 MLR 228.

—— 'Comparative Research in Criminal Justice' in L Noaks, M Levi and M Maguire (eds) *Contemporary Issues in Criminology* (Cardiff, University of Wales Press, 1995).

Zehr, H, *Changing Lens: A New Focus for Crime and Justice* (Scottdale, PA, Herald Press, 1990).

INDEX

abolitionism 269–70
Abrams, D 27
Allen, R 45
anomie 74–5
Anti-Social Behaviour Act 2003 214, 218, 226
Anti-Social Behaviour etc (Scotland) Act 2004 251–2
anti-social behaviour orders 239–42
  in practice 242–5
  in Scotland 251–2
Ariés, P 20
Ashworth, A 141–2, 201–2
attendance centre orders 156
Australia 190, 193

Back to Basics initiative 31, 43
Ball, C 184
BCS (British Crime Survey) 61–2, 143
Beccaria, C 34, 270
Becker, H 79–80, 266
Beckford, Jasmine *case* 254
Bennett, T 112
Bentham, J 34
Blagg, H 197–8
Blair, Tony 82, 154, 220, 236–7
Blom-Cooper, Sir Louis 254
Bowling, B 51–2, 60, 63–4, 69–74, 206–7, 213, 221, 223
Box, S 77–9
Braithwaite, J 179, 181, 199
British Crime Survey (BCS) 61–2, 143
Brown, S 21, 22, 27–8
Bulger case 10, 20, 29–31, 43, 138–9, 150–51, 166, 258
Burt, C 206
Butler-Sloss, Lord Justice 254

Canada 190
Carlen, P 199, 202, 267
Carpenter, Mary 21, 36, 116–17, 118
cautioning 89–95, 96–7
  see also diversion
  caution plus 97, 99
  consistency 92–3, 96–7
  expansion 90–92
  managerial concerns 93–4

practice 96–7
rehabilitative links 97
statutory basis 89–90, 93
Cavadino, M 83, 161
child safety orders 238–9
childhood
  as construction 20
  disappearance 31–2
  historical perspectives 20–22
  pre-sociological 23–4
  as social world 24–5, 32
  sociological perspectives 23–6
  and perceptions 26–32
Children Act 1908 36, 116–17, 132, 193, 245, 253–4
Children Act 1989 120, 151, 159, 166, 212, 214, 225, 230, 238–9, 269–70
  child in need, definition 257
  children as participants 256
  context 253–4
  crime prevention, proactive duties 259
  decision checklist 256
  education supervision order 258
  minimalist approach 255–6
  parental responsibility, breakdown 258
  partnership approach 255
  in practice 259–61
Children Act 2001 (Republic of Ireland) 193–5
Children (Scotland) Act 1995 248–9
children, young 237
Children and Young Persons Act 1931 245
Children and Young Persons Act 1933 127, 132, 151, 243
Children and Young Persons Act 1969 40, 42, 90, 96, 118–19, 124, 164, 173, 246
Children, Young Personsand Their Families Act 1989 (New Zealand) 191–2
Children's Hearing system *see under* Scotland
Christie, N 62–3, 153, 176–7, 180–81, 197, 199, 201–2, 233, 264, 268, 269
Churchill, Winston 270
Citizen's Charter 182
Clarke, Kenneth 166
Cleveland Case 254
Cloward, R 76
Cohen, A 76

Cohen, S 79–80, 162, 266
community orders 155–7
Community Peace Programme (South Africa)
190
community punishment 140–41, 151–5
punitive character 152–5
and social control 161–3
and welfare agencies 157–60
community punishment/community rehabilitation orders 155
community safety orders 236
community service orders 155
conditional discharges 99
conflict theory 77–8, 79
Covington, C 108
Crawford, A 182, 185
Cretney, A 177
crime
see also decriminalisation
and anomie 74–5
conflict theory 77–8, 79
control theories 81–2
'dark figure' 60–61
desistance factors 68–9
deviance amplification 79–80, 110
and drug use 73–4
and education 71–2
extent 63–8
and family life 70–71
labelling process 3–6, 79–80, 109–110, 176
measurement 59–63
and policy conflicts 62–3
official statistics 66, 67
perceptions 82–4
policy conflicts 62–3
and poverty 72–3
research 69–74
social realism 77–8
and socio-economic status 72–3
and strain 75–6
sub-cultures 76–9
surveys 60–62, 63–6
theories 74–82
trends 67–8
crime control model 106–8
Crime and Disorder Act 1998 55, 92, 168
anti-social behaviour orders 240–42
child safety orders 238
curfews 237–8
and diversion 108
and parents 214, 217–19
reparation orders 186–8
reprimands and warnings 98–101
and restorative justice 183
and sentencing 149, 154
and truancy 224

and youth court 120
youth justice framework 158–9
Crime and Justice Survey 65–6, 71, 72, 208
Crime (Sentences) Act 1997 154, 167
Criminal Damage Act 1971 133
Criminal Justice Act 1961 133
Criminal Justice Act 1967 152
Criminal Justice Act 1972 152
Criminal Justice Act 1982 39, 140, 152
Criminal Justice Act 1991 40, 42, 211–12, 219
and parents 211–12, 214–16
and sentencing 140, 142–4, 166, 173, 186
and youth court 119–20
Criminal Justice Act 1993 43
Criminal Justice Act 2003 143–4, 145–8, 157,
173
Criminal Justice and Court Services Act 2000
155, 160, 226–7
Criminal Justice and Public Order Act 1994 43,
78–9, 133, 167
criminal responsibility, minimum ages 9–12
criminalisation *see* crime; decriminalisation
criminology
classical 34
positivist 35, 37
Crook, F 167
crown court 132–9
Bulger trial issues 138–9
juveniles sentenced 134–6
and serious offenders 132–3
transfer procedure 134, 136–8
Crown Prosecution Service 101–5
diversionary discretion 101–2
public interest criteria 102–4
and statutory police diversion 104–5
Cunneen, C 200
curfew orders 156
curfews 237–8
custodial orders 168–9
custody 164–8
see also decarceration
criticisms 169–71
and developmental ideal 165–6
exceptions 164–6
inspection reports 170–71
re-offending 169–70
threshold 146–7

Davin, A 22
de Haan, W 173
decarceration
see also custody
demographic change 38
developmental model 39–40
history 151–4
and legislation 38–9

localised 46
   and magistrates 39
   minimal intervention 44–6
   policy conflicts 40–43, 46–9
decriminalisation 233–4
demographic change 38
Dencik, L 28
detention and training orders 168–9
deterrence 142
developmental ideal 165–6
developmental model 39–40, 204–5, 267–8
deviance 76
   amplification 79–80, 110
differential association theory 206
Dignan, J 161
disorder 234–7
diversion 87–8, 105–6
   see also cautioning; Crown Prosecution
      Service; reprimands and warnings
   due process v crime control 106–8
   formality v informality 108–9, 111–12
   and juvenile court 88–9
   net-widening 109–113
   policy 88–95
   politics 113–14
   practice 95–6
   programmes 190
      Republic of Ireland 193–5
Dobasch, R 267
doli incapax
   abolition 14, 16–17, 19
   legal issues 15–17
   mental capacity 16–17
   minimum ages 9–12
   policy issues 17–19
   presumption 12–14
Downes, D 44
Drakeford, M 8
drug use, and crime 73–4
due process model 106–8
Durkheim, E 74–5
Dworkin, R 177

education *see* schools
Education Act 1996 225
education supervision orders 225, 226–7, 258
eliminative ideal 244
European Convention on Human Rights 127,
   217, 219
Evans, R 109, 112–13
exclusion orders 157

family group conferencing (FGC) (New
      Zealand) 190–93
family life
   see also parental responsibility

   and crime 70–71, 207, 211
Farrington, D 112, 208
Feltham YOI 170
FGC (family group conferencing) (New
      Zealand) 190–93
Fionda, J 171
Foresight 244–5
Foucault, M 162
free will 34

Galbraith, JK 172
gangland culture 76
Garland, D 28, 63, 153, 200, 244
Gelsthorpe, L 187
Giller, H 108, 208
Gillick v West Norfolk and Wisbech AHA 214,
      254, 255
Glassner, B 264
Goldson, B 26
Graham, J 51–2, 60, 63–4, 69–74, 206–7, 213,
      221, 223

Haines, K 8
Hendrick, H 21
Hirschi, T 81–2
Hogg, M 27
Home Office statistics 66, 67
Hough, M 83–4
Howard, Michael 31, 35, 43, 52, 94, 154, 212–13
Hulsman, L 263, 267, 269
human rights 201–3, 217, 219
Human Rights Act 1998 108, 171
Hurd, Douglas 140–41, 172, 211–12

individualisation 35–6
informal warnings 100–101
interactionist theories 76–9, 223
Intermediate Treatment 44–5, 91, 164
Ireland *see* Republic of Ireland

James, A 24
Jenks, C 23–4
Jones, D 222–3
juvenile court
   development 116–19
   and diversion 88–9
Juvenile Liaison Bureau (JLB) 91, 97, 159–60

Kelling, G 52, 236, 239

labelling process 3–6, 79–80, 109–110, 176, 223,
      266
   see also social exclusion
Lee, N 27, 28
Lemert, E 79
Levy, A 167

local authority secure accommodation 169
Lockyer, A 250
Lombroso, C 37
Lushington, Sir Godfrey 164

McConnell, Jack 252
McGhee, J 252
McLaughlin, E 45
magistrates
   minimal intervention 45, 49
   powers 42, 43
Major, John 31, 35, 42–3
managerialism 56–7
Marey, Martin 46–8
Marx, Karl 76–7
Mathiesen, T 162–3, 260–61, 270
Matza, D 81
Maxwell, G 192, 202
mediation 180–81
mental capacity 16–17
Merton, R 75–6
minimum ages 9–12
   international comparisons 11 *Table*
   mental capacity 16–17
   policy conflicts 41
   and punishment 17–19
models, youth justice 34–8, 39–40
   pendulum swings 37–8, 40, 55–6
Morris, A 187, 192, 202
Muncie, J 45, 76
Murray, C 207

National Offender Management Service 160
New Labour, and policy 49
   consultation process 54–5
   discussion papers 50–51
   and diversion 94–5, 113
   influences 49, 51–3
   managerialism 56–7
   public opinion 52–3
   reparation/restorative justice 57, 182–3,
      196–7
   use of models 55–8
   welfare/justice debate 55–6, 57–8
New Zealand 190–93
Newburn, T 182, 185
Northern Ireland 211

official statistics 66, 67
Ohlin, L 76

Packer, H 106–7, 113
parental responsibility 204
   breakdown 258
   for education 225–6, 229–30
   education for 209

legislation 214–19
   policy agenda 209–211, 228–9
   political responses 211–14
   scientific research 206–9
   services for 210
Parkhurst prison 36
Patten, John 211
Pearson, G 28
Perfect, Mark 46–8
physiological defects 37
Pitts, J 161
Platt, A 117, 118
policy
   see also New Labour, and policy
   conflicts 40–44
   and measurement of crime 62–3
   pendulum swings 37–8, 40, 55–6
   v practice 44, 46–9
positivism 35, 37
Postman, N 31–2
poverty, and crime 72–3
Power, M 208, 222
Powers of the Criminal Courts (Sentencing) Act
      2000 129–30, 134, 135, 139, 147, 148,
      155, 168, 186–7, 214
Pratt, J 124, 160, 171
Prevention of Crime Act 1908 117
prevention of crime, proactive duties 259
Probation of Offenders Act 1906 117, 152
probation orders 155
probation service 36–7, 152, 159, 160
proper training 36
proportionality 142–3, 147
Prosecution of Offences Act 1985 101, 103
prosecutor fines 105
Protection from Harassment Act 1997 239–40
Prout, A 24
psychological disorders 37
public opinion, and policy 52–3, 263–6
Public Order Act 1986 240
Puech, K 112–13
punishment
   and minimum ages 17–19
   model 34–5
   theoretical justification 141–2
punishment in the community *see* community
      punishment

Quinney, R 77–8

Ramsbotham, Sir David 170
rational choice 34
referral orders 128–31, 184–6
reformatories 36
rehabilitation
   and cautioning 97

community rehabilitation orders 155
  marginalisation 175
reparation orders 186–8
reprimands and warnings 98–101
  and conditional discharges 99
  criteria 99–100
  informal warnings 100–101
  as restorative justice 188–9
Republic of Ireland 193–5
responsibilization strategy 244
restorative justice
  comparative practice 189–95
  conflicting principles 196–7
  cultural roots 178–9
  ethnocentricity 197–8
  human rights 201–3
  issues 195–6
  and perpetrator 180–81
  practice 181–9
    history 181–4
  and retributive justice 198
  role of state 201–3
  and social cohesion 198–201
  theory 174, 178–81
  and victim 179–80
retributive justice 174, 198
  critisisms of 174–8
Reynolds, D 222–3
Riley, D 208
Roberts, M 83–4
Rousseau, Jean-Jacques 23
Rutherford, A 39, 45, 90, 109, 164–5, 204–5,
    220, 230, 244, 267
Rutter, M 208, 222

Schengen Convention 163
schools
  and crime 71–2, 219–20
  disaffection 221–2
  exclusion 221
  ineffective 222–3
  legislation 223–8
  parental responsibility 225–6, 229–30
  truancy 220–21, 224–8
Scotland 184, 243–52
  Children's Hearing system 37, 124–5
    child-focused approach 250–52
    context 245–7
    procedure 247–50
secure training units 43, 169
Sellin, T 77
sentencing practice
  bifurcatory approach 140–41, 143, 166,
    172–3
  guidance 140–44, 149–50
  principal aims 148–51

proportionality 142–3, 147
  pyramid structure 145–6
  statutory framework 145–8
  Track A/Track B 140–41, 166, 172–3
  welfare principle 150–51
serious offenders 132–3
Serious Organised Crime and Police Act 2005
    243
Shaw, M 208
Shibnall, S 83
Smart, C 27
social contract 34
social control 161–3, 175–6
social exclusion 181, 198–201, 266–7
social realism 77–8
Social Work (Scotland) Act 1968 246
socio-economic status, and crime 72–3
South Africa 190
statistics, official 66, 67
Stone, F 250
strain theories 75–6, 223
Straw, Jack 139, 155, 237
sub-cultures 76–9
supervision orders 155–6
suspended prison sentence 152
Sutherland, E 206

Thatcher, Margaret 141, 172, 254
Theft Act 1968 133
Thompson, Robert *see* Bulger case
treatment model 37–8
tribunals 115–16
  alternative 116
truancy 220–21, 224–8

United Nation's Committee on the Rights of the
    Child 171
United States, juvenile courts 117
Utting, D 209–211, 213, 218, 223, 229

Venables, Jon *see* Bulger case
victims
  interests 176–7, 179–80, 197
  and reprimands and warnings 189
  and youth offending panels 185
Victim's Charter 182*n*

Wagga Wagga (New South Wales) 190
Waitingi, Treaty 190
Waiton, S 163
Walgrave, L 201
Wardhaugh, J 227–8
warnings *see* reprimands and warnings
welfare agencies 157–60
welfare principle 35–7, 150–51, 161, 175
welfare/justice debate 37–8, 40, 55–6, 57–8

White, R 200
Whitelaw, William 38
Wilkinson, C 109
Williams, G. 17
Wilson, JQ 52, 236, 239
Wonnacott, C 131
Wright, M 180

YJB (Youth Justice Board) 46–7, 54, 159, 160,
     169, 189
YLS (Youth Lifestyles Survey) 60–61, 65, 67,
     68–9, 69–74, 208, 222
YOIs (young offender institutions) 169, 170–71
YOPs *see* youth offending panels
YOTs *see* youth offending teams
young children 237
young offender institutions (YOIs) 169, 170–71
young people
  as criminogenic group 59, 67–8, 119–20
  dichotomous labels 3–6
Young People and Crime, Survey 63–4
youth community orders 155
youth court
  development 119–29
  openness and shaming 126–8
  participation 125–6
  philosophical issues 123–5
  practice 120–23

reporting restrictions 127–8
shaming 126–8
youth gangs 76
Youth Justice Board (YJB) 46–7, 54, 159, 160,
     169, 189
Youth Justice and Criminal Evidence Act 1999
     120, 129, 183
youth justice models 34–8
  developmental model 39–40, 204–5
  pendulum swings 37–8, 40, 55–6
Youth Justice Task Force 51
Youth Lifestyles Survey (YLS) 60–61, 65, 67,
     68–9, 69–74, 208, 222
youth offending panels (YOPs) 129–30, 184–5
youth offending teams (YOTs)
  and action plan orders 156
  and child safety orders 238–9
  and custodial orders 168–9
  and custody 46–9
  and parents 218
  in practice 158–60
  reprimands and warnings 188
  role 36
  and schools 224–5
  and supervision orders 155

Zehr, Howard 178–9, 186, 198
zero tolerance 234–7

DATE DUE
